Spotted Tail's Folk

A HISTORY OF THE BRULÉ SIOUX

THE CIVILIZATION
OF THE AMERICAN INDIAN SERIES

Spotted Tail's

A HISTORY

Folk

OF THE BRULÉ SIOUX

by George E. Hyde

NORMAN : UNIVERSITY OF OKLAHOMA PRESS

By George E. Hyde

Corn Among the Indians of the Upper Missouri (with George A. Will)
  (Cedar Rapids, 1917)
Red Cloud's Folk (Norman, 1937. New Edition, Norman, 1957)
The Pawnee Indians (Denver, 1951. New Edition, Norman, 1973)
A Sioux Chronicle (Norman, 1956)
Indians of the High Plains (Norman, 1959)
Spotted Tail's Folk: A History of the Brulé Sioux (Norman, 1961, 1973)
Indians of the Woodlands (Norman, 1962)
Life of George Bent (Norman, 1968)

In Memory of My Father and Mother

GEORGE W. HYDE AND LUCINDA REED HYDE

Library of Congress Catalog Card Number: 61–6497

Copyright 1961, 1974 by the University of Oklahoma Press, Publishing
Division of the University. Manufactured in the U.S.A. First printing,
1961; second printing (new edition), 1974.

Spotted Tail's Folk: A History of the Brulé Sioux is Volume 57 in *The
Civilization of the American Indian Series*.

Foreword

to the New Edition

WHEN THIS VOLUME was first published a dozen years ago, it marked the completion of George E. Hyde's important trilogy on the history of the two southern Teton Sioux tribes, the *Oglalas* and *Sichangus* or Brulés. The other volumes comprising this series are *Red Cloud's Folk: A History of the Oglala Sioux* (1937), and *A Sioux Chronicle* (1956), both published by the University of Oklahoma Press.

Together, the three volumes nicely complement one another, and cover the history of the Oglala and Brulé Sioux more thoroughly than any other group of Plains Indians has been covered. Chronologically, *Red Cloud's Folk* begins in the era of Teton residence in the old Sioux homeland in Minnesota and, concentrating on the Oglalas, continues to the close of the Sioux War of 1876–77. *A Sioux Chronicle* carries the story through the tragic Ghost Dance troubles of 1890, but its focus is broader and includes both the Brulé and Oglala experience during this period. Though its title is similar to the Red Cloud volume, *Spotted Tail's Folk* is more of a biography of Spotted Tail than a tribal history, and deals, time-wise, more closely with the years of Spotted Tail's life, 1820 to 1880.

In order to understand and appreciate Hyde's writings properly, his readers should be acquainted with the tremendous physical handicaps under which this work was accomplished. At an early age he lost his hearing, and the sight in both eyes was seriously impaired. He was able to complete only a formal grade school education before these conditions sharply curtailed a normal boyhood and adult life. Intelligent and vigorous despite his physical limitations, he found, as a young man, that the history of the great plains offered an outlet for his intellectual energies. This was not an unnatural area of interest for him to cultivate, for the Omaha of his boyhood still retained links to the frontier experience. One of Hyde's school friends was the son of E. L. Eaton, a local photographer who had been a companion to Custer, Spotted Tail, Buffalo Bill Cody, and the others who participated in the famous Duke Alexis buffalo hunt in 1872. Years later, while writing *Spotted Tail's Folk*, he recalled that before losing his sight he had played in the attic of the Eaton house, surrounded by equipment and glass plate negatives of photographs for which he was then searching in order to use them as illustrations for this book.

As can be imagined, the combination of being deaf and semiblind posed very special difficulties for Hyde's efforts at historical research. With the aid of strong corrective lenses and a powerful hand reading glass, he was able to utilize his "good right eye" to read nearly everything that was available in books and periodical literature. He was very dependent upon the resources and staff of the Omaha Public Library, and published acknowledgments of their assistance carry more sincerity than many such statements.

Travel for research purposes was impossible, and even Hyde's visits to the library were accomplished only by painstakingly following a route of which he knew every foot. This, too, was curtailed during the winter months, when snow and icy sidewalks made out-of-doors journeys hazardous even for persons with good eyesight. The use of microfilm sources, readily available in his later years, was also barred to him because of his sight limitations. Even personal communication was rather complicated, for to converse with Hyde required the writing of notes which he then read with his hand glass. His replies were made in a strong voice that was understandable, though affected by the lack of tone control characteristic of deaf persons.

Given these limitations, it is certainly significant that Hyde was able to publish eight book-length manuscripts, plus a number of shorter efforts, during his lifetime. Unable to obtain regular employment (although he carried on a surprisingly active new-and-used-book business from his home for many years), he devoted much time to his writing and to the essential process of mulling over and evaluating data, uninterrupted by any sound from activities around him. This life of silence and semi-darkness was undoubtedly an asset of some sort in his literary endeavors, but it was also a condition he would gladly have exchanged for the ability to hear and see.

Hyde never hid behind his physical limitations and the restrictions they placed upon his research capabilities or used them as an alibi when his books were subjected to criticism. He freely admitted that his work had some shortcomings and some day might be supplemented by that of other writers who did have access to research material he could not utilize. He was careful, however, to take positions and make judgments that could be supported by the data available to him. Hyde maintained that the basic story he told would stand up, for the most part, against this newer material. And time has proved the accuracy of this assertion. James C. Olson's *Red Cloud and the Sioux Problem* (1965) covers much the same ground as Hyde's treatment of the Oglala leader in *Red Cloud's Folk* and *A Sioux Chronicle*. Although his book drew heavily upon valuable materials in the National Archives and the Nebraska State Historical Society not used by Hyde, Olson freely stated in his preface that his work *supplemented* Hyde's but was not intended to revise his books. The reviewers of Olson's volume who compared the two authors generally agreed that the newer work was richer in detail and documentation, but at least one such observer also noted that when it came to insight and style, he still preferred *Red Cloud's Folk*.

If limited research was a shortcoming in Hyde's writing, albeit an understandable one, a second feature that has been criticized by some professional historians was his failure to utilize fully the scholarly apparatus of footnotes and bibliography. The absence of documentation was particularly frustrating to others working in the same fields because of Hyde's access to sources of information that were not otherwise available. In most cases, if pressed, he could supply the basis for key statements of fact, either from his vast collection of typewritten notes (frequently filed in old greeting card boxes) or from his usually reliable memory. Readily admitting he was not a trained scholar, he accepted most criticism on these points gracefully. He would become annoyed only when he suspected it came from someone interested in slavish adherence to procedure and not in seeking information. (At times the absence of these features from his books was not entirely his fault. One month after the appearance of *A Sioux Chronicle* he discovered among his papers the unprinted bibliography for the book, and chuckled with delight that both he and his publisher and friend, Savoie Lottinville, had forgotten about it completely.)

Privately Hyde sometimes tended to be too sensitive about his limited formal education and his lack of traditional academic credentials. This sensitivity resulted largely from a fear that these factors would prejudice the reception his books received. Personally I doubted whether any of his general audience knew or cared about his education, and the question of his scholarly ability has never been an issue to any fair reviewer of his Sioux volumes. Still the matter was of concern to him, particularly following some unfortunate contacts with the academic world. In the early 1950's, a prospective eastern publisher gave one of his manuscripts to a holder of the Ph.D. degree from a well-known university to provide "scholarly polish." The results were disastrous. After rescuing his manuscript, Hyde bitterly complained about people with doctorates who didn't know "horde from hoard, practice from practise [and] led from lead." Again, in 1962, a faculty member at a western university wrote and indignantly demanded to know the source for a statement in *Red Cloud's Folk* that a "drunken" Colonel Thomas Moonlight (later governor of Wyoming) ordered two Sioux chiefs hanged in chains at Fort Laramie in 1865. Hyde never wrote this, as anyone reading the passage with any care could see, but his critic had not troubled to do so.

Hyde's difficulties with the academic world became more pronounced in the closing years of his life, when he was writing several books on the early history of the Plains and Woodland Indians. Archaeologists in particular came in for heavy criticism in these volumes, and they replied in kind in reviews and other public statements.

The academic issue in Hyde's life had its lighter side, too. He openly enjoyed the fact that a major book on the Custer battle refers to him as "Professor" Hyde. Persons who knew of him only after reading his Sioux histories frequently assumed what they thought was obvious and addressed him as an academic "Doctor." And the height of this tongue-in-cheek university association occurred for him when some reviewer or publicist referred to him in print as the "dean" of Plains Indian historians. Less humorous but in its own way indicative of the recognized quality in his work was an incident that occurred at the annual meeting of the Western History Association in 1962. The program committee allowed a paper to be delivered under the guise of an original contribution on Spotted Tail that was nothing more than a half-hour summary of Hyde's *Spotted Tail's*

Folk. Imitation may be the greatest form of compliment; but there is little wonder Hyde sometimes looked darkly at a profession that criticized the lack of signs of scholarship but not the absence of its ethics.

In addition to a lively and readable style, George E. Hyde's books on the Sioux contain two other qualities that have made his work, in the opinion of many observers, unmatched in the literature of Plains Indian history. He was fortunate throughout his long years of research to obtain a great deal of information from reliable and knowledgable Indian informants. He was also able to develop, from these contacts and from his own wide knowledge of published sources, a unique appreciation and understanding of the Indian character and way of life.

Hyde's was not a "Parson Weems" view of his favorite Sioux or of the American Indians in general. Rather he saw them as possessing all the strengths and weaknesses of human beings regardless of race. Their leaders were men capable of both good and evil, and the latter quality was not, of itself, the sole product of the influences of white civilization. From his correspondence and his reading Hyde understood as well as any white man could what life was like in the "old days" of the Teton buffalo culture. Against this background, he could write intelligently and with authority about their history and the impact government policies had upon the Sioux, and the response these programs received from the Indians and their leaders.

On the one hand Hyde admired intelligent and farsighted chiefs such as Spotted Tail and Lone Horn, the Miniconjou Sioux headman. He had an obvious affection for the Teton Lakotas as a people whose strength of character enabled them to survive ineffectual government reservation policies that had a brutal impact upon their lives and their native culture. On the other hand he did not ignore the other side of the coin—the cruel traffic in Indian slaves among Plains tribes during the seventeenth and eighteenth centuries; the instances of killing by the Sioux of whole herds of buffalo for only the choice tongues; the ancient human sacrifices by the Skidi Pawnees that continued into the 1830's; the slaughter of Pawnee women and children by Spotted Tail's Brulés at "Massacre Canyon" (Nebraska) in 1873. For Hyde, these incidents were a part of the Plains Indian story that he knew and wrote about. He did not hesitate to criticize Sioux leadership when he felt the evidence justified it, and this "let the chips fall" attitude may not make his books popular with some commentators on the American Indian in our present day. But Hyde was honest in his evaluations. His criticism, like his praise, was well founded and knew no racial boundaries. Even Red Cloud, who at times suffers rather severely by comparison with Spotted Tail in this volume, never came in for a scoring of such magnitude as "The Three Musketeers"—the government land commission of 1882—received at his hands in *A Sioux Chronicle*. As he put it to me on one occasion, "I don't like skunks whether white or Indian."

Hyde's books are ample evidence of his discerning affection for the Sioux people. Perhaps illustrating this further were the efforts he made, poor eyesight and all, on icy and treacherous sidewalks of wintry Omaha to assemble and send parcels to the Brulé Sioux youngsters at the Rosebud Boarding School during Christmas time. These gifts were sent in friendship and not as the result of any maudlin sympathy or pangs of misguided social conscience. His published views about the Indian stemmed from the same attitude.

Letter-writing played a big part in Hyde's life and particularly in his efforts to secure firsthand information from Indian sources. Anyone familiar with field research knows the difficulty of establishing credibility and confidence with an informant in face-to-face encounters. The added problems of doing this solely through correspondence—not always an enjoyable activity for either red or white—were even greater. But this was Hyde's method, and he pursued it with notable success. Undoubtedly he failed on numerous occasions to obtain the information he sought or even to receive a reply to an inquiry. Yet his achievement in establishing lengthy literary relationships, as well as personal friendships, with men like George Bent of the Cheyennes and John Colhoff and Eddie Herman among the Sioux provided him with invaluable research material, much of it unobtainable from the traditional sources utilized by the historian.

This was also the technique Hyde used to contribute to his first book-length publication. *Corn Among the Indians of the Upper Missouri*, written in collaboration with George F. Will of Bismarck,

North Dakota, was entirely conceived and executed by correspondence. During a friendship of some fifty years, the two authors never met. When Will passed away in 1955, Hyde sadly observed, "I have no friends left that I knew in the old days; all gone."

Even before his joint effort with George Will, Hyde had been involved in the production of a book on the Plains Indians as a research assistant to George Bird Grinnell. Hyde's friendship with Grinnell also began through letter-writing in the early years of this century. Later, when Grinnell came west from New York nearly every year to spend the summer among the Cheyennes, he and his wife stopped in Omaha to visit Hyde and his mother, and also in Columbus, Nebraska, to see Luther North, the old Pawnee Scout officer. The major contribution Hyde made as Grinnell's research assistant was in the preparation of *The Fighting Cheyennes* (1915). Grinnell's preface states, rather vaguely, that "Mr. George E. Hyde has verified most of the references and given me the benefit of his careful study of the history of early travel on the plains." Actually Hyde contributed a good deal more.

Grinnell provided him with a large quantity of Cheyenne interviews, transcribed and typed, and Hyde assembled the basic narrative, adding material from his correspondence with George Bent and from published sources. This version was then reviewed and altered by Grinnell to suit his own views. In truth a basic difference existed between the two men on the subject of Indian information. Hyde told me many years later: "Grinnell was one of those who believed Indians always told the exact truth, and he drove me wild by accepting Indian yarns that I thought were fixed up to give the whites a black record. He just would not accept eyewitness evidence by honest and honorable whites, if it went contrary to his darned Indian reports." This problem did not interfere with their relationship, however, for Hyde added: "He was a fine man and gave me work when I was half blind and could not get any other employment. It was his book, but I did help."

My own friendship with George E. Hyde began in 1954 when, while a graduate student, I was writing a history of the Teton Sioux agency at Cheyenne River, South Dakota. With such a subject, it was inevitable that I should approach him for information and help. He generously obliged, and so began an association that continued almost to his death in 1968. We only met face-to-face half a dozen times during this period, but our correspondence was frequent and extensive. The hundreds of letters we exchanged, while containing much of a personal nature, are also filled with a wealth of discussion and detail on Teton Sioux history and on the books Hyde published during these years. Although his physical handicaps could have made him so, Hyde was not negative in personality. His letters are filled with humor and pungent comments on subjects ranging from his own affairs to those of great nations. As a friend he was kind and generous. The assistance I was able to provide for his work was more than repaid by the privilege I had of knowing him.

In return for the interest and encouragement he showed for my studies, I was able to give Hyde access to research material that he did not otherwise have. Information from the rich resources of the National Archives and other manuscript depositories, along with the files of several eastern and frontier newspapers, were effectively utilized in *A Sioux Chronicle* (1956) and to an even greater degree in *Spotted Tail's Folk* (1961). Weaving this new data together with his older material, Hyde gave his account of Spotted Tail and the Brulés a greater dimension than is present in his previous treatment of Red Cloud and the Oglalas.

If *Spotted Tail's Folk* is a better book than *Red Cloud's Folk*, it was also a more difficult one to write. This was particularly true of the early reservation period, when Spotted Tail seemed to take a position that was in sharp contrast to Red Cloud, Sitting Bull, and other popular Sioux leaders. As Hyde himself put it at one point, "It's damn hard to write about a man who deliberately kept out of war; but he was right. He had more brains than any other chief; he noted in New York City in 1870 that more whites entered that one port from overseas in a year than the whole Sioux population amounted to." Hyde continually emphasizes that it was this understanding of the scope and power of American society that gave direction to Spotted Tail's leadership. This leadership was fundamentally conservative and aimed at maintaining for as long as possible the old traditional tribal authority and way of life among the Sioux. While recognizing the futility of military resistances to government policies, Spotted

Tail did everything he could to thwart the introduction of farming, Christianity, and other programs intended to destroy the old ways and establish government control over his people.

Hyde was sensitive to the charge, once expressed by Stanley Vestal in a review of *A Sioux Chronicle*, that Spotted Tail was a "collaborator" for his own gain at the expense of the welfare of the Sioux. (He retorted privately that Vestal was probably "sore on account I hinted his pet Sitting Bull was sort of a wild jackass.") Whenever possible, Hyde sought to use evidence showing that the Sioux themselves looked up to Spotted Tail's leadership. He found particular meaning, for example, in the fact that "the hostiles [the northern Sioux hunting bands of 1870–76] preferred to camp at his agency, even if they went to Red Cloud to raise hell." For Hyde, it was contemporary evidence of this type, not the biased, secondhand information of writers like Charles A. Eastmann, that accurately depicted Spotted Tail's status among the Sioux of his day.

Lieutenant John G. Bourke, himself a keen and knowledgeable student of the American Indian, commented in his book *On the Border With Crook* that a bronze statue of Spotted Tail should some day be erected in his Dakota homeland as a tribute to his greatness. Until Bourke's proposal becomes a reality, this biography by George E. Hyde will substitute as a literary monument—depicting the record of Spotted Tail as both warrior and statesman in the words of one who was truly a *kola* (friend) to the Lakotas.

Milwaukee, Wisconsin   HARRY H. ANDERSON
March, 1973

Preface

FOR MANY YEARS there has been a need for a book on the *Sichangu* or Brulé Sioux, and particularly for an authentic life of the great Brulé chief, *Sinte Galeska* or Spotted Tail. The Brulés were the ancient Teton or Prairie Village of the Sioux during the period when they lived on the Mississippi River in Minnesota, and when they migrated westward beyond the Missouri, they were still termed the Tetons until after the year 1820. They seem to have been looked up to as a kind of parent group by both the Oglalas and the Sioux tribes included under the name of Saone. Their history is well worth recording in detail. Spotted Tail, their great chief, had a strong and colorful character, but every fact concerning him has been so distorted by the Sioux that they have almost destroyed his reputation. He was probably the greatest Sioux chief of his period. His detractors have pictured him as a little man of mean character. They have even cast doubt on his personal courage, when in truth he was as great a warrior in his day as Red Cloud; and Lieutenant Eugene Ware, who knew him on the Upper Platte in 1864, stated that Spotted Tail was considered the greatest war leader among the Western Sioux and that he counted twenty-six coups in personal combat with Indian enemies and white soldiers. He also had a high reputation as a persuasive orator.

The accounts of Spotted Tail that have been given widest circulation come mainly from the Oglala reservation at Pine Ridge, where the Oglala Sioux are strongly inclined to depict Red Cloud and Crazy Horse as heroes and to belittle Spotted Tail. From such a source our standard account of the latter chief has been constructed. It does not even give the correct date of his birth; it tells of a Sioux council on Powder River in 1866 and makes Spotted Tail stand up and utter a plea for peace with the whites (thereby losing the respect of all the Sioux), when in fact Spotted Tail was hundreds of miles away in his own camp and there is no substantial evidence that such a council was held on Powder River.

It is strange that the Sioux in later days, should attempt to picture Spotted Tail as weak and even wicked, because he stood for peace, and stranger still that white authors should follow that lead. The simple truth was that in 1855 Spotted Tail saw General Harney's dragoons and infantry sweep through his own camp, driving the Brulés in panic flight. He fought valiantly against the mounted dragoons, was severely wounded, and was taken to Fort Leavenworth, where he spent a year as a military prisoner; and all this strongly impressed him with the fact that the Sioux would be destroyed in a war with the Americans. He stood for peace with the whites from that time on; but at the same time he led his tribesmen in a vigorous war on the Pawnee Indians of western Nebraska. A strange kind of pacifist, who gloried in the killing of Pawnees by his young men. The Sioux of his day understood his talk of peace with the whites, and those chiefs and camps that had seen the power of the Americans approved of Spotted Tail's stand. The Sioux of later times could only see Red Cloud, Sitting Bull, and Crazy Horse fighting against white encroachment on their hunting grounds, winning battles and losing wars. That was what Spotted Tail was always telling the Sioux: in the long run they could not win against the power of the Americans.

Contemporary opinion, including that of the Sioux themselves, listed the most important man among the Western Sioux in the early 1860's as Little Thunder and Spotted Tail (Brulés), Man-Afraid-of-His-Horse (Oglala), and Lone Horn (Miniconjou). Red Cloud and Sitting Bull were making names as war leaders; but the four big chiefs the Sioux usually listened to were all of them for peace with the whites. They were strongly inclined to be conservative, and when Red Cloud decided on war in 1866, Little Thunder and Spotted Tail withdrew, while Lone Horn planned to make peace with the Crows and take his Miniconjou camp into the Crow country to keep out of war. Man-Afraid-of-His-Horse took as little part in the war as possible. The critics who depict Spotted Tail as being the only leading chief who stood for peace simply do not know the facts.

Born in a wild Sioux camp in the White River country of South Dakota, untaught by white standards of teaching, still believing when he was fifty that the earth was flat and that thunder was caused by the flapping of the wings of a great bird in the sky, Spotted Tail had inborn abilities that, when developed by experience, enabled him to deal on equal terms with presidents of the United States, cabinet members, and generals of the army. He dealt with them and often got the better of the dealings. Frank, good-natured, shrewd, and witty, this Brulé chief made friends of the high officials who held the fate of his people in their hands and obtained from them by friendly persuasion advantages for the Sioux that the fighting chiefs like Sitting Bull and Crazy Horse could not win by war and, indeed, did not value. These things were peace and time and aid to enable the Sioux to change from the hunting life to the ways of civilized existence. The critics of Spotted Tail—Indian and white—seem to assume that being for peace is a weakness and almost wicked. If that is correct, the Brulé chief was certainly a bad man, and so was Red Cloud, after 1877, by which time he had caught up almost level with Spotted Tail as a peace advocate.

It has been said that Spotted Tail did not act for the good of the Sioux Nation, but that he planned selfishly for the benefits of himself and his Brulé Sioux group. There has been too much talk of the Sioux Nation, with the implication that it existed in the days when Spotted Tail and Red Cloud were in their prime. When Red Cloud went to Washington to talk peace in 1870, he told the officials that he represented thirty-two "nations" on Powder River, who had held a council and appointed him to speak for them. By "nations" he meant Sioux camps, some of them with as few as ten families. That was the old-time Sioux idea of a nation: small camps, each independent and thinking and acting in its own interest. When it came to visioning a great Sioux Nation, Spotted Tail was in the forefront of the movement, and was spoken of by the Sioux as the man who was to lead the nation. After his death in 1881, Red Cloud was favored as the grand chief of the nation, but it was too late in the day for such a plan to succeed. The government officials did not desire a united Sioux Nation, and they exerted all their power to thwart the plan.

In the present volume I have not attempted to picture Spotted Tail as anything more than a man of unusual ability and interesting character, who played a leading role during the great crisis his people had to face between 1850 and 1880. On the whole he seems to have played his part better than any of the other Sioux leaders. Ignorant at first of the whites and their ways and of the complicated system of the American government, he was often groping in the dark, trying to grasp half-seen problems. Toward the close of his career he was able to deal with the officials in Washington and best them, a situation which they did not like at all. They preferred their Indian chiefs to be simple-minded and easily controllable.

In preparing this volume, I have been aided by a host of friends, both Sioux and white. From Rosebud (the Brulé reservation) I have had help from Knife Scabbard, Moses Edwards, Stephen Spotted Tail (grandson of the old chief), Sore Eyes, and Joseph La Point. At Pine Ridge, Philip Wells, his son Tom, his daughter-in-law, Flora G. Wells, John Colhoff, and some others have always been ready to give me information or to seek it for me from the older Indians. Eddie Herman, of Rapid City, South Dakota, has given me much information. Harry H. Anderson supplied me with material from the National Archives that was of great assistance. Everett W. Sterling, dean of the College of Arts and Sciences, South Dakota University, sent me extracts from early Dakota newspapers that were very useful. Will G. Robinson of the South Dakota Historical Society has always been friendly and helpful. To the staff of the Bureau of American Ethnology in Washington my thanks are due for the supply of photographs. John C. Ewers of the U. S. National Museum has been liberal with both information and pictures. To Doris M. Quick my thanks are due for a good job of map-making, carried out under rather difficult circumstances. Marvin F. Kivett, curator of the Nebraska Historical Society Museum, took views on the head of White River specifically for this book, for which I am very grateful. Roger Grange, Jr., curator of the Fort Robinson Museum, also made pictures for me and supplied information. To the staffs of the Nebraska Historical Society and the Omaha Public Library I wish to express my appreciation for their constant helpfulness.

Omaha, Nebraska   GEORGE E. HYDE

Contents

Illustrations

MAPS

Spotted Tail's Folk

A HISTORY OF THE BRULÉ SIOUX

Chief Spotted Tail, from an oil painting by H. Ulke, 1877. (Courtesy the Smithsonian Institution)

1. *Indian Paradise*

WHEN SPOTTED TAIL was born in 1823, his tribe was living on White River, west of the Missouri, in what is now southern South Dakota. At that date there were still many old men and women in the tribe who could remember a time in their youth when the Teton Sioux were all east of the Missouri, roving afoot across the vast area of the Coteau des Prairies that stretched from western Minnesota to the valley of the Missouri. These old people had seen with their own eyes the great fortified villages of the Palani or Arikara Indians, their enemies, who at that early period held strongly the land on the Missouri in the vicinity of the Great Bend, below the present city of Pierre. They had seen these villages depopulated by three or more great epidemics of smallpox, and they had taken part in the Sioux attacks that in the end of the eighteenth century had driven the weakened Palanis northward up the Missouri, leaving their lands in the possession of the Sioux.

These Sioux, who had migrated slowly toward the Missouri, all afoot, by 1800 had many horses and were typical Indians of the Plains. The acquisition of horses meant not only that the Teton Sioux became more formidable in war, but also that they could cover a much greater area of country while on their semiannual buffalo hunts, that the women and children no longer had to march on foot, carrying heavy loads, and that the people could have much larger and more comfortable tipis and more camp equipment, clothing, and ornaments than in the old days, when they had had to carry all their possessions on their own backs or packed on the backs of their large dogs. They also had more food now, as it was much easier to find and kill game on horseback than afoot. One result of this new-found comfort probably had been an increase in Teton

Sioux births and a falling off in the rate of child mortality; but this alone could hardly account for the surprising growth of the Teton camps after the people crossed west of the Missouri. The fact seems to be that the new wealth and renown of the Tetons attracted to their camps large numbers of Sioux from bands that still lived east of the Missouri or in Minnesota.

When the first of the Sioux crossed west of the Missouri, they were in two groups: the *Sichangu* or Brulés (Spotted Tail's people), and the Oglalas (Red Cloud's folk). This was the time when the Palani villages were still strong. In crossing the river, these two Sioux groups were, in effect, invading Palani lands and hunting grounds, and some kind of a friendly understanding was evidently made with that alien tribe. Indeed, Tabeau informs us that the Oglalas settled down at the Palani villages, wishing to learn from that tribe how to grow corn and vegetables and how to build permanent earth-covered houses so that they might live among the Palanis. A second group of Sioux, the *Shiyo* or Sharp-tail Grouse people, joined the Oglalas; but a war between the Sioux of Minnesota and the Palanis caused the failure of this Oglala and Shiyo attempt to live in peace at the fortified Palani towns. However, their sojourn among that tribe had familiarized the Sioux with the country west of the Missouri, and when they resumed their wandering life, the Oglalas and Shiyos moved out toward the Black Hills. The Brulés on the other hand were in alliance with the Yankton Sioux, who roved in the lands near the headwaters of the Des Moines River in the district near the red pipestone quarry, extending their hunts sometimes as far west as the Missouri in the vicinity of the Great Bend. Thus when the Brulés crossed the Missouri, they occupied the White River valley, while their Oglala and Shiyo kinsmen were farther north, on Bad River, extending north to Cheyenne River and hunting westward to the Black Hills.[1]

The remaining Tetons in the lands east of the Missouri, who

[1] Pierre-Antoine Tabeau, Narrative of *Loisel's Expedition to the Upper Missouri*, 104, is the only authority for the Oglala and Shiyo attempt to settle down among the Arikaras and grow crops. As the Oglalas claimed that their man, Standing Bear, visited the Black Hills as early as 1775, it must have been at that period, before the Arikara towns were depopulated by smallpox, that the Oglalas and Shiyos came to live at these Indian towns.

were known as Sanona or Saones, were in five groups and were called by the Brulés and Oglalas the Nations of the North. They crossed west of the Missouri at a somewhat later date than the Brulés and Oglalas, and having crossed, they formed five tribes— the Miniconjous, Sans Arcs, Two Kettles, Hunkpapas, and Blackfoot-Sioux. On reaching the Missouri, the Miniconjous (like the Oglalas and Shiyos before them) made friends with the Palanis and attempted to live with that tribe. The name *Miniconjou* means They-Who-Plant-by-the-Water, and it refers to this attempt of that group, in the late eighteenth century, to settle down among the Palanis and grow crops.

Thus by crossing the Missouri into new lands in the West, the old Teton tribe was split up and formed seven new Sioux tribes bearing names which apparently originated in incidents that had occurred during their migration from the Mississippi to the Missouri. An example of this is the new name *Sichangu* or Burnt Thigh, given to Spotted Tail's people. This name originated in an event on the Coteau des Prairies that is set down in the winter-count record of Brown Hat (Wapostangi) under the date 1762–63. According to this winter-count tale, the band was encamped on the shore of one of the long, narrow lakes that are a feature of the country in eastern South Dakota. The grass of the prairie caught fire. A man, his wife, and some children, who were out on the prairie, were burned to death; the rest of the Sioux saved themselves by leaping into the lake; but most of the Indians had their legs and thighs badly burnt, and ugly scars resulted. The band was therefore given the new name of *Sichangu* or Burnt Thighs. The French traders termed them Brulés.[2]

---

[2] The Baptiste Good (Brown Hat) Winter Count appears in the Tenth Annual Report of the Bureau of American Ethnology (1893), pp. 287–328. He was younger than Spotted Tail and was a sub-chief for a time after 1865. His winter count is the only one among the Sioux that attempts to record events before the date 1775. He talked to all of the oldest Brulés and set down a cycle of traditional history going back to a very early time. His references to mounted enemies coming and attacking the Sioux camps on the Coteau des Prairies probably refer to Arikara raids on the Sioux, while that tribe was still without horses and almost at the mercy of mounted warriors. As to the origin of the name "Brulé," Brown Hat and his tale of the prairie fire seems to be correct. Indeed, this version was set

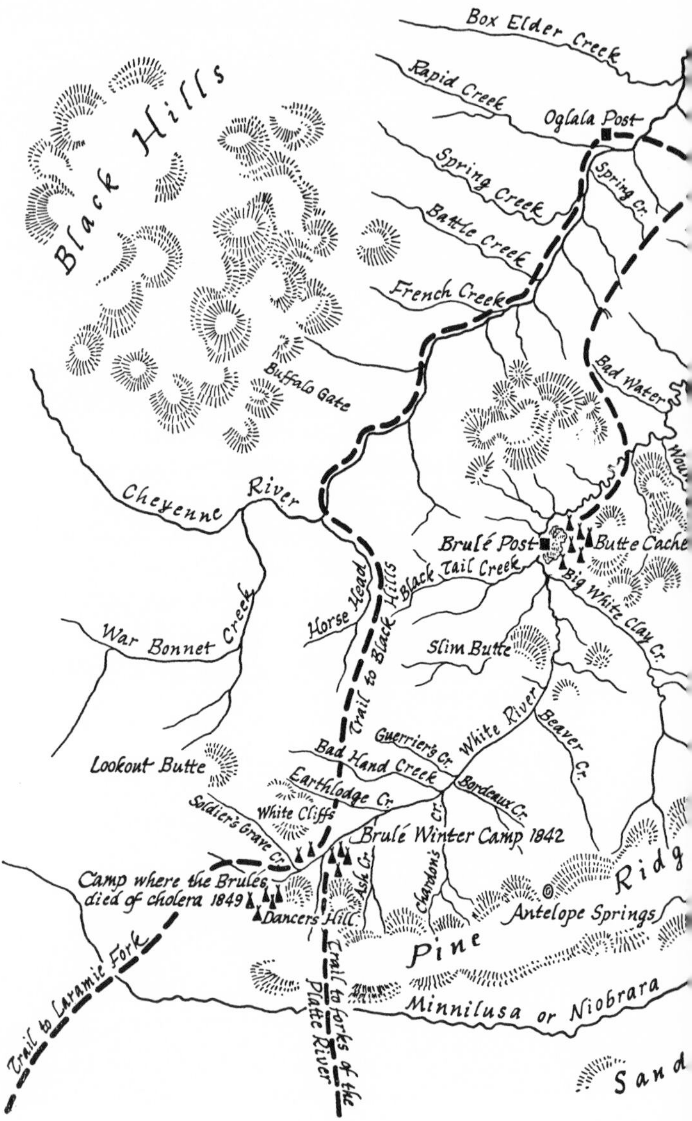
Black Hills
Box Elder Creek
Rapid Creek
Oglala Post
Spring Creek
Spring Cr.
Battle Creek
French Creek
Buffalo Gate
Bad Water
Cheyenne River
Brulé Post
Butte Cache
Black Tail Creek
Big White Clay Cr.
Horse Head
Trail to Black Hills
War Bonnet Creek
Slim Butte
White River
Beaver Cr.
Guerrier's Cr.
Bad Hand Creek
Lookout Butte
Earthlodge Cr.
Bordeaux Cr.
Soldier's Grave Cr.
White Cliffs
Brulé Winter Camp 1842
Ash Cr.
Chardon's Cr.
Camp where the Brulés died of cholera 1849
Dancers Hill
Antelope Springs
Pine
Trail to Laramie Fork
Trail to forks of the Platte River
Minnilusa or Niobrara
Sand

INDIAN PARADISE

The White River Country 1800–35

The White River country of southern South Dakota, into which the Brulés wandered after crossing the Missouri, was probably the finest tract of land for Indian occupation west of and close to the Missouri. A real Indian paradise, it was a land full of buffalo and other game, with a topography that gave the Indians open plains and prairies on which to hunt, many fine streams with groves of timber in which to camp, and pine ridges from which timber for lodgepoles and other uses could be easily obtained. There were vast areas of the finest native pasture on which to fatten their ponies in summer, and a plentiful supply of sweet cottonwood along the streams, which provided bark for feeding ponies in winter. The White River lands also lay close to that other need of the Indians, trade with the whites. French traders from St. Louis began to come up the Missouri into the Sioux country about the year 1785, and from 1800 on, the Brulés of White River could usually find traders at the *Karmichigah*—the Great Bend in the Missouri above the mouth of White River. The Sioux called White River *Makazita Wakpa*, literally, Earth Smoke River. This stream ran in its upper valley through white clay beds, and the water at certain seasons was milky white; but it was from the clouds of white dust that swept along the valley in windy weather that the river probably took its name. The French trader Bourgmont came up the Missouri to this district about the year 1717, and he called White River *Rivière Fumeuse*, Smoky River, a name so similar to that the Indians applied to it that one suspects he simply turned the Indian designation into French.[3]

The lower valley of White River in early times was wide, spacious, and well grassed. The district had abundant timber, and it was swarming with game animals. Above the South Fork, the north bank of the main river for some ninety miles towards the

---

down by Lieutenant Caspar Collins at Fort Laramie in 1863, evidently before Brown Hat made his winter count. Collins obtained the tale from Chief Red Fish of the Miniconjous.

[3] In recent years an attempt has been made to twist this Sioux name for the White River into a new form and to give it the meaning of white water tinged with yellow. The old name, both in Sioux and in other Indian tongues, clearly had nothing to do with the color of the water but referred to *earth smoke;* that is, to dust.

west was shut in by the high wall of the Big Badlands, a region of wasteland which was of no use to Indians. Here towering buttes of the badlands often rose from the very brink of the river, and north of the badland wall the country was cut up into a welter of buttes of fantastic forms, with ravines and little valleys lying between the buttes. In some of the ravines and valleys the ground was strewn with the bones of prehistoric monsters, and the Sioux regarded this vast tract of waste and silent land as the home of spirits, into which no man in his right mind would dare to venture.

It was on the south side of White River, facing the grim badland wall, that the Indian paradise lay. Here, sixty miles to the south, rose the tree-dotted slopes of the Pine Ridge country; and from these distant ridges numerous streams of clear water flowed northward through fine valleys to empty into White River. Here was Corn Creek, where in early times a camp of Sioux first tried their hand at growing crops; Yellow Medicine Root Creek (a name the Sioux had brought from their old home in Minnesota, for along this stream grew the plant whose roots were used as medicine); Bear-Runs-Through-Lodge Creek was named for some incident, long forgotten, of early days; Wounded Knee Creek was named for a chief who was shot in the knee with an arrow in a hunting accident; Porcupine Tail Creek was so called because of a butte at the edge of its valley that was supposed to be shaped like a porcupine tail; Black Pipe Creek was named for a chief; and Big White Clay Creek was so called because it flowed through white clay deposits and, in high water, had the same milky white tinge that marked the flow of White River. With their sources usually in perennial springs in the Pine Ridge, these streams almost always had a good flow of water, and their valleys were well timbered and carpeted by thick growths of fine grass. At its headwaters, for its first twenty miles, White River flowed through a narrow valley shut in between clay hills that at places rose into towering white cliffs; and here, in the district just south of the Black Hills, the Sioux in early days often placed their winter camps, sheltering under the white cliffs from the bitter winter winds.

Take it all around, the White River country, toward the end of the eighteenth century, was the finest hunting ground and camping

9

Running Buffalo, from a painting by Alfred Jacob Miller. (From *The West of Alfred Jacob Miller*, by Marvin C. Ross. Courtesy Walters Art Gallery)

place for Indians to be found west of the Missouri and close enough to that stream for the Sioux to obtain trade with the whites. They had to have trade, for they were dependent on the whites for a supply of guns and ammunition and many other indispensable articles, all the way from needles and awls to camp kettles and axes. In the matter of trade, which was vital, the Teton Sioux had an advantage over the other tribes on the Upper Missouri. If French traders came up the river from St. Louis, the Sioux met them first and had the pick of their stocks of trade goods; if no Frenchmen came up the river, the Sioux could go to Minnesota and trade there among their eastern kinsmen.

This fine White River country had been a hunting ground for the Palanis or Arikaras when that tribe had several fortified villages along the Missouri near the Great Bend. Smallpox destroyed most of the Palanis; the Sioux drove the survivors up the river. The Brulé Sioux then occupied the White River lands. In the west, near the headwaters of the river, the Kiowas, Prairie-Apaches, and Cheyennes had some claims to the hunting grounds; but the warlike Brulés and Oglalas drove them out, and by 1800 the White River country was in the undisputed possession of the Brulés. The fame of this fine hunting ground was spread among all the Sioux camps, and a flow of immigration set in that year by year increased the Brulé population. Sioux families from Minnesota came to visit and remained to become part of the Brulé tribe. The Shiyo or Sharptail Grouse camp left the Oglalas and joined the Brulés; Saone bands came down from the North, and it was in one of their camps that Spotted Tail's father (perhaps his grandparents also) came to White River on a visit and decided to remain with the Brulés.

Spotted Tail's father was a man named *Cunka* (Tangle Hair), a Saone of the Blackfoot-Sioux group. His camp was probably one of the Saone groups that was living with the Brulés when Manuel Lisa's trading expedition came up the Missouri in the summer of 1811. Tangle Hair's band decided to stay on White River, and he married a Brulé girl named Walks-with-the-Pipe and had several children.[4] His son who became a famous chief under the name of

[4] William Bordeaux, *Conquering the Mighty Sioux*. Bordeaux (a mixed-blood Brulé) questioned the old Indians about forty years ago and obtained the names

Spotted Tail was born in 1823 or the following year. The Sioux counted time by "winters," which extended over parts of two of our years; and for this reason it is usually impossible to fix dates accurately by our method. Thus Red Cloud was born in 1822–23, and Spotted Tail in 1823–24, and we cannot state certainly in which of our years the births fell. Dr. Charles A. Eastman (a mixed-blood Sioux and author) stated that Spotted Tail was born in 1833; and most of our writers have given this date, none of them taking the trouble to think or to observe the ridiculous results of such a dating. Thus, following their reckoning, Spotted Tail was born in 1833, was a warrior in 1839 at the age of six, killed a chief in a duel with knives in 1841 and married in the same year, at the age of eight, and was a father in the following year, when he was nine years old. Sioux boys of that period matured early. It was not unusual for boys of thirteen to join war parties and to take part in buffalo hunts; but the precocity attributed to Spotted Tail, when we set the date of his birth as 1833, is really too miraculous to be credited. Dr. Eastman was evidently taken in by one of those careless statements for which Sioux informants are rather notable, and the authors have followed Dr. Eastman, with the idea that, being a Sioux himself, he must know the correct date, were also led astray. Spotted Tail was himself to blame for this, in a way. He was as vain as a woman concerning the matter of his age, and when he approached forty, he usually replied to inquiries by stating that he was thirty. He thus set the date of his birth forward from 1823 to 1833; but when he made two legal affidavits, in 1878 and 1879, in the matter of the killing of cattle by his Indians in western Nebraska, Spotted Tail stated that he was born in 1823 or the following year.[5]

of Spotted Tail's parents and a few more important facts concerning this chief's early life. In Lieutenant G. K. Warren's diary for 1855, it is stated that Spotted Tail's father was present at Fort Laramie when his son surrendered to the military, and that the father was known as *Chomineeshee*, meaning The Grease That Turns Around. The diary adds that Spotted Tail also had the name Jumping Buffalo. The name Spotted Tail seems to be first set down in writing in the Warren diary, 1855.

[5] The Bureau of Ethnology in Washington still retains 1833 as the date of Spotted Tail's birth. The chief stated in an affidavit made in 1878 that he was then 54: born in 1824. In April, 1879, he signed another affidavit and stated his age as 55: born about 1824. Neither Spotted Tail nor anyone else seems to have

It is amazing how completely the Sioux of today have forgotten their famous chiefs. They remember their names, and a few can recount tales (mainly apocryphal) concerning them; but of the births and early lives of such men as Spotted Tail, Red Cloud, and Man-Afraid-of-His-Horse they know practically nothing. Spotted Tail's own grandson, Stephen Spotted Tail, stated some years back that all he knew concerning his famous ancestor was that his boy-name was Jumping Buffalo and that he acquired his warrior-name of Spotted Tail when he was given a ring-striped raccoon tail by a white beaver trapper; hence the name *Sinte Galeska* (*sinte*, tail, *galeska*, ring-striped or, as the Sioux put it, spotted).

The story of the origin of this famous name was given by Stephen Spotted Tail. He said that his grandfather when a boy went off with some other young Brulés, and the party came to a stream where some white trappers were encamped. One of the trappers was skinning a raccoon. The boy who was to become the great chief stood watching the trapper, and the white man began to speak to him, probably in the Indian sign language. He offered the raccoon tail, telling the boy to wear it and to take his name from it. The boy took the black-and-white-striped tail, made a headdress to wear in war, and attached the tail to it. He wore this talisman in his first fights, and—probably convinced that it brought him good fortune—he continued to use the raccoon tail on his head in battle and took the name Spotted Tail. This story is perfectly credible. Here was a big hearty American trapper, amusing himself at the expense of a Sioux stripling, and the boy—just starting out as a hunter and warrior and seeking a talisman to bring him luck—would naturally be much impressed by what the white man told him in signs. No Sioux of that period would go into battle without a talisman of some kind to protect him, and compared with some of the objects they carried for good luck, Sinte Galeska's handsome raccoon tail

---

recorded the month or the exact year, by our form of dating, of his birth; but 1823 or 1824 was the correct period. James McLaughlin (a good authority) in his book gave the date 1823. An article in the Sheridan County, Nebraska, *Star*, July 30, 1942, which is based on Sioux information, gives the date as 1823. The Swift Bear Brulé winter count is the only Sioux count that gives 1833 as the date, and this was probably compiled at a late date by a careless hand.

was a very superior talisman. His family knew this story and repeated it, even after 1935. The soldiers at Fort Laramie had actually seen this chief wearing the raccoon tail on his war headdress in the 1850's and 1860's.[6]

Spotted Tail has been usually spoken of as an orphan, but his father was alive in 1855 and his mother lived to accompany her great son to his first reservation, on the Missouri River at Whetstone, South Dakota, in 1868. There were at least two boys and two girls in the family, and Spotted Tail's brother—a good warrior—was killed in a fight with the Pawnee Scouts in western Nebraska in the middle 1860's. Two of his sisters were married to an Oglala Sioux medicine man named Crazy Horse, and the famous Crazy Horse of Custer battle fame was the son of Spotted Tail's sister.

Dr. Charles A. Eastman's attempt to make Spotted Tail out as a poor orphan boy just does not fit. My friend Harry H. Anderson recently found in the National Archives a letter from Agent Twiss to Indian Superintendent Cumings (October 26, 1855) in which Twiss makes the enlightening statement that Spotted Tail was the cousin of Brave Bear (head chief of the Brulés) and of Brave Bear's full brother, Red Leaf. Red Leaf was Spotted Tail's close friend and companion in arms, and from Agent Twiss's report it is clear that either Spotted Tail's father had a brother who was the father of Brave Bear and Red Leaf or else Spotted Tail's mother's sister was the mother of those two chiefs of the Wazhazha camp. Moreover, Mr. Anderson found that Red Leaf called Spotted Tail his brother-in-law, which suggests that Red Leaf had married one of Spotted

[6] The story of young Spotted Tail and the white trapper was obtained from *Pankeskawin* (Crockery Woman), the widow of William Spotted Tail, a son of the first Spotted Tail. The same story was later given to me by Stephen Spotted Tail, son of William. That frontier liar, George Belden, said in his book, *Belden the White Chief*, that Spotted Tail was given that name because of the tail of a spotted ox which he attached to his bow case as an ornament. This evidently meant the tail of the famous ox whose killing brought on the Grattan massacre near Fort Laramie in 1854; but General J. S. Brisbin, who edited the Belden book, put in a footnote (page 112) in which he stated that Belden was in error and that the name Spotted Tail really referred to a raccoon tail worn on a headdress, and that officers and men at Fort Laramie had seen the chief wearing this raccoon tail on his head when dressed for war. We have no description of Spotted Tail's headdress. He probably gave it to a friendly army officer which he was a prisoner at Fort Leavenworth in 1855.

Expedition to Capture Wild Horses, from a painting by Alfred
Jacob Miller. (From *The West of Alfred Jacob Miller*, by Marvin
C. Ross. Courtesy Walters Art Gallery)

Tail's sisters, or that Spotted Tail had married Red Leaf's sister (or sisters). And again, in the diary of Lieutenant G. K. Warren, for September, 1855, it is stated that the chiefs Man-Afraid-of-His-Horse and Grand Partisan were then present at Fort Laramie, and with Spotted Tail's father with them, gave the information that Spotted Tail (here called by his other name, Jumping Buffalo) was living in a Wazhazha camp of twenty-six lodges, which was the camp of Brave Bear, otherwise known as *Ma-to-i-wa* (Scattering Bear). This most important information indicates that Spotted Tail was most closely related to the Wazhazha group and that, although he went south of the Platte at times, his home was among the Wazhazhas.

From the year 1800 on to 1845 or 1850, the White River country was filling up with Sioux. The first Brulé camps that came to White River in the closing decades of the eighteenth century were clearly a small group; but once they had obtained a foothold in the White River country, immigration from other Sioux groups set in. In 1804, Lewis and Clark listed five Brulé camps; but of these the first camp, *Isanyati*, was clearly a group of Santee Sioux from Minnesota, who had come west and won a position at the head of the Brulé tribe; the fourth band was composed of Wazhazhas, another immigrant group, and the fifth, or *Minnishani*, was a Saone camp, also immigrants. But these immigrant Sioux soon turned into true Brulés. Thus the camp that was known as *Tishayaote*, or Red Lodges, were Miniconjous when they joined the Brulés about the year 1810; but by 1850 they were real Brulés, and after 1865 their chief, Swift Bear, was the second chief in rank in the Brulé tribe. His grandfather was Red War Bonnet (*Tawapasha*), who was a Sisseton Sioux from Minnesota. The son of this man was Lone Dog, chief of the Red Lodges in 1840–55, and his son was Swift Bear. This Red Lodge camp was a superior group, composed of energetic and shrewd people. They had the tops of their skin tipis painted red. They were famous for the fast horses they owned; they captured wild horses in the Nebraska Sand Hills country in large numbers, and every spring they went eastward to trade horses to the Santee Sioux for guns and European goods. Unlike other Teton camps, they thought in times of abundance of lean days to come, and in autumn when food was plentiful they dug big cistern-like caches which they filled with dried meat, pemmican, and dried wild fruits, all carefully packed in rawhide cases, the whole covered and concealed so cleverly that neither water nor thieves could get into the caches. In early spring, when food was often scarce and hunger rife in Sioux camps, the Red Lodge folk returned to their autumn campground, opened the caches, and had enough food to last them until summer.[7]

Thus when Spotted Tail was a small boy, his Brulé tribe was still maintaining some connection with their eastern kinsmen, the Santees, or Sioux of Minnesota. Actually a part of the Santees in early times, the Brulés and other Tetons had drifted off to the west across the Coteau des Prairies; but for a century or more their camps always returned eastward in the spring, so that they might camp with the Santees, whose chiefs they regarded as the heads of the nation. Even after they crossed the Missouri to live, the Brulés and other Tetons kept up the custom of going eastward across the Missouri each spring to visit and trade among the Santees —not all of the camps, but the more enterprising ones. The Santees traded with French and British traders on the Upper Mississippi; then each spring some of the Santee bands brought the trade goods they had obtained to the head of the Minnesota River, and there they held a fair to which the Tetons came to trade furs and horses for guns, ammunition, and other articles. After they had crossed the Missouri to live, it was too far for the Tetons to go to the Minnesota River, and this annual fair was moved westward, to the James River, to a point called *Otuhu Oju,* or Oak Grove, about due east of the mouth of the Cheyenne River on the Missouri. Here in May each year a great gathering of Sioux took place, as many as 1,200 lodges sometimes being present: Tetons, Saones, Yanktons, Yanktonais, and Santees, the last being in the main Sissetons, who seem to have made a business of trading with the Sioux of the west. These annual fairs not only provided the Sioux beyond the Missouri with guns and other needed goods—they kept the Tetons in touch

[7] This account of the Red Lodge is taken from the Susan Bettelyoun manuscripts in the library of the Nebraska Historical Society. Mrs. Bettelyoun was a daughter of the Sioux trader James Bordeaux, and her mother was the daughter of Chief Lone Dog of the Red Lodge camp.

with the Eastern Sioux, whom they regarded as the parent stock of their nation. The Brulés, Oglalas, and Saones of the west were pioneering groups, pushing on into new country and living a rough and free life. They often defied their chiefs and robbed French traders who came up the Missouri; but even among them public opinion had a strong hold; and it was said that the Tetons often resisted the temptation to rob or kill the Frenchmen who came to trade, because they were afraid that when they went to the next fair at *Otuhu Oju*, the Sissetons and other Santees would be angry with them and the great chiefs of the Eastern Sioux would call them bandits and murderers.

Spotted Tail must have been born in the White River country, although William Bordeaux stated that he was born on Laramie Plains in Wyoming and Dr. Charles A. Eastman placed his birth on Republican Fork in southwestern Nebraska. It may be pointed out, however, that the Brulés were all living and hunting in the White River lands at the time of Spotted Tail's birth in 1823, that they never lived on Laramie Plains at any time, and that they did not go to Republican Fork to live until after Spotted Tail was in his teens. It is strongly to be doubted that any Brulés left the White River country, taking their camps and families with them, at this early period, except for occasional trading trips eastward to *Otuhu Oju*. But we may note two exceptions. When Spotted Tail was about five or six years old, the Bent Brothers, Charles and William, who had formerly traded in the Sioux country, established a trading fort on the Arkansas River, near the present city of Pueblo, Colorado, and they sent men up north to invite the Indians to come and trade. The Red Lodge camp went to trade at this new post, and it is possible that Spotted Tail's camp also went. This was about the year 1828. On the return northward the Sioux ran into a camp of Pawnees on the Republican Fork and had a fight with them, in which the Red Lodge warriors captured four fine spotted mules.[8] The second occasion on which the Sioux left White River was in 1830, when

[8] The authorities for this visit of the Sioux to Bent's Fort are Susan Bettelyoun, who states that the Red Lodge went down to trade, and George Bent of the Cheyenne tribe, who states that a large camp of Sioux came to trade, One Horn and his Miniconjous being among them.

the Cheyennes proclaimed a crusade against the Skidi Pawnees and induced the Sioux to join in an expedition against that tribe. The Indians gathered on the North Platte and marched eastward toward the Skidi camp; but in the fight that ensued, the Skidis captured the Cheyenne tribal talismans, the sacred medicine-arrows, and the Cheyennes completely lost heart and fled from the field.

The Sioux were probably never as prosperous and happy again as they were during the period 1780–1820, when they crossed the Missouri, acquired horses, and occupied the fine hunting grounds to the west. The Brulés on White River had an abundance of buffalo, deer, and elk. They captured wild horses in the Nebraska Sand Hills, and they drove whole herds of antelope into traps and killed them. The antelope drives were held in the rough and broken country near the head of White River. The Brulés chose a spot where there was a gap between the hills, and beyond the gap a small cliff or sudden drop to a considerable depth. The Indians built a tall hedge of timber and brush at the foot of the cliff, surrounding a large patch of ground. Part of the hunters concealed themselves behind this hedge; the others, mounted on fast horses, went off into the plain and drove a herd of antelope through the gap. The frightened animals poured through the gap, came to the cliff edge, and leaped over it, falling inside the pen formed by the tall hedge. The Sioux then shot them with arrows as they raced about inside the hedge. On lower Big White Clay Creek near Butte Cache, the Hinman party in 1874 saw one of these old traps, the hedge still there and the ground strewn thickly with antelope bones.

When they first occupied the White River lands, the Brulés did not feel safe from enemies there; and as winter came on, they withdrew their camps to the Missouri, usually crossing the river to winter in safety on the east side; but by the time of Spotted Tail's birth, the White River country was their home, and their winter camps were usually up near the head of the stream. One favorite wintering point was Butte Cache (*Paha Conigna Yanka*, Hill-in-the-Woods), which stands on the south side of White River to the east of the mouth of Big White Clay Creek, north of the present Sioux agency of Pine Ridge. Butte Cache in early times was hidden behind a screen of trees that grew close around its base. Farther

Sioux Encampment, from an engraving by Carl Bodmer, about 1834, with a scaffold burial at the right and another at center background. The woman at the right of the group carries her infant in

her robe. The man with the pipe wears a metal disc hair plate headdress. (From *The Sioux: Life and Customs of a Warrior Society*,
by Royal B. Hassrick. Courtesy Denver Art Museum)

up the river were the White Cliffs, another favorite wintering camp of the Brulés, near the present town of Crawford, Nebraska. After 1830, the Wazhazha band usually wintered at Butte Cache, while the Brulés, including Spotted Tail's band, wintered at White Cliffs.

The Sioux might have kept the White River country as a hunters' paradise if it had not been for their own lack of foresight and the coming of the traders. Some believing souls who have listened to the tales of modern Sioux tell us that the Indian was the first conservationist, that he killed only as much game as was required to feed his family, was very careful not to destroy timber, and had, indeed, established all the rules and regulations of the United States Conservation Service centuries before that office was established. In truth, most of the Sioux of early times were born wasters. They hunted game out of a district and moved on to fresh hunting grounds; they destroyed great numbers of cottonwood trees, cutting off the bark to feed to their horses in winter; and they had a custom of firing the prairies in autumn to insure an early growth of new grass in the spring, caring nothing that the prairie fires they set swept across the country for one hundred miles, burning belts of timber, killing animals, and doing other damage. There were many big groves of fine trees on the streams when the Sioux came to White River which were completely destroyed before 1850.

After the Sioux themselves, the traders were the marauders who spoiled this Indian paradise. At first the Frenchmen who came up the Missouri from St. Louis to trade among the Sioux wanted only beaver, otter, and other fine furs; but after the Sioux crossed the Missouri and acquired horses, most of the men ceased to trap small fur-bearing animals. They were now buffalo Indians, and if the Frenchmen wished to trade with them, they must trade for buffalo robes and for elk and antelope skins. Unwilling at first to do this, the French traders (with cheap water transport down the Missouri to St. Louis) found that there was a profitable market for buffalo, elk, and antelope skins. Then they found a market for salted buffalo tongues; and before long they had the Sioux (already wasters of game) slaughtering huge numbers of buffalo and other game animals to obtain skins to barter for the guns and other goods the French brought up the Missouri. When Spotted Tail was ten years old, George Catlin, the artist, was at the trading post on the Missouri in the Brulé country, and he saw the Sioux kill an entire herd of buffalo, take the tongues to trade at the post, and leave the unskinned carcasses lying on the prairie for the wolves to eat. Not content with the great quantities of robes and skins the Sioux brought to the trading posts on the Missouri, the traders developed a system of branch posts, sending some traders in autumn to build a trading hut near the wintering camps of the Sioux and to remain all winter, urging the Indians to keep on hunting and to bring in robes and skins. This was the season when, if left to themselves, the Indians would have stayed in camp most of the time, hunting only when meat was seriously needed. Now, urged by the traders and plied with bad liquor, they hunted all winter. The branch post, called Brulé Post, was usually at Butte Cache. It was only a temporary hut, which was abandoned when the traders left in the spring to take the robes they had traded for to the main post on the Missouri. Sometimes the traders had a winter post at White Cliffs, where the group of Brulés Spotted Tail's family lived with were wintering.

One of the early traders in the Brulé country was F. A. Chardon, whose name is preserved in a mangled form at Chadron Creek and the town of Chadron, Nebraska. He usually built a big Indian earth-lodge as a trading hut, hence the name Earth-Lodge Creek that used to be given to a northern branch of White River near Butte Cache. Grey Eyes (Frederick La Boue) was another trader who left his name on a creek near Butte Cache. There was a trader, named Yellow Eyes by the Sioux, who married into the Brulé tribe and had a son of the same name and about the age of Spotted Tail. Duck (Charles E. Galpin) was also trading on Upper White River in the period 1820–30, and there was Louis Bissonnette ("Old Bijeau"), who was followed by a younger relative, Joseph Bissonnette, still a Brulé trader in the 1870's. Emilien Primeau, Charles Degueire (De Gray?), and Joseph Juitt (or Jewitt) were traders at the time when Spotted Tail was a boy. P. D. Papin had a small trading hut on Grass-Lodge Creek, high up White River, in December, 1830. Most of these men were Frenchmen from St. Louis.

It was the coming of John Jacob Astor's American Fur Company into the Sioux country, after the War of 1812, that started bitter competition. The French traders were fighting the Americans; both sides had recourse to the use of bad liquor in their efforts to keep their trade going and to win Sioux camps away from rival companies. The Sioux could not resist the poison that was being offered to them; and for some years about the time of Spotted Tail's birth, the Sioux camps were scenes of drunken riot. Red Cloud's father died at this period, a victim of the traders' bad liquor. The Brulés —demoralized by drink—were also often hungry; for game on White River now showed plain indications of being hunted out.

At this time the Brulés had a prominent chief named *Makatozaza* (Clear Blue Earth)[9] who was concerned over this growing difficulty in obtaining meat by hunting. In the early 1830's this chief induced the Brulés to organize their hunts so that every family would have a fair opportunity to obtain a good supply of meat and skins. The organization of hunts was nothing new, but the Brulés had become split up and disorganized by the heavy drinking of the 1820's, and they had to be induced to reorganize the tribal circle. Makatozaza took the lead in this. Each band camped where it chose to in winter; but in early summer when it was time for the buffalo hunt, the bands all met at an appointed place and formed the tribal circle, a great circle of tipis with each band in its appointed place in the circle. Four men called *wakicunsa* (camp leaders) were put in charge. They were not chiefs, but prominent warriors: war shirt wearers of the class the whites called war chiefs. These *wakicunsa* had absolute control, with a force of tribal soldiers to execute their orders. They lived in a tipi in the center of the camp circle, and from there they sent out scouts to locate the buffalo herds, held councils with the chiefs of the different bands, and announced the days on which hunts were to be made. They took charge of the

[9] This name has the same first three syllables as *Mankato*, Blue Earth, the Sioux name for a river and town in Minnesota; *zaza* indicated a clear color. The Sioux today will try to persuade you that no such chief ever lived, and that his name does not mean Clear Blue Earth. In 1851, Makatozaza signed the treaty at Horse Creek near Fort Laramie. After that he evidently lived among the Brulés who kept near the Missouri River, and so he was unknown in the Fort Laramie district. When the amendments to the treaty of 1851 were signed by the chiefs at Fort Laramie, September 15, 1853, Chief Clear Blue Earth's name was set down with the notation "dead."

Bull Bear, from a painting by Alfred Jacob Miller. (From *The West of Alfred Jacob Miller*, by Marvin C. Ross. Courtesy Walters Art Gallery)

Battle Decoration of Buffalo Robe. (From *Ab-Sa-Ra-Ka, Land of Massacre*, by Henry B. Carrington)

hunts, their soldiers ready to whip with their quirts any group that attempted to slip away and hunt ahead of the main party. Thus every hunter had an equal chance to obtain meat and skins before the buffalo herds were frightened away.

Spotted Tail grew to be a hunter and warrior in these years during which Makatozaza revived the tribal circle and worked to restore good order among the Brulés. The tribe was now engaged in war with the Pawnees, a people of alien stock who lived in permanent earth-lodge villages on the Loup Fork branch of the Lower Platte. There were several big Pawnee villages on the Loup. Here the Pawnees planted corn and other crops; but, like the Sioux, they went off on two extended buffalo hunts each year, leaving their villages and crops to take care of themselves. Wandering far to the south on their hunts, they raided the Comanches and other Southern Plains Indians and also made war excursions into New Mexico. In these raids they obtained great numbers of horses and mules; and the Brulés of White River found out at an early date that, by raiding the Pawnees, they could usually count on capturing a large number of good horses. The Miniconjous, who often came down from Cheyenne River to camp with the Brulés, joined in these attacks on the Pawnees.

About 1832 a Miniconjou party, led by Stiff-Leg-with-War-Bonnet, the father of the famous chief Lone Horn, went to steal horses from the Pawnees; but they were discovered, and in the ensuing fight their leader was killed and his war bonnet captured by the Pawnees. The Sioux—always quick to seek vengeance for such a loss—got up a big war party and attacked the Pawnees. In the fight a Pawnee was seen with Stiff Leg's war bonnet on his head, and the Sioux made for him, hoping to kill him and recover the war bonnet; but he got away. In November, 1833, when Spotted Tail was ten, the stars fell. The entire sky was streaked with fire as myriads of meteorites flashed across the heavens, and the frightened Indians thought that the world was coming to an end.

In 1834 two partners in the Rocky Mountain Fur Company, William Sublette and Robert Campbell, built a small trading post on Laramie Fork (Fort William on the site of the later Fort Laramie) and sent men to the Black Hills to invite Chief Bull Bear of the Oglalas to bring his camp down to hunt on the Platte and trade at the new post. This was a direct effort to take the Sioux trade away from the American Fur Company and other traders on the Missouri, and the effort succeeded. Buffalo were no longer plentiful either on the White River or the Cheyenne River, and close to the Missouri the Sioux were at times actually starving for lack of game. The Sioux were ready to move on into better hunting country. Bull Bear took one hundred lodges of Oglalas down to the North Platte, hunting there and going to trade at Fort William; and by the following summer he had two hundred lodges on the North Platte. The Brulés from White River now joined in this southward movement, and the number of Sioux in the Platte country increased with great rapidity.

The lands west of the forks of the Platte were claimed by the Cheyennes and Arapahoes; but these tribes had moved south toward the Arkansas River, in southern Colorado, and they did not object to their Sioux allies coming down to live on the North Platte. East of the forks the country belonged to the Pawnees, the Skidi Pawnees hunting from their village on Loup Fork westward to the forks of the Platte, the other three Pawnee tribes hunting farther to the south, on branches of the Kansas River. The Sioux move to the Upper Platte meant trouble with the Pawnees, and this situation was complicated by the arrival of the Arikara tribe (kinsmen of the Pawnees), who now came down in a body from their lands on the Upper Missouri, from which they had been forced to move because of the hostility of the Sioux and of the white traders and trappers. The Arikaras had gained the hatred of the whites on the Missouri because of their frequent treacherous attacks on white men. Coming down to the Platte, they joined the Skidi Pawnees and at once sent out war parties to seek white traders and trappers traveling through the country, with the object of robbing or attacking them.

The Sioux loved their new lands on the Platte. They called the North Platte Shell River or Shell-on-Neck River; the South Platte was Fat Meat River, for down there the buffalo grew fat and sleek a month earlier than they did farther north. This was a fine country for hunting, and it was much closer to the enemy tribes, such as the

Pawnees, from whom the Sioux could obtain horses by raiding. It was also a land where things happened—happened swiftly and often bloodily—and life in a Sioux camp near the Platte was going to be lively, the way the Sioux liked it to be.

In May, 1833, the Skidi Pawnees captured a Cheyenne woman and sacrificed her to their goddess Morning Star, to insure good crops and good hunting for the season. This practice of sacrificing captured women and girls was a thing that caused the Sioux, Cheyennes, and other tribes to regard the Pawnees as utterly alien and abominable people. The Cheyennes went to seek vengeance; but the Skidi Pawnees now had their hard-fighting kinsmen, the Arikaras, to aid them. In 1835, Colonel Henry Dodge marched up the Platte with a force of dragoons, holding councils with the Pawnees and Arikaras and urging them to keep the peace. He turned south from the Upper Platte and marched to the Arkansas, where he held councils with the Cheyennes and Arapahoes and made a formal peace between them and the Skidi and Arikara tribes, a peace that lasted until the Colonel broke camp and marched homeward down the Arkansas.

The Skidis (evidently aided by the Arikaras) now sent a war party up to the Niobrara River, where Chief Makatozaza and his Brulés were hunting. Spotted Tail, now about twelve and old enough to be a hunter and even a warrior, was in the Brulé camp. The enemy made a sneak attack, rounded up a number of Brulé horses, and made off with them. The Brulés made up a large party and pursued the enemy until they were close to the Pawnee camp. Here a larger force of Pawnees came out and attacked the Brulés; but they were defeated, the Brulés killing twenty-two Pawnees and recapturing the stolen horses. This Brulé war party, on returning home, rode in triumph into the great circle of tipis, carrying Pawnee scalps and other trophies tied to the tips of long sticks and singing war songs as they rode around inside the circle.[10]

---

[10] F. V. Hayden copied the account of Chief Clear Blue Earth from Denig's Sioux manuscript without giving credit. Denig was trading among the Brulés at the time this chief was active, and the Denig account of him is firsthand information. The winter-count records do not mention this chief and are confused about the fight with the Pawnees. The Swift Bear count says "1835–36, two Arikara

That winter, the Sioux had a big fight with an enemy—probably with the Arikaras—on the ice of the North Platte near Ash Hollow. The Sioux were on the north bank, the enemy on the south. Parties of mounted warriors charged across the frozen river, only to be driven back and then to re-form and charge again. The Sioux apparently had the best of it, for after the fight the Arikaras hastily gathered up their camp equipment and fled. They returned to their old home on the Upper Missouri, leaving their Skidi Pawnee cousins to face the Sioux and Cheyennes unaided. The Skidis were hunting buffalo up near the forks of the Platte; the Oglalas and some Brulés were hunting farther to the west. In the winter of 1836–37, a small camp of Oglala Sioux, led by a man named Paints-His-Cheeks-Red, was attacked by a war party of Skidis. Paints-His-Cheeks-Red and some others were killed, and the enemy carried off a number of women and girls as captives. When this war party returned to the Skidi hunting camp near the forks of the Platte, the Skidi chiefs were greatly alarmed. They ordered the camp moved eastward at once, giving up the winter buffalo hunt, as they feared the Sioux would come down on them with a great force, seeking vengeance. The Skidis lost most of their buffalo meat and skins because of this flight eastward. Then they got smallpox from the captured Sioux women and girls, and great numbers of Pawnees died. Nevertheless, the Skidi priests insisted on a sacrifice to Morning Star; and in April, 1838, Haxti, a Sioux girl from the camp of Paints-His-Cheeks-Red was cruelly sacrificed to the Skidi goddess. Meanwhile, among the Sioux, the nephew of Paints-His-Cheeks-Red took a war pipe and went from camp to camp soliciting pledges from the warriors that they would join him in seeking vengeance against the Pawnees. Getting up a very large war party, they went to the Pawnee villages on Loup Fork, attacked the villages, killing Pawnees and carrying off many Pawnee horses and much plunder; but on the return homeward they had to pass through the Nebraska Sand Hills, where there was no game, and they were so hungry that

chiefs killed"; Big Missouri's count says that two Sioux pipe-bearers (war party leaders) stayed behind their party and were killed by the enemy. These two vague statements certainly refer to the big fight with the Pawnees which Hayden pictured as a Sioux victory.

they ate most of the captured Pawnee horses. Spotted Tail, then about fifteen, was probably with this war party.

In his account of Spotted Tail's life, Dr. Charles A. Eastman states that Spotted Tail, Two Strike, and the other Brulés of their generation made their reputations as warriors in fights with the Utes; but the Sioux winter-count records are barren of any references to the Utes, and in none of the contemporary written accounts do we find that the Brulés were engaged in war with the Utes at the period 1835–45. On the contrary, both the winter counts and the written records show that the Brulés at this time were vigorously fighting the Pawnees of the Lower Platte, and our first definite account of Spotted Tail as a young warrior exhibits him as a member of a war party on its way to attack the Pawnees. This story was obtained by George Bent, a mixed-blood Southern Cheyenne, from the old men of his tribe about the year 1910, and the date of the event, as nearly as the old men could figure it out, was in 1839, when Spotted Tail was about sixteen. Some time previous to the setting out of this war party, the Pawnees had killed an entire war party led by the famous Cheyenne warrior Walking Whirlwind. This party had gone to the Republican Fork to find the Pawnee hunting camp and attack it. The Cheyenne party left their camp on a very foggy morning and advanced down the Republican Fork. Moving in a dense fog, they walked into the center of a Pawnee camp before they realized where they were. The Pawnees rushed to arms, drove the Cheyennes into the bed of a creek, and killed them all. The Cheyennes now sent around a war pipe and induced a number of Sioux warriors to join them in seeking vengeance on the Pawnees.

The leaders of the war party selected six men to go ahead as scouts. Only trustworthy and experienced men were chosen to act as scouts; and the fact that Spotted Tail was selected by the leaders indicates that, even at the age of sixteen, he had won a reputation as a warrior. The Brulés selected as scouts Good Bear, Spotted Tail, and Yellow Eyes, the last probably the mixed-blood son of the trader called Yellow Eyes; the Cheyenne scouts were Tall Bull, Wolf Mule, and White Antelope. Of these six scouts, Spotted Tail, Tall Bull, and White Antelope later became great chiefs.

33

The scouts were instructed to do nothing that would bring on a fight near the Pawnee camp and warn that tribe that enemies were near. If they met one or two Pawnees far from the camp, they might attack them, but they must be sure to kill any enemies they attacked so that no one would escape to warn the Pawnee camp. So the six scouts started on their cautious advance, all mounted on fast horses. They had gone a long way across the prairie when they at length sighted a lone Pawnee. He was on foot carrying a large burden on his back, and being on the open prairie where there were no trees or bushes for him to make a stand behind, he looked like an easy victim. The scouts whipped up their horses and made at him, each man eager to win the honor of counting the first coup on their victim. On sighting them, the Pawnee threw down his burden and strung his bow. Then he started running, but to the amazement of the scouts he ran straight at them. With a whoop, Good Bear raced his horse onward to count the first coup, but the Pawnee put an arrow clear through the young Sioux's mount, dropping him in his tracks. White Antelope, a close second behind Good Bear, rushed in and got an arrow in his horse's side. Wolf Mule, a Cheyenne, tried his luck, but when the Pawnee whirled to face him, he turned away and got an arrow in his back. The scouts now drew off to a respectful distance and stood watching the Pawnee. He was a lively person. He was now skipping back and forth, slapping his behind at them and yelling taunts. "Come on!" he shouted. "Kill me! I am a chief! If you kill me, you can boast that you have killed a chief! I am like the sun!" But the six scouts had had enough of him. They started sadly back toward their main party. They agreed that it would be best to say nothing about the devil of a Pawnee, but when they got to camp, it was all too evident that they had been in a fight. They were closely questioned, and the main facts came out. The leaders of the war party were very angry. These scouts had disobeyed orders; they had attacked a lone enemy and then let him escape to warn his camp. The Sioux soldiers gave their three scouts a sound whipping with quirts, and the Cheyenne soldiers tanned their scouts properly. What happened after that is not stated, but the war party probably turned back, knowing that the Pawnees had been warned and were on their guard.[11]

The Cheyennes remembered the story of these scouts and the whipping they received for disobeying orders. It was a nice tale, illustrating the fact that even great chiefs were given to making mistakes when they were young and hot-blooded. The Sioux did not remember the story, but spoke of Spotted Tail's fine fighting deeds as a young man. He certainly was a good warrior; but the Sioux notion, set forth by Eastman, that Spotted Tail distinguished himself in a fight with the Utes and was made a shirt-wearer, or war chief, at the time when he was little more than a stripling, is obviously erroneous. He was a simple scout in 1839, and probably did not win the rank of shirt-wearer for another ten years.

Having made an excellent start as a hunter and warrior, Spotted Tail turned to the third interest of Sioux men and began to court girls. He probably had much success in this new venture, for he was a handsome and bold young man. Soon, in 1841 as nearly as can be made out, he fell in love with a handsome Brulé girl, and she evidently returned his love. But she was being courted by an older man, a chief named Running Bear (*Mato Wakuwa*), who was wealthy and seems to have had the backing of the girl's parents. Spotted Tail, refusing to be warned off, continued to court the girl. Then one day he and Running Bear met outside the camp. A quarrel was started; they fell to fighting with knives, and Spotted Tail killed the Chief, but he was himself badly wounded. When he recovered, he took the girl as his first wife.[12]

11 George Bent told this story to me about 1910, and George Bird Grinnell printed the same tale in his *Cheyenne Indians*, II, 54.

12 Susan Bettelyoun when she was very old and her mind not particularly clear, denied this story of the duel between Spotted Tail and Running Bear, but the story was obtained by William Bordeaux from old Brulés as early as the year 1915, and it is set down by James McLaughlin (a careful writer, who knew the Brulés intimately as far back as 1885), by Dr. Eastman, and by other authorities. This first wife was with Spotted Tail when he was a prisoner at Fort Leavenworth, and she lived to bear him thirteen children.

2. Brisk Young Man

SPOTTED TAIL BELONGED to the most adventurous group of the Brulé Sioux—to a camp that was one of the first to desert the White River and move down to the North Platte. Not satisfied with that, part of them went farther south, joining the Cheyennes and Arapahoes on the South Platte and hunting eastward to the heads of the Kansas River, fighting the Pawnees in their hunting grounds on the Republican and Solomon forks of that stream. With them was the Red Lodge camp, which William Bordeaux terms a Miniconjou group. Bordeaux repeats a story that was told by Swift Bear of this band. The old Chief said that the winter of 1832 was a very hard one and there were no buffalo on White River. The Red Lodge people and other camps were starving. The chiefs decided that the only hope was to reach the great buffalo herds south of the Platte. The Red Lodge and some other groups set out and, after a dreadful march through the snow, found buffalo on the Republican Fork and were saved from starvation.

The other Upper Brulé camps, including the strong Wazhazha group, generally wintered at White Cliffs on the head of White River and in spring and summer hunted down toward the North Platte, going to Laramie Fork to trade and then returning to White River to winter. Spotted Tail's camp and the Red Lodges often wintered on White River with the other camps, but as the years went by, they were more inclined to regard the country from the Platte to Republican Fork as their homeland.

The movement south to the Platte and beyond had split the old Brulé tribe. The bands that took part in this movement were presently being termed *Kheyatawichasha*, meaning "People away from the [Missouri] River." They were more often termed the Highland or Upper Brulés. The more conservative and less venturesome camps that remained on White River and continued to trade at posts on the Missouri were called *Kutawichasha,* "Lowland People," or Lower Brulés. Their interests were centered along the Missouri in South Dakota, while the Upper Brulés became Platte River people, engaged in war with the Pawnees and with tribes farther to the south and in time losing most of their memories of their old close connection with the tribes along the Missouri and their eastern kinsmen, the Sioux of Minnesota. As for the old White River Indian paradise—it was no longer that. The Sioux who hunted on White River had come on bad times; game was often very scarce, and the bold Upper Brulés of the Platte country looked with pity and contempt on the Sioux of the White River and the Missouri, who (for lack of big game) often hunted rabbits and ducks and planted corn and vegetables to add to their slender food supply. These Missouri River Sioux were so lacking in spirit (according to the Upper Brulés) that they actually *bought* horses from white traders! How could Sioux men stoop so low? When the Upper Brulés wanted horses, they rode in force to the Pawnee villages on the Loup Fork of the Platte, charged into the villages, drove the Pawnees into their earth lodges, opened the horse pens between the lodges, and drove out the horses. They lost many a good warrior in these operations, but Sioux who would not take risks and find pleasure in a roaring fight were, in the opinion of the bold Upper Brulés, poor-spirited fellows.

The Pawnees had been masters of the Platte country west to beyond the forks before the Brulés and Oglalas came down from White River and the Black Hills. The fine hunting grounds here on the Platte and those on the head branches of Kansas River were undisputed Pawnee land, and the Pawnee earth-lodge villages on the Loup Fork were safe from enemies, even when the tribe went off on a buffalo hunt, leaving the villages deserted for many months at a time. But when the Sioux moved down to the Platte in the middle 1830's, the era of security for the Pawnees ended. In the 1820's the Pawnee villages were widely separated on Loup Fork, standing in the open prairie close to the river, each village surrounded by cornfields where the women and girls went to work in safety. Then the Sioux came. They came in small parties, slipping into the center of a village at night, opening horse pens and leading out the best mounts. By the time the Pawnees woke up in the morning and noted their losses, the Sioux were usually safely away. At other times a few Sioux would ride suddenly into the cornfields, kill some women and girls, scalp them, and ride off. If the Pawnees pursued the raiders, they ran the risk of riding into an ambuscade and being suddenly assaulted by an overwhelming force of mounted Sioux. By 1840, when young Spotted Tail was actively engaged in

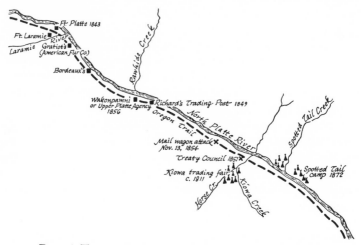

BRULÉ TRADE CENTER ON NORTH PLATTE 1835–65

this war, the Sioux had forced the Pawnees to move their villages to strong positions on the high bluffs, and some of the villages were now surrounded by a deep ditch with a log stockade inside the ditch.

The Brulés had an astonishing hatred for the Pawnees—an alien folk with outlandish customs, including that wicked practice of sacrificing female captives to their goddess Morning Star. That ancient custom had now been abandoned, the white traders and government officials urging the chiefs to give it up; but Spotted Tail and his friends could remember the sacrifice of the Sioux girl in 1838, and they loathed and hated the Skidi tribe of Pawnees who had perpetrated that deed of blood. They regarded the Pawnees as an inferior race, whom the Sioux always defeated with ease. "We killed them like birds" was a common Sioux way of describing a big fight with the Pawnees, and it was useless to remind the Sioux of the many brave deeds of Pawnee warriors, of small parties of Pawnees venturing into Sioux camps and getting safely away with horses and other plunder. The truth lay in the fact that the Sioux had greater fighting forces and that the Pawnees were on the defensive. Both at their home villages and in the hunting field, the Pawnees had to be constantly on the alert, and they never knew whether the Sioux would come with a party of half a dozen warriors or with an overwhelming force of five hundred.

Eastman asserted that Spotted Tail, Two Strike, and their companions-in-arms won their reputations in fights with the Utes. He ignored the Brulé war on the Pawnees. As has been pointed out, there is no record of fights between the Brulés and Utes at the period 1835–55, when these young Brulé men gained renown as warriors. Eastman stated that Spotted Tail and Two Strike first distinguished themselves when the Utes came and made a surprise attack on a Brulé camp, throwing the people into a panic. Young Spotted Tail rallied a party of warriors, turned the enemy flank, and attacked them in the rear, routing them. In the flight a Ute had his pony killed. He jumped up behind a friend on his pony. Two Strike overtook these two men on the one pony, struck and counted coup on both, and then evidently, killed them. For this deed he was given his name *Nomcapa*, Two Strike, or He Who Strikes Two.[1] After this fight, says Eastman, Brave Bear and the other chiefs made Spotted Tail a *tanka-un*, or war-shirt-wearer—a rank usually termed by the whites as that of war chief. Since Brave Bear was killed in the Grattan fight in 1854, this fight in which Spotted Tail won renown must have been before that; but there is no record what-

[1] Two Strike apparently had not heard of his famous bout with the Utes, for he said in 1874 that his name came from a feat he performed when he was sixteen, the killing of two buffalo cows with a single shot. The arrow went through one cow and into the other, killing them both. The name Two Strike was old, as Harry Anderson found a record of a Saone head-soldier of the date 1825 who was named *Nomcapa*, Knocks-Down-Two or Two Strike. In 1874, Two Strike said that he was fifty-three, born in 1821. He had two sons and two daughters, and he died in 1914.

ever of an enemy attack in force on a Brulé camp. The only engagement that at all resembles that described by Eastman was the one with Lieutenant Grattan's troops in 1854. In this affair, a Brulé camp was invaded; Spotted Tail gathered a force of warriors on the flank and rear of the troops and then assaulted and drove them in panic flight. The Eastman account of Spotted Tail's life is full of errors; nevertheless, Eastman was a Sioux, and it seems incredible that he could have confused the Grattan affair of 1854 to such an extent as to describe it as a fight with Utes.

Spotted Tail did have a war shirt, which he treasured and evidently still had in the late 1870's. It was the typical Sioux scalp-shirt that only the most distinguished war leaders could own. Alfred Sorenson, of Omaha, in describing this war shirt, must have repeated information obtained from whites who had seen it in Spotted Tail's possession. He called it a war dress, ornamented with locks of hair from more than one hundred enemy scalps.[2]

It was in the days of his youth that Spotted Tail first became acquainted with Red Cloud, who was of the same age or about a year older. By 1850 both of these young men had won distinction as warriors, and they had both gained the rank of war-shirt-wearers, Spotted Tail among the Brulés, Red Cloud among the Oglalas. While Spotted Tail was fighting the Pawnees in Nebraska, Red Cloud was engaged against the Snakes in the Rockies and the Crows in Wyoming and Montana. Between 1835 and 1855 these two young leaders gained great reputations and took over one hundred enemy scalps each; yet they are not mentioned in any written records of the period, and their own people have forgotten all about their early deeds in war.

When the Oglalas and Brulés began moving down to the Platte to hunt and trade, at the time when the first trading post was

[2] Alfred Sorenson, in *Omaha World Herald Sunday Magazine*, September 21, 1930. Sorenson's information came largely from Captain Jesse M. Lee, who was Spotted Tail's agent in 1877–78. What became of Spotted Tail's famous war dress is unknown. Could he have been buried in it in 1881? His headdress with the raccoon tail attached to it was seen by army men at Fort Laramie in the 1850's and 1860's; he had his scalp-shirt at Spotted Tail Agency in the 1870's. Neither article was described in detail. Red Cloud's war costume is pictured in color in Dodge, *Our Wild Indians*.

built on Laramie Fork in 1834, they came under the influence of
new traders; but the American Fur Company traders on the Missouri regarded the enticing of these Sioux camps down to the Platte
as an attempt of the other traders to steal Indians who belonged to
them, and a bitter trade war was now begun. It was not ended when
the American Fur Company bought out the traders of Laramie Fork;
for new trading companies entered the field, and there were also
the trading companies on the South Platte and the Bent brothers,
whose post was on the Arkansas in southeastern Colorado. As was
always the case when competition for the Indian trade was keen,
the rival companies made free use of liquor. They drenched the
Sioux camps with alcohol; they sold it at a loss and even gave it
away in kegs to the Sioux to win them away from rival traders.
Another period of drunken sprees, accompanied by killings and ac-
cidental deaths, struck the Sioux camps. It was just what had happened on White River when Spotted Tail was a baby; and now,
when he was in his late teens, the same debauchery of his tribe by
traders was being repeated. It is said that he and many of the other
young Brulés took a pledge that they would never taste liquor, and
they kept their word. The efforts of government agents to stop the
flow of liquor to the Sioux camps was of little avail; but changes
in the Indian trade put a stop to this illicit traffic, and by 1844 conditions were much better. Indians could still obtain drink; but they
had difficulty in getting it. They had to deal with traders of bad
repute, and they had to pay a very high price for the stuff.

By moving down to the North Platte, the Brulés and Oglalas had
inadvertently placed themselves across the new emigrant road to
Oregon, a situation that was certain to lead to serious trouble with
the whites. No one could have foreseen what now took place. In
the year following the building of the first little trading post on
Laramie Fork in 1834, the first emigrant train of white-topped
wagons came rolling slowly up the Platte valley, astonishing the
Sioux and their traders. Year by year the flow of emigration up the
Platte grew, and soon the Sioux and Cheyennes were angry over
this intrusion of white people, who were killing the game and destroying the timber and grass along the Platte. The emigrants were
alarmed over parties of Indians coming to their camps to demand

food and to pilfer any articles small enough to conceal under their blankets. Besides this, emigrants who left camp to go hunting were at times caught by parties of warriors, who took their rifles and horses, stripped them of all their belongings, and set them adrift in the plains almost naked. The emigrants wrote to their families in the eastern states, and pressure was exerted in Washington to obtain better protection for emigrant parties from the Indians.

In 1845, Colonel S. W. Kearny was sent up the Platte with a force of dragoons to meet the Sioux on Laramie Fork and warn them not to molest the emigrants. He found the Brulés trading at Fort John (now beginning to be referred to as Fort Laramie), and on June 15 he paraded five companies of dragoons and his artillery, the dragoons making an impressive display, the men mounted on American horses, much larger and stronger than the Indian ponies, and armed with sabers, a weapon strange and frightening to the Sioux. Kearny had his big guns fired and then held a council with the Sioux. Two flags were flying over the council ground: the Stars and Stripes and a Sioux flag (probably the only Sioux flag ever seen, made by the traders for this occasion), a flag with a blue field and two diagonal lines symbolizing winds, above the winds two hands clasped in friendship, and above the hands were nine stars. Old Bull Tail of the Brulés spoke for the Indians. He was very old, and this was his last recorded public appearance. Kearny offered friendship, but cautioned the Sioux to be careful in their dealings with the emigrant families. He distributed gifts to the chiefs, and that night rockets were fired into the skies while the mass of Indians looked on in awe.

Spotted Tail may have been present when Colonel Kearny marched to Laramie Fork, but we do not know that he was. John Y. Nelson stated that Spotted Tail at this period was living in a camp south of the Platte and that he wintered down there, going in early summer to Cottonwood Springs, just below the forks of the River, where the Brulés held their great annual ceremony, the Sun Dance. They then went to the nearest trading post to trade, and after that started south on another buffalo hunt. They were still much occupied in fighting the Pawnees, who every summer and winter came to the Republican to hunt buffalo, bringing their camp,

women, children, and all their horse herds with them. Until the
government appointed a special agent for the Indians on the Upper
Platte, the Little Thunder and Spotted Tail group of Brulé camps
did not have to go to Fort Laramie. There were trading posts on
the South Platte below the present city of Denver, and after 1845
traders began to frequent the Cottonwood Springs locality to trade
with the Southern Brulés in their own lands. Little Thunder (*Waki-
nyan Chika*) was the leading man among these Southern Brulés
after 1845. He is said to have been the son of Black Moon; but
W. T. Hamilton, who met this Brulé camp on the North Platte in
1842, stated that Little Thunder's father was Chief Big Thunder,
who was still the leader of the camp at that time. In 1843, Matthew
C. Field was at Fort Laramie. He did not mention Big Thunder,
but stated that Little Thunder was the most influential chief among
the Brulés, the head of the most important Brulé band. The Chief
was six feet tall, a handsome man, with a commanding bearing.
Bordeaux (then in charge of the trading post) termed Little Thunder the bravest and most honorable of the Sioux chiefs, and he
called the Brulés the best Indians on the Upper Platte. Field did
not mention Spotted Tail in his list of Little Thunder's headmen,
and this fact casts doubt on the assertions of John Y. Nelson that
Spotted Tail was a leader among the Sioux living south of the
Platte at this date. In 1844, Frémont met a camp of these Southern
Brulés on the Arkansas River in Kansas. They were with a Cheyenne
camp.

The other principal camps of the Upper Brulés at this period
were the Corn Band, the Orphans, and the Wazhazhas. The Corn
Band must have had a different name in earlier years. The Swift
Bear winter count states that a white man taught this camp how to
plant corn on White River in 1823–24 (about the time of Spotted
Tail's birth). After that the band was called *Wagmezayuha* (They
Have Corn). The other Brulé bands thought that it was an outrageous thing for any bold Brulés to attempt to cultivate the soil,
and they forced the Corn Band to give up that practice. After 1845
the Red Lodge camp belonged to the Corn Band, and Swift Bear
of the Red Lodges finally became the chief of this camp. The
Orphan, or *Wablenicha*, was another camp that had a different name

in early years. In the 1840's this camp had a bad leader, a chief of poor judgment named Big Raven. In 1844 he led a war party against the Shoshonis, and by carelessness or bad luck the Chief and all the able-bodied men of his camp were killed. The band was now called the Orphans. After 1845 their leader was Grand Partisan (*Blotanhunka Tonka*).[3]

The Wazhazhas were not recognized as real Brulés, although they lived with that tribe. They were a strong camp that wintered on the head of White River and spent the summer and autumn hunting and trading down near the North Platte. With the Orphans and the Corn Band, they formed the group of Upper Brulés that wandered between the White River and the North Platte, usually trading at posts on Laramie Fork.

In the summer of 1843 a party of traders came up the Platte and found a Sioux camp at Cottonwood Springs. John Y. Nelson, then a boy of seventeen, was with this party, and he claimed in later years that he joined Spotted Tail at this time and wintered with him on the Republican and Solomon forks of the Kansas River. Nelson asserted that Spotted Tail was then living with the Oglala group led by Man-Who-Walks-under-the-Ground and Whistler. These men were chiefs of the Southern Oglalas who lived south of the Platte, camping often with the Brulés.

Nelson stated that Spotted Tail at this time was a chief and had five women in his family group, evidently in two lodges. Nelson claimed that during the winter 1843–44, Spotted Tail induced him to marry his thirteen-year-old niece, *Walmbi Zizi*, which he translates Yellow Elk, although the meaning is Yellow Eagle.

The Nelson book is the only printed source that gives any details of the life of Spotted Tail during the obscure years from 1841 to 1854. Unfortunately, Nelson had a reputation as a frontier prevaricator, and although part of what he relates concerning Spotted Tail is obviously true, many of his assertions are clearly manufactured, usually with the object of making himself appear more important than he really was. Nelson depicts Spotted Tail and the

---

[3] His name is signed to the treaty of 1851 as *Belotankah Tangah,* and Rufus Sage (1841–42) calls him Big Eagle. The name might bear that translation, but it was evidently a title of honor, Big Eagle being the rank of a leader of warriors.

group of Sioux he lived among as wintering on the Republican and Solomon forks, hunting buffalo in those lands and fighting the Pawnee tribe, which twice a year came into the same lands on extended hunts, bringing their camps, their women, and their children with them. The Sioux were making it almost impossible for the Pawnees to obtain buffalo meat and skins. Whenever the Pawnees left their camp and set out to surround a herd, the lurking Sioux and Cheyennes came down on them with a superior force and drove the scattered Pawnees in flight back to their camp. The camp itself was often attacked, Pawnee horses were stolen in large numbers, and many Pawnees were killed while hunting.

In summer, the Sioux left the Republican and Solomon and moved up to the Platte at Cottonwood Springs, where they usually held a great Sun Dance in June. They then would make up a war party and go and attack the Pawnee villages on Loup Fork. Spotted Tail undoubtedly took a leading part in such attacks on the Pawnee villages.

Chief Little Thunder, with whose group Spotted Tail was associated, was an unlucky man. The winter counts relate that in 1840–41 five of his brothers were killed by the Pawnees. In the following year, the Sioux got up a big expedition to seek vengeance from the Pawnees. The winter counts do not record the results, but as these winter-count dates are often a year out of line, this Sioux attack on the Pawnee villages may be the one of June, 1843. The missionaries had established themselves on Loup Fork and set to work to bring the blessings of Christianity to the Pawnees. The Pawnees had warned the whites of the danger from Sioux attacks, but the missionaries (some of them fresh from Ohio homes) did not credit the tales of Sioux fierceness.

At dawn on June 27, 1843, a Pawnee chief drove his herd of horses out of the earth-lodge village within sight of the mission buildings, and having placed his animals on good grass, he lay down on the ground and went to sleep again. Some Sioux, lurking in the willows along the river bank, slipped out and killed the Pawnee. They then started to drive his ponies toward the hills. The Pawnees in the village took the alarm, and a mounted force came out and pursued the Sioux; but they suddenly found themselves faced by

three to five hundred mounted Sioux, who came out of the hills
and drove the Pawnees pell-mell into their village. Here the Sioux
killed a number of people before they could find shelter in the big
earth lodges. Some of the Sioux now got on the roofs of the lodges
and fired down through the smoke holes at the Pawnees inside;
other Sioux were opening the horse pens and driving out the Pawnee horses. They set fire to a number of earth lodges and then
withdrew; but as soon as they reached the hilltop which was the
assembly point for their war party, another band of Sioux formed
up and charged down the slope, singing a deep-throated chant and
blowing shrill war whistles. They drove their charge straight into
the Pawnee village and repeated the performance of the first party.
This fight went on for hours, the missionaries watching aghast as
the Sioux made one roaring charge after another straight into the
Pawnee village. When at last they withdrew, they left the village
a shambles. Sixty-seven Pawnees had been killed and twenty-six
wounded, in a village of some eight hundred people; two hundred
horses had been carried off (all that were in the village) and half
of the forty earth lodges had been burned down. The survivors of
the fight fled in panic south of the Platte to join other Pawnee
groups.[4]

Although his name is not mentioned, Spotted Tail was undoubtedly a leader in this fight. Names of the Sioux leaders are not on
record; but a few weeks after the fight at the Pawnee village, young
John Nelson found Spotted Tail in the camp of Sioux at Cottonwood Springs, within easy striking distance of the Pawnee villages.

Nelson went with Spotted Tail to winter in a Sioux camp on the
head of Solomon Fork. In the spring of 1844, the Sioux broke camp
and moved down the Solomon, hunting for the Pawnee tribe but

---

[4] An account of this fight at the Pawnee villages is in Hyde, *The Pawnee
Indians*, 54–55. The Brulés were still holding feasts in honor of the warriors who
had distinguished themselves in this fight in September, 1843, when the hunting
party of Sir William Drummond Stewart came to Laramie Fork. Young Iron
Shell, of the Orphan Band, had killed eleven Pawnees in the fight. A feast was
given in his honor, and Sir William presented the young Indian with a horse. Little
Thunder and his headmen then appeared, in a very bad temper, making rude remarks about the white men honoring "small Brulés" of no importance and ignoring
the really big leaders of the tribe. Matthew C. Field, *Prairie and Mountain Sketches*,
182.

failing to find them. The Pawnees had evidently returned to their villages to plant their crops. In summer they returned to the buffalo range for meat and hides, and, according to Nelson, a great force of Sioux caught them on the Solomon and had a terrific fight with them. The triumphant Sioux then wintered at the Big Timbers on the Upper Republican Fork.

At this period, the Sioux came very near to destroying the Pawnee tribe. The villages on Loup Fork were never safe from the Sioux; the women could not cultivate their corn patches in safety. Almost every week some women were killed in their little fields by lurking Sioux, and horses were constantly being stolen. If the Pawnees pursued the Sioux horse thieves, they often ran into an ambuscade and found themselves face to face with an overwhelming force of Sioux. In the buffalo range near the Republican Fork they were being harassed and prevented from obtaining meat and hides. Every year or so they had a big fight with the Sioux and their allies in the buffalo country and lost from fifty to one hundred men and women. The missionaries gave up in 1845 and abandoned the Loup Fork. The Pawnees deserted their villages there and fled south of the Platte; but by doing this they offended the United States authorities, who wished to keep the Pawnees on Loup Fork, away from the emigrant trail up the Platte. The Pawnees, in deadly fear of the Sioux, refused to return to the Loup, and the Sioux now came and attacked them in their new location on the Platte. In 1848 the military post later known as Fort Kearney was established on Pawnee land on the south bank of the Platte at Grand Island. It was not built to protect the Pawnees but to guard the emigrant trains from Indian molestation.

The triumphant Sioux were pressing the weakened Pawnees hard. The Pawnees had formed an alliance with the Omaha tribe, which had also been much weakened by Sioux attacks, and the Pawnees and Omahas now often joined forces when they ventured into the buffalo range, to present a united front if the Sioux attacked them. This Indian war was causing the government much embarrassment. It was being carried on along the road to Oregon and California, which was usually crowded with emigrant trains.

On July 6, 1849, five hundred Sioux and Cheyenne warriors

struck the Platte road below Fort Kearney. They went to the Grand Pawnee village, found that the Pawnees were away on a hunt, plundered the village, and burned it. Down the road they came on an army transport train; and having surrounded it, they plundered the wagons and robbed the teamsters. They then made off; but farther down the road the wagon train ran into a body of seven hundred Pawnee, Omaha, and Oto warriors, who were hunting for the Sioux and Cheyennes. They evidently failed to find them, as there is no record of a big Indian fight during the summer.[5]

The Sioux, particularly the Southern Brulé and Oglala groups, were elated over their successes against the Pawnees. In little more than ten years, with some help from their Cheyenne and Arapaho allies, they had established themselves firmly in the heart of the hunting grounds the Pawnees had formerly held undisturbed; they had driven this hated tribe from their villages on Loup Fork and now felt that they could soon destroy the last of these enemies. Spotted Tail and many men of his group had won renown in this Pawnee war, and they were filled with pride and confidence in themselves and their people. Ignorant of the world outside their own little orbit, they were confident that they could defeat any foes, including the white people. Indeed, many of these Sioux warriors looked down on the whites, regarding them as inferior to the Pawnees. After all, the Pawnees had many good warriors among them; but the mass of these white emigrants who were pouring westward up the Platte road were obviously not warriors at all. Most of them did not even have horses. They used cows (ox teams) to haul their long trains of white-topped wagons, and even the white soldiers who now occupied the old trading post on Laramie Fork, to guard the emigrants against Indians, had very few horses. The Sioux warriors regarded with contempt these infantry troops. What could walking soldiers do in a fight against mounted warriors? Some of the Indian traders and some of the chiefs warned the younger warriors not to harbor foolish ideas about the power of

[5] Hyde, *The Pawnee Indians*, 171. Spotted Tail must have been a leader in this war party, for John Y. Nelson states that Spotted Tail was with some Brulé and Oglala camps on the Republican, southwest of Fort Kearney, from the spring of 1848 to the summer of 1849, and at this point Nelson is evidently telling the truth, as he had no reason for falsifying the facts.

the whites; but it was impossible to convince Spotted Tail and the other young leaders that the Sioux could not defeat the whites whenever they chose to go to war with them.

No matter how brave in war a Sioux man of the 1840's might be, he could not rise to prominence in the tribe unless he had a strong group of kinsmen to support him. Spotted Tail had his father, brothers, sisters, uncles, cousins, nephews, and nieces in his numerous family connections, and by marriages with other strong families his position as a rising young leader in the tribe was made more secure. Two of his sisters became the wives of an Oglala medicine man named Crazy Horse, who was a member of the powerful Smoke family of that tribe. This man Crazy Horse was the brother of the Oglala chief, Long Face, later known as Little Hawk, and he was the father of the famous Oglala war chief Crazy Horse of Custer battle fame. In the 1840's, Red Cloud—a handsome and bold young warrior—visited the Brulés and carried off a pretty girl, refusing to pay the girl's relatives the usual price in ponies and other property for his bride. Spotted Tail himself made marriage connections with the leading family of the powerful Wazhazha band (the Brave Bear and Red Leaf family) and also with the Man-Afraid-of-His-Horse family among the Oglalas.[6]

When Spotted Tail's Brulé camp first began to frequent the Platte valley, when he was about ten years old, the river was nothing more than the dividing line between the buffalo herds to the north and those to the south, and the establishment of a trading post on Laramie Fork made the Upper Platte a rival point of Sioux trade, competing with the old trade center on the Missouri in South Dakota. The amazing emigration of white families up the Platte valley on their way to the Pacific Coast had swiftly altered conditions, and by 1848 the great valley was being controlled by the government in the interest of emigrants. The heavy travel was spoiling the valley for Indian occupation. The grass was eaten off by the animals the emigrant trains brought with them; timber was disap-

[6] My friend Harry Anderson has found the minutes of a council at Fort Laramie, June 12, 1867, in the National Archives, and the documents show that at this council Spotted Tail called Man-Afraid-of-His-Horse his brother-in-law and Red Leaf gave the same title to Spotted Tail. This would seem to mean that both Red Leaf and Man-Afraid-of-His-Horse had married sisters of Spotted Tail.

pearing, and game was being destroyed. Realizing the growing feeling of anger among the tribesmen, the government built Fort Kearney at Grand Island on the Lower Platte and bought from the American Fur Company the old trading post on Laramie Fork, which was garrisoned by a small force of infantry.

The young men among the Sioux of the Platte country were not impressed by the founding of these two military posts. Their attitude was one of defiance and provocation. They exhibited this very clearly when the war party of five hundred Sioux and Cheyenne warriors attempted to bring war into the Platte valley and almost within sight of Fort Kearney in early July, 1849. They were going to fight the Pawnees and Omahas right there, and if the white emigrants were injured during the fighting, it would serve them right for coming into Indian country where they were not wanted. To make their position even clearer, this war party, one of whose leaders was undoubtedly Spotted Tail, stopped and robbed the wagon train that was hauling military stores to Fort Kearney. This was very close to open war on the whites.

At this very moment, and almost as if the whites had struck back instantly in retaliation, a dreadful blow fell on the proud Sioux and their allies. Asiatic cholera had broken out in the Mississippi valley and had been brought into the Plains—up the Arkansas and Platte roads—by forty-niners on their way to the new gold fields of California. The Sioux and Cheyenne warriors who had robbed the army wagons east of Fort Kearney went home to their camps on the Republican and Solomon forks, and there the cholera broke out with a suddenness and violence that appalled the bravest of the Indians. The Cheyennes broke camp and fled south to get away from the cholera. On the trail they met a Cheyenne camp fleeing north from the Arkansas River, with the cholera killing them as they ran. The Brulé and Oglala Sioux left the Republican and Solomon and fled north. At the crossing of the South Platte, they buried a Sioux chief, dead of cholera, placing his body in a death lodge. They fled on northward. Near Ash Hollow on the North Platte they left five lodges full of dead Sioux, killed by cholera. They fled back to their old home on the head of White River, and there they encamped on a small southern branch of the river. Later another band of Sioux came here and found the lodges standing, all full of dead people. The Sioux gave this little stream the name *Wanagi Wakpa,* Ghost Creek. The whites called it Deadman's Creek.

In the Platte valley, alive with wagon trains moving westward, white men, women, and children were dying of cholera. New graves dotted the roadside. The Mounted Rifle Regiment was marching to Oregon. It reached Fort Kearney in May; but even that early in the season four thousand emigrant wagons had passed the fort with twenty thousand persons, taking the cholera with them. Captain Stansbury, with a small military party, was a few days in rear of the Rifle Regiment. His party reached the North Platte early in July and found five lodges filled with dead Sioux near Ash Hollow. A little beyond this point they met the Sioux trader James Bordeaux with ten lodges of Brulés, probably part of the Corn Band or Red Lodges, for it was to a woman of the Red Lodges that Bordeaux was married. These Sioux were now recovering from cholera, but they had had dreadful losses and were in terror that the mysterious sickness would attack them again. Just west of Bordeaux's camp, Stansbury found thirty lodges of Brulés with Joseph Bissonnette, their trader. Cholera was raging among these Indians, and they begged pitifully for medicines. They had lost faith in their own medicine men, but when Stansbury sent his army doctor among them they received with humble gratitude the medicines proffered, swallowing them eagerly and exhibiting indications of faith that they would now be saved.

It was reported in the following year that half the Cheyenne tribe had died of cholera. The losses among all the tribes affected were very heavy, and the impact of this mysterious disease produced a widespread feeling of hopelessness. The cholera hung on for a year, and was followed by smallpox, which carried off many hundreds of Indians. Recovering at last from these sicknesses, the young men among the Sioux and Cheyennes began to talk of vengeance. To the minds of these people disease was often the work of magicians, and a goodly number of the Indians were convinced that the cholera at least was a wicked magic that the whites had deliberately turned loose among them. The chiefs doubted this view, but many of them had a feeling that their people were doomed. They could see no way to save them.[7]

The government Indian agents and the Indian traders were becoming alarmed over the growing feeling of hostility among the Plains Indians. A plan for a council with the tribes was devised, and as the situation among the Sioux and Cheyennes along the Platte was considered the most serious threat—these tribes being in a position to block the road to Oregon and California—the council was to be held at Fort Laramie. Agents were sent to many tribes and by coaxing and the promise of handsome gifts, delegations of chiefs were persuaded to attend the council. Sioux chiefs came from the Missouri, Crows from the Yellowstone, and a large party of Snakes from their land west of the Rockies. The Pawnees, who desperately needed peace, were for some unexplained reason not even invited to attend this great peace gathering. Congress had voted the sum of $100,000 for this council, and with the money great quantities of food and gifts had been purchased for distribution to the Indians.

This "first treaty council," as the Sioux in later times wrongly termed it (they had held treaty councils with the government officials on the Missouri in 1825 and at St. Louis in 1816), was held in the summer of 1851. Indian Superintendent D. D. Mitchell was in charge of the council. He reached Fort Laramie in August and found great camps of Sioux and Cheyennes assembled. Delegations came from the more distant tribes. Mitchell had to wait for the wagon train carrying the food and other gifts before he could open the council. Day after day passed; the great herds of Indian ponies devoured all the grass within miles of Fort Laramie; game was hunted out; and to support their ponies and obtain meat for their families, the Indians presently moved down the North Platte to Horse Creek, thirty-seven miles below the fort. Here in early

[7] The Indian agent on the Upper Missouri reported that the Sioux talked constantly of all their people who had died of cholera and smallpox and bitterly blamed the whites for introducing these diseases. Hayden (1857) added that many chiefs and headmen had died in the epidemics, tribal control had relaxed, and good order could no longer be maintained in the camps, where hotheads and troublemakers were now free to do as they pleased.

September the council was held and the treaty signed. It was a treaty of peace and friendship between the government and the tribes and between each tribe and all the others. It impressed the Indians greatly. On September 6 one thousand Sioux warriors on fine ponies and wearing handsome war costumes paraded through the great Indian camps in a dense column, four abreast, singing war songs and uttering fierce war cries. Several hundred Cheyenne warriors held a similar parade. The small force of Snake Indians from west of the Rockies watched grimly. They had to be protected by mounted dragoons, for fear the Sioux and Cheyennes would massacre them. The coming of the wagon train put an end to fears of trouble. Free food and gifts were handed out lavishly; each tribe held feasts in honor of the others, the Sioux and Cheyennes feasting their Crow and Snake foes and loading them with handsome presents.

Spotted Tail was certainly at this council, but his name is not mentioned in any of the contemporary reports. He was now a war leader of the Brulés, but not yet a chief. The names of three of the Brulé chiefs were set down on the treaty. First, and as head chief, came *Mato Oyuhi* (Scattering, or Whirling Bear, usually termed Brave Bear or Conquering Bear), who was chief of the Wazhazha band. The second chief to sign was *Makatozaza* (Clear Blue Earth), who may have been Spotted Tail's chief. He died in the following year, or in 1853. The third Brulé chief to sign was *Blotanhunka Tonka* (Grand Partisan), of the Corn band.

Brave Bear's selection as head chief was undoubtedly the work of the government agents and white traders. Rufus Sage had met this Indian in the Sioux winter camps on the head of White River in 1841–42. At that date, Brave Bear was a turbulent warrior who was being paid by the Missouri River traders to harass the rival traders from the Upper Platte, which duty he had performed by stealing the horses of the Platte traders, attempting to set fire to their trading house, and planning to murder them. By 1851, Brave Bear had developed responsibility, and as chief of the Wazhazha camp he was urging his people not to molest the whites and trying to impress them with the fact that in a war the whites would win.

Frank Salway, who was a trader on the Upper Platte in the early

1850's, stated that in 1851 the two big chiefs of the Brulés were Brave Bear and Little Thunder and that the Indians themselves considered Brave Bear to be the stronger chief. The traders and government officials took the same view, regarding this Wazhazha chief to be the best man to recognize as head chief of the Brulé group of the Platte.

The Sioux in later years claimed that under this treaty of 1851 they "lent" the lands along the Platte to the Great Father and that the government then kept the lands and failed to make any payment for them. In fact, the treaty had nothing to do with the transfer of lands. It was a simple peace and friendship agreement. It provided that free annuity goods should be delivered by government agents to each tribe for a period of fifty years. It defined the boundaries of each tribe and implied that the tribes were to respect these boundaries; yet the Sioux in the next few years invaded the fine hunting grounds of the Crow tribe in Wyoming and Montana, drove the Crows out, and took the lands by conquest. The government's only objects in making this treaty were peace and the protection of white emigrants on the California and Oregon road along the Platte. It was a humane program in its main features, and the men (the Sioux Indians and white authors) who have in later years accused the government of bad faith do not seem to realize that the plan embraced in this treaty of 1851 was the most benevolent of several schemes that were under discussion in 1850 for dealing with the crisis in the Plains country. How would the Sioux have liked it if the plan put forward by Superintendent D. D. Mitchell had been adopted? Mitchell was a veteran Indian trader, a man who had the interests of the Indians at heart, and he regarded his plan as the best one for saving the tribes.

The plan was to take all the lands from the Niobrara River in the north to the Arkansas in the south, from the Missouri west to a line near Fort Laramie, and form all this vast tract into a new territory, opening it to settlement by the whites. The head of each Indian family was to be given one section of wild prairie land, and then the Indians were to be left to shift for themselves. Mitchell honestly believed that most of the tribesmen would learn farming from their new white neighbors, and thus the destruction of the buffalo and other game by the whites would not bring disaster to these hunting tribes. He was undoubtedly wrong. The Sioux of that period knew no way of life except that of hunting and war. They despised those tribes that tried to grow crops, and when the Brulé Corn Band attempted to do a little planting on White River, they were fiercely denounced and forced to give up their growing of corn, which the other bands regarded a shameful departure from honest Sioux custom. If Mitchell's plan had been put into effect in 1851, the Sioux would have gone to war the moment the whites began settling in their country, and the tribe would have been destroyed or conquered within ten years. Even if they had submitted and tried to farm, they could not have succeeded. On the reservation after 1865 the government strove desperately to make farmers of the Sioux, and after twenty-five years of effort it had failed to make any considerable number of these Indians self-supporting from the land.

To Spotted Tail, the appointment of Brave Bear as head chief must have been a very important event, for Brave Bear was his cousin, presumably on his mother's side of the family, and this would mean that his mother was a Wazhazha woman.

Brave Bear, the new head chief of the Brulés of the Platte, seems to have made an honest effort to maintain peace with the whites, but everything was against him. The immense and ever growing travel of white emigrants up the Platte valley had produced new conditions which the government officials and the Sioux chiefs could not cope with. With most of the Sioux believing that the whites were spoiling their country and bringing death to their people, the warriors, who believed they were strong enough to destroy all the whites, could not be restrained. The tiny infantry garrison at Fort Laramie could not protect the emigrants or even hold the fort if serious trouble came; yet the young officers at the post considered it to be their duty to send out armed detachments and attempt the arrest of any Indian warriors who were accused of offenses against the whites. Indian Agent Thomas Fitzpatrick, who had been an Indian trader for years before he was appointed agent, was very much disturbed by the conduct of the military officers. The Indian traders had learned by hard experience to leave Indian warriors alone. If a warrior committed an offense against the traders, they took the matter to the chiefs, who dealt with the warriors; but now on the Platte, if an Indian injured the whites in any way, the officers at Fort Laramie marched a little group of infantry into a big Indian camp and attempted to arrest the offending warrior. As most of the Sioux warriors preferred death to arrest, this method of keeping peace was hardly to be regarded as a rational one.

The peace treaty had been in force only a few months when the military brought on serious trouble by attempting to arrest Indians accused of offenses against the whites. There was more trouble in the summer of 1853 when Lieutenant Hugh B. Fleming was sent from Fort Laramie with a detachment of infantry to arrest a Miniconjou warrior. The soldiers marched into a big Sioux camp; the Indians flew to arms, someone fired a shot, and the troops responded with a volley, killing three or four Miniconjous. They then withdrew, having failed to arrest the Indian they were seeking. When Indian Agent Fitzpatrick reached Fort Laramie shortly after this affair, the relatives of the dead warriors were loudly calling for war, and even the friendly Sioux chiefs were infuriated at the conduct of the troops. The Indian agent held councils with the chiefs, quieted them, and even induced them to agree to an amendment of the 1851 treaty which the Senate had made.[8]

In the following August, 1854, the Sioux were at Fort Laramie again in full force, waiting for the Indian agent to arrive and give them their treaty annuities. The Sioux camps were east of Laramie Fork, standing between the Oregon Trail and the south bank of the North Platte River. Trains of emigrant wagons were passing along the road westward. A Mormon wagon train came slowly up the road, passing the Sioux camps. At the rear of the wagons, a

[8] The treaty of 1851 gave the Sioux and other tribes annuity payments in goods for fifty years, but the Senate amended this stipulation, altering the reading to fifteen years. Man-Afraid-of-His-Horse and other chiefs claimed in later years that they had never heard of this amendment, but Man-Afraid's name is written down, showing that he approved the amendment at a council near Fort Laramie in the summer of 1853. The Brulés whose names were signed as approving the amendment in 1853 were (1) Bear Erect (clearly, Brave Bear), (2) Yellow Ears, (3) Standing Bear, (4) Burnt Man, and (5) Eagle's Body; Oglalas, (1) Smoke, (2) Bad Wound, (3) Medicine Eagle, (4) Man-Afraid-of-His-Horse, and (5) Big Crow.

Mormon was leading a lame or worn-out ox. As he was passing the first of the Sioux camps, that of Brave Bear, the head chief, a Miniconjou, High Forehead, shot the ox with an arrow; and the Mormon, afraid of the Indians, abandoned his animal and hurried on to overtake the wagon train. At Fort Laramie, the Mormons reported the incident.

The Sioux Indians have several versions of this affair. Some accounts state that the Mormon was frightened and abandoned his

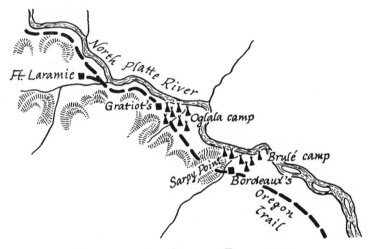

SCENE OF THE GRATTAN FIGHT 1854

ox and that the Miniconjou, who was hungry, shot the animal for food. It is apparent, however, that the Indian meant mischief and that his action was purely provocative. As Agent Fitzpatrick, a veteran Indian trader, used to say, when it came to starting trouble, the Indian was always two jumps ahead of any white man.

Brave Bear went to the fort to talk the incident over with Lieutenant Fleming, the post commander. The Chief regarded the killing of the Mormon's ox as a small matter and wished to have it left for the Indian agent to settle when the agent should arrive at the fort. That would have meant a few days of delay, a cooling-off period; but the young officers at the fort did not wish to wait.

Lieutenant Fleming stated later on that the killing of the Mormon ox was only one of a series of outrages against emigrants that the Sioux had committed in recent weeks, and that it was the opinion of the officers that if something were not done soon, the Indians would get completely out of hand. Fleming, who had tried to arrest a Miniconjou in 1853, had brought on a fight and caused much concern to higher authorities. He now hesitated as to what he should do. Lieutenant J. L. Grattan, a young officer fresh from West Point, was eager for stiff action. He believed that it was his turn to lead some soldiers into a Sioux camp and show what he could do, and he had expressed the view that with a few infantrymen and a fieldpiece or two he could whip the whole Sioux Nation. He kept urging Lieutenant Fleming to issue orders for him to go out and arrest this Miniconjou.

On the following morning, August 19, when the friendly Oglala head chief, Man-Afraid-of-His-Horse, came to the fort, he found that the decision had been taken. Grattan was to lead a party into the Brulé camp to arrest the Miniconjou. Calling for volunteers for dangerous service, Grattan selected two noncommissioned officers and twenty-seven infantrymen. With himself and the post interpreter, they made a party of thirty-one men. He took a twelve-pound fieldpiece and a small mountain howitzer. As the Brulé camp was some eight miles east of the fort, he took a wagon to carry part of the infantry. Some men rode on the gun carriages, and a few borrowed horses to ride.

Crossing Laramie Fork, the little expedition moved down the Oregon Trail, eastward. Four and one-half miles from the fort they passed Gratiot's American Fur Company trading house, in which the Indian annuity goods were stored, waiting for the agent to arrive and distribute them. East of Gratiot's the road passed over a spur or bluff, and from this high point the soldiers had a view down the wide Platte valley. Close below them was the Oglala Sioux camp of three hundred lodges. The Oglalas were driving in their pony herds and preparing for possible trouble. Below the Oglala camp was a small Miniconjou Sioux camp, and east of that a second spur or bluff, Sarpy Point. Just below this point stood James Bordeaux's trading house, and about three hundred yards from

Bordeaux's place was the Brulé Sioux camp, or rather two camps. The first camp was one of two hundred Brulé lodges, and immediately adjoining it was Chief Brave Bear's Wazhazha camp of eighty lodges, in which there was a group of Miniconjou lodges, among them the lodge of High Forehead, who had shot the Mormon's ox.

Lieutenant Grattan had his infantry load their muskets, and farther down the road he halted and had the two fieldpieces loaded. Reaching Bordeaux's place, he called the Frenchman out and asked him to accompany the troops into the Brulé camp; but Bordeaux was not fond of standing up to be shot at. He could smell trouble farther away than most men, and at this moment the odor was very strong. He made excuses, saying that he would come along later and join Grattan at the camp. He urged the Lieutenant to shut the interpreter up. He meant the French interpreter, Auguste Lucien, who was employed by the military. The man hated the Indians, who had run off his herd of horses. He had been drinking before he left the fort, had obtained more liquor at Gratiot's place, and was now shouting insults at the Sioux and riding his horse furiously up and down, to get it out of breath and give it its second wind, as all Indians did before going into battle. To make his meaning perfectly clear, he shouted at the Sioux that the soldiers were going to kill them all and that he, Auguste Lucien, would eat their hearts. Lieutenant Grattan ordered him to shut his mouth, but with little results.[9]

Bordeaux had sent for Chief Brave Bear, and he now came. Man-Afraid-of-His-Horse of the Oglalas, Grand Partisan of the Brulé Corn band, and Little Thunder of the Southern Brulés were also

[9] James Bordeaux in his letter recounting the Grattan killing, written August 21, 1854, gives the interpreter's name as Auguste Lucien. There has been much confusion regarding this man's identity. Some called him Lucien Auguste. The Sioux called him *Yuse*, which is evidently their pronunciation of Lucien. He had a Sioux wife named Ena Tiglak and two half-blood daughters, who married the Clifford brothers and were living in western Nebraska in the 1870's. One of these daughters wrote from her home at Martin, South Dakota, in 1926, and gave her father's name as Augustine Lutice. Matthew Field, in *Prairie and Mountain Sketches*, gives this man's name as Auguste Lucier and says that he was born at St. Charles, Missouri, May 4, 1814. He was employed as a hunter and guide by Sir William Drummond Stewart in 1843. Field describes him as very quarrelsome, particularly when drunk. His father was Antoine Lucier, born in Canada.

present. They all urged Grattan to let the matter rest until the Indian agent arrived, and Brave Bear offered ponies in payment for the Mormon ox; but Grattan refused all offers and stated that he was going to obey his orders and arrest the Miniconjou. He now moved his soldiers into the center of the tipi circle of Brave Bear's camp and formed a line of battle, placing his cannons in position. At this point the Platte river flowed south; the camp circle was on the low ground close to the river, with the dry bed of a creek running through the camp. Brave Bear's tipi was on the east side of the camp, and the tipi of High Forehead, the Miniconjou, was just to the left of the chief's. Beside High Forehead's tipi stood a second one occupied by a Miniconjou family. Just to the rear of these tipis the ground dropped to the lower level of the river flood plain, which was overgrown with willows, bushes, and vines. When the soldiers appeared, the women and children began to slip out of the camp to hide among the willows; and Spotted Tail and a large group of warriors had concealed themselves among the willows, armed and with their war ponies ready.

Lieutenant Grattan was trying to be patient. Since Brave Bear could not induce the Miniconjou to give himself up, the Lieutenant asked Man-Afraid-of-His-Horse to go and talk to the Indian. The soldiers had climbed down from the wagon and gun carriages and were sitting and lying on the ground. After a time Man-Afraid-of-His-Horse came back, and through the interpreter, he informed the Lieutenant that the Miniconjou refused to give up and stated that he wished to die. The chief of his camp, Little Brave, was dead; his two brothers had been killed by the whites, and he wished to die. He was standing in front of his lodge with his gun and bow, waiting for the soldiers to come and kill him. In effect, he intended to commit suicide in the time-honored Sioux manner by dying in a fight. This was regarded as a very brave action. You decided to die, you started a fight, many bystanders were killed, and you escaped to be proud of your brave deed which had cost other people such a high price.

The chiefs again urged Lieutenant Grattan to leave the obstreperous Miniconjou for the Indian agent to deal with, when everyone had had time to cool off; but the Lieutenant had his orders to arrest the man, and he would not alter his determination. Brave Bear and his brother went forward to talk again with the Miniconjou and returned to explain to Grattan what the man had said. The drunken interpreter was misbehaving again, and the chiefs sent a mounted man to urge Bordeaux to come, as the interpreter was twisting their words into a form that angered the officer. Men who were watching from the flat roof of Bordeaux's house thought that the conferences with the Miniconjou consumed about forty-five minutes. Grattan's patience then broke. He gave an order, and the soldiers stood up and leveled their muskets. The men on the roof could not determine whether the first shots came from an Indian gun or an army musket. The sounds were different, but when the shooting started, the reports came with such rapidity that it was impossible to distinguish the first shot. Brave Bear was caught between the troops and Indians and was one of the first to fall, wounded in three places. The first return fire came from Indians in among the lodges; then Grattan ordered the two cannons fired. The guns were aimed too high, and the shots tore through the tops of the Sioux tipis. Grattan was down, and so were some of his men. Spotted Tail led his mounted warriors out of the thicket and charged the troops. The soldiers started to flee, some of them in the wagon, others on a gun limber.

Several hundred mounted Brulés were pursuing the soldiers, and from the upper camps the Oglala and Miniconjou warriors were charging down the road to meet the fleeing troops. The men on the gun carriage got to a point near Bordeaux's and were there overtaken and killed. The soldiers in the wagon got to the point or bluff beyond Bordeaux's, where the Indians stopped the wagon and killed the men. Some eighteen infantrymen kept together and fought their way for a considerable distance, as the Indians had few guns and could not close in on them quickly. The men who watched from Bordeaux's roof stated that Red Cloud, at the head of a force of Oglala warriors, rode the infantry down and killed them all. Only one soldier escaped. He was mortally wounded and died at Bordeaux's place, where he had been hidden.[10]

[10] New details of the Grattan affair are constantly coming to light. The narrative here given has been carefully made from contemporary official reports, from the

Spotted Tail and the other younger leaders among the warriors were highly elated over their extermination of Lieutenant Grattan's little command. These fighting chiefs had taken no part in the efforts of the older chiefs to avoid trouble, and the firing had hardly died down before they began to shout for an attack on Fort Laramie, where they knew only a handful of soldiers stood guard. The older chiefs, including the dying Brave Bear, opposed more killing. Bordeaux was in a tight place. His trading house was thronged with Sioux, who were threatening to kill him and his men and plunder his store. Bordeaux had never been in as tight a place as this during all his years of Indian trading. He had little physical courage, but he was highly skilled in dealing with Indians. He talked all through that terrible night, handing out expensive gifts from his stock to the leading warriors to win them over to his side and placating the angry crowd by giving them supplies from the shelves. In the end, he and the friendly chiefs prevented any more killing, but the Sioux went to the American Fur Company's trading house between Bordeaux's and Fort Laramie, broke in, and plundered the government Indian annuity goods. Having offended the government by killing its soldiers and taking its Indian goods by force, many of the Sioux now became worried. They did not like having their women and children right on the emigrant road where the whites might easily strike back at them. One group after another took down their lodges and crossed to the north bank of the North Platte. Reorganizing their camps in this safer location, they presently moved off into the buffalo plains on their regular autumn hunt.

---

letters of James Bordeaux, and from eyewitness account of Obridge Allen (published in Hafen and Young's *Fort Laramie*). One of the best accounts will be found in *Nebraska History* for March, 1956. The Sioux have been embroidering the plain truth for a century back. One may not object to their attempting to make out a good case for their own people, but they might at least avoid the more obvious forms of falsification. Their elaborate tale of the drunken interpreter hiding in a Sioux death lodge and being dragged out and killed after the fight was over is pure invention. He was one of the first to flee, accompanied by a soldier on Lieutenant Grattan's horse, and they were swiftly overtaken and killed. The Sioux stories concerning Chief Brave Bear become more elaborate and impossible as time passes, and every few years the Sioux invent a new and more improbable explanation of this chief's name.

Spotted Tail and Wife. (From *Ab-Sa-Ra-Ka, Land of Massacre*, by Henry B. Carrington)

Two Strike in Washington, 1872, as a member of Spotted Tail's delegation. (From a photograph by Alexander Gardner. Courtesy the Bureau of American Ethnology)

Red Shirt, son of Red Dog. (From *A Sioux Chronicle*, by George E. Hyde. Courtesy Pitt Rivers Museum, Oxford)

Chief White Thunder of the Loafer Band. (Courtesy Pitt Rivers Museum, Oxford)

3. *The Sacrifice*

THE SIOUX OF 1854 were a fine, bold race of hunters and warriors, but they knew very little about the whites. They had been discussing going to war against the whites for twenty years, but now, in August, 1854, when the killing of Grattan and his soldiers actually began the war, they did not seem to know what to do next. At the moment their camps were on the Oregon Trail and they were in a position to strike telling blows by attacking the emigrant trains, but they became alarmed for fear the whites would attack their camps and kill their women and children. Removing to safer ground north of the North Platte, their leaders could think of nothing further to do than to go off on the usual autumn buffalo hunt. That was their customary way of making war on Indian enemies. Hunting came first—they had to hunt or starve—and at the hunting season they put the war back in the bag, to be taken out and resumed during slack seasons, when hunting did not take up most of their time.

To hunt effectively, they had to separate into smaller groups. The Wazhazha camp thus moved off alone toward the northeast after the Grattan fight. On the Niobrara, near the mouth of Snake River, they buried their dead chief Brave Bear on a scaffold grave. In November the camps assembled again near the head of the Niobrara, held councils, and decided to resume the war with the Americans. They planned it just as they would have planned a raid on the Pawnees or Crows. If it had been June and just after the Sun Dance, they would have sent out a war party of three to five hundred warriors to attack their enemies; but it was November, not the customary season for big expeditions, and, besides, they were divided in their opinion as to the wisdom of attacking the whites. But Chief Brave Bear had to be avenged, and the oldest of his surviving brothers, Red Leaf, acted. He got his half-brother, Long Chin, and his cousin, Spotted Tail, to join him. These three kinsmen, with two boys (described as Red Leaf's brothers), went down to the Oregon road with the purpose of taking vengeance for Brave Bear.

At a point near the treaty council grounds of 1851, on Horse Creek, on November 13, they attacked the west-bound mail wagon on its way to Salt Lake, killing three white men and plundering the mails. In a metal box they found twenty thousand dollars in gold. No one has ever found out what the warriors did with this money; but after the attack, they went up the road to James Bordeaux's trading house. That is the modern Sioux statement; Bordeaux did not report this visit.

On November 29, Colonel William Hoffman, now in command at Fort Laramie, reported that one thousand lodges of Sioux were assembled on the head of the Niobrara—Wazhazhas, Brulés, Miniconjous and Oglalas—and that these Indians were planning to keep up the war on the whites all winter. A similar report came from Indian Agent A. D. Vaughan, from Fort Pierre on the Missouri; but it was the wrong season for Indians to go to war, and the Sioux took no action until the spring of 1855. They then acted again exactly as if they were warring on enemy tribes. Moreover, they evidently had no plan and there was no unity. Every camp acted in its own interest. Only two groups—the Wazhazhas and part of the Miniconjous—seemed to be interested in fighting the Americans. The attacks when they came were, in the main, horse-lifting operations. In April a trader far up the North Platte near Independence Rock had his stock stolen, and John Richards, the Sioux trader at Platte Bridge west of Fort Laramie, lost seventy-five head of animals to a raiding party. These raids were evidently the work of the Miniconjous. The raid on the store of Ward and Guerrier, close to Fort Laramie, may have been made by Wazhazhas. By early summer, the Platte Road was thronged with emigrant trains, but no trouble was reported further than some annoyance from small parties of Sioux. There were no attacks, and by this time many of the Sioux leaders were talking of peace with the whites.

Bordeaux and some of the other traders had warned the chiefs that the government was going to take stiff action in retaliation for the killing of Grattan and his troops and the murder of the men with the mail wagon west of Horse Creek. Most of the Sioux disregarded these warnings. They went about their usual affairs, as if being at war with the United States was a small matter. The Wazhazhas and the Brulé Orphan and Corn bands hunted buffalo north of the Platte, while the Little Thunder camp of Southern Brulés were hunting on the Republican and Solomon. In June this latter group moved northward to the forks of the Platte, where they probably held a Sun Dance. The Sioux, following their regular routine, then got up a war party of about five hundred men and went to seek the Pawnees and Omahas. Spotted Tail was a leader in this expedition, the other prominent warriors being Two Strike, Iron Shell, and White Thunder, all Brulés. On Loup Fork north of the Platte the war party divided, part of the warriors going down to the Platte to seek the Pawnees; but they found the Pawnee villages deserted. That tribe had gone hunting. The second division of the expedition moved on eastward, running into the Omahas who were hunting buffalo. In a fight with the Omahas the Brulés killed Logan Fontenelle, the half-French chief of the tribe. The Sioux warriors came back to Little Thunder's camp late in July with nothing to show other than a few stolen horses and the scalp of Logan Fontenelle.

The War Department had begun preparations for an expedition to punish the Sioux during the previous winter. Brigadier General W. S. Harney, who was in Paris, was summoned home to command the troops. At the moment when the Sioux were frittering away their time in attempting to find and attack the Pawnees and Omahas, Harney was assembling his forces at Fort Leavenworth in eastern Kansas. Meantime a new agent had been appointed for the Indians of the Upper Platte—Thomas S. Twiss, a former officer in the regular army, who seems to have been placed in charge with the idea that he would co-operate with the military in dealing severely with the Sioux.

Reaching Fort Laramie on August 10, Twiss at once held talks with Bordeaux and the other traders and ordered them to send runners to the Sioux camps. The runners were to inform the chiefs that the Platte River was a dead line. Those camps that were friendly were to move south of the river at once and come to Fort Laramie, where he would protect them. The camps that failed to come in would be dealt with by the troops. The men who had led in the Grattan killing and in the raids along the Platte road were known, and they were not to come in with the friendly camps. They were murderers and would be treated as such.

As soon as these messages reached the Sioux camps, it became apparent that the great majority of the tribe had thought better concerning all the loud talk of fighting the whites. With remarkable haste, considering their habit of taking weeks to make up their minds on any matter, the Sioux crossed the Platte and made contact with Agent Twiss. First came the Oglalas, led by Man-Afraid-of-His-Horse.[1] Next came Stabber with a camp of Wazhazhas. This chief had been seen by Francis Parkman near Fort Laramie in 1846. He had just returned north from a visit on the Arkansas River where he had seen U. S. troops on the march for the invasion of New Mexico. Stabber had been greatly impressed by the numbers and equipment of the American soldiers. Now, in 1855, he was all for peace. He told Agent Twiss that he had driven the family of Brave Bear out of the Wazhazha camp. That meant that Stabber took the extreme view held by some of the officials, that Brave Bear had brought on the Grattan killing and was guilty of treachery. The fact seems to be that after the Grattan affair, the Wazhazhas had quarreled, Red Leaf, the oldest of Brave Bear's surviving brothers, wishing to take vengeance on the whites, while Stabber and his followers stood for peace. The camp had therefore divided, Stabber bringing his group to Fort Laramie, Red Leaf remaining with his camp north of the Platte.

By September 8, Twiss had assembled a camp of four hundred lodges of Sioux on Laramie Fork, thirty-five miles above the fort. These were the friendlies whose only wish was to avoid war with the Americans. The number of lodges tells the story. At the time of the Grattan fight, the Sioux had, near Fort Laramie, three hundred lodges of Oglalas, two hundred lodges of Brulés, eighty lodges of Wazhazhas, and a camp of Miniconjous, at least seven hundred

[1] This was Old-Man-Afraid-of-His-Horse, born about 1802, died at Pine Ridge in 1887.

lodges. From the friendly camp Twiss had now established, practically all of the Brulés, half of the Wazhazhas, and all the Miniconjous were absent. Part of the Brulé Corn band had come in. Their chief, Swift Bear, was Bordeaux's brother-in-law and always took that trader's advice. The Orphan band was north of the Platte, and so was Little Thunder's camp of Southern Brulés. Red Leaf was reported to be with Spotted Tail, but the location of his Wazhazha camp is not known.

Little Thunder of the Southern Brulés was in camp on the Bluewater, a small northern tributary of the Platte, just above the forks of the river. Only part of the Southern Brulés were in this camp, the remainder probably hunting in the Republican Fork country far to the south. Little Thunder was usually considered to be friendly toward the whites; but in August, 1855, his camp of some forty[2] lodges on the Bluewater was certainly not friendly. He had in his camp the three outstanding advocates of war on the whites—Spotted Tail, Red Leaf, and Iron Shell.

Why Little Thunder kept his camp where it was is the astonishing thing. This small camp was on the Bluewater only six miles northwest of Ash Hollow, where the Oregon road ran along the southern bank of the Platte. The smoke from the Sioux camp could be seen by emigrant trains passing up the road, and there were reports that Indians from the camp were lurking along the road, molesting but not actually attacking the whites. Little Thunder had been warned by Bordeaux, who had sent a Brulé named Goose to the camp with the news that troops were coming up the Platte. The Sioux account of these events states that the chiefs held a council and decided to keep the camp where it was, because the Indians had been hunting buffalo and the meat would not be dry enough to transport for several days. The Sioux story adds that Bordeaux sent a second and more urgent warning and that the man who brought it was in the camp the day the troops attacked. These supposedly alert Indians did not even take the elementary precaution of sending out scouts to warn the camp of the approach of danger.

General Harney reached Fort Kearney on the Lower Platte on

[2] Forty-one Brulé lodges. A second camp of eleven Oglala lodges was two miles higher up the creek.

August 20, ten days after Agent Twiss had come to Fort Laramie. The General waited four days for more troops to arrive from Kansas and then took the field with a force of about six hundred men, partly dragoons, the rest infantry and some artillery. The troops were accompanied by a wagon train hauling supplies. Harney's orders were to strike swiftly and hard and end the Sioux troubles once and for all. It took him eight days to march from Fort Kearney to Ash Hollow at the forks of the Platte. His guide, Joe Tesson, a Sioux trader, knew where Little Thunder was in camp. On the night of September 2–3 Harney crossed his troops over the North Platte. He sent his dragoons to make a night march, a wide swing that would bring them to the Bluewater above the Sioux camp. At daylight on the third he started his infantry up the creek, advancing openly toward the Indian camp. At this late hour the Sioux awoke to their danger.

The chiefs rode out to try that ancient stratagem of starting a parley and delaying the enemy until the women could pack up the camp and get safely away, but Harney was an experienced Indian fighter and was not to be taken in. When Little Thunder, Spotted Tail, and Iron Shell rode out of the camp, carrying a white flag, Harney was quite willing to talk; but his troops continued to advance steadily, and the alarmed Indian leaders found that their stratagem was being turned against them. They were not delaying the troops, but Harney was keeping them in talk when they should be back in their camp, organizing their people either for resistance or for flight.

In the camp there was wild confusion. The women had just started taking down the lodges and packing up for flight when the dragoons were discovered, moving swiftly down the creek valley toward the upper end of the camp. The Sioux dropped everything and started to run. The chiefs broke off their parley with the General and galloped toward their camp. As they went, the infantry charged after them, firing as they ran. The Indian camp was a wild scene of panic. There was nothing to be done but to run, and it was everyone for himself. The warriors were trying to make a stand, but they were separated into little groups of two to half a dozen and many of them were still afoot. Beyond Bluewater Creek, over to the left, there was rough ground with sand buttes and small ravines. The Indians started fleeing across the valley toward this refuge, where the mounted troops would have difficulty in following or finding them.

Spotted Tail either gave his horse to one of the escaping families or the animal was killed under him. He was afoot when he caught a riderless dragoon horse and mounted it. He is described by Sioux narrators as fighting valiantly against the dragoons and killing some of them. He seems to have been among the last of the warriors to flee, and when he did go, he had two pistol bullets in his body and two severe saber cuts. His family had been lost in the wild stampede. His wife (some Sioux say two wives) and a baby daughter had fallen into the hands of the troops. Iron Shell, another famous fighter, escaped from the camp, apparently unwounded; but his two wives were captured. Little Thunder also escaped.

To modern men, accustomed to great disasters, this affair on the Bluewater may seem a small matter; but to the Sioux of 1855 it was a stunning blow. Never in the memory of living men had one of the big Sioux camps been captured by enemies, and never had they suffered such losses in a fight or seen scores of Sioux women and children carried off as captives. There were about 250 Indians in Little Thunder's camp, and Harney reported that the Indians had 86 killed and about 70 women and children captured. The Brulés also lost many horses, their camp, and all its contents. To Indians who regarded the loss of a few ponies and three or four warriors in a fight as something shocking, the loss in Little Thunder's camp was an overwhelming disaster. The survivors of the defeat were scattered fugitives, without food or shelter. Spotted Tail, at the height of his career as a young war chief, had been struck down and was lying badly wounded in a rude brush lodge among the Nebraska Sand Hills. His wife and one child were in the hands of the troops.[3]

[3] Modern Sioux information states that Spotted Tail had in the camp his wives, his mother, his mother-in-law, and some small children, and that a wife, perhaps two, and three small children were captured, one little girl being wounded in the leg. I am doubtful concerning this Indian information. It is not reasonable to suppose that the Sioux of today who cannot give a straightforward account of either the Grattan fight or the Bluewater battle because of their faulty memory

Harney marched from the Bluewater up the North Platte to Fort Laramie. The Sioux tale that relates how the Sioux women and children were forced to go with the troops, the girls being raped and some of the babies thrown into the river by the brutal soldiers, is pure imagination. The Indian captives were sent down the river in wagons to Fort Kearney, where they were kindly treated. At Fort Laramie, Agent Twiss was acting the part of a dictator in control of the Sioux. He ordered the Indians in the friendly camp on Laramie Fork to do this and to do that. He was preparing to issue the Sioux annuity goods to the friendlies when Harney arrived and ordered him not to do so. Harney also prohibited any dealings of the Indian agent with the Sioux. The General then called the chiefs from the friendly camp to a council at the fort. He spoke very roughly to them, making a curt demand that they should turn over to the commanding officer at Fort Laramie all the warriors who had taken part in the attack on the mail wagon near Horse Creek. The General refused to speak of peace until these warriors, whom he termed murderers, had been surrendered.

Harney now crossed his little army to the north bank of the North Platte and marched through the heart of the Brulé country, challenging any of the Sioux to come and fight. He passed across the head of the Niobrara, where in the previous November a great camp of Sioux had stood, with the chiefs talking over plans for

---

can recall the exact number of Spotted Tail's wives and children. Contemporary accounts in the *Missouri Republican*, October 20, 1855, and in the *Missouri Gazette*, October 26, 1855, report that Spotted Tail was wounded in four places, two balls from heavy dragoon pistols passing through his body, but that he caught a dragoon horse and fought his way out. The modern Sioux tale that Spotted Tail killed about all the dragoons who fell in the fight with his own hand seems to be an embroidery on this newspaper account. Incidentally, these newspapers contain the first naming of Spotted Tail in any written or printed record. The newspapers also explode the Sioux fabrication concerning the Indian women and children's being forced to march to Fort Laramie. General Drum, who was a lieutenant in the Bluewater fight, wrote an account of it in later years, mentioning how he picked up a Sioux baby on the field and how Spotted Tail later thanked him for saving his baby; but Susan Bettelyoun stated that this baby found on the battlefield was Iron Shell's child, meaning perhaps the child that grew up and was given the name Hollow Horn Bear. All that seems to be certainly known is that when he was a prisoner at Fort Leavenworth in 1855–56, Spotted Tail had one wife and a little daughter with him. There may have been two children, or even three.

fighting the whites. He marched through the Wazhazha wintering grounds at the head of White River and on to the Teton or Bad River, down which he proceeded to Fort Pierre on the Missouri. He did not see one Indian during the entire march. The Sioux called him the Hornet, and they very carefully kept beyond the reach if his sting. The only signs of defiance came from the Hunkpapa camps, up the Missouri from Fort Pierre. That Sioux tribe, having never seen any white men except a few traders, was feeling very bold and brave. Harney wished to attack them, but the season was late and supplies short, and he put aside the idea of further operations for the year.

The Sioux of the Platte country were in a dreadful state of mind. Trade had been stopped; most of the traders had left their usual locations and were living at the military posts. There would be no trade until peace was made, and evidently no government annuity goods. The Sioux could not live without trade, and they were in fear that the Hornet would come back and attack them in their camps.

Harney's demand for the surrender of their warriors was another shock. In ordinary times, the Sioux would have paid no heed to such a demand. They were thunderstruck by this order to give up their leading warriors, particularly since the traders had sent them word that these warriors would be taken by the military to a distant fort in Kansas and there hanged. A year or two back the Sioux would have disregarded a demand for the giving up of their warriors, but now the chiefs were deeply concerned. The Hornet had told them that he was coming back with his soldiers in the spring of 1856 and that, if the warriors had not been given up, he was going to be very angry with the Sioux. The chiefs held councils and then begged Spotted Tail and the other warriors whose surrender had been demanded to give themselves up for the good of the tribe.

It took real courage for Spotted Tail and the others to comply with the request of the chiefs. It was a grim business; but the chiefs said that it must be gone through with to save the people, and Spotted Tail and the other warriors steeled themselves to the sacrifice. The Sioux were inveterate procrastinators who quite often put off important decisions for months and then, as likely as not, forgot all about the matter; but on this occasion they acted with surprising quickness. It was little more than two weeks between the time of General Harney's demand and the actual surrender of the men he termed the murderers.

On October 18 the troops and a large body of Sioux were assembled at Fort Laramie when Spotted Tail and his companions appeared, mounted on fine ponies and wearing handsome war costumes. As they advanced slowly, the men were singing their death songs. They dismounted and were taken to the guard house by an escort of infantry. Besides Spotted Tail, the men in the group were the two brothers of the dead Chief Brave Bear; Red Leaf (*Wabasha*), and Long Chin (*Iku Hanska*). Harney had also demanded the surrender of the two boys who had been with the warriors in the attack on the mail party. On October 28, 1855, Agent Twiss reported that the three warriors named above had surrendered, but the boys had not; for one of them was too sick to come to the fort and the other was in a Miniconjou camp north of the Black Hills on the Little Missouri.[4] Later two young warriors, Standing Elk and Red Plume, surrendered in the place of the two boys and were sent down the Platte to join the other prisoners. Twiss reported that in late October Little Thunder's camp was far north, on the South Fork of the Cheyenne River, the Indians being afraid to return to their own lands south of the Platte.

According to Susan Bettelyoun, daughter of the trader Bordeaux, who was born at Fort Laramie, in 1857, Spotted Tail took a young wife with him into captivity and the other prisoners also took their wives. John Y. Nelson stated that Spotted Tail had two wives and three children with him at Fort Leavenworth. The truth seems to

[4] The modern Sioux have caused much confusion by giving conflicting accounts of the surrender of these warriors. They say fifteen men took part in the mail-wagon raid, yet the official reports of the period say three warriors, named, and two boys, who did not take part in the killing. When the two boys failed to surrender, Standing Elk of the Corn Band and Red Plume (unidentified) surrendered in their place. In 1855, "Spotted Elk" was the name given, but in the following year the name was "Standing Elk." There was no Spotted Elk known among the Brulés of that day. Just when Standing Elk and Red Plume surrendered is not stated. General Drum says that in 1856 he visited the five Sioux prisoners and their families at Fort Leavenworth and that all five men were the sons of chiefs. Drum also spoke of the young and attractive wife Spotted Tail had with him.

be that one wife and one to three children were captured in the Bluewater fight and taken to Fort Kearney, and when Spotted Tail and the other prisoners came down from Fort Laramie, the older wife of Spotted Tail joined him and the younger wife and went with him to Fort Leavenworth, taking the children along. Agent Twiss simply stated that the surrendered warriors went down the Platte in an army ambulance escorted by a guard commanded by Brevet Major Edward Johnson. Colonel E. V. Sumner, commanding officer at Fort Leavenworth, reported on December 12, 1855, that the three Sioux Indian prisoners had reached the post the previous day.

This was a strange and frightening journey for the Brulé prisoners. The world they lived in was very limited. Their usual annual round was hunting in southwestern Nebraska and northwestern Kansas and then going up to the Platte near Fort Laramie to trade and get their government annuity goods. Their longest war expeditions were usually against the Pawnees and Omahas in eastern Nebraska. Now they were taken down the Platte road in an army ambulance and with a military guard. At Fort Kearney they were in the country of their Pawnee enemies, who would have been delighted to kill them if they had dared. Below Kearney the road left the Platte and struck southeastward into Kansas, and here the Brulés came into unknown country. It was swarming with whites, thousands of white men, women, and children in camps or on the road, moving in a steady stream westward to the Pacific Coast. There were also settlements here in Kansas, towns of wooden houses; and here were the Kaw Indians, now surrounded by white settlements and forced to live on a reservation, and Shawnees and Delawares, tribes that had formerly roved in the lands east of the Mississippi but had now settled in eastern Kansas. These immigrant Indians lived in houses and planted corn and other crops like white people, and many of the Indian men were dressed like the whites. Looking at these Kansas Indians, Spotted Tail must have realized what fate had in store for his own tribe. Sooner or later, the Brulés would have to give up their wandering life of hunting and fighting and learn to live like white people.

This journey into Kansas was an education to Spotted Tail. He

77

and his friends had been talking about the white people for the past twenty years, and now he suddenly realized how foolish most of that talk had been. The number and power of the whites were frightening. Only a year ago he had been eager to fight the Americans and had imagined that the killing of Lieutenant Grattan and his handful of soldiers would be such a blow that the whites would flee and leave the Platte lands again to the Brulés. Now he began to understand what a very small matter the Grattan fight and even the Harney attack on Little Thunder's camp was to the whites. When the Brulé prisoners reached Fort Leavenworth, the feeling that the Sioux could gain nothing by attempting to fight the whites was overwhelming. This military post was something the Sioux had never dreamed could be possible. Here was a bewildering number of huge buildings, some made of a strange material called bricks, and inside the square of buildings was a vast parade ground, where every day the troops in full dress uniform formed in ranks and marched to the music of a band. There were more soldiers in this post than warriors in the Brulé tribe, and the interpreter told the Sioux prisoners that this was only one of a score of similar military posts. The fort stood near the bank of the Missouri, and on the river steamboats crowded with white people were constantly passing.

This sudden realization of the number and strength of the Americans struck the Brulé captives a stunning blow. It destroyed their faith in their own people's strength. The revelation of white power affected the three men in different ways. Spotted Tail had a sanguine disposition. He loved life and was fond of people. The only humans he really hated were the Pawnees and other Indian enemies, and when some of the officers and their wives at Fort Leavenworth offered their friendship, he met their advances with frank pleasure. Red Leaf of the Wazhazhas was more reserved. He did not like white soldiers, and the killing of his brother Brave Bear by Grattan's troops was an offense that still rankled in his heart. His realization of the power of the Americans threw him into the deepest depression. His younger brother, Long Chin, was apparently a fighting man with just enough intelligence to make him a leader in petty Indian warfare. He sulked and learned nothing from his experiences at Fort Leavenworth.

This difference in character was obviously the reason why Spotted Tail was the favorite with the officers' families. Lieutenant Drum's experience is an example. The Lieutenant went to see the Indians, and the interpreter told Spotted Tail that this officer was the man who saved his baby on the battlefield of the Bluewater. Spotted Tail's handsome and manly face lit up with a look of intense pleasure. He strode quickly forward, placed his hands on Lieutenant Drum's shoulders, and stood for a long time, looking the officer straight in the eyes. Then through the interpreter he expressed to Drum his heartfelt gratitude. Lieutenant Drum understood that it was Spotted Tail's own baby whom he had saved, and he was told by Spotted Tail, as he stated many years later, that Little Thunder was his (Spotted Tail's) father. This does not seem to agree with Lieutenant G. K. Warren's statement in his diary for September, 1855, that Spotted Tail's father was then present at Fort Laramie and that his father was not Little Thunder. Perhaps Spotted Tail called Little Thunder father as an Indian term of respect for the chief whom he followed.[5]

General Harney had certainly intended that these Sioux prisoners should be hanged; but as early as October 18, 1855, Agent Thomas Twiss had urged Superintendent of Indian Affairs Alfred Cumming at St. Louis to apply for a pardon for the prisoners. President Pierce issued pardons on January 16, 1856, but the Sioux remained at Fort Leavenworth through the rest of the winter. In the spring they were started homeward under military escort. They were at Fort Kearney on the Lower Platte in May, 1856. The Sioux who in late years have said that these prisoners were kept in the guardhouse for two years and most severely treated simply did not know the

[5] Drum, in Nebraska Historical Society *Collections*, XVI, 148. The Sioux in recent years had no real memory of the captivity of Spotted Tail in 1855–56. They have invented tales that are almost mythical in their vagueness. In these stories, Spotted Tail is taken to an unknown place in an unknown land by the wicked soldiers, who then try to kill him by magic. There is a bottomless pit that Spotted Tail is told to leap into. He says a prayer to his guardian spirit, and when he leaps, the pit is magically filled up. Taking an idea from performances seen at circuses, the Sioux narrate how Spotted Tail was loaded into a huge cannon; but when the wicked soldiers fired the gun, Spotted Tail prayed, and after whirling off to a great distance, he landed on his feet, unharmed. This is what some of the Sioux of today gravely repeat as authentic history.

facts. Spotted Tail and his companions were treated with kindness, were not strictly confined, and were at Fort Leavenworth for little more than four months.

This was a hard winter among the Brulé Sioux. Trade had been stopped by military order, and the Indians were afraid to approach Fort Laramie or the road along the Platte. The Little Thunder and Spotted Tail camp did not dare to return to their own country on Republican Fork. All the Brulés and Wazhazhas were up north. On Christmas Day, 1855, Agent Twiss reported three Brulé villages on the Cheyenne and White rivers, one on the Niobrara, and two on Rawhide Creek, the last probably being the most friendly camps, the Corn band and another. In midwinter, General Harney sent a peremptory order for Little Thunder to come to Fort Pierre on the Missouri to attend a peace council, and the frightened Chief set out at the end of February, marching through cold and deep snow to obey the order. When the council met at the fort, he was rewarded by being appointed by Harney as head chief of the Brulés. Thus Spotted Tail's own group became the head band of the tribe; the Wazhazhas, who had been the head from 1850 to 1855, were in disgrace with General Harney, and its chiefs were ignored by him. Little Thunder and the other chiefs who wanted peace let their names be signed to a treaty that Harney dictated, but the Senate failed to confirm this document and it was never put into force.

It was just after the signing of this treaty, far up the Missouri at Fort Pierre, that Spotted Tail and his fellow prisoners left Fort Leavenworth to return home. Agent Twiss was evidently at Fort Leavenworth to arrange for the return of the Indian prisoners, and he came up through eastern Kansas to the Platte at the time they did, accompanied by his brother, George Twiss, who had a big freight wagon loaded with Indian trade goods and the first shipment of plows, hoes, and farming tools that are recorded as being taken to the Upper Platte for Indian use. Agent Twiss was urging the opening of farms for the Sioux, and the probability is that he intended to buy the farming tools from his brother. Nepotism was the breath of life of the Indian service, and most of the agents had some close relative near at hand to whom they passed on government contracts and gave special privileges for trading with the Indians.[6]

Spotted Tail and his companions traveled slowly northward through the new Kansas settlements. The road was thronged with emigrant trains and troops were on the move. The Mormons in Utah were making trouble, and a much stronger military force than the one that had been sent in 1855 to deal with the Sioux was on its way to Utah. Watching the military preparations, Spotted Tail became more strongly convinced that it would mean ruin to the Brulé tribe if it went to war with the Americans.

When they reached Fort Kearney the Sioux prisoners were suddenly confronted by a minor crisis. A war party of Cheyennes had come up from their hunting grounds south of the Platte to make a raid on the Pawnees. They had encamped on Grand Island near Fort Kearney, and seeing a mail coach coming along the road, some of the warriors had gone out to beg tobacco from the men in the coach. The white men were apprehensive, and one of them fired a pistol at the Indians, who replied with arrows, wounding the driver. When this affair was reported at the fort, the cavalry prepared to go after the Cheyennes, and the Sioux prisoners were asked to go with the troops as scouts and guides. Red Leaf and Standing Elk agreed to go. They found the Cheyenne war party still in camp, and in a lively fight the cavalry drove the Cheyennes away, killing some and capturing their camp equipment. The angry Cheyennes now found a small Mormon emigrant train on the road and attacked it, killing the whites. Again the cavalry went out, and this time four of the Sioux prisoners accompanied the troops, but they did not find the Cheyennes. Spotted Tail is not named as one of the scouts with the cavalry. The Cheyennes were his friends and allies, and it is not likely that he would serve against them. The Sioux who went with the cavalry were from camps that lived north of the Platte and were not allies of the Cheyennes.

The Sioux prisoners remained at Fort Kearney from May to September, for what reason we are not informed. There were formalities to be gone through. The prisoners had been turned over to the military at Fort Laramie by Agent Twiss in 1855, and the

[6] The Twiss brothers' trip through Kansas in 1856 is referred to in Kansas Historical Society *Collections*, XVII, 491.

requirements of red tape made it necessary for the military now to turn the Indians back to the agent and get a receipt for them. No document has come to light dealing with these formalities, but Agent Twiss was at his Upper Platte Agency at Drips' Trading Post, near the mouth of Rawhide Creek east of Fort Laramie, in September; and Spotted Tail and his companions must have been brought up there under military escort and handed over to Twiss, sometime in October or November, just a year after they had surrendered at Fort Laramie.

Spotted Tail came back to his people with honor, a man who had sacrificed his life, as everyone believed at the time, to save the tribe from further miseries of war. His pardon by the Great Father in Washington had not been foreseen. He had been a leading warrior, a war chief, when he surrendered, with little thought for anything beyond his usual activities of hunting and fighting. He came back very greatly changed by what he had seen and learned, looking to the future and ready to take up the load of responsibility which any true leader must bear.

The trouble of 1854–55 had split the Brulé tribe. Now, in 1856, Little Thunder was recognized by the government as head chief. He and his Southern Brulés were rated as friendly, and as Spotted Tail was strongly inclined to support a friendly policy toward the whites, he now joined the Little Thunder group. In 1854–55 he had lived with his Wazhazha relatives in Brave Bear's camp; but now the Wazhazhas were, in the main, unfriendly—at any rate, unwilling to follow Spotted Tail's plan to be on good terms with the whites. It must have been at this time, late in 1856, that Spotted Tail became the chief lieutenant of the harassed head chief. He was the man needed. Little Thunder was convinced that the Brulés must keep peace, and Spotted Tail now held this same view. He had seen things and learned things during his stay at Fort Leavenworth that enabled him to back up his stand for peace with solid facts. Moreover, he was the outstanding war leader of the Brulés, and he had more influence over the warriors than any of the older chiefs. An able and persuasive talker, Spotted Tail was the best man who could have been found to stand at Little Thunder's side and aid him in avoiding incidents that might lead into war with the Americans.

4. *The Prairie On Fire*

IF THIS WERE A WORK of historical fiction, it might be well at this point to start building Spotted Tail up as a kind of Sioux Hamlet, half-warrior, half-saintly mystic, stalking gloomily about with his mind filled with bitter thoughts on the wickedness of the white race and the virtues of the Sioux. But Spotted Tail, in 1856, was not like that at all. He preferred to seek results by reasonable methods rather than by tying a little blue stone behind one of his ears (as his nephew Crazy Horse is reported to have done) and counting on its mystic power to see him through all difficulties.

When he rejoined the Little Thunder camp late in the autumn, there was plenty to be gloomy about. Spotted Tail had hoped that his tribe could avoid, during his lifetime, the tragedy of having to give up their life of roving and hunting and permit the government to confine them to a reservation; but already in 1856, Agent Twiss was working for the immediate adoption of such a policy. He was urging that the Sioux settle down at once and begin farming. He had chosen a tract of land near the head of White River for the Brulé reservation, and if his scheme was carried out, it meant that Little Thunder's Brulés would have to leave their hunting grounds in southwestern Nebraska and northwestern Kansas and retreat to their old home on White River, where there was no game left and they would have to support themselves by tilling the soil. A return to White River meant defeat and the loss of the Brulé conquests in Nebraska and Kansas; yet the Corn band of the Brulés, now led by Swift Bear, had told the agent that they were eager to grow corn. They had tried that years back, up on White River, and had been forced by the public opinion in the tribe and by angry threats to give up a practice which outraged all the proud feelings of Sioux hunters and warriors. Now they were openly siding with Agent Twiss in his farming scheme, and part of the Oglala Sioux were also talking of accepting a reservation on the headwaters of Horse Creek, southeast of Fort Laramie, where they intended to try their hands at planting crops. Up on Powder River and near the Black Hills the wilder groups of Sioux would have nothing to do with the whites and this new plan for reservations. They said loudly that they would fight any whites, including government men, who came into their country. The Northern Cheyennes had abandoned their northern lands, after having several of their warriors killed in brushes with the troops along the Platte, and had gone to join forces with the Southern Cheyennes on the Solomon Fork in Kansas. They were in a defiant mood and talking of war. The march of the army up the Platte road on its way to deal with the Mormon troubles in Utah had given all the Indians an opportunity to view the military might of the Americans, yet both the Northern Sioux and the Cheyennes were unimpressed and talking war. Spotted Tail must have had a strong feeling that they would soon get the war they seemed to desire. He had learned the ways of the army while at Fort Leavenworth, and he was not surprised when in the spring of 1857 news came that Colonel E. V. Sumner, whose prisoner he had been at Fort Leavenworth, was in the field with a strong column of cavalry and infantry, seeking the Cheyenne camps south of the Platte. Agent Twiss warned all the Sioux camps to keep out of the Cheyenne country if they wished to avoid being drawn into a fresh war.

Spotted Tail's own Brulé group was in a very uncomfortable position. Their hunting grounds were the same as those of the Southern Cheyennes and Arapahoes. They had been frightened by General Harney in 1855 into removing far to the north and wintering up near the Black Hills. They had been cut off from trade by military orders for over a year; and now that they had the hope to return in peace to their lands south of the Platte, their agent warned them not to go. Surely, here was enough trouble to cast any Brulé chief into deep gloom and bitterness, but Spotted Tail was not the kind of man to become the slave of such feelings. He threw himself with fresh zest into the life of his camp, hunting buffalo and planning new attacks on the Pawnees. It has been hinted broadly by Dr. Charles A. Eastman that this chief was a pacifist and fainthearted. A queer kind of pacifist. He was convinced by solid facts that his tribe must not fight the Americans; but war on the hated Pawnees was the breath of his nostrils, and even as late as 1870, when he was in the East and was being petted by the Philadelphia Quakers

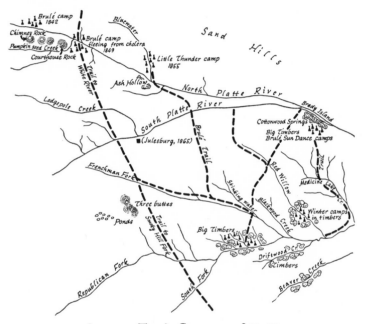

SPOTTED TAIL'S COUNTRY 1833–73

as a great and good lover of peace, the one thing Spotted Tail was proudest of was the fact that his eldest son had recently gone on a war party into Nebraska and taken a Pawnee scalp.

Spotted Tail in 1855–56 had four wives, and according to Susan Bettelyoun, who knew his family at that period, the youngest, *Minniscurrin*, was the sister of the others. It was a common custom among the Sioux for a man who married the eldest sister to take the younger ones when they were old enough for marriage. If for any reason he did not take the younger sisters, they were married to some other man with the consent of the husband of the eldest sister. We may as well say a word concerning these plural marriages among the Sioux at this point. In later years, Spotted Tail was regarded as a kind of immoral monster by certain worthy Christians because of his plural marriages. One cannot blame the Christians, but the army officers and their wives who were intimately associated with Spotted Tail did not hold the Christian view regarding his morals. They thought him a man of the highest character, a good husband, and a loving father. The fact is that these plural marriages among the Sioux were not only approved by ancient custom but were a kind of necessity. A man like Spotted Tail, a leader among his people, had to be very liberal both in hospitality to visitors and in giving charity to the poor of the camp. He could not easily do this if he had only one wife. The wealth of the Sioux consisted largely in tanned and decorated skins and skin garments, which were the work of the women. Part of the products of the women's labor was given away in the form of gifts, part was taken to the trading posts to be exchanged for manufactured Indian goods. There can be no doubt that Spotted Tail was very fond of all his wives, of the oldest as well as of the youngest recruit; but we must take into account that he could not have maintained his position as a chief properly if he had had only one wife. There were, of course, chiefs who had only one wife, but they maintained their rating as givers of hospitality and charity by making their sisters and other female relatives work for them.

The trader Denig records a curious instance of the economic angle of plural marriages among the Plains Indians, around the year 1850. There was a handsome and bold girl among the Crows of Montana who violated all tribal custom by becoming a hunter and warrior. She was a fine hunter and very successful in going with war parties to steal ponies from enemy tribes, but her success only brought trouble to her. She had no woman to tan and decorate skins, and as a warrior she could not do this work. She finally solved her problem by paying several ponies to the parents of a girl and marrying her by tribal custom. This first marriage was so successful that she soon took two more wives. They cared for her ponies, they of the tribe north to join the Mandans above the Heart River. Lewis and Clark visited the same villages on their journey up the Missouri nine years later in 1804.

In 1823, Colonel Henry Levenworth with six companies of men, some mountain men and Sioux besieged the two villages. This was in reprisal for an attack by the Arikara on General Ashley's party of fur traders which had been heading up the Missouri by keel boat. After Levenworth fired some rounds of artillery into the villages, the Arikara attempted to make a truce. Levenworth had failed to take the advantage and both villages were able to escape in the night. The scattered Arikara eventually made their way south to join the Pawnee along the Loup River in Nebraska.

After only a few years in Nebraska, the Arikara returned to the Missouri settling around Fort Clark in what is now North Dakota. In 1838 a smallpox epidemic swept through the villages. Over 2000 died. This greatly decreased their numbers. The Arikara joined the Mandans and Hidatsa at Fort Berthold in 1848.

South Dakota State Historical Society

Office in Soldiers Memorial

Pierre, South Dakota   57501

A Brief History of the Arikara Indians

Courtesy of the Wall Drug Store

The Arikara Indians (sometimes called the Rees) are in language and customs members of the Caddaon group and distinctly different from the other Siouan groups in South Dakota. The nearest 'relatives' of the Arikara are the Pawnee. In the early part of the 17th century the Arikara broke away from the Pawnee in the central part of Kansas and migrated northward to the Missouri River. The earth lodges, pottery, basket making, and agricultural practices of the Arikara all seem to indicate that they originated in the Southwest before settling in Kansas.

With the migration of the Sioux into South Dakota in the mid 1700's the Arikara were driven from the central part of the state. Their fortified villages had lined the Missouri River from Chamberlain to Pierre. By 1795 the fur trader Jean Baptiste Trudeau found the Arikara above the Grand River.

There were only two villages left of what, Trudeau was told, had been over thirty groups of earth lodges. Smallpox, preceding the white man, had wiped out the rest of the villages and driven two divisions tanned and decorated the skins she brought from hunting; she traded the skins for manufactured goods, and soon she was a chief and one of the wealthiest individuals in the Crow Nation, with a very large herd of fine ponies and a wealth of trade goods and other property.

Spotted Tail's youngest wife, who was described in 1855–56 as young and pretty, accompanied him into captivity at Fort Leavenworth.[1] His first wife was a captive at Fort Kearney on the Lower Platte. She went to Fort Leavenworth with him. He had a favorite daughter who was eighteen when she died in 1866. Born in 1848, she was seven when her father was a prisoner at Fort Leavenworth. She must have been the child of his first wife, and she was with her father at Fort Leavenworth and was made a pet of by the officers and their wives. She grew very fond of the military; and now when Spotted Tail was free again and going with the camp up to the Platte to obtain the government annuities and see the Indian agent, he usually visited for some days at Fort Laramie, taking his little daughter about the fort with him. Thus father and daughter kept up their friendship with officers they had known at Fort Leavenworth and Fort Kearney, making new friends among the Fort Laramie officers and their families. Colonel H. E. Maynadier, then a lieutenant with the Raynolds military survey party, wintered at Deer Creek west of Fort Laramie in 1859 and met Spotted Tail and his young daughter. He thought the child pretty and attractive. Between 1856 and 1864, Spotted Tail's camp probably traveled six hundred miles each year on hunting trips and another six hundred on the annual trip from their hunting grounds to Fort Laramie and the Upper Platte Agency and home again. Some years, Spotted Tail made the journey to the fort and agency more than once, and this little daughter nearly always accompanied him.

Late in the year 1856 or early in 1857, Agent Twiss moved the Upper Platte Agency from opposite the mouth of Rawhide Butte

---

[1] This information concerning Spotted Tail's younger wife in 1855–56 comes from the Susan Bettelyoun manuscript in the library of the Nebraska Historical Society. Mrs. Bettelyoun lived among the Brulés near Fort Laramie and states that in 1855 Spotted Tail had four wives. The youngest was then about eighteen. Her children were all girls.

Creek, about thirty miles east of Fort Laramie, to Deer Creek on the south bank of the North Platte, about one hundred miles west of the fort. The Mormons had built a comfortable way station for their emigrant parties at Deer Creek; but during the so-called Mormon war of 1856–57, this station had been deserted, and Agent Twiss established himself in the nice buildings like a jolly cuckoo— himself and his young Sioux wife and their pet bear. Twiss was a West Point graduate and former officer of the regular army; but he had now gone native, marrying *Wanikiyewin,* a girl of the Spleen band of the Oglala Sioux, by whom he had several half-breed children.[2]

Twiss had now turned his back on his own policy of 1856, that of establishing the Sioux reservations and inducing them to settle down and farm. He had allied himself with the wildest bands of the Oglalas, those that hunted and roved in the Powder River and Black Hills country, and he made it very difficult for the more friendly bands that roved along the Platte below Fort Laramie and in the lands in southwestern Nebraska and northwestern Kansas to even come to the agency. The friendly Southern Brulés and Oglalas now had to make a round trip of some six hundred miles to go to Deer Creek for their small quantity of government annuities. But they made the journey at least once a year. Something

[2] Interesting details concerning Agent Twiss and his Indian family were obtained at Pine Ridge by John Colhoff. Louis Twiss and other grandsons of the agent were informants. They said that about 1870, Twiss took up forty acres near Rulo, Nebraska, and started to grow fruit; but he died, and his sister came from the East to settle his affairs. She found his Indian family at the farm and must have been shocked. Retreating, she took a specimen with her—her next to youngest nephew, William. Perhaps she intended to adopt him; but something went wrong, and a year or so later young William turned up at Red Cloud Agency on White River, dressed and looking like a nice little eastern schoolboy. He found his three brothers running wild in the Indian camp, in buckskins and moccasins their long hair in braids, complete with scalp locks. They were being brought up by their mother's brother, He Crow (alias Drags-the-Rope), in the Spleen Band camp, and they were as wild as young wolves. Little William shed his nice clothes and joyously joined his brothers. In 1876 the two oldest boys (Charles and James?) served as scouts with General Crook's forces. In 1879 one of the boys was taken to the Indian school at Carlisle in Pennsylvania. The youngest of the four was Frank. If there were Twiss daughters, they evidently did not count. Paul Twiss, of Pine Ridge, told Colhoff that he has a notebook filled with his grandfather's (Agent Twiss's) notes.

for nothing has a grand pull for most humans, and these Southern Sioux preferred to march six hundred miles, taking their camps, women, and children with them, rather than to be done out of a few free blankets. The chiefs had to go anyway.

Little Thunder was head chief of the Brulés, and it was necessary for him to keep in touch with the government agent to learn what was transpiring and to protect his people as far as possible from the dangers involved in changing government policy. The English traveler, Sir Richard Burton, met old Little Thunder near Fort Laramie in 1860, returning home from a visit to the Deer Creek Agency. The old man complained bitterly that Agent Twiss was stealing the Sioux annuity goods, and it was common talk along the Platte road that the agent's pet bear got more sugar and other free government food than the Sioux, for whom the supplies were purchased.

By moving to Deer Creek, Twiss put himself into close relations with the Indian traders there, John Richards and Joe Bissonnette. These were the men who traded with the wild Oglalas of the Powder River. Like their Indians, these traders scorned the idea of settling the Sioux on reservations and were all in favor of keeping up the wild life of hunting and fighting. Richards had come to the Upper Platte in the 1830's and started smuggling liquor in from the Mexican settlements on the Upper Rio Grande. He had boasted in 1841 that the government would never send out an Indian agent good enough to make him stop selling liquor to the Sioux, and it seemed that the government never had succeeded in doing so. Twiss was hand in glove with Richards, who now was a wealthy man with a fine Indian trading house, an emigrant store, and a toll bridge used by emigrant and government wagon trains to cross north of the river at Deer Creek. He had a numerous half-breed family, including several sons, bold as hawks. Old Joe Bissonnette was also rich now, with an Indian trading house, emigrant store, stage station, and post office, which he ran with the help of his squaws and half-breed children. Twiss seems to have ignored or put difficulties in the way of the traders near Fort Laramie and down near the forks of the Platte—Bordeaux, Robidou, Beauvais, and the Gilman brothers. There were the usual reports to the effect that the agent would

89

not give licenses to traders who were not close to his agency, where he could obtain favors from them and, perhaps, dip his hands into their profits.

The Sioux who had moved down to the Platte from the White River and the Black Hills about 1834 had occupied fine hunting grounds in which there were not a dozen white men. All unaware of it, they had put themselves directly in the Path of Empire, and now they were being overwhelmed by the great stream of white occupation that was pouring westward. Gold had been discovered in the Colorado mountains, and in 1857 the stream of travel to Utah, Oregon, and California had been added to by the rush of 150,000 gold-seekers to Colorado. Not content to use the great roads up the Platte and the Arkansas, hordes of white men went up the Republican and Smoky Hill branches of the Kansas River, straight through the hunting grounds of the Sioux, Cheyennes, and Arapahoes, and a stage line was soon running through these hunting grounds. Denver and other towns were laid out, and the Indians found themselves shut in between the Kansas settlements in the east, the Colorado mining towns in the west, and the great roads along the Platte and the Arkansas to the north and south.

This summer the Sioux held a great council at Bear Butte in the Black Hills, to plan resistance to any further white encroachments into their hunting grounds. The names of Little Thunder and Spotted Tail are not mentioned, and probably they were not present at the council. Their hunting grounds were already infested by whites, and since the chiefs were convinced that the Sioux could not fight the Americans successfully, there seemed to be little sense in talking of a plan to keep the whites out. All the northern tribes of the Teton Sioux were at the council, and as they rode about the great camps, their hearts were strong, seeing how very numerous their people were. The chiefs took a solemn pledge to present a united resistance to any white men, including government officers, coming into their country. Just after the council ended, some of the Sioux discovered a military party led by Lieutenant G. K. Warren near the Black Hills and warned Warren to go away at once. He continued his military survey without seeing another Sioux, and in 1859 Captain W. F. Raynolds led another military survey party through all the Sioux lands, from the Missouri to the Powder River, up to the Yellowstone and down to the Upper Platte, without seeing anything of the Sioux, who had talked so loudly of keeping all whites out of their country.

Meanwhile, the Southern Brulés witnessed another demonstration of the power of the Americans. In the spring of 1857, Colonel E. V. Sumner marched westward, seeking the Cheyennes, who were rated as hostile. The Cheyennes were supposedly ready for him. They had all their strength collected on Solomon Fork, and there, on July 29, Sumner's cavalry in a single charge with sabers drove the Cheyenne warriors off in panic flight. Sumner captured the Cheyenne camp with its contents; he then followed General Harney's example after the Bluewater fight with the Brulés, marching through the heart of the Cheyenne lands and challenging the Indians to fight without finding any takers.

This swift defeat and overawing of the warlike Cheyennes by Colonel Sumner clearly demonstrated that Little Thunder and Spotted Tail were right in maintaining that their Brulés had no chance to win in a war with the Americans. Their lands were the same as those of the Cheyennes and were militarily untenable, for they were now closed in between the great roads along the Platte and the Arkansas, the Kansas settlements in the east and the new Colorado settlements in the west. If the Southern Brulés and Oglalas stayed where they were, their only hope was to keep on good terms with the Americans. It is easy to say that they should have taken the bold move and gone north to join the wild Sioux on Powder River and in the Black Hills country, but such a movement was unthinkable to these Sioux. Their home was on the Republican and Solomon forks, and there they would remain until forced out by military action. Besides, the herds of buffalo on Powder River and in the adjacent country were not inexhaustible; that land was already heavily occupied by Sioux camps, and there can be little doubt that if the southern bands had gone north, they soon would have worn out their welcome and would have been regarded by their northern kinsmen as unwanted guests in the hunting grounds.

There is little mention of Little Thunder and Spotted Tail in the years from 1856 to 1863. Except for journeys to the agency at

Deer Creek and visits at the trading houses on the Platte, the Southern Brulés kept in their own lands far to the south, hunting game and fighting the Pawnees, who still tried to make two extended buffalo hunts each year in the country on the forks of the Kansas River, which before the coming of the Cheyennes and the Sioux had been the exclusive possession of the Pawnees. That tribe had now accepted a reservation on Loup Fork north of the Platte, where they had built new earth-lodge villages and were growing crops. But they raised only a fraction of their food in their little fields, and in order to live, they had to go on two buffalo hunts a year. They spent half of the year on these hunts; and every time they ventured into their old hunting grounds in the Republican River country, they were beset by Sioux and Cheyennes, who followed them from camp to camp, waited until the Pawnee men were scattered on the prairie chasing buffalo and then attacked and drove them pell-mell back into their camp. At night, the Sioux made bold attempts to run off the Pawnee horses and often succeeded in making away with large numbers of animals.

Spotted Tail was still an *ogle-tanka'un*—a war-shirt-wearer—and a *wakicunsa*, or head soldier of his camp. The Sioux maintain that this rank is not that of a chief, although the whites usually referred to men of this rank as war chiefs. Perhaps we might make this clearer by saying that Little Thunder, as chief, was the head of the tribe and that Spotted Tail, as head soldier and shirt-wearer, kept order in the camp and was in charge of war operations. There can be no doubt that Spotted Tail, while constantly warning his people not to risk war with the Americans, was in chief control of the war against the Pawnees, which from the Sioux point of view was very successful. By preventing the Pawnees from hunting, the Brulés and their Cheyenne allies almost starved them; and by making attacks on the Pawnee reservation, they very nearly forced that tribe to flee into the Nebraska white settlements for protection. In 1858 the Sioux and Cheyennes prevented the Pawnees from hunting buffalo on the Republican Fork, and the Pawnees were very hungry. In 1859 the Pawnees decided to play safe and to hunt in the lands north of the Platte, taking the Omaha tribe with them to increase their fighting strength. The Pawnees first became embroiled with the Nebraska white settlers and narrowly escaped being attacked by the troops; then they and the Omahas tried to hunt, and wherever they moved their camp, the Sioux turned up and attacked them. In 1860 the Pawnees had to put up with Sioux and Cheyenne raids on their reservation from April to July, the enemy war parties lurking about, killing Pawnee women in the corn patches and stealing horses at night. On September 14 a big Sioux war party charged into the Pawnee village, killed some Pawnees, and burned sixty earth lodges. The Pawnees had a pledge from the government that they would be protected from enemy attacks; but, having induced these Indians to move to the Loup Fork, the government was contented to let them get along as best they might. The government's one object was to shift the Pawnees away from the great Platte road and the white settlements in eastern Nebraska.[3]

Certain admirers of Spotted Tail's nephew, Crazy Horse, and of Sitting Bull, the Hunkpapa Sioux, have told us in print that Spotted Tail came back from his confinement at Fort Leavenworth in 1856 fat, soft, supine, and a faithful follower of the whites, whom he continued to follow and serve to the end of his life. All this presumably because in 1856 he did not join enthusiastically in the loud talk of the Northern Sioux about fighting the Americans. The fat and supine Spotted Tail let the northern chiefs talk while he led his Brulés in a brisk war that had the hated Pawnee almost finished; he traveled two to three thousand miles each year on horseback to attend to tribal business at the Deer Creek agency, and all these years he had to face the fact that the whites had already established themselves firmly within striking distance of the Sioux camps south of the Platte, with a force of armed white men that amounted to thirty men to each Sioux warrior, not counting the government's military forces at all. Did the Northern Sioux, who had pledged themselves at their great council at Bear Butte to unite to fight any white invasion of Sioux lands, come south to offer aid to the Spotted Tail camps? Not at all. When they talked of preventing white intrusion on Sioux lands, they meant only their own hunting grounds in the Powder River country.

In the autumn of 1859, Spotted Tail went to Deer Creek and

[3] Hyde, *The Pawnee Indians*, 190.

saw what the plan of the Northern Sioux to oppose the whites meant in action. Captain Raynolds had completed an entire summer's work, surveying the Sioux country north of the Platte, and had brought his party to Deer Creek to winter, the purpose being to complete his military survey in the spring. Then Lone Horn, the great Miniconjou Sioux chief, came down from the Powder River in a stormy mood and attempted to frighten Captain Raynolds into abandoning any further intrusions into the Sioux hunting grounds. Raynolds told the angry chief that he had his orders and intended to carry them out. Lone Horn then quieted down and began to give the captain friendly advice, warning him particularly that if he met any group of Sioux when he resumed his survey in the spring, not to shake hands with them. Well, well. So that was the war plan that had come out of the great Sioux council at Bear Butte—the same ancient trick they had used on the unfortunate wagon-train boss at Deer Creek in 1854, some Sioux coming up to him from the front, smiling and holding out their hands, while others slipped around behind and shot him in the back. General Harney called it murder, which was what it was. It was not war, but it was an excellent method for bringing war down on the Sioux, who in 1859 were in no state to carry on war with any hope of success.

It is only in modern books that Sioux chiefs of the period of 1856–65 sit down and hold their heads in black dejection or develop practical plans for united opposition to white encroachments on their lands. The Sioux were too busy living to mourn for any length of time over the probable fate of their people, and they were incapable of presenting a united front with the purpose of holding back the flood of whites coming into their country. Every camp thought first of its own interests, as had been demonstrated during the Harney campaign of 1855 and the Sumner campaign of 1857.

The crisis was fast developing in the Sioux lands south of the Platte. The Cheyenne and Arapaho allies who shared the hunting grounds of the Sioux had been shocked by Colonel Sumner's successes in 1857; and almost immediately thereafter the new settlers in Colorado began to talk of getting these Indians out of the way by placing them on a reservation on the Arkansas River, below Bent's Fort. The officials in Washington took up this plan, and a treaty commission was sent to meet the chiefs at Bent's Fort in September, 1860. There was some hocus-pocus at the fort. The chiefs were coaxed, were given presents, and then some of them were persuaded to permit their names to be set down as agreeing to the treaty and the plan for settlement on a reservation. The treaty was then left in the hands of A. G. Boone, a son of Daniel Boone, who owned the townsite of Booneville on the Arkansas, east of Pueblo. Boone had a direct business interest in getting the Cheyennes and Arapahoes out of the way and settled on a reservation. He induced some of the chiefs to agree to the treaty, which was then declared to be in effect. Part of the Cheyennes and Arapahoes, particularly the bands that hunted with the Sioux on the Solomon and the Republican, denounced the chiefs who had signed the treaty, termed the whole thing a fraud, and refused to be bound by it. The government proceeded to open a reservation for these tribes on the Arkansas, and the agent hired white men to plow land, make small irrigation ditches, and plant some crops. It was hoped that in time the Indians could be coaxed to the reservation, but practically all of the Cheyennes and Arapahoes were determined to continue their old life of hunting, fighting, and roving.

It was now the turn of the Little Thunder and Spotted Tail Sioux group and of their Southern Oglala Sioux allies. On October 28, 1859, Agent Twiss wrote to the Indian Office in Washington suggesting that a fund of money be supplied for the purchase of gifts for the Sioux who lived south of the Platte, for Little Thunder and ten Brulé subchiefs, and for Bad Wound (the chief of the Southern Oglalas) and his fifteen subchiefs. This was clearly the opening move for a treaty with these Sioux which would follow the lines of the Cheyenne and Arapaho treaty and provide for the settling of the Sioux on a reservation. The sweetening of the chiefs by the making of liberal gifts was to be the prelude.

Lincoln's election in 1860 put an end, for the moment, to this plan. Lincoln made the most sweeping removal of Indian agents ever known, replacing the old agents with men whose one qualification was that they were loyal Republicans. The new agent for the Indians of the Upper Platte was an obscure person named Cody. He lasted about a year, and was then replaced by another political appointee, John Loree. The governor of Colorado Territory, John Evans, was much interested in settling the Indians on reservations, and in 1862 he and Agent Loree combined forces to attempt to hold a treaty council with the Sioux, Cheyennes, and Arapahoes who hunted on branches of the Kansas River.

The Civil War had now begun, and nearly all the little garrisons of regular troops had been taken away from the posts on the Platte and the Arkansas to be sent to the scene of war in the East. At this moment the news of the great Sioux uprising in Minnesota threw the whole western frontier into alarm. All Indians were regarded with suspicion and dread. In September a war party of Sioux attacked the Pawnees on their reservation, charging into the Pawnee village and setting sixty earth lodges aflame. The attackers were Western Sioux who had no connection with the Minnesota Sioux, but the entire Nebraska frontier was thrown into panic, and the settlers fled to the towns for protection. A call for military aid was made, and troops were sent up the Platte. These were not regulars but volunteer troops, mostly western men who disliked Indians and treated them roughly.

Agent Loree went to Washington with the scheme for a treaty council with the Indians between the Platte and the Arkansas. He returned to the Upper Platte in June, 1863, with authorization to hold a council. He, Governor Evans, and S. G. Colley (who was agent for the Indians near the Arkansas in Colorado) laid their plans and sent out white traders to inform the chiefs of the coming council, which was to be held on the Arickaree Fork, a head-branch of Republican Fork. One of the traders who had been sent out talked to some of the chiefs and obtained a rather unwilling promise that they would attend the council, but when Governor Evans and Agent Loree reached the council spot on Arickaree Fork, there were no Indians there. Evans was very much disappointed. He regarded the failure of the chiefs to come to the council as an indication that they were hostile. The fact seems to have been that the Indians were determined not to give up their free life of hunting and settle on a reservation, and they forbade their chiefs to attend the council, fearing that they would be coaxed into agreeing to a treaty, just as the chiefs at Bent's Fort had been cajoled in 1860.

Governor Evans, like so many other officials who were not familiar with Indian mental processes, believed that it was a simple matter for Indian chiefs to meet and, after some discussion, come to a firm and unanimous decision and stick to it. He made the mistake of thinking that Indians were like whites and that they made up their minds and acted exactly as white men would. Either in peace or in war, it was almost impossible for these Plains Indians to unite and remain united. The men of each small camp talked, then they either disagreed hopelessly and took no action, or else they agreed and their chief accepted their views. Then the chief met chiefs of other bands and found they held other views, so he was talked around by them; and when he got back to his own camp, his head-men disapproved and forced him to go back on any pledges he had made. There can be no doubt whatever that in 1863 the Sioux south of the Platte and the Brulés up along the Platte were friendly, but most of them were very suspicious of this treaty proposal; and, fearing that in a council their chiefs would be talked around by Governor Evans and Agent Loree, they forbade their chiefs to attend the treaty council. But Loree did not accept the Indian decision. He had moved the Upper Platte Agency eastward, to a point east of Fort Laramie. There he was in close contact with the Brulé Corn Band, and he soon coaxed Swift Bear, the Corn Band chief, into agreeing to accept a reservation and start farming.[4] Swift Bear had only thirty lodges with sixty families, but he started the usual split that prevented the Sioux from remaining united in their stand against going to a reservation. The Brulé Orphans and the Wazhazhas, now hunting up near the Powder River, bitterly opposed; the Little Thunder Brulés south of the Platte were determined to stay where they were and live by hunting.

Little Thunder was now growing old and was leaning more and more on the strong arm of his principal lieutenant, Spotted Tail. This meant that Spotted Tail was in a very favorable position to succeed the old Chief, both as leader of the Southern Brulés and as head chief of the Brulé tribe. There was no other man in the prime of life among the Brulés who could compare with him in ability and popularity. He was head and shoulders above the other

[4] Loree's report, February, 1863, in National Archives.

leaders in his own group south of the Platte. On the North Platte, the Corn Band was split; the old chief, Grand Partisan, was leading the conservative camp of Corn Band folk, who wished to continue hunting and roving. Swift Bear headed the other Corn Band camp, and was for a reservation and farming. He always went to his brother-in-law, trader Bordeaux, for advice, and Bordeaux—a man of peace and little physical courage—usually counseled Swift Bear to be a good boy and do just what his father—the Indian agent—wished him to do. The Brulé Orphans, led by the warlike Iron Shell, son of old Chief Bull Tail, and the Wazhazhas, led by Spotted Tail's brother-in-law, Red Leaf, were up north, closely associated with the wild Oglalas and Miniconjous of the Powder River country.

These Northern Sioux and the Brulés and the Oglalas who hunted south of the Platte were very angry in 1862–63 because the Laramie Loafers and the Swift Bear camp of the Corn Band were making agreements with Agent Loree. The Loafers were the Sioux who had a permanent camp at Fort Laramie. They did not go hunting often, but picked up a living from the garrison and from passing wagon trains on the road. Old Smoke of the Oglalas was generally recognized as the chief of the Loafer camp, although this camp had families of Brulés and even some Sioux from the Missouri River. When the Civil War came and the Sioux of Minnesota rose in 1862, an order was issued in Washington that no more guns and ammunition should be included in the annuity goods sent to the Indians of the Upper Platte. It was necessary to decide what articles should be substituted for the arms and ammunition, and Agent Loree held a council with the Loafers and Corn Band and induced the chiefs to agree that plows, hoes, and other farming tools would be acceptable in lieu of the guns and ammunition. When the wild camps south of the Platte and those up on Powder River heard of this, they were furious. They accused Loree of cheating them and of stealing their goods; and when Spotted Tail went up to the North Platte for his group's share in the annuities in 1863, he had a violent quarrel with Loree. An army officer who was present denounced the agent and strongly advised the Sioux chiefs not to put their *X*-marks down on Loree's receipts; but these Indians had to either take the small quantity of goods offered to them or go without, and they made their X-marks on the paper and went home in a very bad temper. Loree, they said, would not even let them have any trade. He licensed only a few traders, mainly up on the North Platte; and the traders near the forks of the Platte, who were close enough for the Little Thunder and Spotted Tail Sioux to trade with, were either refused licenses or had only small stocks of goods, for which they demanded high prices.

The Gilman brothers had a stage station, ranch, and trading store just below the forks of the Platte near Cottonwood Springs, where heavy Indian trails from the camps on the Republican and Solomon forks struck the Platte. Jack Morrow had a stage station, ranch, and trading store a little farther west, on the south bank of the river just at the forks and up the South Platte, at California Crossing, was Beauvais' trading store. Agent Loree found these traders too far from his agency near Fort Laramie for him to control them, and he tried in every manner to block their Indian trade.

Unlike the wild Sioux on the Powder River, the Sioux south of the Platte were in constant touch with the whites. There was very heavy travel on the Platte road; the Overland Stage was running daily coaches and there was a stage station and ranch every fifteen miles along the road. The Overland Telegraph line had been built along the stage road to connect the Eastern States with the Pacific Coast. Spotted Tail and the other chiefs south of the Platte were going to school, learning the ways of the whites and particularly the tricks and traps employed by Indian agents and traders. Iowa volunteer cavalry had now built a military post at Cottonwood Springs, a favorite old camping ground for Spotted Tail's group, and when Bad Wound, the utterly friendly Southern Oglala chief, appeared with a camp of his people on an island in the river, an officer at the new fort had a howitzer run out and dropped several shells among the Indians. This was regarded by the Iowa boys as a good joke, but old Bad Wound—forced to run for his life—could not see the point of the jest.[5]

These volunteer troops had been rushed to the Platte line when the Nebraska frontier was thrown into panic by news of the Minne-

[5] Eugene F. Ware, *The Indian War of '64*, 75.

sota Sioux uprising in 1862. First the Iowa cavalry was sent to guard the road along the Lower Platte; then in May, 1863, the Eleventh Ohio Cavalry was sent up the road to establish posts from near the forks to the Sweetwater, west of Fort Laramie. Colonel W. O. Collins, commanding the Ohio regiment, was an able and intelligent man; and as an easterner, he did not share the view of the Colorado, Kansas, and Iowa volunteer troops that Indians were twopence the dozen and that shooting them was a public service. He got on well with the Sioux, until the Indian killers among the Colorado volunteers set the prairie afire and brought on a general state of war.

This war came in the spring of 1864. On April 3 it was reported that Indians had run off Irwin and Jackman's herd on the Big Sandy, east of Denver. According to the statements of the Cheyennes, who were supposed to be responsible, they did not raid the herd of work cattle, and they thought the animals had stampeded and the careless herders had then reported an Indian raid to avoid being blamed. Lieutenant George Eayre of the Colorado cavalry was now ordered to go after the Indians, and he marched through the Cheyenne country, attacking all Indians met. The Colorado troops stationed along the South Platte were also soon engaged in fighting the Indians. Little Thunder and Spotted Tail were on the Republican Fork, their Indians busy hunting buffalo. The chiefs were determined to keep out of the Cheyenne troubles. They permitted war parties to go and attack the Pawnees on their reservation in eastern Nebraska, but they ordered the warriors to avoid acts that might involve the tribe in war with the Americans. Despite these strict orders, on May 23 a small war party of Southern Oglalas became involved with a wagon train moving along the road that ran on the north bank of the Platte. The whites had two men killed, and the Iowa cavalry stationed at Cottonwood Springs on the south bank of the river could not cross to assist the party under attack. When this Oglala war party got back to their camp on the Republican, the head chief, Bad Wound, called a council and demanded that the warriors be punished for disobeying orders and attacking white men. The council ordered the Indian soldiers who were the police of the camp to shoot the horses and dogs of the guilty men and burn their lodges; then a herald rode through the camp announcing that any man who injured the whites would be treated in this manner.[6]

General S. R. Curtis, commanding the military department, now ordered General R. B. Mitchell, commanding on the Lower Platte, to summon the Sioux chiefs from south of the Platte to a council at Camp Cottonwood. Mitchell did not think the matter of much importance and did not go to Cottonwood, leaving Major George N. O'Brien, the post commander, to deal with the Indian chiefs. O'Brien sent two traders, Alfred Gay and John Smith, who were married to Sioux women, to find the camps and notify the chiefs. These men left Cottonwood June 2 and found a camp of 40 lodges on Medicine Creek and later a camp of 210 lodges on the Republican, due south of Plum Creek on the Platte. They found the chiefs eager for a council and stating that they had wanted one long ago, but were afraid to venture near Camp Cottonwood, where the Iowa volunteer cavalry had a happy custom of using any Indians sighted as targets for artillery practice.

The council was held at Cottonwood on June 8. Unfortunately, the official report is a brief and colorless abstract, in the form of questions and answers. According to this report, Major O'Brien sharply questioned the chiefs regarding the conduct and intentions of their people and then issued curt orders for the Sioux to keep out of the Platte valley if they wished to avoid war. Old Little Thunder was too sick to attend the council, and for the first time Spotted Tail was delegated to speak for his tribe. He and his life-long comrade, Two Strike, represented the Brulés; Bad Wound and Whistler (*Zoolah*) spoke for the Southern Oglalas. These chiefs stated that they had separated their camps from the hostile Cheyennes to avoid trouble with the whites. They stated that they wished to have a government agency of their own near Cottonwood, because the journey to Fort Laramie for annuity goods was much too long and dangerous. Their agent, Loree, was a bad man, who would allow only one licensed trader for all the camps south of the Platte, a man who had few goods and charged very high prices for poor articles. This brief report pictures the chiefs as submitting meekly when Major O'Brien ordered them to keep their people out of

[6] *Ibid.*, 199.

the Platte Valley; but Lieutenant Eugene F. Ware, who was present, wrote in later years that at this point Spotted Tail lost his temper and told the Major angrily that the Platte valley belonged to the Sioux and that they would travel in the valley whenever they chose to do so.[7]

There can be no doubt whatever that the Sioux chiefs south of the Platte and their councils were very anxious to avoid trouble with the whites; but they had to share the same hunting grounds with the Cheyennes and Arapahoes, and when in midsummer those tribes—goaded into madness by the wanton attacks of the volunteer cavalry on their people—went to war, it was impossible for the Sioux chiefs to control their warlike young men. The Cheyennes had withdrawn their camp to Salt Plain, south of the Arkansas, where they held their annual summer medicine ceremonies; then in June they returned to their hunting grounds on the forks of the Kansas River and at once sent out large war parties to strike the great road along the Platte and South Platte. In this they were joined by their Arapaho allies. Fortune was all in their favor. Having stirred up these Indians to madness, the military authorities had withdrawn all troops from the vital South Platte road that led to Denver, a false rumor of a Confederate force marching northward to invade Colorado having induced General Curtis to order a concentration of forces on the Arkansas to meet the supposed invaders. With the Denver road stripped of defenders, the Cheyenne and Arapaho war parties swept up and down the road, burning stage stations and ranches, killing whites, and capturing big wagon trains of food and other supplies bound for Colorado.

On August 8–10, the Indians shifted their attacks from the Denver road to the Overland road on the Lower Platte, raiding both east and west of Fort Kearney and perpetrating the worst raid in Nebraska frontier history on the Little Blue River, where they burned every station and ranch from Fort Kearney to the mouth of the Big Sandy. The Overland Stage Company suspended its service, and the long trains of big freight wagons halted where they

[7] O'Brien Report, *Official Records of the Union and Confederate Armies*, ser. vol. 63, p. 458. Lieutenant Ware describes three councils with the Sioux at Camp Cottonwood this summer, but the official reports show only one.

were, corralled and prepared to fight for their lives. The little force of Iowa cavalry guarding this line seemed helpless in the face of the violent Indian attacks. Both officers and soldiers were bewildered. Wherever they were ordered to march, the Indians skipped out of the way and drove a hard raid at some point that had been left unguarded. The volunteer officers, who in the spring had held the Indians in contempt and had lightheartedly started harassing them, now admitted their helplessness to stem the Indian attack and called frantically for strong additional forces of cavalry to deal with the situation.

The Cheyenne and Arapaho camps were scenes of wild rejoicing. Scalp dances were kept going in every camp, and war parties were coming in almost daily, bringing more scalps and loads of plunder. These Indians had never dreamed of the riches they were gathering from captured stage stations and supply trains. The camps were filled with foods the people had only known before as the rarest luxuries—wheat flour, sugar, coffee, dried fruits, canned goods, tobacco—all in wholesale quantities, sacks, bales, and cases. Warriors came back from the Overland road and paraded through the camps in the strange outfits of eagle-feather war bonnets with silk opera cloaks and other ladies' finery taken from freight wagons that were carrying goods to the finest stores in Denver and Salt Lake City. Nearly every Indian lodge had bolts of fine dress goods, and the women were making shirts for their warriors from silk of brilliant colors. The Sioux saw all this, and their young men could not resist the temptation. Some of them formed war parties and set out to raid along the Platte road, in defiance of the orders of their chiefs.

George Bent, the half-breed Cheyenne, was in these camps and is our main authority for these happenings. He stated that the "Spotted Tail and Pawnee Killer" Sioux groups joined in the raiding, by which he meant the Southern Brulés, led by Little Thunder with Spotted Tail as his lieutenant, and the Southern Oglalas, led by Bad Wound, among whom Pawnee Killer was a war leader but not a chief. As far as our evidence goes, Spotted Tail was not a chief either, but still a war-shirt-wearer, or war leader. Bent ignores the real chiefs and speaks only of these two war leaders, Spotted

Tail and Pawnee Killer. He never mentions seeing Spotted Tail leading the warriors during the summer, and as Spotted Tail is known to have held strong views against war with the Americans, it is not probable that he took part in these raids.

The Sioux chiefs and leaders still opposed war, but they could not prevent parties of their young men slipping away and joining in the Cheyenne raids. As autumn came, the raiding fell off. The Indians had to hunt and lay up dried meat for winter. This was one reason why leaders like Spotted Tail, who were thoughtful and knew the ways of the American army, had no faith in the Indians' ever gaining ultimate success in a war on the whites. The Indians could only carry on war seasonally. They had to stop the war in early summer to hunt and again in late autumn, or their people would starve. They had their women and children always with them, and most of their attention was distracted from fighting the enemy by the necessity of feeding and protecting their families. In winter they had to find a safe and comfortable location and stay in it, caring for their families.

When the raiding dwindled in the autumn of 1864, the chiefs began to talk peace once more. Black Kettle of the Cheyennes opened negotiations with the officers at Fort Lyon (near the site of Bent's Fort) on the Arkansas in eastern Colorado. This chief was encouraged by the officials to bring his camp near the fort; but Colonel J. M. Chivington, of the Colorado volunteers, was determined to strike a blow at the Indians, and he did not seem to care whether the blow fell on friendly Indians or hostiles. Black Kettle had all of the most friendly families in his camp, and his people had been lulled into the belief that peace was now certain. Chivington concentrated a large force of volunteer cavalry near Denver, most of his men being very rough frontier characters from the Colorado mining camps. He stopped all travel down the Arkansas road to prevent any warning reaching the Indians. Making a swift and secret march, he reached Fort Lyon and threw a screen of pickets about the post, for he feared that some friendly man might slip away and warn his intended victims. At dawn on November 29 his men rode into Black Kettle's camp, taking the Indians completely by surprise and shooting down men, women, and children as they ran out of the lodges. Part of the Indians escaped to the dry creek bed, where they were surrounded and deliberately butchered, the women and children sharing the fate of the men. The survivors of this massacre fled to a Cheyenne camp on the head of Smoky Hill Fork, where they arrived in a pitiful condition. Many of them were nearly naked and had frozen hands and feet; the wounded were in desperate plight.

The Sioux, Cheyennes, and Arapahoes had settled down in winter camps on the branches of the Kansas River when the news of this attack on Black Kettle's camp jerked them to the alert. The story roused their pity and rage, and it alarmed them for the safety of their own camps. The Cheyennes sent war pipes to all the camps, and the Sioux leaders who had stood firmly for peace all through the troublous year 1864 had to give way to the aroused people of their camps. They smoked the Cheyenne war pipes. So did the Arapahoes. The Northern Arapahoes had come south from their own lands north of the Platte to visit the Southern Arapahoes. Finding that that tribe was wintering far south of the Arkansas, the northern group went into winter camp on a head-branch of the Kansas River. Here the Cheyenne war pipes were brought, and the Arapaho leaders smoked them.

It was in December that the Indians all gathered in a great camp of nearly one thousand lodges on Cherry Creek, a branch of the Arickaree Fork of the Republican River. The leaders had made their decision. It was not safe to remain south of the Platte; they would go north, and on the way they would take vengeance for Black Kettle's people by raiding the great road along the Platte and South Platte. Black Kettle's heart was broken by the awful fate that had overwhelmed his people; but he still stood for peace, and when the start was made for the Platte, he took a remnant of his band and headed south. Spotted Tail went with the hostiles. He still believed the Indians could not win a war. He was a man of strong and well-balanced character; but he was also a man of strong passions and sympathies, and the story of the butchery of Black Kettle's people certainly moved him greatly. We have no details as to what happened in the Sioux camps when the Cheyenne pipe-bearers came, but the probability is that each Sioux camp held a council and instructed the chiefs to smoke the war pipes. This created a different situation from that of the preceding summer, when groups of young Sioux had slipped away from the camps to make unauthorized raids. The Sioux had now formally declared war, and Spotted Tail, as war leader, took charge of the Brulé operations.

The Indians obviously had definite plans, talked over and decided on in council. They were going north to join the hostiles on Powder River. Such a march in the dead of winter, taking the camps, the women, children, and pony herds along, was a most difficult operation. The people had to be fed, but such a vast Indian camp would frighten away game, making living by hunting impossible. It was therefore planned to obtain food and other supplies by raiding along the great road on the Platte. Julesburg, in the northeast corner of Colorado, at old Upper California Crossing on the South Platte, was chosen as the first point to attack. Julesburg had a stage station, a store, an Overland Telegraph office, a big stage company warehouse filled with food and supplies, and a military post, called Camp Rankin, garrisoned by a small force of Iowa volunteer cavalry. One thousand warriors were to make the attack, and the plan was the ancient decoy-party trick, which was one of the very few military tactics the Plains Indians had developed.

The Indians reached Julesburg on the night of January 6–7, 1865, and concealed themselves behind the hills to the south. At dawn on the seventh, the decoy party of seven skilled men moved cautiously down a small draw that led across the flat valley to the South Platte River, leading their horses. They got close to Camp Rankin, then mounted and charged a group of soldiers gathered outside the stockade gate, driving them inside. After a time the cavalry, now mounted, rode out and charged the decoy party, who drew them on toward the hills, nearly three miles away. Behind the hills the great mass of warriors was being held in close rank by Indian soldiers, awaiting the signal to charge; but, as so often happened on such occasions, the sound of firing and yelling excited some of the warriors beyond control, and they broke through the thin line of Indian soldiers and rode up on the hills in plain sight, while the cavalry was still some distance off. The cavalry promptly turned and rode for Camp Rankin, their horses at a hard run. The decoy party pursued the fleeing troops, and some of the cavalry had to dismount to stand the Indians off. Warriors on fast ponies now came up from the hills and drove the cavalry and a number of civilians who had joined them back into the military stockade. In this pursuit, the Indians killed fourteen soldiers and four civilians. While this fight was in progress, the westbound stage came into Julesburg, and the passengers and driver alighted to have breakfast. When they saw the great body of Indians charging out of the hills, the passengers, stage hands, and everyone else at Julesburg started running toward Camp Rankin, which they reached just before the Indians drove the flying cavalry in. The whole broad valley was dotted by groups of warriors, riding up and down, shooting and yelling. Indian women with pack-ponies were heading for the buildings at Julesburg, and here the warriors joined them. They systematically plundered the stage station, store, and stage company warehouse, while the troops and civilians at Camp Rankin looked helplessly on. The Indian women loaded hundreds of pack-ponies, and the warriors took as much plunder as they could carry on their own ponies. The work finished, the Indian soldiers took control again and started the march back to the distant camp.

H. H. Bancroft, in his *History of Colorado*, states that Spotted Tail took a prominent part in this attack on Julesburg; and, in the spring of 1865, Major General G. M. Dodge, commanding the troops along the Platte, reported that Spotted Tail had admitted that he took part in the great raids of the previous winter, but made the excuse that he had been forced (by Sioux opinion) to join in a war that he did not think would bring any great gain to his people. With no detailed account of what happened at the councils in the Indian camps, we can only suppose that Spotted Tail did lead in the raids and in planning them, and that in the following spring, when his people wanted peace, he excused himself in speaking to the officers at Fort Laramie.

While the warriors were at Julesburg, the Indians moved their great camp to White Butte Creek, halfway between Cherry Creek and the South Platte. On the return of the raiders, the chiefs announced that the village would start in two days to move to the

South Platte, large war parties going on ahead to raid the road and collect supplies of food and other plunder. Fate still played into the hands of the Indians. After the Julesburg raid, Brigadier General R. B. Mitchell, commanding on the Platte, removed all detachments of troops that were guarding stage stations and ranches and organized an expedition to go south and seek the hostiles in their own country. Marching from Camp Cottonwood near the forks of the Platte, he combed the branches of the Kansas River, finding fresh signs of very large Indian camps but seeing no Indians at all. When he marched back to Camp Cottonwood, he was greeted by the appalling news that the Indians, seven hundred lodges, were on the South Platte, had broken the road, and were creating havoc, attacking and burning stage stations and ranches, forcing all freighting trains to halt, corral, and fight for their lives, and driving off entire herds of cattle. The Overland Telegraph line was down for many miles, the Indians having cut or burned down the poles and carried off the heavy copper wire. Denver was isolated, and there was panic all along the great Overland road.

The Indians were encamped on the north bank of the South Platte, about twenty-five miles west of Julesburg. Their great camp was filled with food taken in the raids. They had an abundance of fresh beef from the stolen herds, while from the captured stage stations and wagon trains they had taken great stocks of white men's food, including everything from flour, sugar, and coffee to fancy canned goods, canned oysters, and olives. The mixed-bloods in camp, who had seen such strange foods before, were constantly being consulted by Indians who wished to know the uses of catsup, candied fruits, and imported cheese. Assured that these were excellent food, they made a huge meal of catsup, candied fruits, and chowchow and were violently sick.

On February 2, the Indians, fifteen hundred strong, attacked Julesburg for the second time. The small cavalry garrison did not dare venture outside its stockade, and the Indians, after plundering Julesburg again, set the buildings afire and withdrew. The camp was now on its way to the North Platte. There the road was not heavily traveled and there were few stage stations and ranches. The Indians sanded the ice in the North Platte and crossed their camp and herds to the north bank. But now they saw troops on the road across the river, Colonel W. O. Collins of the Eleventh Ohio Cavalry having marched eastward from Fort Laramie to seek the hostiles. The warriors streamed back across the ice of the river and had a lively engagement with the Ohio troops, but Colonel Collins corralled his wagons and fought a defensive engagement from inside the corral. Tiring of this, the warriors withdrew.

The Indians now moved northward through the Nebraska Sand Hills, crossing the Niobrara and the head of White River and reaching the Black Hills. All the lands north of the North Platte were empty of whites; there was not even a trading post for Indians in all this vast district. Not a sign of the whites was seen after leaving the North Platte, and it was probably during this march up to the Black Hills that Spotted Tail and the other Sioux chiefs held councils and came to a decision regarding their future action. This great march of the Indians during the worst weather of winter, taking their camps, women, children, and herds with them, was a military feat of the first order. They had taken the whites completely by surprise; the white troops had made a dreadfully poor showing; and the Indians, by raiding, had stocked themselves with great supplies of food, clothing, and other articles. But the Sioux chiefs knew the whites and their ways, and they knew the Sioux and their ways even better. The Sioux had now "put the war back in the bag" and would think no more about it until next summer, when they would make a few raids and then put the war away until the following summer. The whites would come back in the spring of 1865 with greater forces of troops and take the offensive, and they would keep it up endlessly. From the point of view of Spotted Tail, Little Thunder, Bad Wound, and Man-Who-Walks-under-the-Ground, the situation was already very bad. Their groups—the Southern Brulés and Southern Oglalas—had been forced to leave their hunting grounds on the forks of the Kansas River, that country not being safe for their camps and their women and children. They could not venture back to their own lands until peace was declared. They were now in the White River, Cheyenne River, and Black Hills country, where most of the older men had been born and brought up, but these lands were now hunted out. The Northern Sioux had

109

gone farther west into the Powder River country; but there were too many Indians in that land now, and if the southern bands went there, they would find their welcome soon worn out and would be regarded as intruders, eating the buffalo and other game of the Northern Sioux and Cheyennes. The decision made by Spotted Tail and the other chiefs is indicated by the statement of George Bent, the mixed-blood Cheyenne, who was in the hostile camp. He asserted that on reaching the Black Hills, the Cheyennes and Arapahoes decided to move westward to Powder River but that "the Spotted Tail Sioux" left them and moved off eastward. They had decided to keep clear of the hostiles on Powder River and to seek peace in the spring and a return to their own lands south of the Platte. Where they spent the remainder of the winter, we do not know; but in the spring, as soon as the ground was fit for traveling, they turned up at Fort Laramie and declared themselves to be friendlies seeking peace.

Old-Man-Afraid-of-His-Horse. (From *A Sioux Chronicle*, by George E. Hyde. Courtesy Pitt Rivers Museum, Oxford)

Red Cloud, 1875, wearing buckskins and a breast plate and holding a cane. (From *Indian Oratory*, by W. C. Vanderwerth. Courtesy Western History Collections, University of Oklahoma Library)

Crazy Horse (?), from a photograph made by Major Wilhelm, 8th U.S. Infantry, 1874. While no authenticated picture of Crazy Horse is known to exist, this is thought by some to be a photograph of him. (From *Indian Oratory*, by W. C. Vanderwerth. Courtesy Western History Collections, University of Oklahoma Library)

General Crook appoints Spotted Tail chief of both agencies, October 24, 1876, at Red Cloud Agency. The men are shown wearing their reservation hats. (Courtesy South Dakota Historical Society)

5. Spotted Tail
Becomes Head Chief

In the 1830's, the Oglalas had been led by Bull Bear, a strong and tyrannical chief, who was opposed by a chief named *Shota* (Smoke). Smoke seems to have had the better brain, but he was evidently afraid of Bull Bear. His young relative, Red Cloud, was not afraid of any man. In the autumn of 1841, the rival chiefs were in a camp on the Chugwater, a branch of Laramie Fork. Bad liquor had been brought into the camp; the Indians got to drinking, a fight was started, and when Bull Bear rushed out of his lodge to join in the fray, he was shot and killed by young Red Cloud. The Oglala tribe then split into two unfriendly factions. One group was called the Smoke People and was led by that chief; the followers of the dead Bull Bear were called the Bear People and went to live south of the Platte, whereas the Smoke People hunted and lived to the north of the river.

By 1846, Smoke was the leading Sioux chief in the Fort Laramie district, a fat and jovial chieftain, a great friend of the whites, a laugher and maker of jokes. He liked to be near the whites, and when the military took over the old trading post at Fort Laramie, he made the place his headquarters. Most of his part of the Oglala tribe was up north in the lands between the Black Hills and the Bighorn Mountains; but Smoke was getting old, and he preferred to remain with a small camp of followers, at or near Fort Laramie for the greater part of the time. Sioux families from other camps who preferred the easy life at the fort to the dangers and hardships of the wild camps in the hunting grounds came to join Smoke's camp. Girls from Smoke's camp married white men—traders, soldiers, and army officers. In the old days it was considered a very honorable thing for a Sioux family to become connected by marriage with a white trader, and most of the girls who married traders came from the families of chiefs. The marriages of Sioux girls at Fort Laramie and along the Platte road were at first regarded as honorable and advantageous; but by the late 1850's the Sioux in the wild buffalo-hunting camps began to sneer at the people in Smoke's camp. They called them *Waglukhe* (Loafers, Followers, or Hangers-on at the fort) and pretended to scorn them, because they had given up the old Sioux life of wandering, hunting, and fighting to pick up a living from the whites at the fort and along the Platte road.

These Loafers at the fort hardly ever went hunting or took part in war expeditions, and the better of their young men got tired of the tame life at the fort and joined the wild camps up north. Red Cloud lived with his uncle, Smoke, at the fort for a time, then left and made a great reputation as a warrior in the Powder River country. There are at least two sides to every issue, and the people in the Loafer camp returned the scorn of the wild Sioux of the north, treating them like country bumpkins who came to visit the sophisticated Sioux at the fort. These wild bulls from the Powder River were full of airs and big talk about fighting the whites, but what did they know about the whites and their strength? They imagined that a fight among fifty warriors, in which two men were killed, was a big fight. The Loafers at the fort had heard details of the mighty three-day struggle at Gettysburg, and they knew what the white men meant when they spoke of a battle.

Old Smoke died in 1864, at the moment when the Sioux, goaded by the bad treatment of the volunteer troops, were going to war. He was placed on a scaffold within sight of his beloved fort, and Big Mouth, another fat and jovial chief, took his place as the leader of the Laramie Sioux camp. The great raids of the winter of 1864–65 came, and the volunteer troops, unable to strike an effective blow at the Indians, were in a furious temper. The Loafers stayed quietly at Fort Laramie. Fortunately for them, Colonel W. O. Collins of the Eleventh Ohio Cavalry, commanding the post, was a just and humane man. He issued surplus army clothing and rations to these poor friendly Sioux and protected them from rough frontiersmen who had a way of shooting Indians on sight.

Indian Agent Loree now had his Upper Platte Agency on the south bank of the North Platte, east of Fort Laramie and just east of Bordeaux's trading house, which was still where it had been at the time of the Grattan troubles of 1854. In the spring of 1864, Loree had some small irrigation ditches dug at the agency, and white men planted fifteen acres. Chief Smoke approved of this attempt to get the Sioux to start growing crops, but the coming of the Indian war put a stop to the experiment. The friendly Sioux were now moved to a camp on the north bank of the North Platte, about opposite to the agency. This was done to avoid trouble with white men traveling along the Platte road. The rough teamsters with the wagon trains that had been attacked by war parties farther down the Platte were strongly inclined to shoot all Sioux on sight. To control the friendly Indians further, a company of armed Indian police, commanded by Charlie Elliston, a courageous young trader married to a Sioux girl, was organized to police the camp. Big Mouth and his brother Blue Horse were officers of the Indian police. Swift Bear was in this friendly camp with part of the Corn Band all through the autumn of 1864, giving information to the officers at the fort regarding the plans of the wild Miniconjous on Powder River for making raids. This chief took his band off on a hunt north of the Platte in November, and was afraid to return when the great raids started.

The Civil War was ending in the spring of 1865. In the summer of 1864, when reinforcements were so badly needed on the Platte and the Arkansas, not a man was to be spared from the armies in the East; but now, in 1865, great numbers of troops had been set free for service in the West. Regiments of cavalry and batteries of artillery came pouring up the Platte; but these troops had volunteered to put down the rebellion in the South; they had completed that task, and thought that they had earned the right to be mustered out and sent home. Instead, they were ordered up the Platte to take part in an Indian campaign. On the way, some of the troops mutinied, and most of them reached Fort Laramie in a sullen and angry mood. Colonel Collins and his Ohio cavalry were relieved of duty and sent home to be mustered out. New officers and troops, all ignorant of the Indians and in a bad temper, were at Fort Laramie. It was at this inauspicious moment that some of the Sioux who had been drawn into the raids of the previous winter moved in near Fort Laramie, seeking peace. Two Face, an Oglala chief, was one of the first to come. The Sioux state that he had bought a white woman from a warrior who had captured her on the Platte, and he intended to prove his friendliness by taking her safely to the fort; but he now met some Indians from the friendly camp, who warned him of the harsh treatment the troops at the fort were giving to all Indians. Two Face stopped where he was, afraid to approach the fort. Then Big Mouth and some warriors from the friendly camp came and rounded him up. They also brought in Chief Blackfoot (another seeker of peace) and his camp. At the fort the white captive, Mrs. Eubanks, gave a wild and hysterical account of her sufferings and denounced Two Face and Blackfoot. The colonel in temporary command at the fort, who was intoxicated at the time, then ordered the chiefs hanged in artillery trace chains, and this was done.[1]

On April 14, Little Thunder and Spotted Tail came in with sixty lodges and were permitted to join the friendly camp. Swift Bear came in with his group of the Corn Band. Major General G. M. Dodge, the new commander of the military department, knew nothing about the Sioux. He thought all the Indians in the friendly camp were surrendered hostiles, prisoners of war. He was preparing for a big expedition against the hostiles on Powder River, and these Sioux at Fort Laramie were an embarrassment. He telegraphed to Washington for instructions, and was ordered to send the Sioux down the Platte under guard, to be held as prisoners at Fort Kearney.

There were 185 lodges of the most friendly Brulés and Oglalas in this camp near Fort Laramie, with about 700 of the utterly friend-

---

[1] One of the most shocking misstatements of Charles A. Eastman concerning Spotted Tail depicts this chief as handing over Two Face to the military at Fort Laramie to be hanged. Spotted Tail was not present, and Two Face was brought to the fort by Big Mouth's Indian soldiers. Eastman describes Spotted Tail as head chief in the spring of 1865, another astonishing misstatement for a Sioux Indian to make. As the records show, Spotted Tail was still under Chief Little Thunder and may still have been a shirt-wearer and not a chief at all. Eastman obtained his information from Sioux Indians at Pine Ridge around 1890. He says it was the middle of winter when Two Face was hanged, another amazing error.

ly Laramie Loafers. Most of the Southern Brulés (Chiefs Little Thunder and Spotted Tail) were in this camp, and Swift Bear with the friendly portion of the Corn Band. The rest of the Corn Band, under their old chief, Grand Partisan, were with Red Cloud on Powder River.

Thus, Spotted Tail was to go down the Platte road, a prisoner under guard, just as he had done ten years back. During those ten years he had striven constantly to avoid hostilities between his people and the whites, and this was the bitter fruit of all his labors. It was Colonel Thomas Moonlight, a pompous and hectoring Kansas volunteer officer, who supervised the sending of the Sioux friendlies to Fort Kearney. Captain W. D. Fouts, of the Seventh Iowa Cavalry, with a detachment from his regiment, was to guard the Indians on the road. A wagon train of supplies accompanied the Indians; James Bordeaux, the trader, was with the wagons, and in the wagons two or more Sioux who had been in the guardhouse at Fort Laramie were taken, with balls and chains on their legs. Many of the Indians of the Loafer camp had no horses or camp equipment, and they were transported in the wagons. At the first camp on the journey, the Indians were enraged by the soldiers' taking a number of Sioux girls to their camp and keeping them all night. While the soldiers were thus employed, the Sioux were holding a night council and making a plan. Spotted Tail and his followers wanted peace; but they were not the men to put up meekly with bad treatment. They had come in as friends, and now they were being sent as prisoners to Fort Kearney, almost within sight of their mortal enemies, the Pawnees. They had their women and children to think about, and they were determined not to be taken into enemy country and there probably disarmed and left helpless to defend themselves.

Slowly the Indian camp with the wagons and the guard of troops moved down the great Overland road, past Bordeaux's old trading houses, now standing deserted, past Agent Loree's Upper Platte Agency, also deserted. They reached the site of the Brulé village of 1854, where Spotted Tail had led the warriors in the killing of Lieutenant Grattan and his men; and farther down the road they came to the spot where Spotted Tail, Red Leaf, and Long Chin had attacked the mail wagon in November, 1855. At Horse Creek, where the first treaty had been signed in 1851, the Indians camped for the night. The troops and wagons crossed the creek and camped farther down. The troops took with them some Sioux girls and the prisoners with balls and chains on their legs.[2] That night, the Sioux completed their preparations. Charlie Elliston, who was in the Indian camp as captain of the Indian police, told his daughter-in-law in later years that Spotted Tail and Red Leaf made the plans and were the principal leaders. The contemporary records, which are scanty, do not mention Red Leaf as being in the camp. Everything was carefully planned. Black Wolf (Oglala) was to mark the crossing of the North Platte by setting sticks in the water, and he was to be responsible for crossing the women and children safely. He vowed that if *Wakon Tonka* would help him do this, he would undergo the torture in the Sun Dance, and he carried out his vow the following June in the Powder River country. The women had been ordered to leave the lodges standing, as it would be necessary to carry children and old people on the ponies and travel light and fast. Only the most necessary articles were to be packed up and taken along.

At dawn, the Indians failed to break camp, as they had been ordered to do. Captain Fouts left his camp with a few men and crossed Horse Creek to hurry the Indians up. As he rode toward the camp, he was shot dead (the Sioux say the Brulé chief, White Thunder, killed him), and the soldiers with him fled back across the creek. The warriors mounted and rode to the creek to keep the soldiers off, while the women and children and old people crossed the Platte, following the channel marked by sticks. Charlie Elliston's Indian police had deserted. Warned by Sioux friends to get out, he rode to the soldiers' camp, whipping his pony at every jump, and informed Captain Wilcox, now in command, of conditions in the Sioux camp. Wilcox took a cavalry force and attempted to cross the creek, but he was met by Spotted Tail at the head of the warriors and

---

[2] According to the Pine Ridge Sioux, the Indian prisoners in the wagons were Thunder Bear, son of Chief Two Face, Black War Bonnet, Calico (also called Black Shield), and a Brulé named Sand. In later years, Thunder Bear and Calico were judges of the Indian Court at Pine Ridge.

had to draw back to the cavalry camp, followed all the way by a throng of yelling and circling Sioux. Wilcox gathered a picked body of cavalry and frontiersmen and advanced again, getting near enough to see the Sioux women and children crossing the Platte with their loaded ponies, the warriors sitting on their ponies on the river bank, guarding the crossing. They came charging back at the sight of the troops, and Wilcox, finding them much too strong to hold off, again withdrew across Horse Creek.

In this fight the cavalry had Captain Fouts and four men killed and seven wounded. The only Indian killed was a prisoner in the wagons with ball and chain on his legs. He apparently was murdered by the enraged soldiers.[3]

Colonel Thomas Moonlight at Fort Laramie did not get the tidings of the Sioux outbreak at Horse Creek until late in the night (June 13–14). He started next morning with all the cavalry he could collect, marching toward Horse Creek, but on the way a messenger reached him with news that the Indians had crossed north of the Platte. Moonlight turned back to reach the good ford near Fort Laramie, then struck north in pursuit of the runaway Indians. Up near White River, on Dead Man's Fork, he went into camp and had the horses turned out to graze. Experienced Indian fighters protested that the horses should not be left loose in Indian country, but the Colonel paid no attention to them. The next thing

[3] The reports on the Horse Creek affair are in *Official Records of the Union and Confederate Armies*, ser. vols. 101 and 102. The diary of one of the soldiers of the Seventh Iowa Cavalry covering these events is in *Nebraska History Magazine*, Vol. XV, 75 (1934). The official reports state that before attacking the troops, the Sioux fought among themselves and killed four of their chiefs, but the Sioux deny this, and every chief who was known to be in the camp was alive the following year. If any chief had been killed, it would have been for opposing the attack on the troops in the name of peace, and those men would have been Little Thunder, Big Mouth, and Swift Bear. They all came out of the affair unhurt. Agent Loree had been succeeded by a person named Jarrot from Belleville, Illinois. Jarrot got to Camp Mitchell near Horse Creek just as the news of the Sioux outbreak came in. He retired hastily down the Platte to Fort Kearney, a safe spot. Then the military brought in twenty Sioux women and children, prisoners from the Horse Creek affair, and insisted that Jarrot take care of them. The new agent retreated to Omaha, and from there sent the Sioux captives up the Missouri in a steamboat to the Yankton Sioux agency in Dakota. Jarrot seems to have paid one brief visit to his agency near Fort Laramie, when it was safe to do so, and then his name vanished from the list of agents.

he knew the Sioux came sweeping down, yelling, firing, and waving buffalo robes. They stampeded the cavalry horses and made off with them, leaving Moonlight's command to walk back to Fort Laramie, carrying their saddles and equipment. General Dodge then relieved Moonlight of command and ordered him mustered out of the service for failure to take proper precautions.

Some of the escaped Sioux (probably Laramie Loafers) slipped back to Fort Laramie about a month later and reported that the camp of runaways was now at Butte d'Ours (Bear Butte in the Black Hills), where they were reported to have been joined by another Sioux camp. Their plan was to go to the Powder River, where buffalo and other game were plentiful. Later on, Spotted Tail stated that his camp wintered in the Powder River country. Yet Spotted Tail and the other leaders in his camp were not mentioned as taking any part in the fighting that occurred up north during the summer and autumn of 1865. In late June or early July, all the Sioux on Powder River held a great Sun Dance, and Black Wolf (the Oglala who had been made responsible for leading the women and children from the Horse Creek camp safely across the North Platte) carried out his vow to undergo torture in the Sun Dance if he succeeded in taking the people safely across the river. The Sioux marveled at his endurance of the torture.

After the Sun Dance, the Sioux, Cheyennes, and Arapahoes made an attack at Platte Bridge on the North Platte, about one hundred miles west of Fort Laramie. They took about one thousand warriors, led by famous chiefs; but George Bent, of the Cheyennes, who was present, failed to name Spotted Tail or any leaders of his camp as taking part in the expedition. This affair was very similar to the first attack at Julesburg, a decoy party being sent into the valley to draw the troops out of their stockade. The main body of Indians then charged, killing Lieutenant Caspar Collins, son of Colonel Collins of the Eleventh Ohio Cavalry, and a number of his men. The Indians then broke up into small raiding parties and swept along the North Platte road, attacking stations and ranches. They burned Deer Creek Station. Whether John Richards and Joe Bissonnette still had Indian trading houses there or not is uncertain. The Sioux traders had been ruined by the war; trade in arms and ammunition had been stopped in the spring of 1864, and all trade had been ended that autumn and was still suspended. The traders, who had been wealthy men before the Indian trouble started in 1864, lost very heavily, and some of them were reduced to poverty.

The Indians had just returned from their Platte expedition and put the war back in the bag until next summer when the troops invaded the Powder River country. They came in three strong columns from the south, southeast, and east, any one of the columns supposedly strong enough to defeat all the Indians; but, as has been stated, they were volunteer troops who had been sent West to fight Indians when they expected to be mustered out of service and sent home. Except for the troops who marched north from Fort Laramie, under the vigorous leadership of Brigadier General P. E. Connor, the men had no desire to find or fight Indians. Connor, aided by a company of Pawnee Indian scouts, found the Northern Arapaho camp, ran off the Indian herd, and had a big fight with the Arapahoes. The other two columns got lost on Powder River, were found and attacked by the Indians, fought them off, ran out of rations, lost most of their horses and mules from starvation and hardship, and were then found by the Pawnee Scouts and rescued by Connor's command. That ended the futile expedition, which had enough power to smash the Indians but neither the will nor the skill to apply the power.

It was at this time that Governor Newton Edmunds, of Dakota Territory, was given authority in Washington to make a peace treaty with the Sioux. Edmunds and his fellow peace commissioners made a great show and spent a large sum of public money in making peace with friendly camps of Sioux along the Missouri, bands that had taken no part in hostilities. This left the government with a peace treaty signed only by peaceful Sioux and with a mass of Sioux, Cheyennes, and Arapahoes in the Powder River country who were just as hostile as before. To remedy this situation, a copy of the peace treaty was sent to the commanding officer at Fort Laramie with orders that he should do everything in his power to bring the chiefs down from Powder River and induce them to sign the treaty. At this moment, when the army was asked to promote peace with the Sioux, the troops of the Powder River expedition were just back from their fruitless march through the Indian country north of the Platte, and the hostiles of Powder River were in high spirits and determined to go on fighting. No man could be found near Fort Laramie who was willing to risk his life by bearing a peace message to the northern camps; but early in October, Big Ribs and some other friendly Sioux from a camp near Denver were coaxed into undertaking this dangerous mission. They came to Fort Laramie to be instructed by an interpreter and then disappeared into the north. On January 16, 1866, the peace messengers returned to the fort, bringing with them Swift Bear and Standing Elk (Corn band) and some other Sioux leaders for a peace talk with Colonel H. E. Maynadier of the regular army, now in command at Laramie. After the talks the Indians sent runners to the Sioux camps, bearing an invitation for all the chiefs to come to the post for a treaty council in June.[4]

On March 9, Colonel Maynadier reported that Spotted Tail was coming to the fort with his camp, bringing the body of his beloved daughter *Ah-ho-ap-pa* (meaning Wheat Flour). The Chief's message stated that the girl was dying when the Indians with the peace message from the fort reached camp on Powder River, 250 miles from Fort Laramie, and she had begged that when she was dead her body be taken to the fort and placed beside the grave of old Chief Smoke, who had been buried there in 1864. Colonel Maynadier had met this girl with her father near Deer Creek on the North Platte in 1859 when he was a young lieutenant and the child was about twelve. At that time he had been attracted to Spotted Tail and his little girl, and now, when the runner came to the fort, he sent the Chief a friendly message and ordered an ambulance sent to the Indian camp with an escort of one company of cavalry and two howitzers to bring the Chief and his people to the fort. On reaching the post, Spotted Tail went to the commandant's quarters and was happily surprised to find that Colonel Maynadier was the young officer whom he and his daughter had known in 1859. He told the sympathetic Colonel of the troubles that had been forced on his people during the bitter years when the volunteer troops

---

[4] These events are covered by reports of the Office of Indian Affairs, volume for 1866. See also Hafen and Young, *Fort Laramie*, 341–50.

were stationed along the Platte and Arkansas rivers, and as he talked, the tears ran down his weather-beaten cheeks.

The girl whose body he had now brought to the old fort was his favorite daughter, born about 1848. She had gone through the battle on the Bluewater in 1855, when Harney had attacked the Brulé camp, and had shared her father's captivity at Fort Leavenworth, where the officers and their wives had made a pet of her. From that time she had been very fond of visiting at military posts and had always accompanied her father when he was going to Fort Laramie. There was a romantic tale in circulation recounting how this girl had fallen in love with a young regular army lieutenant, fresh from West Point, at Fort Laramie; but she and her father had not been at the fort since 1863, when she was fourteen, except for the brief visit to the friendly camp in the spring of 1865 when the Indians were evidently kept out of the fort. A Sioux girl of fourteen was marriageable, and there was probably some basis for this story of Spotted Tail's daughter loving a young officer, but nothing came of it. Charlie Elliston, who had known this girl from babyhood, stated that she was very proud, always said that she would not marry an Indian but only a *capitan* (army officer), and that her father approved of her decision. The romance makers have been at work on this girl and her story since 1866, and even her name has been left in doubt. Colonel Maynadier's first report called her *Ah-he-ap-pa*, or Wheat Flour; but in the account of her sent to *Frank Leslie's Weekly* the day after the funeral, she is called *Hinzinwin*, or Monica. *Hinzinwin* is there translated Falling Leaf; Monica was evidently a Christian name given to her by the army families at Fort Leavenworth or Fort Laramie. Susan Bettelyoun knew this girl well at Fort Laramie and calls her *Hinzmwin*, clearly the same as *Hinzinwin*. *Win* is the Sioux feminine ending, meaning girl or woman. The name might mean Yellow Girl or Yellow Buckskin Girl. It might mean Yellow Leaf and hence perhaps Falling Leaf. The writers who think it romantic to call a Sioux girl White Fawn or Prairie Flower are imagining a vain thing. The Sioux did not give that kind of pretty names to girls; but Yellow Buckskin Girl or Wheat Flour would be honest Sioux names, and Spotted Tail's daughter—like many of the Sioux—may have had two names.

Colonel Maynadier had a pine coffin made, and the girl's body was laid in it. A Sioux funeral scaffold was set up near that of old Chief Smoke one-half mile north of the parade ground—four posts about twelve feet long were set in the ground in a square, with a platform at the top on which the body was placed, beyond the reach of wolves and other wild animals. Colonel Maynadier ordered military honors for the dead girl, and toward sunset her coffin was placed on a gun carriage, which was followed by her relatives and a group of officers. Behind marched the troops, and a great throng of Indians followed. At the grave, funeral offerings were heaped on the coffin instead of flowers. Colonel Maynadier gave a very handsome pair of gauntlets as his offering. The girl had jealously kept since 1855 a little red-bound Episcopal prayer book with a gold cross on the cover, and the Reverend Mr. Wright now read the burial service from the little book. The coffin was then raised to the platform, covered with a buffalo robe, and tied down with leather thongs. The rites were mainly pagan Sioux. The Sioux believed that their dead traveled to the land of spirits, the poorer persons on foot, the better off on their ponies. They killed the girl's two favorite ponies, cut off the heads and tails, and attached the heads to the two forward posts of the scaffold, the tails to the rear posts, leaving the girl to be carried to the spirit land on the backs of her ponies.[5]

The day after the funeral, Spotted Tail and his headmen attended a council at the Colonel's headquarters, to discuss the signing of the peace treaty. Colonel Maynadier and Spotted Tail both thought it would be best to wait until more chiefs and camps could be brought in before the signing took place. Spotted Tail sent runners out with messages for the chiefs of friendly camps. Swift Bear, with forty lodges of the Brulé Corn Band, came in on March 15 and camped

[5] The account of Spotted Tail's arrival at the fort and the burial of his daughter is taken from Colonel Maynadier's report, March 9, 1866, and from *Frank Leslie's Illustrated Newspaper*, July 30, 1866. When Spotted Tail was given an agency on the head of White River in 1871, he came to Fort Laramie to take the bones of his daughter to his agency. At the moment events prevented his taking the bones; but in the summer of 1876, he came to Fort Laramie again, took the bones to his agency, and had them reburied with much ceremony. Kingsbury in his *History of Dakota Territory*, 770, gives the name of Spotted Tail's daughter as *Pe-he-zi-win*, and he quotes a long description of her appearance, evidently taken from some old account which is unknown to me.

at the trading house of his brother-in-law, Bordeaux, nine miles below the fort. Other small camps began to appear near the fort; but it was decided in Washington that the signing of the treaty should take place in June, as it was hoped by then to induce the leaders of hostile camps on Powder River to attend and sign the treaty.

Spotted Tail and Swift Bear remained near Fort Laramie for some weeks. It was at this time that Spotted Tail was first regarded as head chief of the Brulés.

Little Thunder, the old head chief, was in retirement. In 1843, Matthew C. Field had described him as the finest leader among the Brulés, a man six feet tall, muscular, with a handsome and dignified presence, the most distinguished warrior among the proud Brulés who hunted south of the Platte. When made head chief he had tried to keep peace with the whites; he had failed; but in the spring of 1865 he had come to Fort Laramie with his camp to resume his friendly relations with the Americans. He must have been greatly shocked when the military treated him as a surrendered hostile and ordered his band to be marched to Fort Kearney as prisoners, under guard. After the Indians revolted at Horse Creek, he apparently stayed on the Upper White River during the winter, while Spotted Tail went to Powder River. When the other chiefs went to Fort Laramie in the spring of 1866, Little Thunder stayed away, probably with a small camp of relatives. He had either given up his rank as head chief voluntarily, or the Brulés in a council had set him aside and selected Spotted Tail as the new head chief. Unfortunately, we do not have definite Sioux information concerning what happened in the camps in the spring of 1866, and this has made it possible for some writers to make the sneering remark that Spotted Tail signed the treaty and was rewarded by the officials, who made him head chief. There is no truth in this. Spotted Tail was clearly accepted by the Brulés as their new leader long before he signed the treaty on June 27.

As late as April 1, 1866, the only large camps near Fort Laramie were Spotted Tail's and Swift Bear's. The latter chief clearly accepted Spotted Tail as the head chief, and according to Beauvais, the veteran Sioux trader, Spotted Tail and Swift Bear combined their camps at this time so that they would be strong enough to go hunting. Beauvais stated in 1867 that Little Thunder was the old chief of the Brulé Ring Band, a band name not mentioned by any other authority. He said that in 1866 Spotted Tail succeeded Little Thunder as head of the Ring Band, and then Swift Bear joined forces with Spotted Tail and became, for the time, the second chief of that band. In May these Sioux were given official permission to hunt on Republican Fork far south of the Platte, but the chiefs pledged themselves to be back at Fort Laramie early in June to sign the peace treaty.[6]

The Pawnees in eastern Nebraska had had a much-needed rest from Sioux annoyances after that tribe had joined the Cheyennes and Arapahoes in the winter march to the north in December, 1864. The Pawnees went on a winter hunt on the Republican and obtained great quantities of meat without seeing an Indian enemy, and in 1865 they had good hunts, both in summer and in winter; but the moment Spotted Tail and his Brulés turned up at Fort Laramie in 1866, things were different. In May the Brulés put on a rousing raid at the Pawnee agency. They then went hunting on the Republican and made it impossible for the Pawnees to hunt there. The officials, civil and military, who were trying to represent Spotted Tail as a great lover of peace, were placed in a difficulty by this chief's obvious love for killing Pawnees. In May there were frantic appeals for troops to protect the Pawnees and the white employees on the Pawnee reservation from Brulé raiders.

In June, Spotted Tail and Swift Bear brought their camps to Fort Laramie for the treaty council, but the opening of the council was delayed while the treaty commissioners made strenuous efforts to bring Red Cloud and Man-Afraid-of-His-Horse, with their wild Oglalas, down from Powder River. Obviously, a peace treaty signed only by friendlies with the real hostiles holding aloof would be of no practical value. The hostiles did not wish to sign for peace; but

[6] Beauvais' information, printed in reports of the Office of Indian Affairs, volume for 1867. The meaning of the name Ring Band is unknown, and the Sioux in later years knew nothing of this name. Spotted Tail, when he came to Fort Laramie in March, 1866, had only a part of the old Ring Band in his camp. Other families of the old group joined him later on.

they had had no trade since the spring of 1864, and they were badly in need of many things, particularly ammunition and guns. It was the expectation of treaty gifts and trade that finally induced Red Cloud and the other Oglala leaders to bring their camps to Fort Laramie.

This treaty commission of 1866 was headed by E. B. Taylor of the U. S. Indian Office. The other members were Colonel Maynadier, Colonel McLaren, and a Mr. Wister, of Philadelphia. Taylor was the leading spirit of the commission. He knew almost nothing about Indians but was a fervent believer in the new Indian Peace Policy which had been put forward by idealists and humanitarians and had been adopted as the government policy. Colonel Maynadier, who seems to have been surprisingly misinformed regarding the attitude of the Sioux, encouraged Taylor in his belief that the Powder River Sioux were eager to make peace. One of Maynadier's notions was that Spotted Tail had great influence over Red Cloud, who would follow his advice. The fact was that Red Cloud did not like Spotted Tail and that Spotted Tail had too much sense to attempt to influence the Oglala leader.

Maynadier had striven since March to get the hostile leaders to come to the fort. When Taylor and the other two commissioners arrived from the East, about June 1, only the friendly Sioux were encamped near the fort. Nothing had been heard from the camps on Powder River. Runners were sent north, but the commission kicked its heels at the fort for fifteen days before the Sioux deigned to come in. They had been holding a Sun Dance; which was much more important to them than a peace treaty.

The moment the council was opened and the treaty explained by interpreters, the Powder River chiefs balked. Here was a road in the treaty, running right through their hunting grounds. They would not have it. Mr. Taylor tried to explain the road away. It was not a new road, it was an old one. In fact, a wagon train had come north from the Platte during the Civil War, on its way to the new gold fields of Montana, and the men with the wagons had given the Sioux some little gifts and gone on their way in peace. Now the route the wagons had traveled was put into this treaty. It would not harm the Sioux hunting grounds. Taylor almost succeeded in soothing the angry chiefs and making them believe that the road mentioned in the treaty was a very small matter.

Down the Platte, below the fort, Standing Elk, of the Corn Band, saw a long column of troops with a huge wagon train moving westward. When the troops camped for the night, he sought out the commanding officer, Colonel H. B. Carrington, and asked him where he was going. Carrington told him that his command was on its way to the Powder River and the Bighorn to build posts to protect the new road through that country. Standing Elk warned him that if he went to Powder River to build forts, there would be instant war with the Sioux of that country. Standing Elk now returned to Swift Bear's camp, and within an hour the Sioux camps were buzzing with the news that troops were on the way to build forts and protect a new road through the Powder and Bighorn hunting grounds. The next day in the council meeting Red Cloud made a violent speech, accusing Commissioner Taylor of deliberately lying about the road in the treaty and of concealing the fact that troops were on the way to build forts in his country. He then ordered the lodges in the Oglala camp taken down and an immediate return to the Powder River. The shocked peace commission sent an Indian runner after the departing Oglalas with a placatory message, begging the chiefs to return for further talks. The runner was severely beaten and chased back across the North Platte River.

This sudden breaking up of the peace council stunned the comsioners. Mr. Taylor, a fanatical optimist, tried to gloss the matter over. He now spoke of Red Cloud as an unimportant leader of a little camp, although he had been calling him a head chief and a man of the first rank only a few days back. On June 27 he did the best that he could, bringing the friendly chiefs to the table to make their *X*-marks while their names were signed to the treaty. There were at the moment only one thousand Sioux in the camps at Fort Laramie. Their chiefs signed the treaty in this order:

> Spotted Tail, Brulé Ring Band, and head chief of the Brulés.
> Swift Bear, Brulé Corn Band.
> Dog Hawk, Brulé Orphan Band.
> Hawk Thunder (Thunder Hawk), Brulé.

Standing Elk, Brulé Corn Band.
Tall Mandan, Brulé soldier.
Brave Heart, Brulé chief.

The Oglalas who signed the same day were friendly Southern Oglalas:

Big Mouth, chief of the Laramie Loafers.
Man-that-Walks-under-the-Ground, Southern Oglala.
Black War Bonnet.
Standing Cloud.
Blue Horse, brother of Big Mouth.
Big Head.[7]

Not one hostile Sioux had signed the treaty. The very expensive councils at Fort Laramie had obviously failed, yet Mr. Taylor claimed complete success, and the public was assured that peace had been made with the Sioux. Through some technicality, Congress ruled that the names of the chiefs who had signed on June 27 must be struck out, and the names did not appear on the printed copy of the treaty.

Spotted Tail, by signing the treaty, had taken sides with the whites, or so it could be represented. His own attitude at the time was probably this: The Sioux were not united (which was clearly demonstrated later in the year); his own group must return to their hunting grounds south of the Platte or starve, and the only way they could resume hunting was by making peace with the Americans. He still believed that the Sioux could not win in a war, and this led him to regard Red Cloud's action in breaking up the council as unwise. He did not know (none of the chiefs did) that the government had been saddled with an Indian Peace Policy which meant that, even if the Sioux made open war, no vigorous counter action would be taken by the military. Thus Red Cloud was not risking disaster as Spotted Tail supposed. That chief used his sense and reason and found that he was wrong; Red Cloud acted on impulse and

[7] This list of signers is in "Paper Relating to Talks and Councils Held with Indians of Dakota Territory, 1866–69," a document in the National Archives.

turned out to be right. None of these Sioux chiefs could comprehend the drift of our government's Indian policy in 1866. The situation was so confused that even the officials in charge of Indian affairs must have been bewildered at times. Dr. Eastman and the others who hint that Spotted Tail deserted Red Cloud and made peace because he was fainthearted simply do not comprehend what the situation was. The Sioux were not united. When the camps south of the Platte were forced into war in 1864, Red Cloud's group up north did not help them; when Red Cloud went to war in 1866, Spotted Tail's group preferred to sign peace to secure the right to return to their own country south of the Platte. To criticize these chiefs is unfair. None of them acted alone. Every matter of importance had to be discussed in council, and the council made the decisions. The critics say that Spotted Tail made peace and deserted Red Cloud, but it was the Brulé council that took that action. Spotted Tail undoubtedly spoke for peace. Why shouldn't he? Even the Sioux of Powder River were not united for war, and hardly had the fighting started when the Oglala group led by Man-Afraid-of-His-Horse and the Miniconjous under Lone Horn drew away from Red Cloud and did all that they could to keep out of the war. Like Spotted Tail, Man-Afraid-of-His-Horse and Lone Horn expected the American army to act vigorously and in great force; and like Spotted Tail, they believed that such a war could only end in disaster for their people.

The chiefs of the Brulés and Southern Oglalas undoubtedly believed that by signing for peace they had obtained security for their groups. Either they were unaware that two railroads were being built westward into their country or they failed to understand the implications of that news. They took their camps down into the Republican River country and resumed their old life of hunting buffalo and fighting the Pawnees. North of the Platte, Red Cloud and his allies were indulging in the kind of war the Cheyennes had fought along the Platte road in the summer of 1864—a war of small raids that meant the obtaining of some scalps and plunder at small cost to the attacking war parties. With the army under orders not to strike back, the Indians had many small successes with practically no losses. The raids were confined almost entirely to the new road to Montana, and nothing was done along the Platte, where really effective blows might have been struck. It was the kind of war the Sioux loved, and by midsummer Spotted Tail and Swift Bear sent word to the military commandants on the Platte that many of their young warriors were slipping out of camp to join Red Cloud. The Brulé chiefs were worried. Their idea that the army would attack the hostiles on Powder River now appeared to be incorrect. They could not understand the government policy, but they could see for themselves that it was encouraging the war spirit in their own camps. If this went on much longer, their group that stood for peace would melt away, and all the strength would be held in the hands of Red Cloud and the other Sioux leaders who stood for war.

Here reference must be made to a tale printed in Charles A. Eastman's book, *Great Indian Heroes and Chieftains*. In this work Eastman repeats at two or three points a story of a great council held on Powder River in December, 1866, to decide on the attack at Fort Phil Kearny. He describes how Spotted Tail stood up and made a speech for peace, with all the other chiefs sitting in silent disapproval; Red Cloud then gets up and makes a stirring speech, concluding with the words, "I am for war!" This story has never been called in question, and it has been adduced to exhibit Spotted Tail as a faintheart, or even a traitor who sided with the whites.

Eastman clearly picked up this story at Pine Ridge among the Red Cloud Sioux after 1890. It appears to be an Oglala tale, invented to belittle Spotted Tale. Examining the story critically, we find that the truth seems to be that Spotted Tail was in his own camp far south of the Platte all this winter. Why should he make the long and arduous journey north to the Powder River to make a peace speech to Sioux he knew were for war? There is not a jot of evidence to show that he did. There is no evidence that there was such a council on Powder River in December, and from the Carrington reports we know that the Sioux had made their plan as early as August, 1866. The Cheyenne and Crow Indians both gave information in August that the Sioux planned two attacks: one they called "Pine Woods" (to be made at Fort Phil Kearny), and one they termed "Bighorn" (to be made at Fort C. F. Smith on the Bighorn River). Moreover, Sioux information obtained soon after the Phil Kearny fight indicates that there was no big council in December and that the business was started by White Swan, a Miniconjou chief, who made up his mind in his own small camp and set out with his warriors to go to Phil Kearny. He picked up more warriors from other camps as he went along. This seems to have been the true origin of the Phil Kearny affair, in which the Sioux and Cheyennes set a trap and killed nearly one hundred soldiers. It was the big success of the Indian war in the Powder River and Bighorn country, but there was no council, and Spotted Tail did not go to Powder River to make a peace speech.

Spotted Tail spent the whole of this winter in his camp on the Republican Fork, hunting buffalo. He and Swift Bear had promised to bring their camps up to the forks of the Platte in the spring of meet the new Indian Agent, M. T. Patrick. This they did, and they were informed by Patrick that another peace commission was coming up the Platte. In their anxiety to establish peace with the Sioux, the officials in charge of the Indian Peace Policy were sending out one commission after another to confer with the chiefs. The Brulé chiefs agreed to wait for the coming of the commission. Meanwhile they kept their camp near the forks of the Platte, paying friendly visits to Fort McPherson (old Camp Cottonwood) and watching the amazing doings of the white men in the Platte valley. The Union Pacific line was being built, and the valley was filled with crews of workmen and huge freight wagons hauling supplies. The great numbers of big American horses and mules were a temptation to the young warriors, and despite the strict orders of the chiefs, small war parties slipped away and made raids on the camps of the railroad crews. In one of these raids Spotted Tail's brother was killed by the Pawnee Scouts. The Sioux rode out of the hills and charged down on the railroad camp, singing and blowing eagle-bone whistles; then to their astonishment the Pawnees, whose presence they had not expected, rode out and charged them. In the fight Spotted Tail's brother had his horse killed. He was making off on foot when Bat Bayhylle, a sergeant in the Pawnee Scouts, shot him through the body with an arrow. The brave Brulé pulled the arrow through his body, fitted it to his bow string and shot it back, wounding Bayhylle. He then ran a few steps and fell dead.[8]

When the peace commission arrived, the chiefs met it at a point on the north bank of the Platte near Fort McPherson. After a friendly talk the commission ordered four thousand dollars' worth of food, clothing, and camp equipment distributed among the Brulés. The commission then went on to Fort Laramie.

Spotted Tail, as head chief of the Brulés, was now meeting very important officials—peace commissioners and generals of the army. He went on several occasions to Fort McPherson. He was now on friendly terms with Major General C. C. Augur, commanding the Department of the Platte, and Lieutenant General W. T. Sherman, commanding the military Division of the Mississippi, with headquarters at St. Louis. He knew Major General Alfred Terry, and had renewed acquaintance with his old enemy, General Harney, who was now among the Sioux again, not as a conqueror but in the queer role of a peace-treaty peddler. These high officers all liked Spotted Tail. He was dignified but affable, and his friendliness had nothing of servility about it. He was no orator, but he spoke effectively in council, had good sense, and was witty. He knew the ways of the Americans much better than most of the other chiefs, and thus did not make the mistakes that they often made. When the other chiefs were told by the commandant at Fort McPherson that he did not have the authority to give them what they were demanding, they thought that he was lying. When he telegraphed to St. Louis to pass their requests on to General Sherman and had a reply in an hour, the chiefs thought he was lying again. How could any man send a message thirty days' journey away and get a reply in an hour? But Spotted Tail understood all this and was satisfied with Colonel Carrington's explanations. At this time, in the spring of 1866, Spotted Tail and Swift Bear were taken for a short ride on a Union Pacific train. They rushed by their own camp at the terrific speed of thirty miles an hour, with all the Indians watching them go past, standing dumb with amazement.

In this spring of 1867 there was much concern over the intentions of the wild Cheyennes who shared the hunting grounds of the Sioux on branches of the Kansas River. In April the Cheyennes and part of the Southern Oglalas were camped on Pawnee Fork,

[8] Hyde, *The Pawnee Indians*, 219.

and Major General W. S. Hancock was instructed to learn what the intentions of these Indians were. Hancock might have obtained this information from scouts; but he was a Civil War general who knew nothing of dealing with Indians, and he went about his task in the grand manner of the Civil War campaigns, organizing a column of cavalry, artillery, and infantry, complete with a pontoon-bridge train. He then marched up Pawnee Fork toward the Indian camp with all the pomp of war. The last time a military force had come near a Cheyenne camp was in November, 1864, when Colonel Chivington's Colorado cavalry had massacred Black Kettle's people, killing more women and children than warriors. On hearing that the troops were coming, the women and many of the men in the Cheyenne and Oglala camp became panic-stricken. They left their lodges standing with all their belongings in them and fled in the night northward into their hunting grounds. General Hancock, regarding their flight as proof that they were hostile, turned loose Custer's Seventh Cavalry to pursue them. The Cheyennes on their way northward raided the Smoky Hill stage line, killing white men and carrying off horses and mules.

Up on the Platte near Fort McPherson, Indian Agent Patrick and Colonel H. B. Carrington had persuaded Spotted Tail and Swift Bear to stay in camp at Brady Island, just below the forks, and keep out of the way of possible trouble. The Indians were to be fed on government rations, as they would have no game to hunt near Brady Island. This arrangement had hardly been made when fugitive Oglalas, running away from Hancock and Custer, appeared on the Platte and went to see Colonel Carrington. The chiefs were alarmed and bewildered. They came to Colonel Carrington, asking anxiously what they were to do. He suggested that they join Spotted Tail, stay north of the Platte, and live on government rations until this trouble was ended. The chiefs returned to their camps on or near Republican Fork and prepared to move north; but then Custer appeared with his command on the Platte, and the Sioux grew very suspicious.

By this time neither the military officers nor the chiefs could make out whether they were at peace or at war, and every man mistrusted every other man. Spotted Tail and Swift Bear were in a grand muddle. They had signed the peace treaty; they had been assured that they could hunt in their lands south of the Platte in perfect security; and now they were barred from their hunting lands because a war with the Cheyennes was going on there. Red Cloud seemed to be having all the best of it. No troops were sent to drive him out of his hunting grounds. He could hunt in peace, hold a Sun Dance, and then take the war out of the bag for a time and make attacks on the white soldiers. They would not strike back. Custer could strike hard, but he was being kept south of the Platte, to harass the Sioux who had signed the treaty.[9]

On July 20, 1867, Congress passed an act providing for a new and larger peace commission, whose purpose should be to induce the Indians to leave their hunting grounds and go to reservations, thus assuring the unhampered building of the new railroads and the safety of the Kansas and Nebraska settlers. If the Indians refused to sign a treaty and go to reservations, the President was authorized to employ troops to drive them to the proposed reservations and hold them there. This new act was a challenge to the idealists and humanitarians who had invented the Indian Peace Policy and had been loudly proclaiming that all of the Indians wanted peace and that kind treatment was a sure preventive of Indian wars. These peace advocates were now given one more chance to make real peace with the tribes, but if they failed, strong measures were to be adopted. This shift in Indian policy vitally affected the Sioux; yet one suspects that the chiefs were either not clearly informed of the change or else they failed to understand. They clung to the pledge that had been given that their people could return to their hunting grounds south of the Platte as soon as the Cheyenne troubles were ended, and they do not seem to have given a thought to the talk that they must go to a reservation.

Spotted Tail, without seeking it, was getting more publicity than any white man who has lived in Nebraska since 1867. The *New York Herald* had Henry M. Stanley (in later years the great African explorer) in Nebraska as special correspondent and was receiving almost daily wires from him and from other correspondents. These

[9] For detailed accounts of these events, consult Carrington, *Ab-sa-ra-ka: Land of Massacre*, 268–82; Grinnell, *The Fighting Cheyennes*; Hyde, *Red Cloud's Folk*.

reports showed that the Chief was having a hard time keeping his people north of the Platte, as he had pledged himself to do. On August 10 the *Herald* reported that his camp was breaking up and that Two Strike with his band had crossed south of the river and was said to be on his way south, to join the hostiles. On the thirtieth, Spotted Tail had a council with Indian Superintendent H. B. Denman and agreed to send a party of his warriors to the hostiles who were in camp on the head of Republican Fork to summon them to attend the council with the peace commission at Fort Laramie at the time of the full moon in September. The Chief selected ten of his best men, and Denman gave each man a new rifle, a horse, saddle, bridle, picket rope, blue Indian leggins, blue cavalry jacket, cavalry hat, black silk cravat, and new blanket. They had ten yards of scarlet Indian cloth each, and each man had eight squares of plug tobacco wrapped in a yard of scarlet cloth. These were for gifts to chiefs in the Republican Fork camps. Each warrior had a military pass stating that he was a friendly Indian on a peace mission.

Spotted Tail told Denman he could not hold his Indians. They were determined to go hunting; so Denman consented, gave the chiefs passes and white flags with the wording SPOTTED TAIL'S FRIENDLY BAND, to be carried on the march and put up over the tipis in camp. He gave twelve days' rations to the Sioux, and they moved off southward. On September 4, Iron Shell came to North Platte with 180 Indians of his Orphan Band from Powder River, probably seeking arms, ammunition, and supplies. On September 9 a wire was sent to the *New York Herald* from Omaha stating that Spotted Tail had ransomed three white women and three children who had been taken captive by the Cheyennes. He brought the six captives to North Platte and handed them to the peace commission on September 19.

When the new peace commission reached Omaha in September, they received news that Red Cloud and the Powder River chiefs had refused to come to Fort Laramie to meet them. The commission spent several days in rather futile debate about what they should now do. They had already formally called all the Indians to meet at Fort Laramie, but Red Cloud and his friends had ruined the plan for a great peace council. In the end the commission took the Union

Pacific train for North Platte to go through the same old futility of making peace once more with friendly Indians only. But the Sioux they met at North Platte were not particularly friendly at the moment. When the council opened, the chiefs burst into angry accusations and took turns at denouncing the whites in a council that resembled a riot more than a peace meeting. Big Mouth accused the whites of setting the prairie on fire, that is, of starting a war; and all the chiefs clamored for guns and ammunition with which to hunt. The military members of the commission suspected that the arms were wanted for hunting white men, and for a long time they refused to consent to supply the Sioux with guns and ammunition; but in the end the humanitarians on the commission talked them into ordering the issue of the weapons, "for the sake of peace."[10]

These were critical times, and neither the chiefs nor the peace commission members could judge what might happen next. Those writers who have criticized Spotted Tail and some of the other chiefs have not exhibited much judgment. Every matter that came up was discussed in council, and the chiefs were then instructed by the council regarding what action they should take. The chiefs could advise, but they could not act without the council's decision. Most of the chiefs were bewildered by the confused situation; and as they do not appear to have understood that a plan was being formed to send their people to a reservation in Dakota, their main purpose was to obtain the right to return to their hunting grounds south of the Platte. This they achieved.

At this North Platte council, the commission broached the subject of the Sioux's accepting a reservation in Dakota. The commission planned to go to Fort Laramie in November in the hope that Red Cloud and the other hostile chiefs would at last consent to attend a council at the fort, and the chiefs at North Platte were given until November to consider the peace conditions the commission had spoken to them about. But Red Cloud and his friends failed to come to Fort Laramie, and there was no council at the fort in November.

All this summer and autumn of 1867 the Sioux, gathered from

[10] Report of the Peace Commission, in *Report of the Commissioner of Indian Affairs*, 1867, 26; H. M. Stanley, *Early Life and Adventures*, I. Stanley was at the North Platte council as a *New York Herald* reporter.

the hunting grounds south of the Platte, were camped near the new town of North Platte, drawing rations and supplies. It was their first taste of being cared for (and controlled) by the government, and the two to three thousand Indians in the camp were very discontented and often threatening to leave. Spotted Tail and Swift Bear had a hard time keeping their followers from defying the officials and returning to Republican Fork to hunt buffalo. The camps were near each other above the town on an open plain, where it was so windy that the Indians had to dig trenches and pile dirt up on the edges of the tipi covers to keep the wind from blowing their dwellings away; and Captain L. H. North of the Pawnee Scouts said in later years that the earth circles where the Sioux tipis had stood could be clearly seen for some months after the Indians left the place.

The hostiles up north lost strength in 1867. Families and entire camps were coming south to join Spotted Tail and the other friendly chiefs. Practically all the Brulés, except for a part of the Orphans and the Wazhazhas, who were not rated as real Brulés, were now with Spotted Tail, and large numbers of Oglalas had also come down to the Platte. Red Cloud was said in this year to have had only forty-five lodges in his camp, and Man-Afraid-of-His-Horse, the old Oglala head chief, had only thirty-five lodges. Red Dog of the Oglala Oyukpa band had one hundred lodges. Red Cloud and the other northern leaders were now beginning to learn what Spotted Tail had found out in 1855: that the Sioux could not remain united or fight a protracted war. Even with the army under orders not to attack the Sioux in the Powder River and Bighorn country, the Indians could not accomplish the obvious purpose of their war—to drive the whites out of their hunting grounds. These Northern Sioux were enthusiastic for war in 1865; but one little success at Platte Bridge satisfied them. They put the war back in the bag until next year, and by 1866 half the camps were tired of war and kept out of it. In 1867 nearly all the Northern Sioux had only one main interest—to trade with the whites, particularly for guns and ammunition.

The friendly Sioux stayed at North Platte until after the council with the peace commission. They obtained guns, ammunition, new camp equipment, and blankets, and in late September returned happily to their hunting grounds on the Republican Fork. There they attacked the Pawnee tribe that was also hunting on the Republican, preventing the Pawnees from obtaining buffalo meat and skins for winter use. This was like the good old days, with the Sioux free from meddling white officials, living their own way, hunting buffalo, and mauling the hated Pawnees. Having finished their autumn activities, the Sioux in the Republican River country settled down in winter camps, free for a time from the annoyances of peace councils and the obnoxious activities of Custer and the other white military leaders.

In November the peace commission made the long journey to Fort Laramie to meet Red Cloud and the other hostile leaders, only to be disappointed again. Not one Northern Sioux chief was at the fort to meet them. This new snub was too much for Generals Harney and Sanborn. They proposed that columns of troops be sent to the Powder River to give these insolent Indians a drubbing. General Sherman now asked General Augur, commanding the Department of the Platte, how many men he would require for a war on the Sioux, and Augur, after considering the matter, said 20,000 troops, half of them cavalry, would be needed. General Terry, commanding in Dakota, was asked this question and replied that he would need the same number of troops to carry out his part in a Sioux war. Sherman thought it over and told the peace commission that the government had nearly all the army on duty in the Southern States and it was not possible to provide the troops necessary for a Sioux war. So Red Cloud and the Northern Sioux won again. They could defy the government and make the little raids they called war indefinitely. The government was not going to strike back at them.[11]

[11] The military commanders in the Plains probably exaggerated the requirements in troops for dealing with the Sioux and their allies in November, 1867. Custer, with a small column and in a single winter campaign of brief duration, knocked most of the Cheyennes and Arapahoes out of the war; and General Augur, with a small force of cavalry and Pawnee Scouts in 1868–69, drove all the Sioux and Cheyennes in panic flight from the lands between the Platte and the Arkansas. On the Powder River, Red Cloud and Sitting Bull were the only out-and-out hostiles. Red Cloud in 1867 had a camp of less than fifty lodges, perhaps around

Red Cloud had won his war, because the United States government declined to fight him. In March, 1868, the final shame was accomplished, President Grant ordering the abandonment of the army posts in the Powder River and Bighorn country in a last bid to appease Red Cloud and the other hostiles. But the Northern Sioux demanded all their pound of flesh in advance. They refused to sign any treaty until after the troops were removed from their country and the forts abandoned. The peace commission now met at St. Louis and wrote a new treaty that would give the hostile Sioux everything they desired, or so it was supposed.

The Sioux south of the Platte knew nothing of the government's new peace plans. In the spring of 1868 the camps came up to the forks of the Platte, and at once the summer activities of holding peace councils were resumed. The chiefs met the entire peace commission and were given handsome quantities of Indian goods, including the usual supply of guns and ammunition; and for all this they had only to promise to go to Fort Laramie for a peace council, at which it was supposed the Northern Sioux chiefs would be present. But when the peace commission reached Fort Laramie, it found that neither Red Cloud nor any of the other Northern chiefs had heeded the urgent messages to come in for the grand council. They had not even bothered to reply to the commission's messages. Iron Shell, with his Brulé Orphans, and Red Leaf, with his Wazhazhas, had come in, and that was all. On April 29, the Brulés signed peace all over again, Iron Shell being permitted to sign first. As a reformed hostile, he rated higher with the peace commission than the friendly head chief, Spotted Tail.

The peace commission could not spend the entire spring and summer waiting at Fort Laramie on Red Cloud's whims. They left agents at the fort with a copy of the treaty and departed. One Northern Sioux camp after another was tolled in by promises of the com-

one hundred warriors, and Sitting Bull probably had about the same strength. The Northern Cheyennes were hostile, but did not have more than a few hundred fighting men. The rest of the Indians in the Powder River and Bighorn country were tired of the war and starved for trade, and all the Indians up north were in great need of arms and ammunition. All that was needed to bring peace was a stiff winter campaign, to hit Red Cloud and Sitting Bull in their own camps at the season when they felt safe from attack.

mission's agents, to be coaxed into signing the treaty. They were given quantities of gifts, including guns and ammunition. Some realist (perhaps old General Harney) had suggested this quaint method for making peace. It was open bribery, rooted in the old frontier belief that Indians were children and could be led into agreeing to anything if given a proper quantity of gifts.

The friendly Sioux, after signing the treaty at Fort Laramie, had returned to Republican Fork to hunt buffalo. Not one of the chiefs apparently had an inkling of the fact that the treaty they had signed included a provision that they were to take their people to a new reservation in Dakota. The Laramie Loafers, most friendly of all the Sioux, were the first to learn what the new treaty really meant. Hardly had the Loafer chiefs signed the document when they were brusquely informed by the officers at the post that they were no longer welcome to live there but must go at once to their new reservation on the Missouri in Dakota. This was apparently the first the Loafers heard of the reservation. Stunned, they made no move to go. The fort had been their home for the past twenty-five years, and they had several hundred mixed-blood children in their band to demonstrate their friendship with the whites. But they had to go. The government agents had planned carefully for this. They had hired a number of Indian traders and white men married into the Loafer Band to put pressure on the Indians, and presently—led by these men and pushed vigorously from behind by the military—the unhappy Sioux bade farewell to their old home and started on their long and sad journey. Many of the families had lived at the fort so long that they had lost the old Sioux ability to travel. They had no horses or camp equipment, and the army had to load them into wagons and transport them. They reached North Platte on June 30. Here another group of tame Sioux was added to their number, and they set off again, accompanied by a wagon train loaded with rations. On the Keyapaha River near the end of their long journey, the unfortunate Loafers went down with smallpox and lost a large number of their people before the epidemic left their camp. Swift Bear lost most of his Indian relatives in this smallpox attack.

The military (charged with getting rid of the friendly Sioux as quickly as possible) now turned to a more difficult task: that of inducing the wilder Sioux in the camps on Republican Fork to go to the new reservation. That frontier worthy, John Y. Nelson, tells us how the army set to work. He states that he and other squaw men who were hanging about at Fort McPherson near the forks of the Platte were suddenly ordered to go to the Sioux camps on the Republican and induce the Indians to start the move to the Missouri River. These men were told that if they did not do as they were ordered, they would be thrown in the guardhouse and roughly treated. Nelson gives no date, but this was in the summer of 1868. He and some of his friends unwillingly went to Republican Fork, where they found a camp of two thousand Sioux, probably the Spotted Tail and Swift Bear camp.

Just what happened next we do not know, but the chiefs probably called a council to consider this amazing order that their people should quit their hunting grounds and move to a reservation they had never heard of until this moment. Knowing that they were in a trap, surrounded by troops stationed at new posts, the chiefs evidently decided that they had no choice but to comply with the order. They were now closed in between two new railroads, with white settlements all around them. They were not in the fortunate position that Red Cloud's Northern Sioux occupied—far from the railroads and settlements and not under military threat. The Southern Brulés and Oglalas were in a trap, and the chiefs knew it.

Perhaps the Brulé leaders thought that they could hold a council with the officials at North Platte and get the order for them to go to the Missouri revoked; but times had changed since spring and early summer, when no Indian camp could come to North Platte or Fort McPherson without running into a peace commission or some other group of friendly officials, ready to hand out liberal supplies of rations, blankets, guns, and ammunition. The Indian agency at North Platte was closed up. There were no more free rations and supplies, and the military at Fort McPherson were no longer friendly. They had just one thing to say to the chiefs: Go to the Missouri, or the troops will drive you there.

Spotted Tail, Swift Bear, and the other Brulé chiefs were in a dreadful position. They had urged their followers to peace and friendliness with the Americans, and this was the result. They had signed the treaty in April, evidently without the faintest suspicion that they were to lose their hunting rights by doing so. The treaty protected those hunting rights, and nothing had been said (as all the chiefs later claimed) even to hint at a removal to the Missouri. The fighting men in the Brulé camps were furious, and the chiefs must have had a terrible time controlling them. Tribal soldiers were probably put on duty, policing the camps. Holding grimly to it, the chiefs got the camps across to the north side of the Platte and started toward the Niobrara and the White River. The Brulés were in retreat. They had conquered the lands south of the Platte from the Pawnees, and now, on an order from the whites, they were retiring, going back to the old Indian paradise (no longer a paradise, but a land stripped of game and timber) on White River, where most of them had been born, and back to the Missouri, which their tribe had crossed over a century ago in their bold advance westward into unknown country. The plain, ordinary warriors in the Brulé camps could not understand all this. They had not been beaten by the whites, not in open war. They had been overwhelmed by swarms of whites coming into their country, opening roads, building iron trails, forts, and towns, and pressing in on them ever more strongly. The chiefs said it was better to go to the hated Missouri than to fight a hopeless war. The Brulés accepted the opinion of the chiefs, but they crossed the Platte in a sullen and bitter mood, and some of the younger warriors slipped away from the camps and made raids along the Platte to show the whites that they were neither beaten nor afraid.

6. *Whetstone*

WHETSTONE CREEK (Sioux: *Izuza Wahkpala*) is a small stream that empties into the Missouri from the west, twenty-three miles above Fort Randall in South Dakota. On the north bank of this creek in the summer of 1868 an agency was built for the accommodation of the Brulé and Oglala Sioux of the Platte; and at the time when these Indians signed the peace treaty at Fort Laramie in April and May, preparations were made for feeding and caring for them at Whetstone, although the Sioux seemed unaware that they were expected to leave their own lands and go to the distant Missouri River. Congress had put control of Whetstone and the other new Sioux agencies on the Missouri in the hands of the military; these agencies had been formed into a military district, and grim old General Harney, who had ridden roughshod over the Sioux in 1855, was put in command of the Sioux district with headquarters at Sioux City. Harney had not altered much except in age since 1855. When interviewed at the Northwestern Hotel in Sioux City in 1869, he expressed a low opinion of the Sioux. Indians, he said, were children and should be treated like children. He had been a member of the treaty commission, but he seemed to regard all the solemn councils and the bribing of the Sioux with hundreds of thousands of dollars' worth of Indian goods as nothing more than a good joke. With a twinkle in his eyes he said that he did not expect to go among the Sioux again, as the Indians would probably start asking him where were all the horses, cows, chickens, and other gifts promised to them by the treaty commission.

When Spotted Tail's camps of Sioux reached Whetstone, late in the summer of 1868, after being forced to leave their hunting grounds south of the Platte by military threats that they would be attacked if they did not start for the Missouri at once, they did not find any of the fine gifts which the peace commission had so liberally promised them—off the record. Instead, they found an amazing assortment of strange machines, which indicated that the government was in earnest when it told the Sioux that they must suddenly cease to be warriors and hunters and go to work earning a living by farming. At the new agency there were batteries of heavy breaking-plows for tearing up the virgin prairie sod—plows much too heavy for little Indian ponies to pull—cross-plows, cultivators, horse rakes and harrows, expensive threshing machines, and patent corn-planters. There was a gristmill for making flour, a sawmill, and huge log-carts with immense wheels and a wheel base much too wide for any Dakota road. These carts had been made for handling great logs in the big woods. What they were doing in the prairie at Whetstone only a government purchasing agent could have explained. The newspapers reported that even before the first Indians came, General Harney had ordered thousands of acres plowed at Whetstone. Everything was ready for starting farming on a grand scale. Everything except the Sioux, most of whom had no intention of touching a hand hoe, and a hand hoe was as complicated a farming tool as any of these Indians were capable of using. The grand collection of farming equipment was waste material and proof that the officials in Washington knew nothing whatever about the Sioux.

The Sioux came to Whetstone in a sullen mood. Only a part of Swift Bear's Corn Band had any wish to live on the hated Missouri. This district near Whetstone was in the eastern edge of the Indian paradise into which the warlike Brulés had pressed about the year 1780, when they had started to drive the Arikara tribe farther up the Missouri and take possession of the Arikara hunting lands. Spotted Tail's grandparents and parents had lived in these lands; but by 1868 the old hunting paradise was stripped of buffalo, and although there were still deer and antelope to be found in places along White River to the west, this was not a country in which Indians could live by hunting. The Brulés and Oglalas had gone a long way since they had crossed west of the Missouri, over a century back; and during that advance to the west and south, they had become people of the high and dry plains. To their way of thinking, the lowlands here near Whetstone were utterly alien and obnoxious, and from the moment of their arrival on the Missouri, their principal desire was to get back to their own beloved high country.

During the time of trouble and danger from 1865 to 1868, Spotted Tail and Swift Bear had combined their camps; but as soon as he reached Whetstone, Swift Bear left Spotted Tail with most of his Corn Band people and settled close to the new agency. So did the seventy-five white men who had married into the Sioux tribe, the five hundred mixed-bloods, the Laramie Loafers, and the small Oglala camp headed by Chief Fire Thunder. Spotted Tail, with the main Brulé camp, halted on White River, thirty to forty miles west of the agency, and here his people stubbornly remained, refusing to go near the detested river and agency.

General Harney had established Sioux agencies at Whetstone, Cheyenne River, and Grand River and had placed an army officer in charge of each agency. A Major Chambers from Fort Randall was in charge at Whetstone when the Sioux arrived, but he was presently replaced by Captain A. E. Woodson, also from the Randall garrison. Spotted Tail was on bad terms with both these officers. The Chief was having the greatest fight of his life, trying to hold his wild followers together and to prevent their flouting government orders and leaving the reservation to resume hunting and fighting. He was in a bitter mood, feeling that he and the other chiefs had been deceived by the treaty commission, and he was in no humor for being ordered about by army majors and captains. Major Chambers, and later Captain Woodson, ordered the Chief to bring his Indians to the agency to avoid the trouble and expense of sending rations to the distant camp, where in winter it would be next to impossible to send wagons loaded with supplies. Spotted Tail explained the situation. His people refused to come nearer to the Missouri, and if an attempt was made to force them, they would run away. There was also the problem of drink. The camps close to the agency were already flooded with whiskey, which enterprising Dakota citizens smuggled across the Missouri into the Indian lands. The Chief was determined that his own camp should not be demoralized by the whiskey peddlers, and he refused to bring his camp nearer to the river.

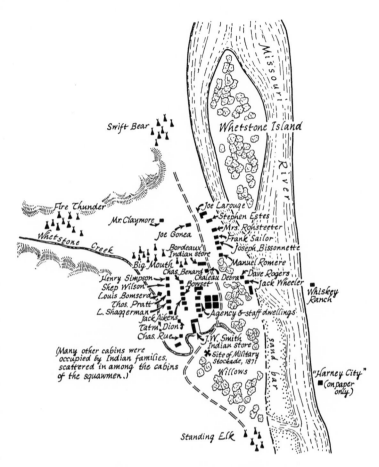

Swift Bear

Missouri River

Whetstone Island

Fire Thunder

Mr. Claymore

Whetstone Creek

Joe Gonea

Big Mouth

Bordeaux
Indian store

Chas Benard

Henry Simpson
Shep Wilson
Louis Bomsera
Thos. Pratt
L. Shaggerman

Chateau Debra
Bowset

Jack Aikens
Tatm. Dion
Chas. Rue

(Many other cabins were
occupied by Indian families,
scattered in among the cabins
of the squawmen.)

Joe Larouge
Stephen Estes
Mrs. Rohsteeter
Frank Sailor
Joseph Bissonnette

Manuel Romere

Dave Rogers
Jack Wheeler

Whiskey
Ranch

Agency & staff dwellings

J. W. Smith
Indian store

Site of Military
Stockade, 1871

Willows

sand bar

"Harney City"
(on paper
only.)

Standing Elk

WHETSTONE AGENCY 1868–71

Based on maps in Wi-iyohi, the monthly publication of the South Dakota Historical Society, Volume 8, Number 2, 1934. Many of the houses shown were not built until after Big Mouth's death and the breaking up of his camp.

Another matter that caused bad feeling between the Chief and the army officers was the order from the Indian Office in Washington to cease giving special treatment to chiefs and to deal with the Sioux through the heads of families. This plan for discarding chiefs had been devised by the high-thinkers of the Christian and humanitarian groups of the Eastern States who were meddling in government Indian policy. Knowing nothing about the Sioux, these crusaders had decided that Sioux chiefs were selfish tyrants, enriching themselves at the expense of their people and holding the common Indians back from any progress toward civilization. Spotted Tail, who was holding councils day and night to prevent his Indians from running away from their first glimpse of civilization at Whetstone, was infuriated when the army officer in charge of the agency attempted to ignore his position and authority as head chief of the Brulés. The Sioux had a tribal government that kept control and good order in every camp. It was a government approved by the common men of the tribe, and probably every bit as democratic as the American government. A chief could take no important action until after it had been approved by the council; and far from battening on the common Indians, the chiefs by long established Sioux custom had to give away most of their possessions to maintain their reputation and standing. Among the Sioux a great man was one who kept openhanded hospitality for all visitors. In the free life of the hunting camp, Spotted Tail always had large supplies of buffalo and other meat, fine garments made of dressed skins ornamented with dyed porcupine quills and beadwork, and ponies taken in war from the Pawnees and other tribes. He treated all visitors hospitably and gave each man a handsome gift when he departed. The government officials had recognized the need of the chiefs to keep up such hospitality, and all through the years 1865–68, the treaty commissions had given extra supplies of rations and goods to the chiefs so that they could maintain their position as leaders. Now, the minute the Sioux were on the reservation, the Indian agents were ordered to treat the chiefs as common Indians. Every chief at Whetstone was enraged, and most of the common Indians were angry and alarmed. The idealistis in the East who had thought out this chief-breaking scheme to benefit the common Indians had been unaware of the simple truth, that the common Indians could not think for themselves. They were constantly going to their chief to ask his advice and help, and the very thought of not having a chief to go to in time of need frightened them. And why not? After all, this theory that was supposed to benefit the common Indian, if extended to the American population, would have caused the discarding of mayors and all civic leaders. It meant anarchy, and the Sioux chiefs at Whetstone knew it and fought against it.

Before they came to the reservation, most of the Sioux chiefs were honest men and reasonably good men. At Whetstone they discovered almost at once that if they expected to survive, they had to fight, and that it was a new kind of fighting in which trickery played an important role. These chiefs knew nothing of the American government and its methods, but every chief had several white men who had married Sioux women living in his camp, and these squaw men were only too pleased to increase their own importance by acting as advisers to the chiefs. Some of these men were real geniuses in devising plans for getting around the agency rules, for thwarting the agent's orders, and for cheating the government. Spotted Tail occasionally took advice from some squaw men. He preferred, however, dealing directly and frankly with his agent; but during all his years on the reservation, come fine weather or foul, he managed somehow to get the extra supplies of food and goods necessary to maintain his position as head chief.

The agency buildings stood on the north bank of Whetstone Creek, on the second or higher terrace of the Missouri River bottom lands. A group of warehouses and other buildings had been constructed of rough, unpainted planks. There was an agent's office and a large council room under the same roof, carpenter and blacksmith shops, and small, rude dwellings for the agency employees. There were between four and five thousand Sioux at this agency in 1868–70, and they had to be fed, clothed, and supplied with all they needed by the government. The supplies were shipped up the Missouri in steamboats. Between the agency buildings and the landing on the river bank was the first bottom or flood plain, one-quarter of a mile wide and densely overgrown by willows interlaced with vines. In the river just above the agency was Whetstone Island, which had a good growth of timber, from which much of the lumber used in constructing the agency had been cut. There was some timber on Whetstone Creek; the rest of the district was open prairie with a line of low bluffs set back one mile or more from the river. The agency was to some extent sheltered by the bluffs, which swung in close to the river at two high points, some four miles apart. Enclosed between these points or bluffs, the agency had about two thousand acres of good bottom land fit for farming, and part of this land had been plowed by white employees before any of the Indians arrived.

Just west of the agency buildings was a scattered cluster of rude cabins, occupied by some of the squaw men and their Indian families. The remainder of the seventy-seven squaw men and the five hundred mixed-bloods lived in the Indian camps. The Laramie Loafers —never happy if separated from the whites—had a tipi camp just west of the squaw men's cabins; about half a mile farther west on the north bank of Whetstone Creek, Chief Fire Thunder had a little camp of Oglalas, not more than a dozen tipis. Swift Bear, with part of the Corn Band, was north of the agency in a tipi camp which was about opposite to the northern end of Whetstone Island in the river. Standing Elk, of the Corn Band, had a camp south of the agency.

That first winter at Whetstone (1868–69) was hard on everyone. The Sioux were unhappy under the new conditions; they missed the action and excitement of life in a hunting camp and also the abundance of food. They were big eaters, especially of meat, and they complained of the scanty rations doled out to them. Part of the government rations, such as wheat flour and pickled pork, were either distasteful to them or else the women had no means of preparing such food. You cannot do much with flour if you have no equipment beyond a kettle simmering over an open fire of sticks. Rations were issued once in five days, and the hospitable and improvident Sioux invited friends to feasts and cooked and ate until everything was gone. They then went hungry until the next ration day, blaming their deprivation on the government.

As Spotted Tail's people would not come to the agency, their rations had to be hauled thirty to forty miles to their camp, and when snow was deep, the wagons loaded with rations could not get through. Sometimes the Indians came to the agency with ponies and packed their rations to camp. The cattle for beef rations were driven to the camp, where the Sioux turned the animals loose and hunted them like buffalo, killing them with arrows and bullets. Because of transportation difficulties, the rations for Spotted Tail's camp were issued once in ten days, and the chief and his headmen usually came to the agency a day or two before to induce the agent to alter the rations. These talks took place at the agent's office. Spotted Tail would start in by saying his people did not like wheat flour and wanted shelled corn in its place. They could make hominy. The army captain who was acting as agent would reply through the interpreter that the rations were fixed by law, and there was no shelled corn on hand, even if it could be substituted for flour. Spotted Tail would argue that point for a long time. He would then say his people wanted twenty more head of cattle and a dozen extra sides of bacon in their ration issue and less of other articles. The agent would explain again that the rations were fixed by law and could not be altered. This would go on and on until the exasperated and worn-out agent would give in enough to let the chief have two head of cattle and two or three sides of bacon more than his official rations for his camp. Spotted Tail would go home pleased after one of these small victories, leaving the unfortunate agent to listen to the howls of rage from all the chiefs of the camps close to the agency. Spotted Tail had been given additional rations; now the agent must add to the rations of all the camps.

Haggling with the army captain over rations for his camp, quarreling with him over his refusal to issue extra supplies to him as head chief so that he could keep up his position, Spotted Tail was still doing the government splendid service by keeping his wild followers from leaving the reservation. He was not doing this for the government; he was still angry over the deception the peace commission had been guilty of when it had induced the chiefs to sign what they thought was a simple peace agreement and had then ordered the Sioux to go to the reservation. He was trying to keep his people at Whetstone because he was convinced that they would be attacked if they left the reservation, and he was finding the task a man-sized job.

During the winter some Sioux from the hunting camps came to Whetstone to visit, and they told of the abundance of buffalo both in the Powder River country and down on Republican Fork. Spotted Tail's followers were hungry half of the time; their clothing of tanned skins was wearing out, and so were the tanned-skin covers of their tipis. The men were bored and angry at sitting about camp in idleness, and they kept demanding that the chief permit them to go hunting. He and the camp council ordered them to stay where they were, explaining over and over that if they left the reservation, the troops would attack them—if they went down to the Republican. If they went to the Powder River, where it was safe, the Sioux there would not welcome them. All the hunting lands were supposed to be free for any Sioux to hunt in, but if any large group from Spotted Tail's camp had gone to the Powder River, they would have been regarded as intruders on the hunting grounds of the local Sioux camps. Spotted Tail and his camp council put the Indian soldiers on duty, policing the camp to prevent any groups' leaving. Despite these precautions some small parties of warriors slipped away and went down into Nebraska to raid the Pawnees. They came home with a few Pawnee scalps and some Pawnee horses, and nothing was said about it. Spotted Tail and the other chiefs hated the Pawnees, and it was too much to expect that the warriors would remain idle in camp with the Pawnee villages on Loup Fork, within raiding distance. It was about this time that Spotted Tail's eldest son, a boy still in his teens, went off secretly with a war party and came home with a Pawnee scalp. The Chief was a proud man and made a big feast in honor of his son's achievement of the rank of warrior.

When spring came, despite the watchfulness of the Indian soldiers in the camp, a group of families got away and went to Republican Fork to hunt. Spotted Tail was worried. Other groups would probably follow the first one, and presently his camp would melt away. But before anything of that kind could happen, the runaway families came home in a much chastened mood. Down in the Republican hunting grounds, they had been surprised in camp by Pawnee Scouts and had been driven in frantic flight north of the Platte, having several persons killed and wounded and losing their camp and all its contents.

This affair lifted Spotted Tail's standing among his people. He had been right in warning them of the danger of leaving the reservation. This was demonstrated still more strongly in the next few months. General C. C. Augur, commanding the military Department of the Platte, sent strong forces of cavalry and Pawnee Scouts into the field, combing the Republican Fork country for camps of Indians who had failed to heed the warnings to go to the reservation. The Southern Oglalas, who had stayed in their hunting camps when Spotted Tail and his Brulés had unwillingly gone to the reservation, were now surprised in their camps and driven north of the Platte. They lost their camps and everything in them, and many of these Oglalas soon turned up in Spotted Tail's camp, poor, hungry, and much disillusioned about their ability to fight the Americans. Their arrival ended for the time being the urgent demands of Spotted Tail's people to be permitted to go hunting. Not buffalo hunting but farming became the burning question of the day.

The Christian and benevolent groups who were planning the lives of the Indians, and the Washington officials who were trying to carry out the plans, miscalculated the attitude of the Sioux. These Indians had been hunters and warriors since the beginning of time, and the plan for turning them rapidly into farmers was moonshine. Yet the government had adopted this scheme and was spending huge sums in an effort to carry it out. Most of the Sioux had an ingrained opposition to trying to make a living by wounding Mother Earth with metal tools. No good could come of that, and the spirits would probably punish the tribe most severely if it attempted such wickedness. A few of the Sioux bands, such as the Brulé Corn Band, had attempted to grow crops in the past and were willing to try the experiment again, but their idea of farming was a fraction of an acre dug up with hand hoes by the women and planted with Indian corn and a few vegetables. Even in these so-called progressive camps, the men had no intention of touching a farming tool. That was women's work. As for the very costly outfit of big plows, horse harrows, horse rakes, corn-planters, and threshing machines the government had bought and shipped to Whetstone, that was simply proof that officials loved to throw away public money.

The government employees had plowed a common field in 1868

and fenced it, a strong board fence one and one-half miles long. In the spring of 1869 some of the white men who were married to Indian women planted small fields inside the fence. The Sioux were angry. These men were enrolled as members of the tribe, and from the Sioux way of looking at it, they were insulting the tribe by working with their hands. Worse than that, Chief Swift Bear of the Corn Band was up to his old tricks. He had always listened to his brother-in-law, the trader Bordeaux, and even in the old Fort Laramie days had wanted to try his hand—or rather the hands of his wife and daughters—at farming; and now, in 1869, he dared to do it. Some of the angry Sioux wished to "soldier" him—to cut up his tipis and shoot his ponies for insulting the tribe by such conduct, but the other chiefs did not wish to start fresh feuds and restrained their angry followers.

The spirits, however, did not hold their hands. They let Swift Bear's women plant their little field—Ree squaw corn, pumpkins, squashes, and field beans. Then, following the usual Indian ideas of farming, Swift Bear left the crops to take care of themselves while his band went off wandering, seeking deer and antelope. At harvest time they moved back to the agency and found their field dead as a doornail. While they had been away, the Dakota climate had produced first drought, then blistering hot winds and swarms of hungry grasshoppers; and by the time the farmers came home to harvest, their field was bare. Swift Bear stood in the middle of the desolated corn patch, looking sadly about him, and at that moment one of the officers at the military stockade that now guarded the agency fired a shot and the bullet thudded into poor Swift Bear's side, wounding him quite badly. It was clearly an accident, but the Sioux would not accept that view of it. The spirits that looked after the interests of the tribe had punished Swift Bear for daring to depart from ancient custom and wound Mother Earth.[1]

---

[1] The first attempts of the Sioux to plant crops at Weststone in 1869–70 are covered by Poole, *Among the Sioux of Dakota*. Swift Bear's account of how his crops failed and how he was shot in his own field is given in Turner's *Red Men Calling on the Great White Father*, 122. The corn the Sioux planted was little spotted Ree corn ("squaw corn"), which produced roasting ears in about eight weeks; but even that very tough variety of maize was wiped out by drought and grasshoppers.

The Sioux were better off than the unfortunate Dakota pioneers, who had also lost their crops through drought and a plague of grass-hoppers. The Sioux, by giving up their way of living as free hunters and surrendering most of their lands, had obtained by treaty free rations, clothing, and other needs for a period of years. They did not need crops. The government was obligated to take care of them. But it was not doing so in a manner to satisfy the Sioux, who complained that the rations were "too small" and not the right articles. But most of all they complained about the annuities. Annuities were blankets, clothing, camp equipment, canvas for tipi covers, and a host of other articles. In the old days, the Sioux had hunted and had traded skins and other products of the hunt at the trading posts for all the trade goods they required. Now they received such goods under the treaty from the government in an annual payment. There had been no annuities handed out at Whetstone in 1868, and the Indians were both angry and anxious. Their clothing was becoming ragged and their tipi covers and camp equipment were wearing out. They had little to trade at the two agency trading posts for new goods, and from the time the ice went out of the Missouri in the spring of 1869, they anxiously watched every steamboat that came up the river, hoping that it was carrying the annuity goods. But spring, summer, and autumn dragged by and no annuities came. Congress had not even voted the money. However, the Sioux had rations, and ration day was the event that broke the monotony of life at the agency. The issuing of rations had not yet become a dull routine. It was a gamble, and many kinds of loaded dice were being used. Every chief was intriguing to obtain more rations and a better selection for his camp, and already (with the Sioux on the reservation less than a year) the trick of juggling with numbers was being worked. The Sioux could not count to ten without using their fingers or a notched stick to help them out, but chiefs were claiming rations for more people than they had in their camps, and families were borrowing the neighbors' children to enable them to claim a larger quantity of rations. The agent and his clerks, attempting to combat such claims, had poor success. All the Sioux were armed, and persons who might have come forward as witnesses to the truth restrained their inclinations. They had no desire to be shot.

At Whetstone in 1869 the rations, except among the Laramie Loafers, were issued to the chiefs of camps, and that was the way the common Indians wished it to be done. They expected their chiefs to take care of them, and they were cold to the plans of the whites to break the chiefs and make every Sioux head of a family his own representative.

Ration days were the time when the Sioux women—usually kept at home—came to the fore. Each band formed a circle near the commissary building in which the rations were stored, and the women sat in front in the circle. The men were at the back, for they would not demean themselves by taking any active part in the handling of rations. That was the women's work. Then the white employees brought the rations and piled them in the center of the circle, and as the work proceeded, the women would begin to exclaim with pleasure. Then they would start singing, chanting the praises of the white men, calling them by their Sioux names:

> See, See, Red Head brings the sides of bacon;
> See, see, Big Nose brings the bags of beans;
> Now comes Little Whiteman with the sugar sacks;
> Chatka is carrying the coffee bags!

The men sat quietly watching, but if they thought their family was not getting a fair share, they complained later to their chief and he carried the matter to the agent. These agency bands had their beef issued to them on the hoof. The Texas longhorns were very wild; they could run as fast as elk, and the Sioux had a glorious hunt, riding them down and shooting them. Only the Laramie Loafers were left out. That band was used to the army method at Fort Laramie, and a white butcher had been employed to serve them with meat, dressed and cut. The other Sioux looked on with pity. There were many parts of the animal the Sioux loved to eat that a white butcher threw away.

Chief Big Mouth (*Eh Tonka*) of the Loafers was a big, plump Indian. He had been a notable warrior in his younger days; then he had taken over control of the Loafer camp at Fort Laramie after Old Smoke's death in 1864 and had grown fat and soft from living at the fort. He had become a hard drinker of bad whiskey, but he was a relative of the great Red Cloud and probably the most effective orator among the Sioux of the Plains. He was an ambitious man; and as soon as the Indians came to Whetstone, he began to make claims that the agency was his property and that he was the head chief. In effect, he was attempting to shoulder Spotted Tail out of the way, and he seemed to have a good opportunity to do so, as Spotted Tail was far to the west in his own camp, one or two days' hard ride from the agency.

But Big Mouth, despite his loud pretensions, was not a strong chief. His own followers would not trust him to divide up the rations and other free supplies fairly, and the Loafer Band was the only one at the agency in which the distribution was made direct to the heads of families. Neither the Sioux nor the agent trusted this chief, and a number of families who felt they needed an honest chief to take care of them left his camp and joined one of the others. Despite this, Big Mouth persisted in his demands that the agent recognize him as head chief, and he kept sniping at Spotted Tail and making belittling remarks about him. Spotted Tail ignored him in public but was watchful. Every important Sioux chief knew that sooner or later he would have to deal with some man of the Big Mouth type who would attempt to pull him down and supplant him.

This summer it was proposed that the government make a peace between the Whetstone Sioux and the small Ponca tribe that lived on a reservation in northeastern Nebraska, a short day's ride below Whetstone. The Brulé Sioux and the Poncas had been at war for over a century, and the Christian Friends of Indians wished to see this shocking state of affairs ended. The Ponca agent induced his suspicious Indians to agree, and he then took two hundred Poncas up to Whetstone. The Brulés wanted no peace, but the chiefs wished to please the officials. They agreed to a peace, and having accepted the idea, they made peace with much ceremony, feasting the Poncas for a week and giving every Ponca man a Brulé pony as a peace gift.

The summer wore on. The Sioux at Whetstone were bored with inactivity, and presently a war party slipped away and made a horse-lifting raid on the Poncas. That tribe had been given by the government a number of big American horses, the idea being that Indian ponies were too lightweight to pull plows and that the Poncas (who were farming one to two acres for each family with hand hoes) needed big horses to aid them in their labors. The Brulés stole some American horses and went home. Pleased with this success, they sent out one war party after another until they had stolen every American horse the Poncas had. They then set to work and stole back all the Sioux ponies that had been given to the Poncas as peace gifts. This performance charmed the editors of certain Dakota and Nebraska newspapers. They recommended that the Brethren (which was their name for the Christians who were meddling in Indian policy) should make some more peace treaties between the Sioux and neighboring tribes. It kept the Sioux busy and happy, and it left them little time for raiding the white settelers.

During the summer, Captain Woodson was relieved and Captain DeWitt Clinton Poole, Second Infantry, was ordered to come from his station in Georgia to assume the duties of acting agent at Whetstone. Poole took an instant liking to Spotted Tail. He found that this chief had more good sense and good will than any other chief at the agency. Spotted Tail did make demands, but he was open to persuasion; and when the matter had been explained to him, he would accept a fair arrangement with good humor and friendliness. He was utterly unlike the bumptious Big Mouth, who claimed that Whetstone Agency was his, that all the supplies piled up in the warehouses belonged to him, and who threatened that if he was not given all he demanded, he would use force and take what he pleased.

Big Mouth was playing up the discontent of the Sioux. No annuity goods—blankets, clothing, canvas for tipi covers, kettles, and camp equipment—had been delivered in the full year the Indians had been at Whetstone. Big Mouth harped on this fact, and as he lived at the agency, he was able to make endless trouble for Captain Poole. The Sioux said angrily that if the government did not carry out its treaty pledge and supply them with clothing and other needs, they would return to their hunting grounds, where they could clothe and supply themselves. In the end, Poole appealed to Newton Edmunds, superintendent of Indian affairs for Dakota Territory, and Edmunds applied the old principal of robbing Peter to pay Paul. The Brulés of Whetstone were wild and were threatening to go off the reservation. Up the Missouri at Crow Creek, Edmunds had a lot of tame Sioux—poor Indians of little spirit—so he borrowed the annuities the Crow Creek Indians were in sad need of and had Poole issue the goods to the Whetstone Sioux. The amount was not one-fifth of what the Whetstone Indians required, but the issue of blankets and other goods quieted their threats of leaving the reservation immediately.

Spotted Tail's education was much broadened by his first year on a reservation. He was learning about the different types of white men and their ways. There were some very low types, he found. That frontier hero, John Nelson, had followed the Sioux to Whetstone, where by right of living with a Sioux woman he was enrolled as a member of the tribe with full rations, clothing, and other supplies. As he stated in his book, he at once formed a partnership with the Cliffords and a worthy he called Toad Randall, and they started running whiskey across the Missouri and peddling it in the Indian camps. Spotted Tail used his Indian soldiers to keep these men away from his camp. There was no money in the Indian camps. The whiskey trade was barter, mainly for government rations, clothing, and other supplies, and a Sioux who had acquired a taste for drink would strip his family naked and leave it to starve to satisfy his craving.

Some of the squaw men spent all of their very great leisure in thinking up swindles to try on the agent or the chiefs. They were not all like that. There were many honest and hard-working men living with the Sioux, but when a shrewd and unscrupulous squaw man set to work in earnest, it was a liberal education to have him working on you.

Spotted Tail was also learning what it meant for free people to put themselves under the care of government officialdom. Already in 1869 the officials were meddling in every phase of Sioux life and attempting to twist the Indians into new and officially approved shapes. Spotted Tail set his face against these efforts to break the tribal form of government to pieces, put the Sioux under white control, and force them to change their way of life. Fine talk did not deceive him. His people had been free and had been supporting themselves when they had been cheated into signing a treaty which, unknown to the chiefs, provided that they must give up hunting and trust the government to take care of them. The government was not doing that. His people were ill clothed and not half as well fed as they had been in the hunting camps; and he resented bitterly the new attitude of the officials and of Congress—the pretense that the Sioux were paupers being cared for by a kindly government, people who should be ashamed to complain or to resist government orders. His tribe had been forced to give up vast tracts of land and their means of supporting themselves and come to this reservation— not to please themselves but to satisfy the demands of the whites. The government owed them under the treaty every blanket and pound of food they were getting. Spotted Tail did not brood. He kept busy and usually cheerful. He liked Captain Poole personally and got on well with him, but he was on the watch and ready to defend his people's interests if the officials attempted to infringe on them. He had no faith in the scheme for turning the Sioux suddenly into successful farmers. That would be the work not of a few years, as the officials imagined, but of generations. The Yankton Sioux had accepted a reservation below Whetstone on the Missouri in the late 1850's, and for nearly twenty years the government had labored to turn the Yanktons into farmers. Every honest man in Dakota knew that if rations were stopped, the Yanktons would starve. They were not farming, but gardening. It was the same with several tribes that had been planting corn on the banks of the Missouri for two to three centuries. Deprived of their main source of food in the hunting field, these tribes, despite all the government efforts to teach them, were still gardening and depending on government rations and beef for their real support.

It would be false to depict Spotted Tail at this period as a leader bent under a load of work and worry in behalf of his people. He did take his responsibilities as head chief seriously, but he was a man who loved life, and he was finding interest and enjoyment at Whetstone during the time he could spare from tribal business. He appears to have made the long ride to the agency about once every ten days or two weeks, spending a day or two there and then returning to his camp. He had become warmly attached to Stephan Estes, a young man who was acting as chief clerk, and when the chief was staying at the agency, he messed and bunked with "Stevaness." Whenever a steamboat stopped at Whetstone, the Chief went on board to look the strange machine over, eat with the captain, and stand and wonder at the antics of the Negro deck hands. He went down to Fort Randall to extend his acquaintance among the officers and their wives, for he still thought more highly of army officers than of any other group of white men.

He made no objection when Captain Poole, pushed vigorously on by the Washington officials, opened a little school with his own wife as the first teacher. Mrs. Poole could not understand Sioux and the children could not understand English, so one of old Bordeaux's half-blood daughters was employed as assistant teacher and interpreter. Spotted Tail and the other chiefs seem to have thought that a school was a place where kindhearted (and evidently softheaded) white persons fed and cared for children whose families were too poor to do the job properly. The head chief would probably have been angry if anyone had attempted to open a school in his camp. His people were able to feed and clothe their own children, and they needed no school. The agency school pupils were from the Loafer camp. That was just like the Loafers, to swallow their Sioux pride and accept any help that was offered. The school served meals to the children; and when winter came it was a popular institution, with many Sioux men attending school regularly, to sit near the hot stove and add greatly to the expense of the school meals by absorbing free lunches and coffee.

Spotted Tail was learning a great deal about his own tribe, probably more than any other living Sioux. He was being visited by leaders from many Sioux agencies, ranging all the way from the tame Christian Santees, who had a small reservation down in Nebraska, to the wild Sioux on the Grand River, far up the Missouri. These Sioux leaders often came to discuss the crisis caused by the intrusion of the whites into their country; and even in 1869 some of them were seeking a means of organizing all of the Teton Sioux into a united group, with a head chief and council, but it was already too late for that. The government would never permit any such united action of the Sioux, the policy being to break up tribal groups and treat these Indians as individuals under government control.

One of the criticisms of Spotted Tail, made by authors and by Sioux Indians, has been that he gave in to the whites and went to the reservation in 1868 while Red Cloud defied the whites and remained in his hunting grounds. As has been stated, the army's orders were to act against the Indians south of the Platte only, leaving Red Cloud to do as he pleased on the Powder River. One camp of Spotted Tail's followers did not believe in the military threats and slipped away to hunt in the spring of 1869, only to be surprised in their camp south of the Platte. They had several persons killed or wounded, lost all their property, and fled back to Spotted Tail's camp. Next, the Southern Oglalas, who had ignored the order to leave the lands south of the Platte, were attacked by cavalry and Pawnee Scouts and driven north in panic flight. Led by Little Wound, Pawnee Killer, and other chiefs, they joined Spotted Tail's camp on White River and settled down to eat free government rations. The way it was going it looked as if Spotted Tail had been wise to go to the reservation in 1868. Red Cloud, in no danger of being attacked by the troops, was losing people to Spotted Tail. Red Leaf and his Wazhazha camp left Red Cloud and joined Spotted Tail on August 26; then Grand Partisan, with the portion of the Brulé Corn Band that had lived with Red Cloud since the late 1850's, joined Spotted Tail, bringing a report that Red Cloud's camp was near the Black Hills and that Red Cloud was attempting to coax his followers to move to the reservation. With the situation developing in this manner, it is really difficult for any fair-minded man to say, "Here is the fainthearted chief who gave in, and here is the hero who held out."

In 1869 both Spotted Tail and Red Cloud stood for peace with the Americans. Spotted Tail's main difficulty was that his followers were demanding the right to go hunting, while Red Cloud's principal trouble lay in the cutting off of trade. The military had stopped all trade with the Sioux on the Upper Platte when the Indian war had started in the summer of 1864, and despite all their talk of peace and friendship, the treaty commissioners had forgotten to permit the resumption of trade. The truth was that the main object of the government was to keep the Sioux away from the Platte and the new Union Pacific railroad. There was some talk of establishing a trading center in the Black Hills for the hunting camps in the Powder River country, but this plan got lost in the maze of Washington offices and red tape. Red Cloud's camp was starving for trade goods, and particularly for guns, ammunition, blankets, and camp equipment; and his people could get none of these articles without going to the reservation. They had been making and piling up fine buffalo robes and other products of the hunt to trade for manufactured goods for the past five years, and they were clamoring for trade, but most of them were too wild and too suspicious of the whites to go to the reservation.

The Indian agent, Captain Poole, met the chiefs from Powder River—Red Leaf, his lieutenant, Black Horn, old Grand Partisan, and that wild Miniconjou chief, Roman Nose (alias Crow Nose), when they came to the agency to trade at the stores kept by John W. Smith and the Bordeaux family. Poole was much struck by the difference in appearance of his agency Indians and these wild fellows from the free camps. The Sioux near the agency were the tamest bands, and life on the reservation had softened them up, for they had been sitting in idleness for a year. The clothing of tanned skins they had brought from their hunting grounds was wearing out; through government neglect they had received very few new blankets and other articles, and after trading all their best things to whiskey peddlers, they looked ragged and dirty. The men from Powder River were all clad in fine skin garments, handsomely ornamented with dyed porcupine quillwork and beads. They were lean, alert, and bold, watching the whites at the agency with quick eyes and ready to fight instantly if interfered with. The men of Spotted Tail's camp were between the agency Indians and those from Powder River. They were growing ragged from lack of hunting, but they were as bold and independent as any of the men from Red Cloud's camp. Part of the Powder River Indians went home after trading at the agency and eating free rations for a time in Spotted Tail's camp, but Red Leaf and his Wazhazhas wintered with Spotted Tail.

Big Mouth, like most big talkers, did not seem to have much sense. Unable to control the Indians in his own small Loafer camp, he was bent on pulling Spotted Tail down and taking his place as head chief at Whetstone. That would have been fine for the Whetstone Indians. Here is an example of the kind of leadership Big Mouth would have provided. There was a whiskey ranch on the east side of the Missouri, about fifteen miles below Whetstone and fifteen above the Yankton Sioux agency. The white man who ran the ranch had a Yankton woman for his wife. Big Mouth had been obtaining whiskey from this man, but now had nothing left to trade for whiskey. His credit was thoroughly bad, so one night he went down to the ranch with a party of his bold warriors and chased the ranchman and his wife off into the brush. The Indians then drank an entire barrel of whiskey, went out to hunt the ranchman and his wife in the brush, and fired several shots at them. They wrecked the interior of the log cabin, tore the door off, and finally departed. When accused at the agency of this deed, Big Mouth treated the affair as a good joke, admitting the truth of the story.[2]

On October 27, 1869, Big Mouth was holding a feast and drinking party in the Loafer camp, and the agency resounded with the singing, drumming, and yelling of the Sioux. Spotted Tail was at the agency on business, and Big Mouth had invited him to the feast, twitting him and implying that it was a dare. A wagon train was being loaded with rations for Spotted Tail's camp, and the chief was with the agent, completing the arrangements for the starting of the train the following morning. He had with him two men from his camp (probably Two Strike and another minor chief).

Late in the day, Spotted Tail and his friends went to the Loafer camp. It is not clear whether the feast was in a large tipi or in a log house, but the Spotted Tail party went in and spent some hours eating with Big Mouth and his followers. As the night wore on, Big Mouth began to press whiskey on Spotted Tail, who refused to drink. The Loafer chief got more and more boisterous and insulting in his language, and finally Spotted Tail and his friends got up and went out. Big Mouth followed them, and, according to eyewitnesses, he drew a revolver from under his blanket, aimed it at Spotted Tail, almost touching his body with the muzzle, and pulled the trigger; but the percussion cap misfired, and before the Loafer chief could cock his gun and fire again, Spotted Tail whipped out a re-

[2] Poole, *Among the Sioux of Dakota*, 81.

volver and shot him in the head. As he fell, Spotted Tail's two friends counted coup on him. This was the Sioux custom. They struck Big Mouth with their revolvers, not to injure him but to count the coup.

A crowd of frantic Sioux had snatched up weapons and were preparing to fight. Neither side daring to fire the first shot, they stood and howled at each other. The wagon train boss ran to the agent's office and pounded on the door with the butt of his gun, shouting that the Sioux were fighting; and Captain Poole, awakened from sleep, came and opened the door. "Here they come!" shouted the wagon master, and ran into the office to hide. The Sioux came pouring in, all yelling and brandishing weapons. They pushed Poole through the office and into the large council room, where he was dumped into a chair, and Spotted Tail sat down on the floor beside him, his blanket drawn closely about him, alert and cool. Big Mouth's brother, Blue Horse, started a violent harangue in the Sioux language. He had a rifle in one hand and a strung bow and a bunch of arrows in the other, and when he dropped his blanket, two navy Colts and a big scalping knife could be seen in their sheaths at his belt. He was in a raving fury, leaping and bounding about the room as he hurled accusations and threats at Spotted Tail. The head chief seemed calm, but he was watching Blue Horse intently. He now had a rifle, and at one point in the Oglala's violent harangue he cocked the gun. Agent Poole was frozen to his chair. The room was thronged with enraged Sioux, all armed and evidently itching for a fight. If they started shooting, Poole was in a wonderful position to field most of the bullets and arrows.

A pale and scared squaw man slipped in and stood beside Poole's chair. Blue Horse raged on and on; but in the end he had to stop from sheer exhaustion. Thigh, a Loafer chief, then took up the tirade, emphasizing his points by waving a big pistol in Captain Poole's face. Unlike Blue Horse, he was not blaming Spotted Tail; he shouted that this tragedy was all the fault of the whites, who made whiskey and brought it among the Sioux. Had it not always been like this, ever since 1841, when the Sioux had got drunk on Chug Creek and Red Cloud had shot and killed Chief Bull Bear? Thigh quieted down a little as he talked and ended his harangue on a rather less warlike note. He sat down; Spotted Tail stood up. He said that Thigh was right—whiskey was to blame—and that he was sorry about Big Mouth. The Sioux should not kill each other. They were here now in the council room, and Captain Poole should advise them how to settle this matter. Poole had no ideas, but the squaw man who acted as his interpreter knew the tribal custom, and he coached Poole to suggest that Spotted Tail pay for shooting Big Mouth. Poole had been driven almost to distraction by Big Mouth's outrageous demands, trickery, and lawlessness, but he now spoke sadly of the passing of this great and noble chieftain. Yes, Spotted Tail must pay for what he had done. Coached again by the interpreter, Poole suggested ten ponies as a proper price. He then said that since the gentlemen had been up all night, it might be well for everyone to go home and sleep. In the morning they could settle this trouble in a peaceful manner. To his amazement the Sioux, who a few minutes before had been on the point of starting a general fight, got up and left quietly.

Big Mouth died toward dawn. Some hours later Blue Horse came to the office and told Poole that he felt so sad over the death of his great and good brother that he would have to wash off the paint he had put on his face for the feast the day before and begin mourning. The interpreter warned Poole that if this Indian washed his face and started mourning, it would mean the reopening of the feud and more shootings. The agent should give Blue Horse two fine blankets; that would comfort him, and he would refrain from washing his face and going gunning for Spotted Tail. The blankets were handed over, and the grieving brother went quietly away.

Captain Poole was far from being in a quiet mood. Nearly all the agency employees were gone, half of them still in the hiding holes they had jumped into when the trouble had started the previous night, half of them on the east side of the Missouri, where they had fled for safety. The wagon train boss was afraid to start for Spotted Tail's camp, as the Loafer warriors seemed to have a plan for attacking the train in revenge for the killing of Big Mouth. The women in the Loafer camp were keening the death of the chief. They dressed Big Mouth in his buckskin war costume, laid his bow and quiver at his side, and wrapped the body in a fine blanket.

He was then placed on a Sioux burial scaffold standing outside the Loafer camp. Spotted Tail paid the ponies to the Big Mouth family and rode off with his men to his distant camp. A company of infantry, hastily summoned by Poole, had marched in, the white employees came out of hiding, and by evening on the twenty-eighth the danger seemed ended.[3]

[3] This account of the killing of Big Mouth is taken largely from Poole, who obtained the details within a few hours from eyewitnesses. The Captain obviously was not grieved over the taking off of Big Mouth, and he did not blame Spotted Tail. In the *Handbook of Indians*, published by the Bureau of Ethnology, there is, under the heading *Big Mouth*, a wonderful example of the kind of wicked nonsense that has been made up to besmirch Spotted Tail. This standard authority states that the killing was in 1872 or 1873, when the correct date had been recorded over and over as October 27, 1869. This account states that at Whetstone, Big Mouth's influence increased so greatly that Spotted Tail was alarmed for his position as head chief. The reverse is true. Big Mouth was drinking so hard that the Sioux lost respect for him. This handbook tale makes Spotted Tail plot the death of his rival. The reverse is true. The account ignores Captain Poole's eyewitness narrative and the statements made by William Welsh, the highly reputable Philadelphia merchant, who visited the agency a year later. Welsh states from witnesses who were present that Big Mouth was drinking hard all day and repeatedly attempted to provoke a fight with Spotted Tail, concluding the performance that night by drawing a pistol suddenly and attempting to murder his rival. (Welsh, *Sioux and Ponca Indians*; pamphlet, p. 19, Philadelphia, 1870.)

7. *The Great Journey*

IN THE EARLY SPRING OF 1870 there were two matters that the Sioux of Whetstone Agency were greatly interested in—going to Republican Fork to hunt buffalo, and government annuity goods. Agent Poole was talking up farming; but, except for Swift Bear's group of the Corn Band, the Sioux had no intention of touching a farming tool. Spotted Tail was still keeping a careful guard to prevent any of his people from going to the Republican Fork to hunt. General Harney had been relieved from duty as controller of the new Sioux agencies, and the civilian Indian Office in Washington was now in charge; but General Sherman had made an announcement that any Sioux outside the reservation were still under military control, and, as far as the Republican Fork country was concerned, any Sioux who went there to hunt would be driven back to the reservation by the troops.

The annuity goods that had been expected in the spring of 1869 had been shipped so late in the year that they had been caught by the closing of navigation on the Missouri. A wagon train had brought the goods up from Sioux City in February, 1870, and the half-naked Sioux had been made happy for a time. Then they had begun to complain bitterly. It was the old story of letting a government office take care of people. Urged on by visionaries who thought it high time the Sioux should take up civilization, the officials in Washington had sent 1,500 pairs of trousers, 1,500 dress coats, 700 greatcoats, and even a large shipment of felt hats. There were only 800 blankets, which were the principal article of clothing for the Sioux of both sexes; the hats and clothing sent were old army surplus, the coats with army brass buttons still on them. The Sioux were furious. They cut the hated military buttons off and bought new buttons at the traders' stores; they cut the seats and fronts out of the pants, turning them into Sioux leggings, and they cut up most of the other garments, using the cloth to make proper Sioux wearing apparel. For every year during the next decade, the Sioux were cheated out of about $50,000 worth of proper Indian clothing by the smug officials who sent civilized clothing in the absurd belief that they could turn the Sioux into white men overnight by putting them into coats and pants.

Captain Poole kept talking up farming. The chiefs were polite and said that they were interested in farming; might try it; next year, or maybe the year after. Meanwhile a Yankton newspaper editor (probably with his tongue in his cheek) was predicting that the Sioux would have surplus crops to market after providing all their own food needs this year. The true situation at Whetstone was that a group of families of Swift Bear's Corn Band were permitting the women to plant little plots, total thirty acres, less than one acre for each two hundred Indians at the agency. As the Indians had carried away and burned the farm fence for fuel and the indications were that another Dakota drought was coming along, the prospects for a good farming year at Whetstone were not bright. However, the government was building a small house for Chief Swift Bear, who was determined to become a farmer and live like a white man. That was progress, at least a glimmer of progress.

Late in the spring the western newspapers began to print rumors that the Sioux were preparing for war. Spotted Tail and the other chiefs were puzzled. Who were the Sioux who were planning war? Certainly not the Sioux at the new agencies on the Missouri, whose one great desire was to go off the reservation to hunt buffalo. There were many families from Powder River in Spotted Tail's camp, and from what they said, the wild Sioux of the hunting camps had only one desire—trade with the whites. The Sioux of the Powder River badly needed guns and ammunition; they had not traded with the whites since 1864 and were not equipped for war.

The church leaders and humanitarian groups in the East who had taken a leading part in the development of the Indian Peace Policy now had achieved an official standing by inducing Congress to authorize a Board of Indian Commissioners and then influencing

President Grant to appoint the high priests of the Peace Policy groups as members of the board. This board was to watch with one eye the wicked War Department and with the other the officials of the Indian Office and to guard their Indian brothers from all harm. When the rumors of a new Sioux war began coming in, the leaders of the peace groups grew alarmed. They held conferences, and Benjamin Tatham, of New York, suggested the plan of bringing Red Cloud and the other chiefs to Washington for friendly settlement of all differences. Someone on the Upper Platte must have sent a message to the Sioux in the Powder River country, for now these Indians got word to the commanding officer at Fort Fetterman, on the North Platte west of Fort Laramie, that the chiefs wished to visit the Great Father in Washington. At first it was said that Man-Afraid-of-His-Horse was to lead this Sioux party, but that chief refused to leave his own lands, and after holding a council, the Sioux chose Red Cloud as the leader of the delegation that was to go East.[1]

In Washington the officials decided to extend this plan to include the chiefs from the agencies on the Missouri, and Captain Poole was ordered to bring Spotted Tail and others from Whetstone, while the military agent at the Cheyenne River Agency was to bring a delegation from there. During the previous winter, Captain Poole had induced Spotted Tail to move nearer to the agency because of the impossibility of sending rations to his distant camp. Spotted Tail persuaded his unwilling people to move to the bank of the Missouri, near a high bluff overlooking the river, some eighteen to twenty miles north of Whetstone Agency. In April the chiefs of this camp shut their eyes and permitted a party of two hundred warriors to slip away and make a raid on the Pawnee Indians on Loup Fork in Nebraska. It was probably in this raid that Spotted Tail's eldest son (Young Spotted Tail of 1880) killed a Pawnee. The warriors had been at home for only a short time when Captain Poole came up from the agency to inform Spotted Tail that he was expected to go to Washington with a delegation. Poole reported that Spotted

---

[1] When he reached Washington, Red Cloud stated that "thirty-two nations" (meaning Sioux bands) had held a council, selecting him to represent them and instructing him about what he was to say in Washington.

Tail at this time had five wives, and this report is confirmed in a letter a member of Poole's party sent to a Yankton newspaper. The head chief had his large family in several tipis which stood in a cluster; in front of the chief's own tipi the fine peace flag General Sherman had given him in 1868 was flying at the tip of a long and slender cedar pole. Unlike the riotous camps at the agency, Spotted Tail's camp was in perfect order, the Indian soldiers on duty as police. Poole and his party were invited to a feast, where they met Two Strike, Little Wound, Pawnee Killer, Black Bear, and White Eyes. The chiefs were very friendly; they promised to hold a council and discuss the proposed journey to Washington.

Later on, Spotted Tail came to the agency with some of his camp leaders. He and Swift Bear, now the principal chief at the agency camps, were unwilling to go to Washington. They said that it was too far away. Poole's orders were imperative. He appealed to Spotted Tail and Swift Bear to consent to the journey in the interest of their people, and after talking together for some time, the chiefs agreed. Each was to take a warrior or head soldier with him. Poole states that Spotted Tail chose Fast Bear, and Swift Bear took Yellow Hair.[2]

Captain Poole, with his Indians and interpreters, left Whetstone on May 17 for the seven-day journey to Washington. They rode horses to White Swan, a stage station south of the agency, and there took the stage to Yankton. In Yankton, Poole purchased black suits and complete outfits for the Indians. They were all wearing handsome buckskin costumes, but it was the deplorable taste of officialdom at that period to dress all visiting Indians in black suits, white shirts with starched fronts, uncomfortable shoes, and hats. Spotted Tail and the others refused to put on shoes, which hurt their feet and made it almost impossible to walk, and they covered their hated black suits by keeping wrapped in handsome blankets. They went on to Sioux City and there took the train east. Another party from the Cheyenne River Agency was on the way east—Miniconjou, Two Kettle, and Sans Arc Sioux.

[2] The Yankton newspaper reported that Swift Bear took Black Pipe (Wazhazha leader) with him to Washington. Yellow Hair was a Wazhazha soldier, who in 1880–81 was groomed by the opposition party to supplant Spotted Tail as head chief.

Not one of these Sioux had ever been outside the Indian country west of the Missouri. Spotted Tail was the most experienced traveler, having been taken as a military prisoner to Fort Leavenworth in 1855. The chiefs had little knowledge of the extent of the lands east of the Missouri or of the great population of white people in those lands. If they were alarmed at being taken on this journey into an unknown world, they did not show it. They faced the strange new conditions calmly and were dignified and polite. At every big city in which they stopped they were offered entertainment, but they refused all invitations, stating that they were going East on tribal business and that it was not a pleasure trip. Spotted Tail always stood in the front of the party and usually spoke for them. He was the recognized leader.

The Whetstone chiefs reached Washington ahead of the Red Cloud party, which was coming from Wyoming. Captain Poole took his Indians to see the Secretary of the Interior. Spotted Tail was not in the least impressed with the sacredness of a member of the President's cabinet. He started right in, to Captain Poole's dismay, scolding the great official. The government, he said, was not carrying out its part of the 1868 treaty. His Indians had a right to hunt on Republican Fork, and they were being prevented from doing so by the use of troops. They had a right to decide for themselves in which part of the reservation they were to live, and the government was forcing them to live on the Missouri where whiskey peddlers were ruining them. The rations were too small; the annuities were not right. The great secretary listened to the interpreter's translation of the chief's words, and then he started to lecture Spotted Tail. "Tell him," he said to the interpreter, "that a man must expect some trouble in his life and should face it in a manly way, not by complaining." When the interpreter translated this, Spotted Tail began to laugh. "Tell him," he said, "that if he had had as much trouble in his life as I have had in mine, he would have cut his throat long ago."[3]

Spotted Tail was taken to the White House to see the Great Father—President Grant. Grant had a beautiful new meerschaum pipe with the bowl carved into a horse's head and a handsome silver

[3] Poole, *Among the Sioux of Dakota*, 117.

matchbox. The two big chiefs sat and smoked in amity for a time; then, through the interpreter, the Brulé chief started the same talk he had already given to the Secretary of the Interior, stressing two points: his people did not wish to remain on the Missouri River and they demanded the right to go hunting. The President replied mildly that it would be a good idea for Spotted Tail to go home and start farming. He also spoke of the value of education and offered to send one of Spotted Tail's sons to school. The chief politely declined. He said that his sons were to be warriors; the eldest, sixteen, had recently taken a Pawnee scalp. He told the President that he had three wives and eleven children.[4]

At the Indian Office, Spotted Tail developed his theme more fully. He told the Little Great Father (the Commissioner of Indian Affairs) that it was impossible for him to hold his Indians at the agency on the Missouri. They must be permitted to choose an agency site of their own liking, high up White River near the Black Hills, and they must be permitted to hunt buffalo on Republican Fork, as the treaty of 1868 gave them the right to do. The commissioner (who was determined to keep the Sioux on the Missouri and make them farm) was polite. He even made half-promises, not realizing that Indian chiefs, like small children, have a devilish way of turning half-promises into solemn pledges.

Brigadier General John E. Smith, commanding officer at Fort Laramie, reached Washington on June 1 with Red Cloud's big delegation—over thirty chiefs and headmen and some women. Trouble at once developed between Red Cloud and Spotted Tail. The Oglala leader, according to Captain Poole, was very angry over the killing of his relative, Big Mouth, by Spotted Tail. He was also assuming that he was Spotted Tail's superior, a point that the Brulé chief rejected with scorn. At this time, in 1870, Red Cloud does not appear to have been recognized as a chief by his own tribe on the Powder River. He was a war leader or *ogle tanka'un*—war-

---

[4] This is a newspaper report. Captain Poole states that Spotted Tail would not touch tobacco in any form and did not even smoke in formal councils. He says Grant merely gave the pipe and matchbox to the chief, the worst selection for a gift that could have been made. On the other hand, there is a photograph of Spotted Tail taken on the Platte about 1866 showing him holding a Sioux red stone pipe and beaded tobacco bag.

shirt-wearer. (He left his war shirt with his nephew, He Dog, when he started for Washington.) Spotted Tail was a head chief. Moreover, there was a tradition among the Teton Sioux that the Brulés were the old parent group, the head of the tribe, while Red Cloud's Oglalas were an off-shoot, or junior branch.[5] General Smith, Captain Poole, and the white men with the delegations took the angry chiefs into a room in the Washington House, the hotel in which the Indians were staying, and let them have it out. Red Cloud was haughtily determined to take the lead; Spotted Tail, impressed by General Smith and Captain Poole with the fact that the officials wanted Red Cloud to be treated as the principal leader, gave way with his usual good sense. He said that the interests of the Sioux people were most important, and that if the Sioux would benefit by his keeping in the background, he would do it. But he clearly had little use for Red Cloud, who was stiff with superiority and determined to have his way, come what might. Ever since the Fort Phil Kearny massacre in December, 1866, the whites had regarded Red Cloud as the great chief of the Sioux. Now, in 1870, the officials had only one main purpose: to induce Red Cloud to keep the peace and come to an agency on the reservation. Spotted Tail had been driven to an agency in 1868 by the threat of the use of troops against his people; Red Cloud had not been threatened and had been left to roam freely in his hunting grounds. Now the officials were going to bring Red Cloud to an agency, not by the threat of military action but by cajolery and the making of handsome promises. With their usual ineptitude, the officials had gotten off on the wrong foot. They had provided Spotted Tail's little party with horses so that they could ride about Washington in true Sioux style. Red Cloud now demanded horses for all his big party. The officials had no fund from which to pay for such a large number of horses. They tried to persuade Red Cloud that riding in official carriages behind handsome teams was much more impressive than riding on horseback, but the Oglala angrily rejected the idea. He said that these shiny black wagons were good enough for women, but his Oglalas were

[5] Poole, *Among the Sioux of Dakota*, 118. The Brulés were still called the Tetons as late as 1825, and the Tetons were one of the original seven Sioux tribes in Minnesota, going as far back as 1650.

warriors and wanted horses. They were promised horses and saddles when they got back to Omaha on their way home, but that did not satisfy Red Cloud, and he continued to nurse a grievance because Spotted Tail had been given horses.

On June 3, Red Cloud's party was taken to call on the Secretary of the Interior and then in carriages to tour the city. These wild people from the Powder River refused to enter any of the huge stone buildings. The whites were very clever at piling up big stones to a great height, but the Sioux were afraid the buildings would tumble down on them. On the fourth they were taken to the arsenal, where they saw more weapons than the Sioux had supposed the whole world possessed. They were more impressed by the suits of ancient armor than by the most modern firearms. But the fifteen-inch Rodman gun that sent a huge shell screaming off and skipping over the water four or five miles away did impress them, and so did the dress parade of a full regiment of marines. Spotted Tail and Red Cloud protested about all this sight-seeing. They said they had come on tribal business and wished to get it finished and go home.

On the evening of the sixth they were taken to dine in state at the White House, where they met the cabinet and members of the diplomatic corps. The officials were in formal dress, the ladies in evening gowns; most of the Sioux were in fine buckskin costumes. Two of the women of Red Cloud's party were at the dinner: Sans Arc Woman (wife of Chief Yellow Bear) and White Cow Rattler (wife of the warrior named Sword). The old-time Sioux names for girls and women were far, far removed from the ideas of romantic writers, who called one of Spotted Tail's daughters Prairie Flower and another White Fawn. Red Cloud and his wild men were too much overawed by the splendors of this banquet to speak a word; but Spotted Tail was perfectly at ease, and kept up a flow of talk through his interpreter. The Brulé chief was clever and witty. He remarked that the white people certainly did have handsome things, fine tipis, and grand food. The officials were not missing a chance to put their farming propaganda over, and one of them remarked that if Spotted Tail would go to work at farming, he also could soon have many fine things. The chief, his fine eyes twinkling, replied that if they would give him a tipi as fine as the White House, it might encourage him to take up farming as a career. President Grant burst into a hearty laugh, but did not offer to trade tipis with the chief.

On June 7, Red Cloud and his chiefs were taken to the Indian Office for the first business session. These chiefs had been brought to Washington for the avowed purpose of preventing a Sioux war. Red Cloud told the officials that he did not want war. He pictured the land of his group of Sioux as an island surrounded by white people. In this island were two hills—the Black Hills and the Bighorn Mountains, and now the whites were seeking gold and wanting roads through his land to the hills. He would have no new roads. Fort Fetterman had been built on the north side of the North Platte on his land, and he demanded that the fort be taken up and moved off his land. The officials brushed aside his talk and began urging him to leave his island and go to the reservation. Red Cloud brushed that aside. He said his people wanted trade; they needed many articles, particularly guns and ammunition. The whites need not fear a war. He and the other chiefs now realized that, compared with the teeming whites, the Sioux were but a small handful. They needed guns for hunting. He forgot his haughtiness and spoke in a conciliating tone. "I think I must in time go to farming, but I can't do it right now." Like all the chiefs, when he said, "I," he meant his people.

On the ninth, Red Cloud and his chiefs were taken to the White House for another talk with the President. Red Cloud now knew that the main object in bringing him to Washington was to talk him into going to the reservation. "I have said three times," he announced, "that I would not go to the Missouri, and now I say it for the fourth time." He told President Grant that the treaty of 1868 gave him the right to trade at Fort Laramie and to have an agency there. Grant made a mild and rather dull reply to the chief, and the Indians left the White House.

It was now apparent that the officials must explain the treaty of 1868 to Red Cloud, and in a general council on the tenth, the Secretary of the Interior began to do this. He demonstrated from the terms of the treaty that Red Cloud was wrong. The Sioux under the treaty had no right to trade at Fort Laramie or to have an agency in that neighborhood. Red Cloud, listening to the interpreter, became furiously angry. He shouted at the astonished cabinet official to put that lying paper away. It was all lies and a swindle. When he had been coaxed into signing that paper at Fort Laramie in 1868, he said, a lying curly-headed interpreter had assured him that the paper was nothing more than an agreement for peace. The other chiefs from the Powder River backed Red Cloud. Not one of them would admit that he had been told any terms in the treaty beyond the simple making of peace. Spotted Tail looked on. This was old Wooden Head's show, and he wished him luck in his efforts to argue the officials down or to frighten them. In the end they would force him to accept their view of the treaty. Meanwhile, without any shouting or displays of temper, Spotted Tail was painstakingly nudging the officials into accepting his view of the treaty and giving him what he desired: an agency far from the hated Missouri and the right to hunt on Republican Fork.

After this council on June 10 some of Red Cloud's chiefs attempted to commit suicide in their rooms at the Washington House. They said that they were ashamed to go home alive to tell the people how they had been lied to and cheated into signing the treaty in 1868. From Red Cloud down, they now all demanded to be taken home at once, for they considered their mission a tragic failure.

The high priests of the Indian Peace groups were aghast. If Red Cloud and his chiefs went home in their present mood, they said, a new Sioux war was certain to come. They swiftly evolved a plan for taking the chiefs to New York and having them speak before a great gathering of peace advocates at Cooper Union. Red Cloud refused to go. He said that he had had enough of towns and wished to go home. The chiefs were now practically kidnapped and put on a train for Philadelphia, where the Quakers and other Indian Friends were planning a great welcome for them. But when the party reached Philadelphia, the chiefs were in such a temper that General John E. Smith, who was in charge of them, decided that it would be better not to take them off the train. They went straight through to New York.

The great meeting in the hall of the Cooper Union on June 16

179

had been planned by church and humanitarian groups to put pressure on the government to give in to the Sioux and thus insure peace. Red Cloud was the central figure and hero of this public spectacle. The great audience adored him. When he got up on the platform and prayed to his pagan god, the Christians rose from their seats and prayed with him. They wept when he spoke of the children in his Indian camps whom he wished to see live, as if the government were planning to carry out a massacre of the innocents. Red Cloud was earnest and sincere, but his white listeners were too ignorant of conditions in the Sioux country to judge what was truth and what delusion in his speech. They did not wish to judge; they wished to have fervent faith. Dr. Crosby, a Protestant minister and most effective speaker, took Red Cloud's words from the interpreter and turned them into fiery English phrases. This added greatly to the effectiveness of the Sioux leader's address. A literal translation of what he was saying would have been more honest but not nearly as effective. One would like very much to know exactly what Red Cloud said about Spotted Tail and to what he was referring. He was reported as saying, "I am not Spotted Tail, to say one thing one day and to be bought for a pin the next." Spotted Tail was not wanted at this meeting; he was given no opportunity to speak; and it is impossible to even guess when and where he was bought with a pin. All the chiefs—including Red Cloud—had been bought in 1868, not with a pin, but with hundreds of thousands of dollars' worth of guns, ammunition, blankets, Indian goods, and food. Within a few weeks after this Cooper Union speech, Red Cloud was bought again, this time with an entire railway-train load of Indian goods.

After the speech-making the chiefs were shown the wonders of New York, but they kept demanding to be taken home. They went by way of Buffalo and Chicago to Omaha, where Red Cloud's party remained for two days, getting the horses and saddles promised them in Washington. Reaching Fort Laramie, they found that one thousand lodges of Sioux from Powder River were awaiting the return of the chiefs, in perfect faith that now they would be permitted to trade. General Smith reported by telegraph that if these Indians were denied trade, it would endanger peace. The officials gave in again. They had refused this right to trade at Fort Laramie in every council with Red Cloud, but now they granted it.

During the councils in Washington and the visit in New York, Spotted Tail had played a minor role in public. He was friendly and no one had to appease him; but while Red Cloud and his church and Quaker allies held the center of the stage, the Brulé chief worked quietly and persistently to right the wrong that had been done to his people when they had been forced by armed threats to leave their hunting grounds and go to an agency on the Missouri. It is true that he only managed to force half-promises from the unwilling officials; but he had learned enough about officials by this time to realize that half-promises might easily be turned into whole victories.[6]

The chiefs returned to Whetstone on July 7 and told the Indians that they had obtained permission to move the agency far from the Missouri, after which there was high hope that the Sioux could return to Republican Fork to hunt buffalo. The Indians were wild with delight. Captain Poole tried to stop the celebration by stating that the officials had made no definite promise, but were only considering the matter. The Sioux grew angry and said loudly that if not permitted to move from the river, they would go without permission. Poole wired to Washington that his Indians were getting out of hand and that he feared they would leave the agency and go off in a hostile mood. The worried officials conferred and wired to Poole that the permission to move the agency to a new location of the Indians' choice was granted.

Spotted Tail had won his two-year fight to get away from the Missouri River, but it is to be doubted that he foresaw any of the more striking results of his success. The Washington officials and the leaders among the whites of Dakota Territory had no idea of what was in the offing either. Curiously, it was only a small group of squaw men and Indians in Swift Bear's Corn Band that caught a glimpse of what the future had in store. These men vigorously

---

[6] For further details concerning this visit of Red Cloud and Spotted Tail to the East in June, 1870, see Hyde, *Red Cloud's Folk;* Turner, *Red Men Calling on the Great White Father;* Poole, *Among the Sioux of Dakota;* and General John E. Smith's report in the *Report of the Commissioner of Indian Affairs for 1870,* 324.

opposed removing the agency from the river. They said that there was very little land fit for farming on the Upper White River, where the new agency was to be located, and that once the agency had been established some two hundred miles west of the Missouri, the wild Sioux from Powder River would flock in and use force to prevent any man's shaming the tribe by attempting to work with his hands. That would mean the death of the government's main policy—to induce the Sioux to begin farming at once and learn to support themselves.

Certain squaw men and members of the Corn Band accused Swift Bear of helping Spotted Tail to scuttle the farming program. He denied it. He was as much in favor of farming as ever, but two years on the Missouri had convinced him that, if the Sioux stayed there, they would become too debauched by the whiskey sellers to farm or to do any other work. One of his sons had died recently and the chief had gone into deep mourning, cutting off his scalp lock and going about the agency barefooted and with nothing on except a ragged old black blanket. Spotted Tail was probably in the same state, as one of his younger wives, his favorite, is said to have died while he was in the East. These two chiefs had achieved the almost impossible felicity of becoming popular among the Dakota whites, who as a rule hated Indians wholeheartedly; but now the Dakota editors were enthusiastic over the chiefs' plan to remove the agency to a point far west on White River, because the move would give handsome profits to the Dakota contractors who obtained the work of transporting supplies in wagons to the distant agency. Moreover, the new agency would be only sixty miles from the Black Hills, and the Dakota leaders told each other jubilantly that this agency would be the gateway through which white men could get into the hills and exploit their reportedly rich gold deposits. One would have thought from the way some of these Dakota worthies talked that Spotted Tail had gone to Washington solely to gain favors for them. Clasping Whetstone on the Missouri in their hand, they let it fly away, thinking that they had a thread tied to its leg; and when they found later on that there was no thread, they hated Spotted Tail.

No Sioux belonging to separate bands could settle anything without quarreling, and from July to October, 1870, the Whetstone Sioux quarreled. A tiny minority wanted to remain on the Missouri; one group wanted the new agency at the forks of White River; but the majority wanted to go far west and place the agency at or near Butte Cache at the mouth of Big White Clay Creek, which had been a famous camping place for the Brulés when Spotted Tail was born. While this quarrel was in progress, another matter came up that made the Sioux very angry. Congress was again delaying the Indian appropriations, and no annuity goods had been sent to Whetstone. The Sioux were eager to move away from the Missouri, but they could not go until they were outfitted for the coming winter by the arrival of the annuity clothing. They were in such a temper that William Welsh, a member of the Board of Indian Commissioners, who was visiting in Dakota, was urged to come to Whetstone and talk to the Indians. William Welsh was a typical Christian philanthropist of his period. He gladly came to help his red brothers at Whetstone. He gave them soothing syrup, and let himself be sold on the idea of moving the agency two hundred miles up White River. These Christian meddlers in government and Indian affairs were amazing. Welsh was sold on the removal of the agency because it would take the Sioux far enough from the Missouri to end the whiskey-peddling menace. Neither he nor any of his Christian friends realized that the removal would kill the farming plans which they considered vital.

Spotted Tail and Swift Bear were away when Welsh visited the agency. They had been taken down the Missouri to visit the Christian Santee Sioux on a little reservation in Nebraska. The Santees were all Christians. They had placed themselves absolutely under the control of their missionaries, and they had little thought for anything in the world beyond piety. Swift Bear may have been a bit impressed, as he had some leanings toward Christianity; but Spotted Tail was only shocked that this little remnant of the Santees, once the leaders of the Sioux Nation and looked up to by his own Brulés, should have come to this condition, making themselves into imitation white people, and the praying kind of white people at that. He went home to Whetstone, and when he heard of William Welsh's visit, he wrote Welsh a letter, dictating it to a squaw man, November 15, 1870. This was the first known letter ever sent through the mails by a chief of the Western Sioux. Spotted Tail's education was advancing. He wrote to William Welsh to gain his backing for the removal of the agency to the Upper White River, and he tried to please Welsh by asking for missionaries and stating that the location chosen for the new agency was in a fine district for farming. This was wicked deception; but Spotted Tail had been deceived by the whites in 1868, when they had sugar-coated the treaty and trapped his people into going to the reservation, and he was now using the same tactics to get his people out of the trap they had been led into. William Welsh had helped make that treaty and was now fair game. Spotted Tail even sold him on the idea of shifting the Whetstone base of supplies from the Missouri to the Platte; and on his way home from Dakota, Welsh stopped off in Omaha and found that the Union Pacific Railroad was willing to make a special low rate for hauling Spotted Tail's supplies by rail to Cheyenne, Wyoming, from which town they could be taken in wagons via Fort Laramie to the agency. That was exactly what Spotted Tail desired—to renew his old friendships and alliances with the whites near Fort Laramie. He was not in the least interested in saving the government money on transportation. He did not even realize that he was stabbing the Dakota whites in the back by taking their transportation profits from them. (Nor did Brother Welsh.)

In this letter the chief said, "In my camp I have three villages: one Ogalalla, say 200 lodges, Black Bear is their chief; the Brulé Wanagi [Ghost] camp 150 lodges, Red Leaf is their chief; the Upper Brulés 225 lodges, Spotted Tail is their chief." "Wanagi" is a name not elsewhere mentioned; they were the Wazhazhas under Red Leaf. Spotted Tail did not include the Corn Band and other camps at the agency, only the Indians in his camp up on White River. He listed 575 lodges. In the spring of 1865 he had come down from Powder River to Fort Laramie, a broken chief with a tiny camp of very poor people. He had built that little camp up to its 1870 numbers mainly through the fact that he was the one chief with an outstanding ability for leadership among the Sioux on and south of the Platte.

Setting aside the taffy put into this letter to please the taste of the

Eastern church and humanitarian leaders, Spotted Tail disclosed his true objectives. His main purpose was to put on the brakes. The white officials and their self-styled Indian Friends advisers wanted to take control of the Sioux and suddenly change their way of life completely. By urging that squaw men be put on the agency employee list and given the transportation contracts, the chief was planning to whittle down the authority of the government agent and make it impossible for him to carry out the government plan to destroy the power of the chiefs. Squaw men were the chiefs' men and would act in the interests of the chiefs they followed. Spotted Tail's plans were not constructive. He did not intend them to be; for he had his mind made up that the sudden changing of his people along the lines planned in Washington would be a tragedy, and he was hoping to stave off these changes or slow them down during his own time.[7]

[7] This letter is printed in William Welsh's pamphlet, *Sioux and Ponca Indians* (Philadelphia, 1870). The letter has Spotted Tail's name signed to it "per Bissinett."

8. The Fruit
of Appeasement

DURING THE FOLLOWING THREE YEARS at the new Whetstone Agency on the Upper White River, the government's Indian Peace Policy, a policy of appeasement toward the Sioux, met the acid test and was proven to be false coin. The plan to buy the friendship of these Indians failed, the farm program failed, and the plan to break the power of the chiefs and put the Sioux completely under the control of white agents also failed. Instead of peace this appeasement policy was bringing on a new Indian war. All this was the result of permitting the Sioux to move to a point on White River near the Black Hills, and Spotted Tail was mainly responsible for obtaining the consent of the officials to make that move. Yet it is perfectly clear that he was not planning war. He had become more convinced than ever during his visit to Washington that it would be madness for the Sioux to go to war with the whites. The Peace Policy was one he approved of; yet he took a leading part in destroying it, simply by demanding the right to move away from the Missouri River. William Welsh, a high priest of the Peace Policy, also had a hand in pulling that policy down, but, like Spotted Tail, he did not realize what he was doing.

It is difficult to believe that Spotted Tail really intended to encourage his Sioux to farm. Farming was a talking point in his plan to obtain permission to leave the Missouri, and he used that point adroitly. He employed it in his talks with the officials in Washington, and in his letter to William Welsh, he convinced that trusting gentleman that the main object of removing from the Missouri was to find better farm land up White River. Welsh heartily approved of this, Captain Poole approved, the Dakota editors were enthusiastic over the plan, and only a few squaw men and mixed-bloods (who knew that the White River country was a very poor locality for farming) objected. These men really wanted to farm, and they opposed Spotted Tail's plan with all their strength. But they were a small group, and no one bothered about them—no one except Spotted Tail and Swift Bear, who made it clear that if they continued their outcries, they would be soldiered by the warriors who kept order in the camps. Being soldiered was not amusing. Your horses were shot and the windows of your cabin, if you had one, were shot out, and if you did not take the hint, you were shot.

Swift Bear's support of Spotted Tail is a curious feature of this movement. This Corn Band chief wanted to live like a white man and was eager to farm. Part of his own band bitterly opposed moving the agency away from the Missouri. They agreed with the squaw men and mixed-bloods that any such move would kill all hopes of getting started at farming. But there was another side to the problem. Swift Bear was convinced that if the Indians remained on the Missouri, they would be demoralized by the whiskey peddlers, but if the agency was moved two hundred miles to the west, it would be impossible to run whiskey in any quantity to the new location from the Missouri. Swift Bear therefore supported Spotted Tail and helped him to deal with the incipient revolt of the minority in the agency camps that opposed removal.

Spotted Tail wished to keep Captain Poole as his agent. He liked army officers; he liked Poole and his wife, and he urged William Welsh to speak for Poole, saying that it was poor policy to remove a good agent and replace him by an inexperienced man. But by this time President Grant had been persuaded to put the churches in control of the appointment of agents, and in November the Episcopal church chose J. M. Washburn for the new agent at Whetstone, and he was appointed. Captain Poole was detailed to command the infantry that guarded the government property at the old agency on the Missouri; Agent Washburn came out and went up White River to visit the Sioux in their winter camp at Butte Cache, at the mouth of Big White Clay Creek. Stephen S. Estes, Poole's chief clerk and Spotted Tail's close friend, was at Butte Cache, acting as subagent. He had already started issuing rations and beef. On December 21, 1870, the Yankton newspaper reported that the majority of the Sioux were at Big White Clay Creek, but on January 4 the paper reported that 125 lodges, or 1,000 Indians (Corn Band and Loafers), were still at the old agency, and Spotted Tail was there, too sick to make the winter journey up White River. This newspaper was very happy over the move. It stated that the new agency was only forty-nine miles from the Black Hills, and would be the natural gateway for white men to pass through to reach the hills and their golden treasures. Spotted Tail, by insisting on moving the agency from the Missouri, had initiated "a grand step toward opening up that country" to white settlement.[1]

This new Whetstone Agency, high up White River in the winter of 1870–71, was not a real agency, but simply a Sioux winter camp near which the chiefs wished to have their new agency built. Spotted Tail and Swift Bear had picked as good a location as was to be found on the Upper White River. The land near the mouth of Big White Clay Creek was not good; but higher up the creek (where Red Cloud's Sioux were settled in 1878 at the new Pine Ridge Agency) there was good farming land, and to the eastward was even more good land along creek valleys, with good water and a fair stand of timber. The new Whetstone Agency should have been built here on Big White Clay Creek, but no one took the trouble to examine the land higher up the creek and along the other streams to the east, and in June the agency was moved to a site that was impossible; in 1872 it was moved to another bad site; in 1874 it was moved to a good site but off the reservation and in Nebraska, where it could not remain. Commissions sent to the agency to investigate wrote scathing reports on the folly and waste of each removal.

Spotted Tail, by cornering the Washington officials and getting them to approve the removal of his agency to White River, had put his tribe on the wing, and whether he had foreseen that or not, it was a situation that pleased him. Each removal of the agency meant the spending of great sums and the letting down of all the government controls for the time being. He objected to government con-

---

[1] Most of these details are taken from the Dakota newspapers of the day. I am indebted to Harry H. Anderson and Dean Herbert S. Schell of the Graduate School, University of South Dakota, for the extracts they have kindly sent me from these old newspapers.

trol; he objected to the plan for hurrying his Indians into making an effort at self-support through farming; and how could the Sioux farm when their agency was mounted on wheels and was being rolled away to a new location each year?

Agent Washburn spent only a few days with his Indians at Butte Cache in December, 1870. He then returned to the agency on the Missouri, went from there to visit his family in Yankton, and his Sioux did not see him again until April, 1871. He then returned to the old agency to order the removal to the new one. At this time, in April, "the Frenchmen of Whetstone" were shouting themselves hoarse in opposition to removal. By "Frenchmen," the Yankton newspaper meant the former Indian traders, who were in the main French. A number of American squaw men were with them, and just as bitter over the removal of the agency as the French were. But Washburn had his orders from Washington. He called for bids on a contract to haul supplies and heavy property from Whetstone on the Missouri to Whetstone on White River, a distance of over two hundred miles, and John W. Smith, the principal trader at the old agency, got this contract. Another bit of business was the asking for bids to supply the new Whetstone Agency with 3,962,000 pounds of fresh beef during the year 1871.

The move up White River now began. On May 10 the last of the squaw men who had insisted on remaining at the old agency gave in and started for White River. On June 10 it was reported that Washburn had found the location of the new agency unsatisfactory. The soil was barren and dry; Swift Bear and his "Corn Planters" were eager to farm; Spotted Tail was blocking any attempt at progress. The Yankton newspaper now called this the Black Hills Agency and reported that it was 210 miles from the old Whetstone Agency by a good road.

There was a fight in progress at the new agency. A proposal was made to move about fifty miles higher up White River and to establish the agency there, but we do not know whether Spotted Tail proposed the move or the agent was talked into making it by Swift Bear and the "progressives," which was a newly coined name applied to those Indians who were willing to try farming. The new location suggested for the agency was on or near Little White Clay Creek, near Crow Butte and close to the present town of Crawford, Nebraska. This neighborhood was the one the Sioux called White Cliffs, and it had been a favorite winter camp of the Brulés from about 1820 until after 1860.[2]

Washburn and the Indians reached Little White Clay Creek on June 24, and work was started at once, putting up warehouses and other agency buildings. The agent reported that this was a good farming district, although the soil was burned by drought. No one told him that this was the usual condition and that in this region one good crop in four years was considered good fortune. The truth was that if anyone had benefited by removal to Little White Clay Creek, it was Spotted Tail, who did not intend to encourage farming. His object was to reopen friendly relations with the traders and other white men he knew down on the Platte, then to resume hunting on Republican Fork, and the new agency was as close to the Platte as he could get without leaving White River.

The Dakota editors now began to suspect that someone had basely deceived them. Their dream of Dakota men growing rich from supplying Spotted Tail's agency high up White River were disturbed by the news that the annuity goods for Spotted Tail had not been sent up the Missouri, to be hauled in Dakota wagon trains to the agency, but had been shipped along the Union Pacific to Cheyenne, Wyoming, to be sent thence to Fort Laramie in wagons. The Dakota newspapers promptly forgot how highly they had approved of the agency's being moved up White River; the removal, they said, was a scheme of the human cormorants in Nebraska and Wyoming for depriving Dakota men of their rightful profits and enriching themselves by having the base of supply for Spotted Tail shifted from the Missouri to the Platte. They suddenly discovered that all the

[2] There has been a deal of controversy about the location of this agency of 1871. It was removed in the following year, the buildings taken down and hauled to a new site, and the old location was left almost without a mark to indicate it had ever existed. To add to the confusion, the winter camp had been on Big White Clay Creek, the agency on Little White Clay Creek, and men who spoke of the two places got mixed up, calling the stream near the new agency Big White Clay Creek and imagining it the stream of that name over fifty miles farther down White River. The agency does not appear to have been on Little White Clay Creek, as it is usually stated that it was twelve miles below the later Red Cloud Agency. On a map, Red Cloud Agency is nearer to being five miles above Little White Clay Creek.

Indians were dissatisfied with the new location, and they started a movement to have the agency moved back to the Missouri. But it was too late. Spotted Tail and a majority of his people loved the new location. They would never return willingly to the Missouri. And Spotted Tail had two handsome aces in the hole that would defeat any such play. His first ace was Red Cloud; his second was (of all the unlikely persons) the Grand Duke Alexis of Russia.

When Red Cloud had started homeward from New York in June, 1870, he had been in a very glum mood and angry with both the white officials and Spotted Tail. The Peace Policy leaders were so afraid that he would start a new war that they induced the officials to appoint a commission of two good men and send them out on the trail of the angry Oglala chief. A trainload of Indian goods was also sent to put the Sioux in a happier mood. In September, Red Cloud's people came to Fort Laramie, were given all the gifts, and held councils with the two commissioners. Red Cloud was urged to accept an agency and free rations and clothing for his people, but he would not have an agency anywhere except at Fort Laramie, and the government refused to permit that.

Still fearing that Red Cloud would start war, the officials gave in sufficiently to establish a temporary agency at Fort Laramie for his Indians, and in 1871 the Sioux flocked down to the fort to draw free rations and supplies and to trade. An agent for Red Cloud, J. W. Wham, now arrived at the fort; more councils were held with the chiefs, and in the name of peace, Mr. Wham forgot the government's decision never to permit Red Cloud to have an agency on the Platte and agreed to establish the agency on the north bank of the river, just west of the Nebraska line. Thus Red Cloud and Spotted Tail were at agencies within easy reach of each other, and for a season the two chiefs forgot their differences and became allies.

Spotted Tail was having wonderful luck. The Grand Duke Alexis of Russia was planning a journey to the western plains with a large entourage for the coming autumn or winter. The Grand Duke had expressed a wish to hunt buffalo and to witness an Indian hunt; and the officials in Washington, forgetting that it was a main point of policy to make Spotted Tail remain at his agency and farm, had the chief notified that he and his people were to go to their old hunting grounds on Republican Fork, there to meet and entertain the imperial guest from Russia. Spotted Tail had been told in 1868 that if he did not leave those hunting grounds, the troops would attack and drive him to the reservation. He had been firmly repulsed in all his attempts to obtain permission to hunt; and now the officials were asking him to go back to his lost hunting grounds as a special favor to them.

The Brulés were greatly excited and filled with pleasure. They were going back to their hunting grounds, and they were going in glory. Every man in the Spotted Tail camp bankrupted himself to obtain a handsome costume and new weapons, new tipis, and camp equipment. Even Agent Washburn and Swift Bear forgot the sacred farming program. They left the agency to take care of itself and set off for the Platte.

They were to arrange for the hauling of the annuity goods to the agency, and Spotted Tail intended to visit his old haunts at Fort Laramie and take the bones of his daughter, who had been buried at the fort in the spring of 1866, to his new agency.[3] The annuity goods had been shipped on the Union Pacific to Cheyenne, Wyoming, and had there been loaded on a wagon train and sent up to Fort Laramie. The wagons were to cross the North Platte near the fort and go on northward to Whetstone Agency on the head of White River; but when Washburn, Spotted Tail, and Swift Bear got to Fort Laramie, the wagons were halted and did not dare to cross the Platte. Red Cloud and his Indians were carrying out their part of the program. The Sioux were staging a new threat of war. They said that the land north of the Platte was theirs, the treaty of 1868 provided that no white men should come north of the North Platte, and if these wagons and the white men with them crossed the river, there would be a big fight. Riding up and down in large bands, the Sioux whipped themselves into a fury.

The commanding officer at the fort and the boss of the wagon train appealed to Agent Washburn, but Washburn could see no solution of this difficulty. Spotted Tail was wonderfully friendly

[3] The wagon-train trouble prevented Spotted Tail's taking the girl's remains home at this time. He came back to Fort Laramie in the summer of 1876, had the bones packed, and took them to his agency. See Hafen and Young, *Fort Laramie*, 384.

but declined to interfere. He rejected the proposal that he and his warriors guard the wagons, and he gave his opinion that if the wagons crossed north of the Platte, there would be war. Spotted Tail and Agent Washburn then left Fort Laramie, but Swift Bear remained and presently offered to obtain permission from the Indians for the train to go through. D. J. McCann, the freighting contractor, accepted this proposal with relief, and Swift Bear went off to make contact with the Sioux. He was to be back in eight days, but he failed to return or to send a message. McCann then applied to the commanding officer at the fort for a military escort, and was granted one. Then Richard Smith, who was representing Agent Wham of the Red Cloud Agency at the fort, wrote a formal protest to the commanding officer, stating that the instant his troops crossed north of the Platte, the Sioux would attack them. The commandant knew that this was true. He telegraphed to department headquarters in Omaha, asking for instructions, and Richard Smith telegraphed to the Indian Office in Washington, warning that a Sioux war was imminent and asking if, for the sake of peace, Spotted Tail's people might not be given permission to come down to the Platte to get their goods. At this period the officials would do anything for the sake of peace with the Sioux. They telegraphed the necessary instructions, and the war was over.

The wagon train took the goods to the new Red Cloud Agency on the north bank of the North Platte, and Spotted Tail came down from his agency with 465 lodges of Sioux, leaving Agent Washburn at the agency on White River with practically no Indians to care for. At Red Cloud Agency the Brulés received their treaty annuities, the delivery of which had almost brought on a war. Among the articles in this shipment were included 2,450 pairs of fine Indian blankets. (The Sioux were very particular about size, quality, and color of these free blankets. The men preferred dark colors—dark blue, dark green, and dark red.) There were cases of fine blue Indian cloth and cases of red, nine huge cases of prints, two of Melton cloth, eight of blue drill, forty-eight cases of camp kettles, forty-eight dozen axes, and many additional articles of camp equipment. There were boxes of tobacco, and a score of cases of shirts, socks, pants, coats, and hats. All of these articles of white men's clothing the

Sioux did not want; but the officials were determined to turn them into imitation white men. Their success was minor, as the Indians traded most of the articles of clothing for ammunition or whiskey or cut the garments up and made them over into proper wearing apparel for the Sioux.

The government had planned since 1866 to remove all Indians from the Platte and the lands to the south; it had used troops to drive some of the Sioux out; it had sternly forbidden Spotted Tail's and Red Cloud's Indians to come to the Platte, and had forbidden all trade in that district. Spotted Tail, by a little planning, and Red Cloud, by his stubbornness, had wrecked the government's policy. They were all back on the Platte once more; and as soon as Spotted Tail had received his annuities, he crossed south of the river, taking his own people and nearly all of Red Cloud's with him, and went down to Republican Fork on a buffalo hunt. His new friend, Red Cloud, went with him; so did Little Wound with his Southern Oglalas, who had been chased out of their camp down near the Republican in 1869 by troops and sent in panic flight north of the Platte. Even Red Leaf and his Wazhazhas now joined Spotted Tail and went south to hunt. In the four camps were a total of 6,000 Sioux. It was impossible to hunt buffalo with such a big group operating together. Spotted Tail made camp on the Stinking Water Fork of the Republican; he had 1,200 Brulés and also the Red Leaf Wazhazha camp with him. The Oglalas camped at the forks of the Republican, sixty to seventy miles from Spotted Tail's camp.

Agent Washburn had now been at Whetstone for nearly a year, or (to be more accurate) he had paid occasional visits to the agency during that period of time. He was probably the good Christian and honest man the Episcopal church authorities had stated him to be when they had nominated him to be agent, but during the whole of his time at Whetstone he had not done or said one thing to indicate what his true character was. He had his family at Yankton, about three hundred miles from the agency, and he spent much of his time traveling to Yankton to visit his family. When he was not thus employed, he was making journeys to Washington at public expense. Spotted Tail and Swift Bear needed an agent who would stay at the agency—a man they could respect and like, one who would give them advice and at least attempt to make them take it. Washburn was not the man to do that. When Spotted Tail started for the Platte, Washburn appointed his friend, Trader Yates, to go with the Indians as subagent. Washburn then went to Yankton to see his family, and as soon as he had gone, Spotted Tail brushed Yates off and appointed as his subagent "a disreputable white man named Todd Randall." Randall was married to the sister of Yellow Hair, a Wazhazha head soldier. He was a shrewd and rather able man who knew the Sioux very well, gave advice to the chiefs, and (when he had to) took orders from them. As subagent in this hunting camp, he let Spotted Tail take control. Thus for the time being, Spotted Tail threw off all government control, and from August, 1871, to April, 1872, he and his people were free again, supporting themselves by hunting; and all the labor and the millions of dollars expended by the officials in their effort to control the Brulés proved ineffective.

In January, the Grand Duke Alexis and his entourage came out along the Union Pacific to North Platte, where Generals Sheridan and Custer met him and made the final arrangements for the hunting trip to Republican Fork. Spotted Tail had several hundred of his warriors splendidly equipped and was awaiting the arrival of the Russian party and their military escort. Twenty-five big wagons loaded with food went from Fort McPherson to the Brulé camp, and letters were sent to the chief to make final arrangements. Spotted Tail dictated replies to General Sheridan, Todd Randall writing the letters, which was apparently all the work he did to earn his pay as official subagent. Red Cloud and the other important Sioux chiefs sulked in their distant camps. Why had Spotted Tail and his plaguy Brulés been chosen to mingle with all these white officers and king's sons in glittering uniforms, and why had twenty-five wagons loaded with fine food been sent to the Brulé camp and none to any of the other camps?

The Grand Duke's party left the Platte on January 13, escorted by Generals Sheridan and Custer, with a picked force of cavalry, including a Negro troop. They met Spotted Tail with a picked camp of six hundred Brulés on the Red Willow and proceeded to hunt buffalo. The Brulés had their families with them, and both the people and the camp were spick and span, with fine tanned-skin clothing and new tipis. The chief and eight picked warriors accompanied the Grand Duke on all the hunts, and one day the Brulé men made a surround of a herd in the old Sioux fashion, pursuing the buffalo on horseback and killing them with bows and lances. In the camp at night the Indians entertained the Grand Duke and his party with dancing and feasting. Custer flirted shamelessly with Spotted Tail's sixteen-year-old daughter, and the Grand Duke gave the chief and all the members of his family handsome gifts. To each Brulé warrior he gave a fine hunting knife with an ivory handle. These knives were made specially for the Czar's imperial huntsmen and to be given to distinguished guests at the Czar's hunting parties in Russia.[4]

This was a cold winter with much snow, and after the hunting in December and January, the Sioux settled down in their camps. They were not altogether happy; the chiefs, at any rate, thinking of the future, and it was not to their liking. When they had last been in these hunting grounds in 1868, it had been an Indian country. Now, in 1871–72, the white cattlemen were taking over and were running large herds. The last of the buffalo herds would be destroyed very soon, and then this would be a white man's country in the lands south of the Platte.

This winter some of the Sioux killed cattle when they ran out of buffalo meat. When spring came, some of the cattlemen turned up in the Sioux camps—John Bratt, men representing the Coe and Carter Company, and others—and they got hold of Todd Randall, who was with Spotted Tail, and Leon Palladay, who was trading in the Oglala camp, and got written statements from them. They also induced Spotted Tail and other chiefs to put their *X*-marks to papers admitting that their Indians had killed some cattle. One of the cattle companies put in a claim for four hundred head at $45 a

[4] The best account of the Grand Duke's hunt in Nebraska will be found in the Lincoln, Nebraska, *State Journal*, December, 1871, to January, 1872. Paine's *Pioneers, Indians, and Buffaloes* reprints some of the reports from this newspaper. Agent Wham, of the Red Cloud Agency, was the one who reported that Spotted Tail rejected Yates as subagent and appointed Todd Randall in his place. Spotted Tail's own camp was first on the Stinking Water, then in December on Blackwood Creek, and in January on the Red Willow.

head—$20,250, and the others followed the lead. The government paid the bills; but later someone talked too much, and in 1877 the U. S. district attorney at North Platte brought suit against the cattlemen for fraud and won the case. Spotted Tail made an affidavit. He said in this document that among his own people he was known as Speaks-to-the-Woman but that the whites called him Spotted Tail. He stated that he thought his camp killed about fifteen head of cattle that winter but that Todd Randall had him sign a paper which increased the number of animals killed by twenty. The other Indians signed similar affidavits.[5]

Spotted Tail brought his Indians back to Whetstone Agency in the spring of 1872. Agent Washburn now appeared, but stayed only long enough to induce Spotted Tail, Swift Bear, Two Strike, and another chief to go to Washington with him. In 1870, Spotted Tail had maneuvered the officials into permitting him to move the agency from the Missouri to the Upper White River; now, in 1872, the officials, informed that the new location was not fit for farming, were begging the chief to permit them to move the agency to a location where the soil was more fitted to the growing of crops. Agent Washburn had not been at his agency in summer for any length of time and had done nothing about farming; Spotted Tail and the majority of his Brulés were using pressure on the Corn Band to prevent their planting even small patches of corn, yet the Eastern Friends of the Indians and the officials clung to their dream of making all the Sioux self-supporting from the soil in three or four years. They now proceeded to bribe Spotted Tail and the other chiefs with handsome promises to induce them to agree to removal to a better location. Spotted Tail got back to White River in mid-

[5] This case is covered in Paine, *Pioneers, Indians, and Buffaloes;* also in *Nebraska History Magazine*, Vol. XV, No. 1. Spotted Tail's name, Speaks-to-the-Woman, is not mentioned elsewhere. It was probably a nickname, making fun of the chief for talking to women. In Sioux, "to talk to a woman" meant to court her, most of the Sioux warriors being too proud to speak to a woman for any other purpose. Spotted Tail evidently was pleased with the name, or he would not have referred to it in his affidavit. He was not ashamed of liking women and talking to them, even in public. In Washington, while being shown the wonders of the Corcoran Gallery of Art, he shocked the cultured gentlemen who were conducting him by stating that he would rather be out on Pennsylvania Avenue watching the pretty women go by.

summer and at once prepared to take his Indians south of the Platte on another buffalo hunt, to remain all winter. Meantime, Agent Washburn was relieved, and D. R. Risley, of Omaha, Nebraska, was appointed agent. Risley, like Washburn, had been nominated by Bishop Whipple of the English Episcopal church as an intelligent, energetic, and honorable man. These two agents may have been all that, but they knew nothing concerning Indians, and in the whole term of their service they did not perform one outstanding action that would indicate what type of men they were. Washburn was away from his agency most of the time, but Risley bettered his record, for it was reported that he was at the agency exactly thirty-six days during the year he acted as agent. What was the sense of spending great sums of public money on a scheme to rush the Indians quickly into self-support and to put them under government control when the agent left his agency for most of the year to be run by the chiefs and their squaw-man advisers?

Captain Poole, while he was agent, had found both of the leading chiefs friendly, willing to co-operate with him, and ready to consider any plan that they regarded as intended to benefit their people. Now, in 1871–72, the church-recommended agents left the chiefs to be advised by squaw men and other whites whose object was to make money, usually by shady activities. Neither Spotted Tail nor Swift Bear had had any training in the ethics of civilized life; they had difficulty in judging what was right and what wrong, and they were easily talked around by the white men at the agency. It was the same at the new Red Cloud Agency, where the squaw men were busy hatching schemes for getting money out of the government and inducing Red Cloud and the other chiefs to support their plans. The Sioux at these agencies had taken care of themselves in their hunting camps, the men working at hunting, which was hard work and often dangerous, the women doing all the camp labor. Now on the reservation neither the Indian men nor the women had any real work. It was a pleasure jaunt to ride a few miles to the agency on their ponies for their rations, no trouble to cut and carry wood for the campfires; yet the squaw men developed a swindling scheme to have themselves employed to haul rations to the Indian camps and to cut and haul wood for the Sioux.

The squaw men and the wagon-freighters were charging the government so much per hundred pounds for given distances, and they usually were permitted to make their own estimate of the number of miles hauled. Even the agents nominated by the churches did not seem to care. Termed honest and intelligent, they did not think it important whether the distance charged for hauling was really seventy miles or only thirty-three. They kept no proper books, gaily handing out about four million pounds of beef and the same weight of other rations at Whetstone each year, taking the Sioux's word for the number of Indians to be given rations, and rarely bothering to weigh anything. No wonder the Sioux (and the squaw men) called Whetstone and Red Cloud "fat agencies." The government was paying for great quantities of flour and pickled pork that the Indians simply threw away. Even the Indian dogs were getting so many beef pickings that they had grown choosy and would not touch the pickled pork that was being left on the ground.

In 1872 the great object of the planners in Washington was to move Whetstone to a good farming location and to move Red Cloud Agency from the North Platte northward to White River. They were so intent on this that they failed to notice that the agencies on White River would be outside the Sioux reservation and in Nebraska, where they had no legal right to be. They also overlooked the vital fact that in order to control these Sioux and try to induce them to go to work, it would be necessary to separate each group widely from the others. They were concentrating the Sioux in a mass on White River, where they were sure to lose all control over them. But Red Cloud would not move north. He claimed that all the land north of the Platte belonged to him, that no white man, not even the government agent and his employees, had any right to come north of the Platte, and he was demanding that his agency should be moved south of the river. He threatened war, and Agent J. W. Daniels had to ask for troops from Fort Laramie to protect the lives of the whites at the agency and the government property. No troops came. The official policy was still to appease the Sioux.

In June of this year the officials had Spotted Tail and a large delegation come to Washington to talk of removal of the agency to a site favorable for farming. Someone had suggested the mouth of the South Fork of White River, a point less than half the distance from the base of supply on the Missouri than the location of Whetstone in 1872. Spotted Tail took his favorite wife and her baby on this trip East, and in Washington they were all three photographed. Whatever the chiefs said in Washington, the move to the South Fork of White River was never heard of again, and when Whetstone was moved, it was placed in a location at the mouth of Beaver Creek that was unfit for farming. Spotted Tail was reported to have insisted on removal to this site. Again he had had his own way.

During this visit in Washington another subject was discussed: the sale of Sioux hunting rights in Nebraska. Standing Bear, a Sioux author, states in his book that Spotted Tail sold the Sioux lands in Nebraska in a secret agreement and kept the money. This is an example of the stories the modern Sioux relate concerning their own great chief. The truth was that Standing Bear's own father was a member of the delegation that went to Washington with Spotted Tail and took part in all the talks. No agreement was reached. The matter was discussed openly in councils until 1875, when the Sioux (again in open council) approved the sale. Red Cloud and the other chiefs have been the target of these modern Sioux stories that tell of chiefs' secretly selling lands and slipping by at night, carrying bags of gold under their blankets. These are not even good bedtime tales for little tots.

Spotted Tail and most of his Indians were hunting on Republican Fork when Agent Risley moved Whetstone to the new location, late in the year 1872. The government had gone to great expense to induce the chiefs to agree to this removal; yet when the move came, it was bungled. There was a terrific scandal about it in the following year. The contract for moving the agency was given to Dr. Graves— a shadowy figure, a friend of someone higher up. Graves turned over the job to the trader Yates; Yates hired squaw men with teams and wagons to do the hauling; someone handed the haulers' vouchers, and Yates, as he claimed, paid the men and then could not get payment from the government. The new location was on the south bank of White River at the mouth of Beaver Creek. The distance from the old agency to the new one was less than forty miles, but the men were paid for a haul of from seventy-five to eighty-seven miles. The amount of haulage was padded, and the Sioux (who were perfectly capable of moving themselves and their camp equipment) were hauled in wagons at a cost of so much per hundred pounds of Indians, charged to the government. Agent Risley was reported to have been away during this fine performance; to add to the scandal, the new site was no better than the old one, and as a farming location just as worthless.[6]

At the time of this removal Agent Risley was pleased, the officials in Washington were satisfied, and there was not a word of criticism; but presently the air was filled with loud and angry voices, and most of them were blaming Spotted Tail. This highhanded chief had moved his Indians to a locality where it would be impossible for them to farm, because he was personally opposed to all progress in civilization. The fact was overlooked that the main body of his Indians were just as opposed to progress as he was and that they were getting out of hand—so much so that Spotted Tail was having difficulty in controlling them. The insidious poison of the government appeasement policy was at work among the Brulés. These Indians had stood for peace and friendly relations with the whites; but they were being led by the government's policy of giving in and giving in to a conclusion natural enough from their ignorant point of view. They imagined that the whites were afraid of them. Spotted Tail was friendly, and he knew what his followers did not know— the power of the Americans. He had had his eyes open while he was in the East in 1870; he had noted several cities that held more white people than all the Sioux Nation put together, and he had found in New York that in that one city more white people came

---

[6] If this had been a private business enterprise, several men would have gone to state prison; but in 1872 (and today) men accused of defrauding the government rarely have to pay a penalty. In 1873 two retired army officers, Alvord and Kemble, were sent to investigate this agency removal and other affairs at Whetstone. They shouted fraud and accused Agent Risley of absconding, taking his chief clerk and all the agency books, just before they reached the agency to start their investigation. Agent Daniels of Red Cloud Agency was then ordered by Washington to investigate. He found Risley and his books at Omaha, made a careful investigation, and exonerated Risley. Like so many government investigations, there was a great deal of shouting and pointing of accusing fingers, and then the public and the Washington authorities forgot the whole affair. The papers are printed in *Report of the Investigation of Affairs at Red Cloud Agency*, 1875.

across the sea every year to add their numbers to the population of the Americans than the Sioux could number in their tribe. By moving away from the Missouri River to his present location, he had hoped to slow down the government's efforts to force his Indians to abandon their old ways suddenly and adopt those of the whites; but now, in 1872, it was beginning to look as if the Brulés were turning the tables on Washington and had the officials treed. Spotted Tail was facing a new problem. Was he to side with the officials and, perhaps, be treed along with them, or was he to lead his tribe along the uncertain way they were heading, which might end in war? What the Brulés needed at this moment more than anything else was the appearance of a regiment or two of cavalry close to their camps, to exhibit to them the fact that the Americans were not all fools and weaklings.

When the agency was moved to the mouth of Beaver Creek in the winter of 1872–73, Spotted Tail (supposed by the later official view to have been directing the removal) was far to the south, hunting buffalo on Republican Fork. So were all the leading chiefs, even Swift Bear, that good progressive. Most of the Indians were in the hunting camps. Agent Risley was in Washington, pulling wires to get the contract for moving the agency approved and paid for.

Spotted Tail and his buffalo hunters came back to the agency in the spring of 1873 in time to put pressure on anyone at Whetstone who wished to try farming. They did not have to make any very loud threats. Even Agent Risley was not able to work up any real enthusiasm for planting crops. He was being relieved, and a new agent, E. A. Howard, had come to take over. Meantime the agent at Red Cloud took advantage of the fact that the main body of his Indians were absent on a hunting trip and moved the agency suddenly from the Platte some seventy-five miles to a point on White River, about ten miles west of where Whetstone Agency had stood in 1871–72 and some forty miles west of the new Whetstone Agency.

By moving Red Cloud and his wild followers to White River, the government was unknowingly doing its best to defeat its own purposes. The two great Sioux agencies were now only forty miles apart. As each Indian camp was miles away from the agency (Spotted Tail's own camp was on Bordeaux Creek, ten miles west of his agency, and some of the Red Cloud camps were on Chadron Creek, only five miles from Spotted Tail), the Sioux of the two agencies were now combined into a single mass, and the sight of their numerous camps made their hearts strong and encouraged them in their growing hostile attitude toward the whites.

Even the Eastern church group and Friends of the Indians were beginning to falter in their belief that the Sioux were all friendly and good people. When the leading Indian Friends had helped to write the Sioux treaty of 1868, they had firm faith that if the Sioux were given a helping hand—free rations, clothing, and other needs —for five years, at the end of that period they would all be self-supporting through farming. The period of five years expired in 1873, and not one full-blood at these two agencies was even gardening or doing any work with his hands. They were hunting for part of each year and living on wild meat plus abundant government rations. They were rich, and rich Indians do not have to work. They not only had clothing and other needs provided by the government, but they were trading buffalo robes, deer and elk skins, and hides from beef cattle to the agency traders for Indian goods, and they traded horses (mostly stolen from the Pawnees, some from the whites) to unlicensed traders on the Platte for Winchester rifles, Colt revolvers, and ammunition.

The avowed purpose of these agencies was to promote peace and to teach the Sioux to support themselves by farming, but by 1873 even the friendly Sioux were mistaking the government's kindness and forbearance for indications that all white men were fools and afraid of the Sioux. To make matters worse, the wild Sioux of the Powder River and the Bighorn country, who were openly hostile, were permitted to flock to the agencies, where they fiercely demanded, and were given, beef and blankets in unlimited quantities, repaying the agent for his kindness by inciting the agency Sioux to war.

As an example of government in business, these Sioux agencies are instructive. The government was spending over $2,000,000 a year on the Sioux, which was a great deal of money in the 1870's. The agents had salaries of $1,500 a year. For this sum they lived among wild Indians, who might kill them at any moment. They were almost sure to lose their reputation for honesty. The lack of system put a premium on dishonesty. It was almost impossible to keep proper books, and the pretense of business methods was mainly government red tape. You could steal anything from a pound of bacon to a carpenter shop with all its tools if you filled in the official forms properly. Weights were usually just estimated. Beef, which was supposed to be weighed, was issued at the rate of one steer to each five tipis, four times a month, the agent guessing the number of tipis, because the Sioux refused to be counted. Rations, blankets, and supplies were all issued in exactly the same slapdash manner.

The atmosphere at these agencies was thick with intrigue. Everyone, from the agent down to the Indian women, was hatching schemes for getting the better of someone, and the someone was usually Uncle in Washington. The chiefs became adept at this game, the rather dull-witted Red Cloud and the keen-minded Spotted Tail both taking part. The contractors were constantly being accused of dishonesty, and it was rumored that honest businessmen could not be induced to touch an Indian contract. You had to be a gambler to do that. You invested large sums if you took a contract to supply millions of pounds of beef or flour, and you never knew when you would be paid. With luck you got your money promptly; more often the officials, for reasons of their own, made you wait a year or perhaps three years. The officials made a great pretense of protecting the government in every way, but it was largely pretense. The government paid for hauling all supplies to the agencies at so much per hundred pounds, per hundred miles; yet for three years the distance of the hauls was unknown and the contractors collected on their own estimate of distance. At last the officials had an odometer attached to a wagon wheel to get the exact mileage; but, as it was reported, the wagon-train boss set one of the teamsters the task each evening in camp of jacking up the wheel the odometer was fastened to and spinning the wheel for an extra hour. But the teamster did his chore too well, turning out a total mileage that no one could believe, and the government went back again to the old method of paying on an estimated distance which was known to be exaggerated.

The agencies stood in the open, sun-blistered valley of White River: clusters of rude, one-story buildings constructed of rough lumber or logs, the buildings surrounded by tall log stockades, for the white men at the agencies were often in danger, and in times of stress they were actually besieged. Near the stockades were log cabins occupied by a squaw man and mixed-blood families, but most of the wild Sioux were in camps miles away. In every direction herds of Indian ponies could be seen, grazing on grassy hillsides, guarded by small boys and large Indian dogs. If a white man rode out of the stockade, the Indian boys would signal by waving blankets, or some boys would mount ponies and ride off to warn the nearest camp. Then a band of mounted warriors would come sweeping over a hill and bear down on the white man, ordering him fiercely to go back to the stockade. At Whetstone the squaw men (who were not afraid of the Sioux) took advantage of this situation. They got the agent to hire them to haul rations to the distant Indian camps, and then they insisted on an armed guard of agency warriors paid to protect them on their journeys.

There were at least five investigations of these agencies between 1871 and 1876; notorious scandals were uncovered, and nothing was done to improve conditions. The Alvord-Kemble report and the Bishop Hare report accused Spotted Tail of being responsible for most of the misrule at Whetstone. They accused the chief of forcing the agent to move twice to new locations unfit for farming, because he was determined that none of his Indians should even try to farm. The truth seems to have been that a majority of the Sioux hated the very thought of farming, and Spotted Tail, as head chief, had to accept that fact and take the lead in preventing farming. Spotted Tail was certainly learning much about the running of an agency, and with weak agents in control, it was a constant temptation to this strong-willed chief to take charge. If he was permitted to do this, it was the government's own slackness that was to blame. At bottom, Spotted Tail was both friendly and reasonable. His Indians were running wild, and with the agent too weak to act and half the time absent, the chief took over the controls.

In July, 1873, Spotted Tail's Indians got ready for another extended buffalo hunt on the Republican Fork. By moving the agency to the Upper White River, they had regained their freedom. In the old days they had gone on a hunt, then returned north to the Platte to trade dressed skins, dried meat, and other articles at the trading posts for the manufactured goods they needed. Now they obtained nearly all the goods they required from the government, plus free rations; and still they were free again to hunt, obtaining meat for extra food and dressed skins to trade for articles at the agency store. They were so well off now that they were trading for modern Winchester repeating rifles and Colt revolvers (obtained from unlicensed traders along the Platte), and they had never been so well armed before.

Spotted Tail and his people had their way about this buffalo hunt. Agent Howard was induced to appoint Spotted Tail's friend, Steve Estes, as trail-agent, to go along and represent the government in the hunting camp. At the same time, Chief Little Wound of the Southern Oglalas was preparing to go hunting from Red Cloud Agency, and he obtained an Oglala trader of former years, Antoine Janis, as his trail-agent. The Sioux set out from both agencies in July, crossed the Platte, and entered the buffalo range near the Republican.

The Pawnees were also going to hunt on the Republican. That country had been their hunting lands long before the Sioux had come and invaded it. The Pawnees were friendly Indians and therefore of little importance to the government, which left them to make a living or starve. The Sioux, with generous rations, free clothing, and supplies, had no real need to hunt buffalo, but the Pawnees had to hunt or go hungry. Their Quaker agent was trying to force them to stay on their reservation and plant crops, although the Pawnees had always obtained the main part of their food by hunting. In the summer of 1873, the Quakers refused to permit any large number of Pawnees to go hunting, but a hunting party of 250 men, 100 women, and 50 children left the Pawnee reservation at about the time the Sioux came south to hunt.

The Pawnee hunters struck the Republican Fork, found buffalo, and killed fifty. They dried the meat and packed it in rawhide cases for winter use and prepared the buffalo skins. Moving up the Republican they met a party of white hide-hunters. These white men, armed with modern repeating rifles, were slaughtering the buffalo, taking the hides, and leaving the meat for the wolves to eat. The white men warned the Pawnees that large forces of Sioux were in the lands north of the Republican, and the Pawnees turned to the southwest, but found few buffalo in that direction. Turning north, they reached the Republican and again met white hunters who warned them of the Sioux. John Williamson, who was trail-agent for the Pawnees, advised them to take the safe course and turn eastward. They now had their ponies packed with the dried meat and skins of eight hundred buffalo, and he told them that they should not take risks. Fighting Bear, a pugnacious Pawnee chief, accused Williamson of cowardice. He said that the Pawnees had never been afraid of the Sioux and that these white men were lying. There were no Sioux; the white men were trying to keep the Pawnees out of the good hunting grounds so that they could have the hunting for themselves. Most of the Pawnee men sided with Fighting Bear, and the camp was now crossed north of the Republican.

Led by the men, the Pawnees went up a little northern tributary of the river. It was a small ravine, and after riding up it for about three miles, they came out on an open prairie dotted with small bands of grazing buffalo. The men started hunting. They made a good kill and dismounted to skin the buffalo they had shot. They were scattered out all over the prairie, when a compact band of about one hundred Sioux charged over a prairie hill and came down on them, killing Sky Chief and some others. The Pawnees mounted and fled to the ravine, where the women and children were bringing up the heavily loaded ponies. Here the Pawnee men rallied. They then came out on the prairie and started fighting the Sioux off.

The fight went on for about an hour; and then suddenly the whole prairie was covered with bands of mounted Sioux, from eight hundred to one thousand warriors, riding into the fight. The Pawnee men took one look at this great force of enemies and made for the ravine. The Sioux rode along both sides of the ravine, pouring bullets and arrows into the mass of fleeing Pawnees. Here the Pawnees had thirty-nine women, ten children, and an unknown number

207

of men killed. They fled the three miles down the ravine and out into the broad, flat valley of the Republican. Turning eastward they fled down the river, parties crossing to the safer south bank. The Sioux, massed in force, were just preparing to cross and resume the attack when a bugle rang out and a troop of cavalry rode out of a grove of trees. Some white hunters had brought the news of the Sioux attack, and the officer in command of the troop, in camp near by, had started a march toward the field of action, to stop the Indian fight. The Sioux took a good look at the advancing cavalry, turned their ponies, and rode northward, vanishing from the scene.[7]

In this bloody affair, the Pawnees had about one hundred killed and many wounded. The Sioux captured eleven women and children, about one hundred ponies, and the dried meat and skins of eight hundred buffalo, all the Pawnee camp equipment, and some Pawnee guns and other weapons. The Sioux scouts had discovered the Pawnee hunters, had reported to the Sioux chiefs, who had then deliberately planned the attack. The only excuse for the Sioux lay in the fact that they were wild Indians who had been at war with the Pawnees for nearly one hundred years, that they hated the Pawnees, and that the Pawnees hated them and would have butchered them gladly if they had had the men and arms necessary to do it.

We do not know whether Spotted Tail personally led in this attack. We cannot single him out and place all the blame on his shoulders. The other chiefs were equally guilty, but not from their own way of regarding the matter. They were proud of defeating the Pawnees and killing them. The chiefs were all rated as friendly by the government officials. Spotted Tail always stood for peace—with the whites—and so did Little Wound, who led the Oglalas in this Pawnee attack. Two government trail-agents were with the Sioux, and did not lift a finger to prevent the fight. Steve Estes, who was with Spotted Tail, attempted to excuse the Sioux by pretending that the Pawnees had invaded the Sioux hunting grounds; Antoine Janis, who was with Little Wound, left that chief to do

[7] See Hyde, *The Pawnee Indians*, 244–47. This was Spotted Tail's last fight, but it is not recorded whether he led the warriors or remained in his camp.

the explaining, and Little Wound's excuse was that his agent had warned him not to attack the Pawnees on their reservation, but these Pawnees were off the reservation in the hunting grounds. The agents at Red Cloud and Whetstone evidently considered the Pawnee slaughter a matter of no importance. On the frontier even the bloodiest Indian fight did not concern the whites, unless white men were killed; but a flutter of telegrams from Washington, demanding explanations, soon waked the agents up to the fact that in the East the Sioux slaughter of the Pawnees was viewed with horror. By this time, however, the agents had fresh trouble on their hands that made the Pawnee affair seem of little account.

The wild Sioux of the Powder River and the Bighorn country still had no trade with the whites; and when Red Cloud Agency was established on the Platte, they flocked there in winter to trade at the agency stores, to obtain free blankets, rations, and other supplies, and to express their gratitude to a kindly government by creating such a situation that troops had to be asked for from Fort Laramie to save the lives of the white men at the agency. But it was contrary to the government appeasement policy to use troops. Now in the autumn of 1873, Red Cloud and Spotted Tail had their agencies near each other on White River, and the Northern Indians (as they were called at these agencies) came down from the Powder River in unusual numbers in October. They were in a bad humor because the whites had invaded their hunting grounds, sending a survey party escorted by troops to lay out the line for the Northern Pacific Railroad. The Sioux had attacked the troops and forced the survey party to turn back, and now they came to the agencies, angry with the whites and bent on making all the trouble they could. Lone Horn of the North and Roman Nose were there with Miniconjou camps; the Sans Arcs had a camp, and there were families from all the other Northern camps. They started moving back and forth, from one agency to the other, fiercely demanding beef and blankets in unlimited quantities and forcing the agents and their men to fill all their requirements. They were openly talking war, and they soon had most of the younger Sioux in the agency camps supporting them. Red Cloud was joining in the war plans; Spotted Tail held to his old view, that it would bring disaster on the Sioux if they went to war, but he was in no position to control the warriors.

Rumors of the dangerous condition at the agencies seeped out. General John E. Smith, commanding at Fort Laramie, heard that the Sioux were forcing the agents to issue beef in such quantities that the meat was being left on the ground, the Sioux only wanting the hides to trade at the agency stores for goods. In the East the Friends of the Indians—who could believe no wrong of the Sioux—had a report that the trouble was being caused by the agents' starving the Indians. The agents were in a very tight place. They had been nominated by the Episcopal church, and if they asked for troops, they would be pilloried by the church people and would probably lose their appointments as agents.

Dr. J. J. Saville, the agent at Red Cloud, seems to have been particularly anxious to hold on to his $1,500-a-year salary. He pretended to be in control of the situation.[8] Agent Howard, at Whetstone, kept very quiet. He was being protected by Spotted Tail. The worst trouble was at Red Cloud, where that chief was backing up the wild Sioux. At Whetstone, Spotted Tail was using his tribal soldiers to prevent the Northern Indians from going too far. He could not prevent their forcing the agent to hand out beef and blankets, but he would not tolerate any attempt to kill the whites.

One day in February, 1874, the men at Red Cloud Agency heard singing, and going outside the stockade they beheld a column of two or three hundred Northern warriors advancing slowly, four abreast, the men chanting a war song as they came on. The Sioux and their ponies were painted for war, and the men were wearing all their war finery. The white men ran for cover, and the Sioux rode in through the agency gateway. They whipped their ponies into a run and went sweeping around and around, whooping and firing. They shot out all the windows, narrowly missing some of the hidden whites, and then they rode wildly out of the gateway and away over the hills. This was probably the war party that made

[8] Deer, the trader at Red Cloud, let some of the truth out. He was a friend of Saville's and secretly in a business partnership with the agent, but he was very much frightened and accused Saville of risking the lives of all the white men at the agency in order to hang on to his $1,500-a-year salary. See *Nebraska History*, Vol. VII, 26–28.

the raids south of the agencies. They killed Lieutenant Robinson and Corporal Coleman, of the Fourteenth Infantry, near Laramie Peak, a hunter on Laramie Fork, and a teamster on the Niobrara. This was open war.

It was about this time that a young Hunkpapa warrior decided to distinguish himself by murdering Agent Saville. He got inside the Red Cloud stockade at night and stood in front of the agent's office, hallooing to attract Saville's attention. But it was the agent's clerk, young Frank Appleton, who opened the door and stood in it, holding up an oil lamp in his hand. The Indian, mistaking him for the agent, shot him dead and escaped to the camp of Roman Nose near Whetstone Agency. There Spotted Tail's Brulé warriors found and killed him.

Agent Saville now sent a messenger to Fort Laramie, asking for troops, but he kept the matter very quiet, perhaps fearing that the church people would demand his removal for calling in the soldiers. In his February reports he stated that his agency was under good control, the Sioux having held a council and decided against war. Even Red Cloud was now for peace, stating that if his men were given one hundred good guns, they would protect the agency and also induce Crazy Horse and the wild Oglalas of the north to come in and settle at the agency.

But by this time the government had decided to act strongly. General John E. Smith was given orders, and he organized a column, including cavalry, infantry, and artillery, with a wagon train to haul supplies, and set out from Fort Laramie for the agencies. The wild Sioux were queer people. Left undisturbed, they might have whipped themselves up to the point of starting a real war in the spring of 1874, but at the news that troops were approaching the agencies, they fell into a panic, took down their tipis, and fled. Most of them fled to the safety of the badlands north of White River, taking part of the tamer agency Sioux with them; but part of the wild Sioux fled to the camps of the agency bands. There were wild scenes at both agencies, but hardly a shot was fired and no one seems to have been hurt. The wilder Sioux blustered and made threats. They rode their ponies up to the sentries that had been set about the agencies, insulting the soldiers and crowding their ponies against them; but they were very careful not to start a fight, and gradually the situation quieted.

The troops had come to stay. Appeasement was ended and the government was now determined to maintain order at the Sioux agencies, by force if necessary. The Christian Indian policy of brotherhood and kindliness simply did not operate when applied to the wilder Sioux, who kept brotherhood for a little group strictly inside their kinship circle and who regarded kindliness from a stranger as a sign of weakness and fear. They knew only one way of dealing with alien people who showed signs of weakness, and that was to kill them and plunder their goods.

Spotted Tail, his wife and daughter. (Photograph by W. R. Cross, Norfolk and Niobrara, Nebraska, about 1879.)

Spotted Tail (*left*) and part of his family. (Photograph by W. R. Cross, Norfolk and Niobrara, Nebraska, about 1879.)

Spotted Tail, Captain Pratt, and Quaker ladies at Carlisle School, June 1880. (From *A Sioux Chronicle*, by George E. Hyde. Courtesy New York Public Library)

Spotted Tail and his children at Carlisle, June, 1880. *Seated, left to right,* are William, Chief Spotted Tail, Pollock; *standing, left to right,* are Oliver and Max. (Courtesy South Dakota Historical Society)

Sioux chiefs at Carlisle, June, 1880. (Courtesy New York Public Library)

Red Cloud and Mr. Blackmore, of London. (From *Ab-Sa-Ra-Ka, Land of Massacre*, by Henry B. Carrington)

Agent McGillycuddy (*center*) at Pine Ridge, about 1884. With
him are Sword, chief of police (*seated, left*); Standing Soldier, lieutenant of police; Billy Garnett, interpreter; and Young-Man-
Afraid-of-His-Horse (*seated, far right*). From *A Sioux Chronicle*,
by George E. Hyde. Courtesy C. I. Leedy)

Chief Swift Bear and Charles Jordan. (Courtesy South Dakota Historical Society)

9. *The Black Hills Crisis*

SPOTTED TAIL's EFFORT to slow down or block the government's farming program and other plans for forcing the Sioux quickly into self-support almost won him in 1874 the reputation of being the head and front of the hostile faction at the two great Sioux agencies on the Upper White River. Contrary to the view set forth by some of the modern Sioux, he was not condemned and ostracized by the Sioux in 1868–78 because he had first gone to the reservation and had then always sided with the whites against his own people. The reports made in 1873–75 show that the wildest of the Sioux— those from the camps in the Powder River and Bighorn country —looked up to and respected Spotted Tail and preferred him to Red Cloud. When they came to the agencies, most of their camps went to Spotted Tail, and it was their liking for him that almost cost him his reputation for friendliness among the whites.

In the winter of 1873–74, Spotted Tail's wild visitors from the north created anarchy at his agency. When a commission was sent to the agencies in March, 1874, headed by Bishop Hare of the Episcopal church, the commission investigated affairs at both agencies and reported that there had been more turmoil at Spotted Tail's agency than at Red Cloud's. Bishop Hare was strongly inclined to place all the blame on Spotted Tail's shoulders. He reported that this highhanded chief had forced his agent to locate the agency in the midst of a "repulsive barren," where there was little timber, the narrow bottom lands often bare of soil, and the water almost undrinkable. This the chief had done to prevent any farming. The Bishop's charge seems true enough, only it was the majority of the Brulés who opposed farming, and Spotted Tail's fault, if it was a fault, amounted only to his giving effectiveness to the wishes of the majority. Farming at the two agencies was not a practicable matter in 1874. At Red Cloud Agency, which the Bishop reported was in a beautiful location, the Sioux opposition to farming was even stronger than at Whetstone.

Spotted Tail seems to have kept his head better than any of the other chiefs during the riotous winter of 1873–74. While Red Cloud sided with the Northern Indians and talked of war, Spotted Tail told the wild Indians from Powder River that he would not tolerate the killing of any white men. When the Hunkpapa warrior murdered Frank Appleton at Red Cloud, Spotted Tail sent the Brulé warriors to hunt the murderer down and kill him. When the troops arrived, Red Cloud was furious and demanded that they leave. Spotted Tail went to see the commanding officer and had a friendly talk with him. The result was that the military kept their force at Red Cloud's agency, where they soon built Camp Robinson and settled down to stay. They trusted Spotted Tail to keep order at his agency, waiting until that agency was removed to a more suitable location before establishing a military post near it.

The Bishop Hare commission had one council with the Sioux. The commission had to be escorted by a troop of cavalry. They found several hundred Sioux warriors assembled at the camp, all armed with Winchesters. Seated in a semicircle around the good men of the commission, the Sioux scowled at them, every now and then bursting out into fierce yelling and firing their rifles. Bishop Hare said in later years that he had been in more danger during this council than at any other time during his long experience among Indians. In his report in 1874 he denounced Spotted Tail. "The claims and conceit of this chief know no bounds, and being himself settled with his band near Bordeaux Creek (some twenty-five miles from the barren agency site) having abundant wood and water and receiving government rations he lives at ease." Spotted Tail persistently opposed the Hare commission's proposals—to remove the agency to a site fit for farming, and if that was not done, to remove the entire Sioux Nation to Indian Territory! This mad scheme of the Eastern planners was first broached to the Sioux by the Hare commission, and the Sioux turned the plan down as too nonsensical for consideration, which was exactly what it was. Bishop Hare stated that Spotted Tail's influence among the Sioux "towers above that of all other chiefs," which is a flat contradiction of the assertions of some present-day Sioux that in 1874 Spotted Tail was looked down on and mistrusted by the Sioux because he always sided with the whites. The Bishop stated that this chief always sided against the government and was keeping his own agent shut up inside the Whetstone stockade, forbidding him even to ride out to look for a better site for the agency. The Corn and Loafer bands were camped at the agency. *They* were the ones who sided with the whites. The Bishop wished a census of Sioux to be taken so that rations could be issued on a basis a little more businesslike than just taking each chief's word for how many people he had in his camp. The Corn and Loafer chiefs at once agreed; Spotted Tail (like Red Cloud) refused point blank, adding that he would use tribal soldiers to prevent a census in the Corn and Loafer camps if the chiefs in those camps did not have the sense to forbid a count. The Bishop, in a quite unchristian mood, recommended strong punitive action against Spotted Tail and his band.[1]

The government was trying to purchase the Sioux hunting rights in Nebraska to prevent further trouble caused by large camps of Sioux going on hunts to the Republican Fork. In 1872, Spotted Tail and some of the other chiefs had been taken to Washington, and this subject of the hunting rights had been discussed, but the chiefs refused to make any commitment before they had held councils with their people. In the winter of 1873–74, Congress voted the munificent sum of $25,000 for the purchase of the hunting rights, and in May the chiefs, including Spotted Tail, were again dragged off to Washington for consultations, with the same result. The chiefs would agree to nothing until they had held councils with their bands. In the end the Sioux held the councils and decided to sell. By 1874 there were not enough buffalo left in western Nebraska to support any camp of Sioux even for a few weeks, and in another year or two the white hide-hunters would kill the last of the buffalo.

Spotted Tail was back at his agency in June, and now the officials were pressing hard for removal of the agency to a location where

[1] Bishop Hare's report is in the *Red Cloud Investigation* report of 1875, 807–12.

farming would be possible. The chief was not interested in farming, and he had a poor opinion of the Washington officials, who kept harping on farming and could not see that the most urgent problem at the two agencies was to preserve order and prevent the wilder of the Sioux from killing all the whites at the agencies and starting war. He talked to the army officers at Camp Robinson and (passing over the heads of the Washington officials) made a private agreement with the soldiers. The chief agreed to the removal of his agency if the army helped to choose the new location. There seems to have been an agreement concerning the changing of the agency name also. Spotted Tail had felt slighted when the government named Red Cloud Agency for that chief. He wished to have his name given to his agency, and now this was to be done and Whetstone was to be known officially as Spotted Tail Agency. The military officers picked a site on upper West Beaver Creek, some ten miles south of where Whetstone stood near the mouth of the main Beaver Creek. The new site had good water, good stands of timber, and plenty of land fit for farming; but during this summer surveyors ran the northern line of Nebraska, finding that both Red Cloud and Spotted Tail agencies were in Nebraska, and almost at once an agitation was started in the Nebraska legislature to have these Indian agencies removed from Nebraska soil northward to the Sioux reservation. Thus, after three removals of his agency, Spotted Tail had hardly reached the latest site when talk of removal was resumed.

But even before the agency was moved to West Beaver Creek, the Sioux had something much more exciting to talk about than a new removal. Custer had invaded the Black Hills with 1,200 white men, marching across the prairies from Fort Abraham Lincoln on the Missouri in Dakota, and this, as the Sioux chiefs angrily asserted, was an open violation of the treaty of 1868. This Black Hills expedition was another straw in the wind indicating that the government policy toward the Sioux was stiffening. The treaty barred whites from the Sioux reservation; the Bishop Hare commission had recommended that the main purpose in 1874 should be to conciliate the wild Sioux in the Powder River and Bighorn country and to establish a new agency (perhaps in the Black Hills) to which these Indians could be coaxed. General Sheridan had recommended the building of a military post in the Black Hills, obviously for the purpose of controlling the wild Sioux by military force; and now Custer had been sent to the hills with the announced object of making a military survey, and when Bishop Hare warned President Grant that such an expedition would arouse the rage of the Sioux and make conciliation impossible, he was ignored, and Custer was given his orders to march. He took with him the whole of his Seventh Cavalry, two companies of infantry, sixty Arikara Indian scouts (deadly foes of the Sioux), some artillery, and the new rapid-fire Gatling guns. He had a train of 110 wagons and was accompanied by a number of scientists and a party of Dakota gold-seekers. Ever since 1864, the Sioux had kept gold prospectors out of their lands, and now the miners were going into the Black Hills under military protection. On reaching the hills, Custer sent out enthusiastic reports on the placer gold deposits that had been found, and a wave of gold excitement spread to all the frontier communities. Parties of prospectors prepared to set out for the hills, ignoring the official announcements that it was illegal to trespass on the Indian lands.

The anger among the Sioux over this invasion of the Black Hills was rapidly increasing when, in October, the wild Sioux from the north made their usual appearance at the agencies. They found conditions changed from the previous autumn. Red Cloud now had the garrison at Camp Robinson little more than a mile from his agency; Spotted Tail had moved to a new location on West Beaver Creek and also had a military post (Camp Sheridan) within sight of his agency. The warriors from the Powder River and Bighorn country were not eager to fight the soldiers. They were, in a way, guests of the agency Sioux, to whom these agencies belonged, and the code of Sioux manners forbade them to start trouble. They must wait and join in after their agency hosts had started the fight.

Spotted Tail was siding with his agent, at least in the matter of keeping decent order at his agency; but Red Cloud was quarreling with Agent Saville and welcomed the reinforcements that the Northern camps had brought to him. In October, Saville tried to put up a flagstaff at the agency so that he could fly the American flag, and this apparently innocent project brought on a violent outbreak during which a troop of cavalry was sent to the agency and came very close to being massacred by a great throng of enraged Sioux. In November there was another outbreak when Saville—urged on by the officials in Washington—tried to take a census of his Indians. Most of the Northern Indians stampeded in terror at the prospect of being counted, fleeing northward into the badlands and taking a goodly number of Red Cloud's agency Indians with them. The beef herd for Red Cloud Agency was also stampeded, supposedly by the Sioux.

Lone Horn and his big band of Miniconjous were camped with Spotted Tail, but most of the Northern camps were with Red Cloud. Spotted Tail seems to have enforced good order, while at the other agency, forty miles away to the westward, Red Cloud kept the Indians stirred up much of the time.

Spotted Tail's agent, E. A. Howard, was a quiet man, so quiet that he attracted little notice and was hardly more than a shadowy figure seen dimly in the background. We know little concerning his character or views. His relations with Spotted Tail seem to have been friendly, but it may be surmised that Spotted Tail dealt with Howard as he did with all his other civilian agents, protecting him from the Sioux and at the same time controlling most of his actions. This is shown by Bishop Hare's remark that Spotted Tail ordered Howard to remain inside the agency stockade and forbade him to ride to the several camps to carry out the Washington orders to take a census of his Sioux. When the investigation of affairs at the two agencies was in progress in 1875, Spotted Tail defended Howard and wished to retain him as agent, although a large group of the Sioux at the agency wished to have him removed. At this moment, Red Cloud was denouncing Agent Saville and demanding his removal. When Saville was removed, Howard remained.[2]

[2] The only instance I know of in which Agent Howard took a notable stand was during his quarrel with some of the squawmen in 1875. He reported to the Indian Office that these men were making trouble and should be removed from the agency. He was instructed to request the military to remove the men and did so, but the army failed to take any action. Howard was the one agent who stuck it out as Spotted Tail's agent for more than a year or so. From 1868 to 1880, Spotted Tail had ten agents and acting agents. Howard held the position from April, 1873

The winter of 1874–75 was a hard one, and there were bitter complaints from the Sioux at both agencies over the scantiness and bad quality of the rations. Just what was wrong is in doubt. Some said that Congress, in a fit of economy, had slashed the Sioux appropriations; others, that the Indian Office was deliberately cutting down on the amount of food provided for the Sioux. The quality of part of the rations was undoubtedly very low, but men connected with the business of contracting for Indian supplies knew that the prices the government was willing to pay meant that the food for the Indians had to be a very low grade, unfit for sale to white people. There was undoubtedly much suffering among the Indians that winter, and large crowds of Sioux hung around the two military posts, begging for food for their families.

While this was going on at the agencies, a big camp of Sioux, almost all Southern Oglalas from Red Cloud Agency, were in a hunting camp down near Republican Fork. The ever thoughtful officials had established a special base of supplies at Julesburg above the forks of the Platte, and sent wagon trains regularly to the hunting camp with rations and other needs. There were reported to be five thousand Indians in the hunting camp, and during the entire winter they killed a total of about one hundred buffalo. The white hunters had almost wiped out the herds, and in the spring of 1875, the Sioux went home to their agency with the conviction that they had seen their last buffalo hunt.

Spotted Tail's new agency on West Beaver Creek was located with much more care than any of the previous agencies. A commission was sent to consider the site carefully, and the military took a leading part in the selection of the site, wishing to have the agency where the army post could be placed in a proper and comfortable location. This work was done in September, 1874, the troops reaching the new location September 9 and locating their new post, Camp Sheridan, on September 12. They put up log barracks and stables.

until he was removed by the military in the summer of 1876. Colonel Anson Mills in his book, *My Story*, seems to be referring to Howard when he states that the Spotted Tail agent was dismissed and accused of fraud. The fact is that the Indian Office transferred Howard to the Ponca reservation, as a strong agent was wanted to take the place of Agent Lawrence, who was regarded as unfit to handle the Ponca crisis of 1877.

At this time most of the Brulés were encamped on Chadron Creek. Agent Howard started removing the agency from the mouth of Beaver Creek in late autumn and finished the move during the winter. The new agency was reported to be ten miles south of the one at the mouth of Beaver Creek and twelve miles south of the Nebraska line. The agency was at first one-half mile above Camp Sheridan, but in 1875 the military abandoned their log buildings and built a new post of sawed lumber one-half mile above the agency. An infantry officer is said to have commanded Camp Sheridan when the post was established, but in April, 1875, Colonel Anson Mills, of the Third Cavalry, took command of the post.

The officers at Camp Sheridan took a strong liking to Spotted Tail on sight, and they also got on well with Agent Howard. The situation was very different from that at Camp Robinson, where the military heartily disliked Agent Saville and were feuding with Red Cloud half the time. At the new Spotted Tail Agency the Indians were in the main friendly, and their chiefs and the agent tried to co-operate with the army officers. Agent Howard was badly worried during the winter when deep snows delayed the wagon trains bringing rations from the distant base of supplies on the Missouri and even the driving of beef cattle to the agency was much delayed. The Sioux were hungry and flocked to Camp Sheridan, begging for food. It was the temporary failure of their meat ration that hurt the Sioux most, and the commissary officer at the post did what he could to tide the Indians over this bad time.

Among the officers at the post was Lieutenant Jesse M. Lee of the Ninth Infantry,[3] who was later appointed Spotted Tail's agent during the Sioux war of 1876 when the military took over the agencies. Lieutenant Lee and his family at once became very friendly with Spotted Tail, and when Colonel Mills took command of the post in the spring of 1875, he and Mrs. Mills also took a strong liking to Spotted Tail, who was a favorite dinner guest at the com-

---

[3] It is difficult to give these officers their proper rank. Most of them had been officers during the Civil War and had won rather high ranks, but at the close of the war they were reduced in rank in the regular army service. On retirement their rank was increased again. Jesse M. Lee was a captain or major in the Civil War, was reduced to the rank of lieutenant in the regular army, then became a captain, and rose to the rank of brigadier general by 1902.

manding officer's quarters. The officers' families also liked White Thunder, a handsome and bold head-soldier or subchief of the Brulé Orphan Band, and Standing Elk, an intelligent and friendly chief of the Corn Band. Swift Bear was very friendly, but he was an older chief who lacked the handsome presence and outstanding qualities of character that Spotted Tail possessed. Colonel Mills described Spotted Tail as a handsome man, fine looking, with engaging manners, always speaking for peace and telling his Indians that they could expect nothing but misery from going to war with the Americans. Mills spoke of this chief's perfect loyalty. Some of the military officers stressed the loyalty of Spotted Tail and other chiefs toward the government, and by doing so, they exhibited the fact that they did not understand these chiefs. Spotted Tail was friendly, but if he felt any loyalty, it was toward his own people. The government was not his affair. He never said "loyalty," but spoke of feeling responsible, and toward his people, not the government.

A Brulé chief named No Flesh (*Konika Wanika*) was eager to be friendly with the army officers and, incidentally, to be invited to dinners. He made a great effort to gain the good graces of Mrs. Mills, the commandant's wife, but his appearance and personality did not make a good impression on the lady. Failing with his social qualities, No Flesh took to making crude colored paintings on tanned skins, which he presented to Mrs. Mills, but as an artist he failed even more completely to win her esteem. As an army wife she was fond of soldiers, and all of No Flesh's paintings had to do with his personal triumphs in killing soldiers. One painting depicted him mounted on a fine war pony with a long-tailed eagle-feather war bonnet on his head, two buffalo horns attached to the headpiece of the bonnet, and killing a cavalry captain with his bow and arrows, while all around the border of the painting lay heaps of dead soldiers—very dead and gory. Perhaps this was No Flesh's version of his part in the Fort Phil Kearny massacre. At any rate, Mrs. Mills did not regard the painting as a tasteful gift to present to an army wife, and her dislike for No Flesh was increased.

At this time, in May, 1875, Captain McDougall, of the Seventh Cavalry, came to Camp Sheridan with a scouting party for a brief stay, and Mrs. Mills invited Spotted Tail, Standing Elk, and White

Thunder to dinner to meet the visiting officer. The watchful No Flesh noted the preparations for a party and invited himself. The guests had just gone into the dining room when the maid came in to announce No Flesh. Mrs. Mills made a prompt decision and told the maid to seat Mr. No Flesh in the front room. There he sat, listening to the lively talk and the clink of tableware in the next room as the meal progressed. Every now and then he would say in the Sioux language and in a loud and annoyed voice that he was exceedingly hungry, but Mrs. Mills ignored him. After this unsuccessful social evening, No Flesh spread it about that Anson Mills was not a proper soldier-chief, but a poor creature, ruled by a woman who neglected to show hospitality to important guests.[4]

By the spring of 1875 the invasion of the Black Hills by white gold-seekers was the absorbing question at the Sioux agencies. The Sioux were angry, threatening to drive out or kill the white men, and the government, by ordering the troops to remove the whites from the hills, admitted that their presence was a violation of the Sioux treaty. But once the gold fever had started, there was no stopping the flow of prospectors to the hills; and when the troops did remove some miners and turn them over to the frontier sheriffs, the men were promptly released and returned at once to the hills. Left with apparently only one way out of this dilemma, the officials had the Sioux chiefs brought to Washington in May to discuss the sale of the hills; but the chiefs refused to take any action until they had held councils with their people. The treaty of 1868 provided that any future sale of Sioux land had to be approved by three-fourths of the adult male Indians. This provision had been written into the treaty by the Friends of the Indians to protect the tribe from any future attempt to take land by the old method of obtaining the approval of a few chiefs. In theory this was an excellent precaution; in practice it broke down, for the theorists in the Eastern States had failed to observe that the common men among the Sioux could not think for themselves and wished to have their chiefs make all decisions. Another point that the theorists had overlooked was the fact that if the Sioux were brought together in a great mass

[4] Colonel Anson Mills, *My Story*, 158–62. Mills has his dating wrong, placing events in the wrong month and even the wrong year.

to hold councils and make a decision, the result would be endless quarreling and perhaps an outbreak of killing.

Spotted Tail was greatly concerned over the Black Hills invasion. Red Cloud was more interested in a feud with his agent. In the autumn of 1874 he had played a handsome trick on Agent Saville by giving a set of samples of rations to Professor Marsh, of Yale University, who was at the agency collecting bones of prehistoric mammals in the badlands. Red Cloud had someone make up the samples of rations very carefully. The sample of very low-grade flour had some handfuls of White River clay dust added to it; the coffee had all the good beans removed and only the bad left, and so it was with the rest of the samples. Professor Marsh was so shocked by the thought that human beings should be expected to live on such repulsive food that he took the samples to Washington, where he exhibited them and demanded a thorough investigation of Red Cloud Agency affairs. When the Sioux chiefs reached Washington in May, 1875, Professor Marsh was there, ready to champion Red Cloud and support his charges that Agent Saville and the contractors were robbing the Indians, but Red Cloud now had taken to evasive action. He denied making charges against his agent or giving the ration samples to the professor. The fact was that his own subchiefs were not supporting him; they had split, and a factional quarrel was in progress. One of the head soldiers of the Oglala tribe, named Face, turned on Red Cloud at a council in the Indian Office in Washington and said fiercely, "I told you just how this matter would be when we commenced it! We came here far apart [divided]; we have done nothing, and we have no one to blame but ourselves! Our Father [the agent] is a good man. He is a brave true man. We tried to break him down and we could not. He is the man we ought to take back with us and keep!"[5]

But Red Cloud was stubbornly determined to be rid of Agent Saville. He returned home to prepare for the investigation which everyone knew was now coming. While he was thus engaged, Spotted Tail grew more and more concerned over the crisis caused by the white invasion of the Black Hills. He did what none of the other agency chiefs had the mentality or enterprise to do. In

[5] Hyde, *Red Cloud's Folk*, 232.

May the government, wishing to learn the exact truth concerning gold deposits in the Black Hills had sent Professor W. P. Jenney with a group of mining experts to make a thorough examination in the hills, and in August, Spotted Tail went into the hills with a party of his headmen to make his own investigation on the spot. He came back to his agency convinced that the hills were rich in gold and with his mind made up that the hills were of great value and that the Sioux should refuse to sell them. Spotted Tail took Agent Howard and twelve headmen of his tribe on this trip to the hills.

The great investigation of affairs at Red Cloud and Spotted Tail agencies was in July and August. Both agents were accused of dishonesty and of collusion with dishonest contractors who supplied beef, rations, and other needs for the agencies. The main battle was at Red Cloud, where that chief was determined to be rid of Agent Saville. The Spotted Tail Agency was less involved, and Spotted Tail wished to keep Agent Howard; but for the first time since he had become head chief in 1865, he was outvoted in the tribal council, and a group of malcontents (led by little men of no importance) was for the moment in control. Spotted Tail must have been very angry; but backed by a council vote, the little men, who in ordinary times did not dare to speak in his presence, put a shut-up order on him, and when the Brulés met the investigation commission in council, Spotted Tail had to sit in silence while such nonentities as Brown Hat (alias Baptiste Good) and Good Hawk complained to the commission and tried to get rid of Agent Howard. Swift Bear, the second chief at the agency, had also been shut up by order of the council. After the commission had listened to the malcontents at this public meeting, they held a private talk with Spotted Tail, Swift Bear, Two Strike, and other leading men. Swift Bear was siding with Spotted Tail. He said that Brown Hat and Good Hawk had formerly been minor chiefs but had been "thrown away." The malcontents had stacked the tribal council and voted for these little men to speak for the tribe. Spotted Tail remarked that these men spoke jealously and foolishly and that, as he had been ordered not to speak, he had "looked with my eyes shut." He admitted that these men were right about the rations being bad, but he said that this was not Agent Howard's fault. As usual, he spoke with good sense and exhibited an understanding of matters which seemed to be beyond the comprehension of the minor chiefs. He said that the provision in the treaty for free rations had expired two years back and that he knew the Sioux were getting rations now only because of the good will of the government officials. This was a point that the common Indians and minor chiefs just could not comprehend.[6]

In the end the great investigation into affairs at Red Cloud and Spotted Tail agencies was no more helpful than such investigations usually are. It ended in talk. The two chiefs got what they wanted. Agent Saville was removed, or permitted to resign, and Red Cloud was pleased; Spotted Tail got his desire and kept Agent Howard. The report stated that Spotted Tail Agency was in better condition than Red Cloud. Pretty clear evidence of wholesale robbery of the government and the Indians by a score of contractors and their assistants was uncovered, but no one was brought into court and accused.

In June, the Sioux held a great Sun Dance midway between Red Cloud and Spotted Tail agencies. This is the first Sun Dance recorded as taking place at these agencies, and at the conclusion of the savage rites the Sioux followed the old custom of forming a large war party and setting out to attack their enemies. As the Pawnees on the Loup Fork in Nebraska were the nearest enemies, the warriors headed in that direction, for they did not know that the government had removed the Pawnee tribe to Indian Territory. They also did not know that General George Crook, commanding the Department of the Platte, was determined to prevent the repetition of the raids made on the Upper Platte from the agencies in the spring of 1874, and that troops were in readiness to march. This was at the time when Spotted Tail and the chiefs were in Washington for the Black Hills conference, the chiefs getting back to the agency just after the warriors set out. Spotted Tail was very angry. He sent messengers after the war party, ordering the Brulés to return at once. They sent back a defiant answer. The angry chief

[6] Council at Spotted Tail Agency, August 16, 1875, in *Red Cloud Investigation* report, 502.

then sent tribal soldiers with a pipe—symbol of tribal authority—and most of the Brulés unwilling left the war party and came home. After they left, the other warriors were surprised by a detachment of the Seventh Cavalry, commanded by Captain McDougall, and were routed, losing one man killed and having fifteen ponies captured by the cavalry. The warriors then returned to the agencies in a terrible temper. They started organizing a party of five hundred to go back and whip the Seventh Cavalry, but again Spotted Tail and other chiefs intervened and stopped the proposed expedition. This was one reason why Spotted Tail was outvoted in the tribal council when the investigating commission came to the agency. The angry warriors, combined with other malcontents, voted that Spotted Tail should not speak in council and put up some little men to speak in his place.

The commission that had been appointed to treat with the Sioux for the sale of the Black Hills now sent its secretary, J. C. Collins, to the agencies for preliminary talks. Collins got Red Cloud to agree to the government plan that the council should be held at an agency on the Missouri River; but when he went to Spotted Tail Agency, that chief brushed aside the government plan. He said that the Brulés and the Oglalas had kept and guarded the Black Hills, that these two tribes were the most important ones among the Teton Sioux, and that this great council should be held at a point between his agency and Red Cloud's. "The Missouri River Sioux must come here to council," he told Collins, and he refused to budge from his stand.

If there was one Sioux chief in the summer of 1875 who realized the seriousness of the Black Hills crisis, that man was Spotted Tail. While Red Cloud stayed at his agency and squabbled with his agent, Spotted Tail persuaded his agent to go with him and the minor chiefs to the Black Hills. He thus turned his visit into an official affair and insured that he and the other chiefs would be treated with respect by the rough miners in the hills, for Agent Howard was at his side to support him and to aid him in learning the facts of the situation. Howard was later severely blamed for giving Spotted Tail an idea about the real value of the gold deposits in the hills. The chief found this out for himself. He also found that the government pretense of removing white miners from the hills was no longer being kept up. The troops who were supposed to remove the miners were camping with them in perfect friendliness. If the Sioux tried to drive the miners out, the troops would undoubtedly defend the miners.

Coming back to his agency, Spotted Tail prepared for the councils, but with little heart. The Sioux were already split into quarreling factions, some favoring the sale of the Black Hills, others bitterly opposed and talking of war. The common Indians did not understand the seriousness of the situation. They did not even comprehend that the free government rations and other supplies, under the treaty of 1868, had been for five years only, and that they were no longer entitled to free supplies. They were talking of getting great sums for the Black Hills and spending the money, at the moment when the Secretary of the Interior was instructing the commission to bear in mind that most of any money offered to the Sioux for the hills would be spent in supplying food and other needs for the Indians, and the remaining funds would go toward training the Sioux to support themselves by farming and for education—two things the Sioux did not value in the least.

By the time the Black Hills commission reached the agencies in September, masses of Sioux had come from the Missouri River agencies and from the wild camps in the Powder River and the Bighorn country. The land for miles about was covered with Sioux camps and great herds of grazing ponies. There were said to be 20,000 Sioux assembled at the two agencies; they were wild, all armed, and all in a bad temper. The chance of having orderly negotiations with these Indians was nil, and Spotted Tail knew it and also knew that at any moment a spark dropped might produce a violent explosion. In the past all government negotiations had been with small groups of chiefs, with some chance of friendly agreement. The government, and the Sioux, owed the present situation to the high-thinkers among the Eastern humanitarians and idealists who had put the provision for a three-fourths vote of the adult male Sioux into the treaty of 1868 because they regarded the chiefs as tyrants who did not represent the will of the tribe.

Reporters from eastern newspapers had come with the commission, and one of them tried to interview Spotted Tail. The chief stood looking at him in amiable silence while he asked one question after another through an interpreter. After some minutes of this, Spotted Tail asked a question and the interpreter said, "He wants to know if you get paid for talking." "Why, yes, of course," the reporter replied. "Then he wants to be paid for talking," said the interpreter. The reporter looked hard at the chief, shook his head, and handed over five dollars. Spotted Tail pouched the money and answered several questions; then he dried up. "What's wrong now?" demanded the reporter. "Oh, he says he has talked five dollars' worth," the interpreter told him. The reporter looked long and grimly at the chief, then handed over another five dollars. *"Miye un wopida!"* said Spotted Tail ("I am thankful!") and pouched the money. The interview was then resumed.[7] Spotted Tail took much pleasure in playing such tricks on brash white visitors. He always gave the money collected to needy families in his camp.

The Black Hills commission reached Red Cloud Agency on September 4, expecting to leave in two or three days. The Sioux quarreled fiercely among themselves from the fourth to the twentieth. On that day the exasperated commission called a council with the Indians and made proposals for the purchase of the Black Hills. The chiefs asked for one day to ponder the proposals, and then the Sioux quarreled for four more days.

On the twenty-fourth the commission went to the council ground to hear the reply of the Sioux. The party was staying at Camp Robinson near Red Cloud Agency, and it came to the council ground in an army ambulance escorted by a troop of cavalry and a band of mounted Oglala tribal soldiers.[8] Meantime, Spotted Tail was coming from his agency, accompanying Colonel Anson Mills.

[7] Alfred Sorenson, in Omaha *World-Herald* Sunday Magazine, September 21, 1930.

[8] J. S. Collins, who was secretary to the Black Hills commission, told me that the council was held on Chadron Creek, and I so stated it in my book *Red Cloud's Folk;* but Anson Mills states that the council was in a grove eight miles northeast of Camp Robinson, and another evidently reliable account states that the council was in a plain north of Crow Butte and eight miles east of Red Cloud Agency. This would seem to place the council very near the point where Spotted Tail's Whetstone Agency was located in 1871.

Mills had a troop of his Second Cavalry with him, but Spotted Tail was so alarmed over the threats the Sioux had been making that he took a large force of Brulé warriors to escort the Colonel and his cavalry. The chief told Mills that it was madness for the commission to meet the Sioux in open council. He said that the white men should remain at Camp Robinson, where they were safe, and deal with a few chiefs only. But that would have ruined the democratic experiment of the idealists who wanted a vote of approval from three-fourths of the adult male Indians before any Sioux land agreement could be termed legal. The men in the East who had invented that scheme should have been present on September 24 to witness the new Sioux democratic setup in action.

The commissioners sat in chairs under the shade of a tent-fly that had been rigged up in front of a large army tent. Back of them the cavalry and Indian soldiers sat their horses, waiting. Off in the distance thousands of Sioux could be seen, walking or riding about or just sitting on the hilltops to watch. A great cloud of dust suddenly billowed up from behind the hills, and a force of Sioux warriors rode into view, all mounted on splendid ponies and each man wearing his war finery. They swept down toward the commission's tent in a column, then whipped their ponies into a run and began circling madly around the seated white men in a whirl of dust, whooping and firing their rifles. Presently they drew off and formed a line facing the commission; then their chief dismounted, walked forward, and sat down facing the white men. A signal was given, and another band of warriors emerged from the hills and repeated the performance of the first band. Band by band the Sioux rode proudly out of the hills, until at length seven thousand warriors were drawn up in a great circle surrounding the commission and its little guard of cavalry and Indian soldiers.

Red Cloud was just ready to open the council when the circle of thousands of warriors began to seethe with sudden excitement, and out from among the massed Sioux shot Little Big Man, a warrior from the camp of the hostile Oglalas up north. He was mounted on a splendid iron gray horse which had no saddle on its back and only a lariat tied to the lower jaw in place of a bridle. The warrior was naked except for a breechclout and an eagle-feather war bonnet, whose long tail sailed out behind him in the wind. He had two big revolvers in holsters at his belt; in one hand he gripped a Winchester, in the other a fist full of brass rifle-cartridges. Riding boldly into the open space between the seated chiefs and the seated commission, where he had no right to go, the warrior announced in a stentorian shout that he had come to kill the white men who were trying to take the Sioux lands.

A group of tribal soldiers rode out from behind the tent, closed in on him, and hustled him away, but the Sioux had been roused to a frenzy of rage by his performance. The warriors were moving in on the cavalry and tribal soldiers. Loud Sioux voices were calling for a charge. Spotted Tail, ignoring the decorum customary at formal councils, left his place among the seated chiefs and hurried up to the commissioners, telling them through the interpreter that they had better get back to the safety of Camp Robinson before it was too late. General Terry acted instantly, bundling his fellow commissioners back into the army ambulance. The cavalry and Indian soldiers surrounded the vehicle. Young-Man-Afraid-of-His-Horse ordered the mass of enraged Sioux that was pressing in on the white men to go back to their camps and stay there until they had cooled off and had some sense. There are several stories as to who saved the commission and their cavalry escort, but no one doubted that it was touch and go until the commission was back at Camp Robinson.[9]

The commission had had enough of attempting to get a vote of approval out of the mass of temperamental Sioux. They had no taste for the role of dead martyrs, and it was clear enough that if they met the Sioux in another open council, they would all be killed. They had also discovered the fact that time meant nothing to these Indians. They would talk and quarrel for months and never come to an agreement. Abandoning the democratic process for obtaining a three-fourths majority vote, the commission summoned a few chiefs to Camp Robinson and attempted to deal with them as the lawful representatives of the Sioux Nation; but the chiefs were as split in their views concerning the sale of the Black Hills as the

[9] Part of this account of the council with the Sioux is made from information J. S. Collins gave me. I have also used Anson Mills' lively narrative, printed in *My Story*, 167–68.

mass of their followers were. They made endless harangues in front of the exasperated commission. Then Spotted Tail came forward with a sensible request that the commission put its proposals into writing for the consideration of the chiefs. The commission gladly accepted the suggestion and set down in writing an offer to lease the Black Hills mining rights for $400,000 a year, the government retaining the right to cancel the agreement on two years' notice; they also proposed to purchase the hills outright for $6,000,000. The chiefs returned to their camps and considered these offers, and after some further quarreling, they united long enough to reject the commission's offer. That ended the matter.

The Sioux were pleased over the failure of the Black Hills councils. They imagined that they had gotten the better of the whites this time; but Spotted Tail could not see it that way. The whites already had possession of the hills and were laying out new towns. The government would not dare to employ troops to drive its own citizens out of the hills. It would take some other way out of this difficult position. By treaty the government was pledged to keep whites off the Sioux lands. It could not keep that pledge; but it must take some kind of action.

Soon after the Black Hills councils Spotted Tail obtained his first house. When Camp Sheridan was established in 1874, log barracks and houses had been constructed, but in 1875 the post had been rebuilt on a site one mile away, the new buildings being constructed of sawed lumber. When the log quarters were abandoned, the commanding officer, Captain Anson Mills, held a ceremony and turned over his log house to Spotted Tail. The next best house he gave to Swift Bear, and each of the other chiefs was given a house. Thus suddenly the Brulé tribal leaders became homeowners, and they were very proud men that day. The news delighted the leaders among the Indian Friends in the East. Now the Brulés were started on the road to civilization, and from here on progress would be rapid. But it was not as simple as that. The Brulé women just could not solve the mysteries of brooms, dust rags, and stoves. They knew of only one method of cooking: over an open fire and mostly just simmering food in a kettle. A bed on the earth floor of a tipi was one thing; a bed in a house, with a wooden floor, was another.

Set in their simple ways, they found the problem of living in a house beyond them. In a tipi, when dirt accumulated, you just moved the tipi to clean ground, and in half an hour your house cleaning was finished. You could not clean a big log house in that manner. Presently the chiefs' families regretfully moved out of their handsome log residences, back into tipis. Civilization had lost the first round, but the chiefs were still very proud of their houses and kept them to show to Indian visitors and for use on ceremonial occasions. For everyday comfort, they stuck to tipis.

Spotted Tail had now been head chief of the Brulés for ten years. When he had taken charge in 1865, the Brulés had been scattered, most of them up north in the Powder River camps of hostiles, some small camps hidden away in the White River country southeast of the Black Hills. He had only a little camp at Fort Laramie, and then Swift Bear joined him with another small camp, they had had to combine their camps to be strong enough to go to Republican Fork to hunt buffalo. Ever since that dark year, Spotted Tail had feared two things: a war with the whites that would destroy his tribe, or (what would be even worse) an attempt of the government to force his people to give up their old way of life and to change themselves suddenly into imitation whites, living and working like the whites. He had avoided war by coming to the reservation, and on the reservation he had slowed down or stopped every attempt of the government to change his people. He knew better than any other Sioux chief that these changes must come, but he wished them to come slowly and naturally, not as the result of a sudden and violent social revolution.

The Brulés in 1875 were facing new conditions. The old free life of the hunting camp and the war trail was gone forever. In July of this year, the Brulés and Southern Oglalas had signed away their hunting rights in Nebraska. There was no hunting left for a large camp of Sioux. In less than five years white hide-hunters armed with modern rifles had exterminated the buffalo herds, and the buffalo range down along Republican Fork was already stocked with domestic cattle. The Brulés still had plenty of fighting spirit, but now they had no one to fight. The government had removed their ancient enemies, the Pawnees, to Indian Territory, and Brulés who were seeking a fight now had to go to the Powder River and the Bighorn and join the Sioux up there in a raid on the Crows or Shoshonis, or perhaps on a horse-lifting expedition against the whites in Montana. But even the slow-witted Red Cloud knew now that hunting and raiding in the Powder River and the Bighorn lands would be ended within the next few years. Then there would be nothing left for the Sioux but the confined life of the reservation and the slow shift to living like white people.

That was inevitable, a thing that fate had decreed; but without the sudden shocks of war, the change would be relatively slow. The Brulés had been on the reservation for seven years, and the only real change was that they were now getting used to the reservation, were a little quieter, and could look at a white man without itching to kill him and take his horse and other belongings. The progress in civilization that the Eastern Friends of the Indians and the Washington officials were harping on and wasting huge sums of money to promote was a dream. Farming at Spotted Tail's agency consisted in keeping a white farmer on the payroll. The Sioux kept him cooped up at the agency, threatening to kill him if he even attempted the preliminary work of riding out to locate a parcel of good land that could be plowed. The English Episcopal church had sent a missionary and teacher, but he, like the farmer, was a prisoner at the agency with no chance to till the spiritual and educational field that he longed to get to work on.

Spotted Tail, when he had first been brought face to face with the certain changes his tribe must undergo, had had another dread: the fear that his Brulés would melt away, as so many other tribes had done. The once very numerous Mandans of the Upper Missouri were now gone, almost exterminated in a few weeks by small-pox, the formerly strong Poncas, Omahas, and Arikaras were reduced to little and weak groups; the once mighty Pawnees of Nebraska had been decimated by their contacts with white civilization, and the remnant of their tribe now had been forced by the government to move to Indian Territory, where they were dying in shocking numbers from having to live under new conditions in a new country. But the Brulés were holding their own, perhaps actually gaining. In 1865, when the Brulés were at the height of their strength in their free hunting camps, they had been estimated at 350 lodges, and that included nearly 100 lodges of Wazhazhas. At Whetstone on the Missouri in 1869, Spotted Tail had 225 lodges of Brulés in his own camp, and including the camps close to the agency, there were over 300 lodges, with the Wazhazhas and part of the Brulés on the Powder River. In the summer of 1871 when Spotted Tail took his agency camps to hunt south of the Platte, he had 450 lodges, still with the Wazhazhas and some Brulés absent. In 1875 there were added to his agency camps "429 Northern Brulés," recently come from the Powder River to live at the agency. And still there was a Brulé camp up north and the Wazhazhas were living at Red Cloud Agency and being counted there. Part of Spotted Tail's increased population was due to large numbers of Lower Brulés coming to live at his agency, for this separate tribe of Brulés was not satisfied with conditions at the Lower Brulé agency on the Missouri and preferred Spotted Tail's "fat agency." Spotted Tail's own camp in 1872–75 held at least 300 lodges, the largest number he had ever had.[10]

Thus Spotted Tail no longer had to fear that the Brulés would rapidly decrease in numbers. In the early winter of 1875 he had one main concern, and that was the Black Hills crisis. When Congress met, there would be angry talk and President Grant would perhaps be forced to take some stiff action, which would almost certainly mean action against the Sioux.

[10] The numerous estimates of Upper Brulé population from 1865 to 1877 are very confusing, but I think the main fact is that the estimated population made by experienced traders in 1857—350 lodges, 3,950 people—and the actual count taken in 1877—6,004 people—indicate the trend well enough. As to how the Brulés were divided up, I know of no better way to show it than to say that in 1875 fourteen bales of blue three-point blankets were issued at Spotted Tail Agency, divided up eight bales to Spotted Tale's band, five to Swift Bear's combined Corn and Loafer bands, and one bale to the mixed-bloods and squaw men families. With no accurate census, the dividing up of these coveted blue blankets shows the relative strength of the bands. Most of the Orphan Band was now at the agency, living in Spotted Tail's camp.

10. *War*

WHEN THE GOVERNMENT ACTED in the Black Hills matter, it took every man at the Sioux agencies completely by surprise. President Grant in November, 1875, held a conference with the Secretary of the Interior, the Assistant Secretary of the Interior, the Secretary of War, and the Commissioner of Indian Affairs and decided to send a message to the wild Sioux of the Powder River and the Bighorn country ordering them to come to the Sioux agencies with all their camps by January 31 and informing them that if they did not do this, they would be turned over to the military and would be driven to the agencies by troops.

This order to the wild camps was an astonishing reversal of the soft policy toward the Sioux that had been in force during the decade from 1865 to 1875. It obviously was the result of the refusal of the Sioux to sell the Black Hills, but the official line of reasoning is difficult to follow. The wild Sioux from up north had not attended the Black Hills council near Red Cloud Agency in any large numbers, and even if they had, the refusal to sell the Black Hills was hardly a proper reason for setting the army on them. George W. Manypenny, a former commissioner of Indian affairs, asserted that this decision to act against the Sioux was first taken in Washington and that after the decision was made, an excuse for the action was found in a report made by Indian Inspector E. C. Watkins, dated November 9, 1875, in which he accused the wild Sioux of raiding the Crow Indians of Montana.

In the early summer of 1874 Bishop Hare's commission had recommended the establishment of a Northern agency, probably in the Black Hills, to which the wild Sioux were to be coaxed by the proffer of free food, clothing, and other supplies. President

243

Grant had seemingly favored this plan; then Custer had marched into the Black Hills, and after that the whites had swarmed into the hills and taken possession. The plan for a Northern agency and a soft policy toward the wild Indians was then forgotten. The whites wanted the Black Hills and did not want an agency for wild Indians in or near the hills. Then came the astonishing order for the wild Sioux to go to the old agencies by January 31.

The Sioux agents received this message just before Christmas, with orders to send Indian runners with the message to the camps. The thing was amazing. If white men in the Powder River and Bighorn country had been served with such a message, they might have realized that the officials in Washington were in earnest; and by acting at once and with speed, they might have reached the Indian agencies by the deadline set for January 31. But the wild Sioux were not like that at all. They had little understanding of government messages; they would not comprehend what this matter really meant, and they would sit around their winter campfires and talk of the matter from time to time, perhaps deciding to go to the agencies next summer or a year from next summer to talk the matter over with the agents and the agency chiefs. The officials at the Indian Office in Washington must have known that the wild Sioux would take no action on this strange order in time to meet the deadline; the military officers certainly knew it; and before there had been time to receive any reply from the Indian camps, Major General George Crook went to Fort Fetterman on the North Platte, west of Fort Laramie, and began the work of organizing a column to go and drive the Sioux out of their winter camps on the Powder River. Thus the order for the wild Indians to come to the agencies was in fact a declaration of war, although it was dressed up to have a different appearance.

The runner from Standing Rock Agency on the Upper Missouri went to the Powder River camps and did not get back to his agency until February 11, 1876. He traveled much faster than an Indian camp could possibly move, and this exhibited clearly that the time limit in the message did not give any of the wild Sioux a chance to reach the agencies by January 31. This runner reported that Sitting Bull was encamped near the mouth of the Powder River, had received him well, and had sent back a friendly message. A typical Sioux friendly message: the Sioux would consider the order, but could not move camp at that time. Later on. Maybe next summer. A similar report came from the Cheyenne River Agency. The runner from there had been well treated in the wild camps and had brought back a friendly message. Spotted Tail's agent reported that he had sent out runners but nothing had been heard from them when the time limit expired. J. S. Hastings, agent for Red Cloud, reported that his runners had found Black Twin and Crazy Horse with an Oglala camp near Bear Butte at the edge of the Black Hills and that they had seemed friendly but had said that they could not move their camp to the agency because of snow and cold. Snow and cold did not prevent their moving their camp a much longer distance to the Yellowstone, where they were reported to be in the following March. Summing it up: the Sioux did not take the message sent to them very seriously; they had no realization that it was an ultimatum and a threat of war. They went about their usual winter affairs, just as if nothing had happened.

General Crook left Fort Fetterman on March 1 for the purpose of driving the wild Sioux out of their winter camps and forcing them to go to the agencies. He was an experienced Indian campaigner, and he had organized a strong and mobile column of ten troops of cavalry, two companies of infantry, a body of mixed-blood Sioux scouts (mostly from Red Cloud Agency), and a train of pack mules that could move quickly with the troops. A wagon train loaded with extra supplies also accompanied the column.

At dawn on March 17 part of Crook's cavalry under the command of Colonel J. J. Reynolds surprised a camp of sixty-five lodges on Powder River, ten miles above the mouth of the Little Powder. This camp is said to have consisted of fifty-five lodges of Northern Cheyennes and ten lodges of Oglala Sioux. Part or all of the Cheyennes had recently come north from Red Cloud Agency, equipped with new canvas lodge-covers and new blankets and clothing, given to them by the Red Cloud agent. Driven from their camp, the Indian warriors rallied and came back fighting with such spirit that the troops had to abandon the camp without destroying it, which their orders required them to do. Colonel Reynolds retired up the

Powder River, his movements slowed by the presence of wounded and frostbitten men in his command. The enraged Indians followed him, and in a night attack got back the herd of seven hundred ponies the troops had captured at their camp. General Crook was very angry with Colonel Reynolds, whom he charged with bungling his attack on the camp. The general now made up his mind that it was useless to continue the operations. The Indians in other camps would be on the alert, the weather was atrocious, and supplies were running short. He therefore took his troops back to Fort Fetterman.[1]

This was a surprising kind of Indian war. The main body of the Sioux and Cheyennes were at the agencies, supposedly friendly, certainly not regarding themselves as involved. Camps from the Powder River had wintered at the agencies, as was their custom, and when spring came in 1876, they went back to Powder River. General Crook at this moment did not seem to care how many agency Sioux might be going to the hostile camps. In Arizona, some years back, he had had much success in hiring Apaches to fight Apaches, and he was now attempting to enlist agency Sioux to fight their kinsmen in the hostile camps. He came very near to succeeding in this; but Red Cloud and the other chiefs, and Agent Hastings, blocked the plan, and apparently Agent Howard at Spotted Tail Agency did the same. Crook was angry and complained of the actions of the two agents, stating among other things that arms and ammunition for the hostiles were coming from these agencies. Agent Hastings denied this; Howard, at Spotted Tail Agency, stated that there had been no trade in arms and ammunition at his agency for the past two years.

Considering that a war was supposed to be in progress, the two agencies on the Upper White River were astonishingly quiet in the spring and early summer of 1876. At Spotted Tail Agency

---

[1] When I wrote *Red Cloud's Folk*, I was misled by modern Indian information into stating that the camp Colonel Reynolds attacked was Crazy Horse's own camp. In the present brief description of the fight, I am using the report made by a brother of Chief Bull Eagle, who came to the Cheyenne River Agency in mid-April and gave Lieutenant Ruhlin a statement. He said that Crazy Horse the day of the fight was in a large camp at the mouth of the Rosebud on the Yellowstone and that the camp Reynolds struck was one of fifty-five Cheyenne and ten Oglala lodges. Lieutenant Ruhlin's report, April 19, 1876.

the chiefs were still amusing themselves by playing with the nice log houses Colonel Mills had handed over to them. Agent Howard was immersed in building the new agency warehouses. The agency stood on the high bank of West Beaver Creek, a clear brook of cold spring water with pleasant groves along its banks. There was now an Episcopal chapel and mission school in the charge of the Reverend W. J. Cleveland and two young women assistants, Miss Mary J. Leigh and Miss Sophie Pendleton. They had 160 pupils on the school rolls, probably nearly all mixed-blood children. The Reverend Mr. Cleveland was not very hopeful concerning the prospects of the mission. Swift Bear was the only important chief who was at all interested in Christianity and education, and there was a rumor that the agency was to be moved all the way back to the Missouri early in 1876, which would mean the dispersion of the school pupils and the chapel congregation.

Conditions at the agencies were so quiet that in June Spotted Tail went on a visit to Fort Laramie. His beloved daughter had been buried there in March, 1866, and he had always longed to bring her bones to his agency. He had gone to the fort in the summer of 1871 for that purpose, but at the time there was a threat of war and he had to give up the project. Now, in June, 1876, he went to the fort, then down into Colorado to visit friends in the Denver district, probably some of the old Indian traders who had a little colony there. Returning to Fort Laramie, he took the box containing his daughter's remains to his agency, where he had them reburied with much ceremony, the new bell at the Episcopal chapel being rung for the first time during the burial services.[2]

In early May, General Crook was waiting on the Upper Platte for more troops before starting the summer campaign. On the Upper Missouri, General Terry was collecting troops, including Custer's Seventh Cavalry, to march westward. In Montana, General John Gibbon was forming a third column, mainly infantry, to march

[2] Mrs. Cynthia J. Capron, in *Illinois Historical Society Journel*, Vol. XIII, 487. Mrs. Capron described Spotted Tail as a handsome man, his hair smooth and black, green cloth leggins with Indian beading down the sides, a dark blue blanket neatly disposed about his upper body with a wide white stripe extending down the center of the back of the blanket.

eastward down the Yellowstone. The Sioux and their Cheyenne and Arapaho allies were to be caught between these three columns.

To all appearances unaware that a war was on, the hostiles went hunting, and having laid in a stock of dried buffalo meat and skins, they came together in a great camp on the Rosebud to hold the annual Sun Dance. Here on the Rosebud parties of wild Sioux who had wintered at the agencies came into camp, bringing some agency Indians with them. They were well fed, nicely outfitted with new blankets, clothing, canvas tipi covers, and some arms and ammunition. They must have brought information concerning the activities of the troops, but if this information led the Sioux and Cheyenne chiefs to decide on any course of military action, the plans made have never been disclosed. As was customary, war parties left the camp when the Sun Dance ended, probably to go and steal ponies from the Crows and Shoshonis, and it was one of these war parties that discovered Crook's column near the head of the Rosebud, the warriors promptly returning to the main camp to report to the chiefs. The next morning, June 17, the Sioux and Cheyennes caught Crook two hours out of camp, unwarned despite his large force of Indian scouts, and in a roaring fight they mauled Crook's troops so severely that he gave up his plan to advance and remained in camp for some weeks, waiting for reinforcements.

Meantime the hostiles moved from the Rosebud to the Little Bighorn, and there Custer found their great camp on June 25. Dividing his command to prevent the Indians from getting away, Custer made a swift march down stream, intending to attack the lower end of the village; but the Sioux and Cheyennes crossed the stream, drove his troops back to the ridge, and there surrounded and killed them all. Meanwhile they had driven Major Reno's command out of the upper end of the village and back across the stream to high ground, where they kept Reno besieged until they learned that the troops of Terry and Gibbon were approaching. The Indians then took down their tipis and withdrew.

In these two battles against Crook and Custer, the Sioux and their Cheyenne allies exhibited superb fighting spirit and skill. They had abandoned the old Indian tactics of circling the enemy with their ponies at a hard run, shooting and whooping and giving up the fight if they lost a few warriors. In June, 1876, they swept down on the troops in a mass, each group led by a prominent warrior. They charged home, breaking the line, knocking the cavalrymen off their horses, and riding over them. When they hit Crook's well-ordered line, they threw it into confusion, and from that time on, the General was largely occupied in striving to reform his line of battle. The same thing happened to Reno on June 25, and it probably was the same in the Custer fight. But, fine as the fighting of the warriors was, the Indians had little in the way of general leadership. The tactics employed in battle were so simple that every leader of a small group of men knew what to do and did it, but when it came to leadership that could plan a campaign, the Indians had nothing to offer.

Having defeated Crook and destroyed Custer, the hostiles withdrew toward the Bighorn Mountains the moment they found that Terry and Gibbon were advancing up the Bighorn River. The leaders did not even plan to harass the advancing troops. Following the age-old custom, they put the war back into the bag for this season, broke up their assembled strength, and each camp when off to pursue its usual late-summer activities: going into the mountains to cut new lodgepoles and then resuming hunting. There were enough troops in their country to defeat them, but the Sioux had put the war away until next year, in the beautiful faith that the white soldiers would do the same.

Crook and Terry were simply waiting for reinforcements and supplies before resuming operations, but when they were ready to march again in August, they could not find any Indians to fight. The Generals joined forces on the Lower Powder River, then separated and started out to find the Indians. Part of the Sioux were now taking their camps to the agencies, where they fondly believed they would be fed and cared for all winter and permitted to return to Powder River in the spring of 1877 for another happy summer of hunting and fighting. Marching southward at the head of Crook's column, Colonel Anson Mills and his cavalry ran into one of these camps at Slim Buttes, north of the Black Hills. Mills took the Indians by surprise and captured the camp, but finding the Sioux hard to deal with, he sent a message to Crook asking for reinforcements. In this fight the chief, American Horse (alias Iron Shield), was killed and a number of women and children were captured. The camp contained trophies from the Custer battle and also papers showing that these Indians had wintered at Spotted Tail Agency and were regarded by Agent Howard as good folk. They said that Crazy Horse with a big camp was over to the west, on or near the Powder River, and would come to their aid, but the Oglala leader failed to make an appearance with his warriors. Crook, whose troops were worn out and short of rations, now decided to end the expedition and marched southward toward the Black Hills settlements and Camp Robinson.

Up near the Yellowstone, Colonel Nelson A. Miles, with a force of infantry, caught up with Sitting Bull, but after a brisk fight the Sioux got away northward. Miles then caught another Sioux group, mainly Miniconjous and Sans Arcs, and forced them to give a pledge that they would take their camps to the Cheyenne River Agency on the Missouri. The Sioux left some chiefs as hostages in Miles' hands, but most of the Indians failed to keep their pledge. Some of them did go to an agency, but it was Spotted Tail Agency that they chose. With Miles' operations, the campaign ended.[3]

Lieutenant General P. H. Sheridan, who had the top command in the operations against the Sioux, was furious over the failure of the troops to defeat the Indians and force them to go to the agencies. The country had been profoundly shocked by the news of the Custer disaster, and there was a strong feeling that the Indians must be punished. Unable to strike a blow at the hostiles, Sheridan demanded that the peaceful agency Sioux be turned over to the military, and in mid-August this was done. On August 15, Congress at last passed the much-delayed appropriation bill to provide for feeding and caring for the agency Sioux for the next year; but attached to this bill was a provision that no further funds should be voted for the Sioux until they gave up the Black Hills and the Powder River

[3] The story of the Sioux war of 1876 has been told so many times and in such detail that the brief account I have given here seems sufficient for the purposes of this volume, which deals mainly with Spotted Tail and his Brulés, who were not engaged in the war.

and Bighorn country, and agreed to remove to the Missouri, where they could be controlled and compelled to start farming.

Sheridan was impatient for Crook and Terry to bring their columns back from the field so that he might concentrate strong forces at the agencies and take stiff action against the Sioux. He sent an order to General Crook to leave his command, then in the Black Hills, and come down to the Union Pacific line for a conference. Red Cloud was disobeying his new military agent, and Sheridan was determined to teach him a lesson. The agency Sioux were greatly alarmed. As one of the chiefs said, this was a war the whites had started, and having failed to defeat the wild Sioux, they were now going to treat the agency Sioux as conquered people and force them to give up the Black Hills and the hunting lands in the Powder River and Bighorn country.

One of the first acts of the military after they took over the Sioux agencies was to make a census. Agent Hastings at Red Cloud was claiming that he had 12,873 Indians under his care, while Agent Howard at Spotted Tail claimed 9,170; but the new military agents in late August found by count only 4,760 Indians at Red Cloud and 4,775 at Spotted Tail. It was then claimed that these figures disclosed two things: first, that the civilian agents had been falsifying their returns and defrauding the government by representing that they were issuing rations and goods to a great many more Indians than they actually had, and, second, that large numbers of agency Indians had gone to join the hostile camps, this supposed fact explaining why the Sioux had exhibited such astonishing strength in their battles with Crook and Custer in June.

To be fair to the civilian agents, we must observe that they had no means of enforcing an accurate census, but most of the agents seem to have done the best they could to make fair estimates of the number of Indians under their care. The number fluctuated violently, for the Sioux were on the wing, moving their camps away from the agencies and back again seasonally. Another fact was that the Sioux were greatly alarmed when the military took over the agencies, and large numbers of the Indians ran away, many of the camps going to the Powder River to hunt, but moving too late in the season to take part in the battles of June. We have definite information that a number of Miniconjou and Sans Arc camps left the Cheyenne River when ordered by the military to move in close to the agency and be counted. The same thing probably happened at Spotted Tail and Red Cloud. From Red Cloud some 800 or 900 Northern Cheyennes fled to the Powder River; but they went too late to take part in the June battles, and their reason for running away was that the government had ordered their rations stopped in an attempt to force them to go to Indian Territory. Their leaving the agency had nothing whatever to do with the war then going on.

When Spotted Tail returned to his agency from his trip to Fort Laramie in late June, the news of the Crook and Custer battles had reached the Indians, who were greatly excited. The chief seems to have kept them under good control, as there was not a whisper of any trouble at his agency in July and August. Red Cloud was defying his agent and assuming an attitude of hostility toward the whites, but Colonel R. S. Mackenzie was at Camp Robinson within sight of Red Cloud Agency with eight troops of cavalry, and Red Cloud did not venture more than to talk war and flout his military agent's orders. When Spotted Tail was given a military agent, he was assigned Lieutenant Jesse M. Lee, who had been stationed at the agency for about a year and was a close personal friend. Spotted Tail had been a frequent guest at the Lee quarters; he had made a pet of Lieutenant Lee's small daughter, Maude, and she often went to the Indian camp to play with one of the chief's daughters who was about her own age.[4] Thus from the moment Lieutenant Lee was made agent his relations with Spotted Tail were of the best, and there were no signs of the bad feeling and plotting which were so much to the fore at Red Cloud Agency.

The Sioux at Spotted Tail and Red Cloud agencies had their attention turned toward the Powder River country, where the hostile camps and the troops were in movement in September, when

---

[4] Ten years ago, I exchanged letters with Maude Lee Rethers, of San Francisco, who told me what she remembered of Spotted Tail and his family. She had a scrapbook which I never saw containing articles which her mother had published in an Indianapolis newspaper during the years she lived among the Brulés—1876–78.

the new treaty commission arrived at Red Cloud and started operations to induce the chiefs to sign away the Black Hills and the Powder River and Bighorn hunting grounds. The Sioux were stunned
by this unexpected development, and they eyed the treaty commissioners with suspicion, calling them the praying men and liking
them no better because they pretended to be the good friends of the
Sioux, who had come to save them by taking from them all their
valuable holdings of land. The government was attempting to get
around the provisions of the treaty of 1868, which said plainly that
no Sioux lands could be ceded to the government in the future except by the approving vote of three-fourths of the Indian adult
males. To avoid this provision, the new treaty was termed an agreement and was to be approved only by the chiefs. It was an agreement, drawn up in Washington without consulting the Sioux or even
notifying them of what was going on; and it was to be approved
by the chiefs without the altering of a single word. To call it an
agreement was a shocking misuse of the word. It most closely resembled peace terms proffered by conquerors to the conquered at the
close of a victorious war. The government had not won the war.
It was not even dealing with the hostile Sioux, but with the friendly
agency Indians who had taken no part in the war.

Bishop H. B. Whipple, of the Episcopal church, and Newton
Edmunds, former governor of Dakota Territory and an old hand
at talking Sioux chiefs into signing treaties, were members of this
commission. They and some of the other members were supposed
to be the friends of the Sioux; they emphasized this in all the
councils, and they had agreed among themselves on a new wildcat
scheme for saving the Sioux (and incidentally the government) from
the very troublous situation they were in, by removing the tribe to
Indian Territory. When this plan was broached to the chiefs, they
shied violently away from it. One of the chiefs said reproachfully
to the commissioners: "You speak to me about another land, a country far away from this. I think you should not have mentioned this
to me at all. My grandfathers and relations have lived here always.
There is no blood on this paper [meaning the agreement was not
one ending a war]; we are not at war with you; and therefore
when you speak of a strange land, a land where we were not brought

up, a land far away, my chiefs and soldiers are very much displeased, and they wish me to say that they are displeased with the mention of that land." This splendidly worded rebuke should have stopped the talk of removal to Indian Territory; but the men on the commission, filled with righteous faith that they knew best what would be good for the Sioux, went on pressing for removal. Turned down by all the chiefs, they ignored that and announced that a delegation of chiefs was to be taken to Indian Territory to see the land and decide on removal.

The councils at Red Cloud Agency were opened by Bishop Whipple, who prayed fervently for the unhappy Sioux. He and Newton Edmunds assured the Indians that they were their friends, who had come to save them from destruction. Assistant Attorney General Gaylord then spoke menacingly, explaining to the Sioux just what destruction meant. They must sign this agreement or their people would have no more rations; they would starve; they would be turned over to the military, and then they would be removed, either to the Missouri River or to Indian Territory.[5]

The chiefs at Red Cloud were all unwilling to sign the agreement. Most of them complained that the whites had taken their lands, piece by piece, and now this new paper was to take in one

[5] The plan for removing northern Indian tribes to Indian Territory was highly favored by the Eastern Christian and benevolent groups who were meddling in Indian welfare work in the 1870's. The dreadful death rate and misery caused to such tribes as the Nebraska Pawnees when forced to move to the Territory did not in the least deter these visionaries. Newton Edmunds does not seem to have been particularly eager to have the Sioux sent to the Territory. As a Dakota business leader he is said to have preferred the plan to remove the Sioux to the Missouri River in Dakota, where the Indians would be a source of steady profit to Dakota men, who would get the contracts for supplying the Sioux. In northeastern Nebraska this plan was not approved of, as the Nebraska settlers had no wish to see the wild Sioux settled near at hand in great force. The editor of the Niobrara, Nebraska, *Pioneer*, violently objected to having Spotted Tail's thousands of "outlaws" settled on the northeastern Nebraska border. In his issue of April 5, 1877, he said that Newton Edmunds had taken a leading part in the shanghaiing of the peaceful little Ponca tribe, which had been sent unwillingly to Indian Territory so that Spotted Tail's Sioux could have the Ponca reservation on the Missouri, and he hinted that Agent James Lawrence was to be rewarded for helping to ship the Poncas south by being made Spotted Tail's new agent. This appointment was actually made; but for some reason Mr. Lawrence after some hesitation refused, and another man was appointed as Spotted Tail's agent.

great bite all the best lands they still had. They wished to have the military garrisons removed from the Sioux reservation so that they would be free again; but they were not mentally equipped to comprehend that the presence of troops on the reservation was a small matter compared with the things that had been inserted into this falsely termed agreement. Ever since they had come to the reservation, the Sioux had opposed the government plans to destroy the chiefs. This agreement provided for by-passing the chiefs and having the government agent ignore them and deal with the head of each Sioux family. Ever since 1868, Spotted Tail and nearly all the other leaders had opposed the government scheme to force the Sioux to go to work at farming. The agreement provided that no Sioux who was able to work should receive rations and other free supplies if he did not start farming. This meant work or see your family starve, a curious plan for Eastern Christians and humanitarians to approve of. It was not as if the Sioux were ordinary lazy people. They believed that they had been robbed of lands sufficient to pay for free rations for many years to come, and this would give them the opportunity to accustom themselves to a new way of life and work. That at least was what chiefs like Spotted Tail thought. They wanted no forced labor in an effort to make the Sioux immediately self-supporting.

The commission went to Spotted Tail Agency and found the Indians just as unwilling to sign the agreement as those at Red Cloud. Mr. Gaylord, the assistant attorney general, then put pressure on the chiefs. He spoke grimly of what would happen to the Sioux if the chiefs did not sign. Rations would be stopped; the Indians and their families would starve; the troops would take over and treat the Sioux roughly; they would be removed from their present lands by force. Standing Elk, of the Corn Band, a friendly and reasonably progressive chief, lost his temper at this point. He said to Gaylord: "My friend, your words are like a man knocking me in the head with a club. By your speech you have put great fear upon us. Whatever the white people ask of us, wherever we go, we always say *Yes—yes—yes!* Whenever we don't agree to what is asked of us in council, you always reply: *You won't get anything to eat!—You won't get anything to eat!*" Spotted Tail said that they might be compelled by pressure to let their names be signed to this paper, but that he would not touch the pen. That meant that he would not legalize his signature by holding the end of the pen with his fingers while his name was written down and attested. He jumped up, left the council, and went to speak to Red Cloud and his chiefs who were waiting outside, but the conference brought no relief to the Brulé chief's worried mind. He came back into the council and said to the chiefs and headmen: "If our friends above [Red Cloud's Indians above on White River] had not already signed it, I would help them in holding out; but as they have signed it, I now ask all good men who feel responsible to come up and sign." He then went to the table and held the end of the pen while his name was signed. The other chiefs and headmen followed him.

Thus in a few days the commission, by warning the Sioux that they were facing disaster, by assuring them that the commission was made up of friends who had come to save them, by coaxing and praying, by making dire threats, turned the overwhelming disapproval of the agreement into almost unanimous assent. The commission then left to go to the Sioux agencies on the Missouri and repeat their performance there.

In recent years the Sioux brought a suit against the government, still pending before the Indian Claims Commission, for the illegal taking of the Black Hills and other lands in 1876. The government is doing as it always does in such cases—diligently piling up counter claims; so many millions for free rations and free supplies given to the Sioux, so many millions for education, so many millions for teaching the unwilling Indians to farm. In the end the Sioux will probably not receive one dollar for their lands, but they will have the satisfaction of a court decision that the praying men of the 1876 commission robbed them.

Bishop Whipple described Spotted Tail at these councils in September, 1876, as "a picture of manly beauty, with piercing eyes, self-possessed, a man who knew what he wanted to say and said it." One cannot doubt that if Red Cloud and his chiefs had not signed first Spotted Tail would have opposed signing. He said in council that he would not sign until he and the other chiefs had been given the opportunity to go to Washington for a conference with the

President. It was the Gaylord threats that the Sioux would be starved, dragooned, and forcibly removed either to the Missouri River or to Indian Territory that finally convinced the chief that the agreement must be signed. When he spoke of good men who felt responsible, he was exhibiting his idea of good leadership. In the position in which the Sioux found themselves, to oppose the government's will would be perhaps a noble action, but it would be an irresponsible one that would bring down on the helpless people starvation and other miseries.

Red Cloud was still bent on making trouble. It seems a pity that he did not realize that an excellent opportunity for doing so was presented to him in this Black Hills agreement. If he had held out, Spotted Tail would have done so and the Washington officials might have been highly embarrassed by the public scandal of the two best-known Sioux chiefs loudly proclaiming that their people were being threatened and robbed. But Red Cloud missed that chance, and as soon as he had led the Sioux in signing the detested agreement, he returned to his favorite activity of disobeying or ignoring his military agent. Ordered to move his camp close to the agency where it would be under observation, he moved over twenty miles away to Chadron Creek, taking Red Leaf's camp of Wazhazhas with him. There the two chiefs established their camps and ignored the order to move in near the agency.

Colonel R. S. Mackenzie, in command at Camp Robinson, was alarmed by rumors that Red Cloud and Red Leaf were planning an uprising. He reported the facts, and when General Crook went down to the Union Pacific line for his conference with General Sheridan, the matter was discussed. Crook wished to wait until his column of troops could be marched from the Black Hills to Camp Robinson before he dealt with Red Cloud, but Sheridan thought the situation dangerous and urged immediate action. A force of Pawnee Scouts had been recruited in Indian Territory to serve against the Sioux and had been brought out along the Union Pacific to Sidney Barracks, near the forks of the Platte. Here Major Frank North, commanding the Pawnees, received orders to march northward and join the cavalry from Camp Robinson in the operation aimed at the camps of Red Cloud and Red Leaf. On October 23

257

the Sioux of these two camps went to bed and slept soundly. At dawn on the twenty-fourth the Pawnees charged the camps, taking them completely by surprise and running off the pony herds. The Sioux, finding themselves afoot and facing a superior force of cavalry and mounted Pawnees, submitted and were ignominiously marched off, under guard, to the agency.

At this moment a subcommittee of the treaty commission came back to Red Cloud Agency to collect a delegation of chiefs to go to view Indian Territory. Red Cloud was still regarded by the public as the most important Sioux chief, and the committee wished to have him on the delegation; but when they arrived at the agency, they were informed curtly by the military officers that the army was engaged in an operation concerned with Red Cloud and that they could not see or speak with that chief until the army gave permission. Red Cloud and Red Leaf, as it was reported, were at the moment in the guardhouse as prisoners.

Spotted Tail was furious over this persistence about removal to Indian Territory. During the councils in late September the chiefs had turned down this proposal firmly, yet now in late October the whites were taking it for granted that the Sioux were willing to consider the matter. They were not. But Spotted Tail knew that if he and the other important chiefs refused to go to look at Indian Territory, this committee would make up a delegation of Sioux nonentities, take them to the Territory, talk them round, and then pretend that the Sioux nation had decided on removal. General Sheridan was using all his great power in favor of immediately shipping all the Sioux south. He was so blinded by anger that he even pretended that Spotted Tail and the other chiefs had only signed the agreement in September as a ruse to delay removal to Indian Territory. Faced with this situation, Spotted Tail said grimly that he would go to the Territory on this delegation, but that during the journey he would keep his eyes shut, his ears shut, and his mouth shut. He would say nothing that might be twisted into approval of this wicked plan to remove his people from their own land.

But he was of too lively a disposition to sulk and keep silent for any length of time. This was his first journey into the south, and he was very much interested to see the southern lands and to find there the famous tribes of old—the Delawares and Shawnees, the Cherokees, Chickasaws, and Seminoles. He enjoyed his visit and made amiable short speeches, but he was very careful to say nothing that might be represented as approval of taking his tribe to the Territory to live, and he seems to have warned the other chiefs on the delegation to take the same precaution. How right he was! The committee was fervently in favor of removal, and it presently made a written report in which it pretended that the Sioux were favorably inclined toward removal. There never was a falser statement made.

It must have been just after his return from Indian Territory that Spotted Tail met the nun who came to his agency, seeking to recruit Indian girls to be educated at her convent in Kansas City. Spotted Tail was not interested in Christianity and education, and he was doing what he could to make life miserable for the Episcopal church missionary and his two devoted virgin assistants, who had come to start a chapel and school. The chief called the Episcopalians White Robes and the Catholics Black Robes, and when members of either color of robes turned up, he generally threw cold water over them. At the request of the Protestant churches, President Grant had parceled out the Sioux agencies to the different denominations, and in this distribution the English Episcopal church had been given the Spotted Tail and Red Cloud agencies as mission and school fields. There was a kind of gentlemen's agreement that no church was to trespass on the field of the other, but the Roman Catholics were trying to slip in wherever they could find an opening. A priest came to Spotted Tail Agency to scout the ground. He was attempting to use the fact that Father De Smet had baptised a number of Brulé infants at the 1851 treaty council to support a claim that the Roman Catholics had been first among the Brulés. Through an interpreter he kept asking Spotted Tail about the children De Smet had sprinkled water on—who were these children, what had become of them in the years since 1851? Spotted Tail was bored by all this talk. At this time it was very rainy—it rained nearly every day. Spotted Tail, after listening to the priest for a long time, lost patience. "Tell him," he said to the interpreter, "that I do not know anything about the Brulé babies that Black Robe threw water on at the old treaty council, but recently God Almighty has been throwing a great deal too much water on all of us, and I wish that someone would ask him to please let up on us."

But to return to the nun who visited Spotted Tail Agency in the autumn of 1876. She and the young novice who was with her were entertained by Mrs. Anson Mills, the wife of the commanding officer at Camp Sheridan, and Spotted Tail was invited to the house to meet her. Lemonade was served, and the nun (who appears to have been a lively lady) sprang up laughing, holding out her glass toward Spotted Tail and dancing toward him. The chief instantly jumped up and began dancing toward her, holding out his glass. In the center of the room the two met, clinked glasses and stood laughing and drinking. That was the beginning. Presently the nun had a promise from the chief that he would give her one of his daughters to take to the Kansas City convent to be educated. That would mean success for the venture, for the minute the other Indians knew that Spotted Tail was sending a daughter to the convent, they would forget their prejudices and be willing to let the nun take some of their daughters.

The girl Spotted Tail was going to sacrifice to the white men's god called Education was *Chau-hu-luta*: Red Road. The army officers and their wives called her *Chankoo*. Maude Lee, the daughter of Lieutenant Jesse Lee, remembered her very clearly in recent years. She described Red Road as a pretty girl, tall and dignified and as proud as a princess. This description also fits Spotted Tail's daughter who died in 1866 and was buried at Fort Laramie. These two girls were very proud of being Spotted Tail's daughters, and they both had a lot of their father's dignity and spirit. Colonel Anson Mills stated that Red Road was seventeen in 1876; but the official records show that she was only eighteen in 1879. Sioux girls looked older than their years, and they were marriageable at thirteen or fourteen.

Colonel Mills, in his account, states that Red Road and her mother were present when the nun and Spotted Tail danced together. The subject of sending Red Road to the convent was then broached, and Spotted Tail agreed to it. Red Road sat with face stiff with astonishment or outrage and said never a word. Colonel

Mills suggested to the chief that it would be better to ask the girl's approval, but Spotted Tail brushed that aside, saying carelessly that it was all right, the girl would do as he told her to. He forgot that she had part of his own brain and spirit in her. She was given three days to prepare. On the third day, instead of bringing her to Camp Sheridan and turning her over to the nun, Spotted Tail sent a glum message to announce that Red Road had eloped with a young warrior named Lone Elk and had gone off to some distant Sioux camp where her father could not find her.

Red Road soon tired of Lone Elk. She came home, and a year or two later was married to Charles Tackett, a young half-blood at the agency of whom Spotted Tail had a good opinion. Education still pursued poor Red Road. In the fall of 1879 her father made her go with her husband to Carlisle Indian School in Pennsylvania, not as a learner but as matron in charge of the Sioux children who were being taken to the school.[6]

The Sioux had put the war away until next year after the Custer battle on June 25; but General Sheridan was in no mood for playing at war in the Sioux fashion. Returning from the field in October, General Crook began preparations for a winter campaign. Demanding more scouts from Red Cloud and Spotted Tail agencies, he obtained some. He also had the Pawnee Scouts. While Crook was preparing to take the field, Colonel Nelson A. Miles, up on the Yellowstone, was sending messages to the Sioux hostiles urging them to surrender to him. In October he told the Miniconjous and Sans Arcs that if they surrendered, an agency would be established for them at the forks of the Cheyenne River, just east of the Black Hills, and a military officer would be made their agent, who would treat them generously. Thus Miles was making use of the Northern agency plan which Bishop Hare had urged on President Grant in the spring of 1874, as the best means to assure peace with the Sioux.

---

[6] Anson Mills, *My Story*, 184–86. Maude Lee Rethers remembered Red Road as a tall, pretty and proud girl, too old in 1876 to play with her and with Spotted Tail's younger daughter. This girl's name is one quite common among the Sioux: *Chanku* (Road) *luta* (Red). She was then eighteen and married to Charles Tackett. Recently Harry Anderson found the name in the 1879 records of the persons who went to Carlisle School from Spotted Tail's agency that fall: Chau-hu-luta: Red Road (Mrs. Charles Tackett), age eighteen.

At that time the officials in Washington had pigeonholed the agency plan and preferred to send Custer on a military expedition to the Black Hills; and out of that move had come war. In November, 1876, some of the Miniconjous and Sans Arcs joined Crazy Horse's camp on Tongue River, and they brought to the camp Colonel Miles' offer of an agency for the surrendered hostiles, but the leaders in the Crazy Horse camp were not at all inclined to surrender. They talked war. They had a medicine man in their camp who had taken Custer's Sioux name of Long Hair and pretended that he was holding daily conferences with the spirit of the dead General, who seems to have been sending Crazy Horse advice to keep a strong heart and continue to fight.

Crazy Horse kept a strong heart, but did no fighting. From September on, he had a wonderful opportunity to strike at the whites in the Black Hills; but the only plan his war *junta* had was to go hunting and to bully those families in the camp who were weak enough to wish to go in to the agencies and surrender. Crazy Horse's Indian soldiers shot the ponies of these families, cut up their tipis, and threatened to kill the men if they tried to leave camp.[7]

When Crook struck in November, it was not at the Crazy Horse group but at the Northern Cheyennes. This seems a pity, for these Cheyennes do not appear to have been out-and-out hostiles. They had run away from Red Cloud Agency in June, too late for the Crook and Custer battles, and mainly because the officials had ordered their rations stopped in a wicked attempt to starve them into leaving their own land and removing to Indian Territory. The troops, under the immediate command of Colonel R. S. Mackenzie, surprised the Cheyenne camp, hidden away in a canyon on the Red Fork of the Powder River, at dawn on November 25, and after a long and fierce fight, captured the camp with all the Cheyenne winter supply of food and clothing and most of the Indian ponies. The Cheyennes fled northward in bitter weather and, according to In-

[7] I am under much obligation to my friend Harry H. Anderson for new material from the National Archives on the events of October, 1876–March, 1877. He found the Miles offer of an agency in the archives, also the report on Long Hair, the medicine man, and on Crazy Horse's bullying of the families that wished to leave his camp and surrender.

dian information obtained by Crook, went to Crazy Horse, who turned the hungry and freezing Cheyennes away, thereby winning their hatred. After this fight on Powder River, Crook directed his march toward the east, on information his scouts had picked up from Cheyenne women, who said that a large Sioux camp was on the Belle Fourche, northwest of the Black Hills. The weather was severe, and when Crook failed to find any indications of a Sioux camp on the Belle Fourche, he gave up the expedition and returned to his base.

Crook now went to Camp Robinson at Red Cloud Agency, where he had a strong force of troops. The Sioux had been forced to move in close to the agency, and the valley of White River was filled with their camps. We have little information concerning conditions at Spotted Tail Agency during the winter, but the Indians were probably camped close to the agency, where the troops at Camp Sheridan could keep a watch on them. Spotted Tail was often with General Crook, eating with the officers in the mess. Red Cloud was also a frequent guest at meals, and the two chiefs were distantly polite to each other. Spotted Tail had been made head of the Indians at both agencies when Red Cloud was brought back from Chadron Creek as a prisoner on October 24, and apparently this situation continued all winter. It did not matter much, but it hurt Red Cloud's feelings dreadfully. He was now as friendly as he could be in his dealings with the army, but Crook and the other officers preferred Spotted Tail. Captain John G. Bourke, of Crook's staff, described Spotted Tail in 1876 as dignified but affable and friendly, easy to please but sharp as a briar; a good talker, witty and sensible, with his views carefully thought out and well expressed. He could understand a little English, enough to get along in simple talk. Bourke expressed the belief that one day a bronze statue of this great chief, the friend of two races, would be erected in Nebraska or Dakota. Well, well. . . . Times change, and today it is the morose and savage Crazy Horse who is being honored as the man of peace and typical American Indian by having a memorial to him carved on the side of a mountain in the Black Hills.

The Sioux themselves were not admirers of Crazy Horse in November and December, 1876. He was soldiering them to keep them in the hostile camp where they did not wish to stay. At Red Cloud Agency, where the Crazy Horse cult is strong today, the talk was that most of the people in the hostile camp were ready to come in and surrender and that the one chief at the agencies whom they most respected and would be most willing to listen to was Spotted Tail. General Crook had Colonel J. W. Mason, a particular friend of Spotted Tail's, open negotiations with that chief, who expressed a willingness to go to the hostile camps, but not unless he had from General Crook's own lips a pledge that the Sioux would be given liberal terms of surrender, specifically stated by the General in person. The exasperated Crook had to drop important business and come, either from Omaha or Fort Laramie, all the way to Spotted Tail Agency for further talks with the chief. The terms of surrender he offered were agreed to, but Spotted Tail insisted on another point. He said that he must take a strong force of armed Brulé headmen and warriors with him to insure that he would be received in honor at the hostile camps and should not be exposed to the sniping operations of Sioux die-hards. Crook agreed that this was wise, and he instructed the commanding officer at Camp Sheridan to give Spotted Tail the ammunition, rations, and other supplies he needed, so that the success of his visit to the hostiles would be assured. The chief even obtained a number of army pack mules to transport his supplies, and having made all preparations, he set out with 250 armed Brulés in February, 1877, to go all the way north to the Little Missouri and the Powder River under weather conditions that made it impossible for the troops to move.

During the conference with General Crook, Spotted Tail refused to go to the hostiles to talk peace, unless the General would pledge his word now that he would use his great influence in Washington to have the order for the removal of the Sioux agencies to the Missouri set aside. The General gave such a pledge, and the chief then agreed to go to the hostile camps. Those critics who have described Spotted Tail as subservient to the whites and a self-seeker should ponder this. The removal of the Sioux to the Missouri was to be the entering wedge for the plan to remove the tribe to Indian Territory, a fatal decision for the Sioux and probably for the whites. This was a matter more important than making peace with the hostiles, and Spotted Tail was the only chief wise enough to know it.

Meantime, Colonel Nelson A. Miles, from his cantonment on the Tongue River, had been attempting to induce the hostiles to surrender to him. His terms were unconditional surrender, but even so, many of the Indians exhibited a strong inclination to give up. They wanted food and warm clothing for their families, and only the fierce opposition of Crazy Horse and his Indian soldiers prevented a general movement toward peace. In mid-December, just about the time when Crook's officers were trying to persuade Spotted Tail to go on a peace mission, the group called the Crazy Horse hostiles were encamped near the head of the Tongue River. From this camp a large party went to Colonel Miles' cantonment, seeking peace. When they approached the cantonment, the Sioux were marching in a column, and some distance ahead five chiefs and headmen were marching abreast, carrying peace pipes. Unfortunately the Crow Scouts at the cantonment were the first to discover the Sioux and get mounted, and before any white officer could stop them, they made a fierce charge and killed all five of the Sioux leaders. The rest of the Sioux fled. Miles was furious. He dismounted the Crows and sent all their ponies to the Sioux, with tobacco and a peace message, but the Sioux had had enough of that kind of peace negotiations.

The reports of the Sioux who came from the hostile camp to surrender at Cheyenne River Agency during the winter contain curious details concerning the situation among the hostiles. There are five of these reports in the National Archives. Crazy Horse had about six hundred lodges—his own Oglalas, a Cheyenne camp, camps of Miniconjous and Sans Arcs, some Hunkpapas (the Four Horns camp?), and some small groups of mixed Sioux. A majority of the Indians wished to go to the agencies or to surrender to Miles, and Crazy Horse was using his Soldiers Lodge to intimidate those groups that sought peace. Red Horse, a chief and member of the Miniconjou tribal council, was infuriated. He warned Crazy Horse to keep his soldiers out of his camp and said angrily that he was going to Cheyenne River Agency and would fight the Crazy Horse soldiers if interfered with.

The Indians were quarreling the whole time. In December part of them went to make peace with Miles, but the attack by the Crow Scouts broke up their plan. In early January, Sitting Bull came down from the north with a group of his people to confer with Crazy Horse. He brought fifty-four boxes of fixed ammunition and a quantity of new blankets, probably obtained by trade with the Canadian Red River half-bloods, which he gave to Crazy Horse. The character in the Crazy Horse camp who called himself Long Hair, after Custer, and pretended to be in nightly contact with the spirit of the dead officer, was also producing a box of fixed ammunition each night, pretending he obtained it by making medicine. Everything possible was being done by the hostile leaders in this camp to keep the war going—everything except to go out and attack either Miles' troops or the thousands of miners in the Black Hills.[8]

In early January, Miles upset Crazy Horse's arrangements by sending a column of five hundred infantry to attack his camp. Crazy Horse tried the same old decoy-party trap that all Sioux leaders seem to have produced as the only stratagem in their box of tricks, but the infantry avoided the trap. On January 8, the mounted warriors who had overwhelmed Custer's cavalry in the previous June were defeated by the despised walk-a-heap soldiers of the infantry, who drove them five miles up the Tongue River through snow and cold toward their camp. Crazy Horse now moved his camp to the Little Powder, and the Miniconjous and Sans Arcs sought safety even farther away on the Little Missouri. Four Horns took his Hunkpapa camp north of the Yellowstone, and in the spring he crossed the line to find safety in Canada. The Sioux might talk, but the war was ended.[9]

[8] The reports of the Sioux who came to Cheyenne River Agency in the winter and spring indicated that in September–November, 1876, the less hostile chiefs, such as Touch-the-Clouds, Roman Nose, and Red Bear, had very little influence in the Crazy Horse camp, where the Indian soldiers and the war party were in full control; but hunger and cold and the defeat by Miles' infantry brought a change, which caused the Miniconjous and Sans Arcs, who now desired peace, to leave Crazy Horse and go to the Little Missouri. Even in Crazy Horse's Oglala camp the desire for peace was strong.

[9] Here are some additional items from Harry Anderson's notes taken from the Sioux statements made in January and February. It was Crazy Horse's Oglalas and the Cheyennes who tried to force the other Sioux to remain in the hostile camp

One might suppose from the remarks of some of Spotted Tail's critics that this Brulé chief was the only man among the Sioux who wanted peace in the winter of 1876–77. They either ignore or never heard of the peace movement in the hostile camp, which had a good start in October, 1876, or of the talk among Oglala relatives of Crazy Horse at Red Cloud Agency, which resulted in Sword's leading a party of Oglalas to Crazy Horse's camp to urge the hostile leaders to give up and come to the agencies. Sword was Red Cloud's nephew. His party was in the hostile camp in January. The documents in the National Archives do not show just what Sword did among the hostiles, but Chief No Water brought his camp to Red Cloud Agency and surrendered, March 19, 1877, perhaps as a result of Sword's peace talks.

Spotted Tail, with his 250 Brulé warriors, left the agency about February 15 and started for the hostile camps. Just north of White River they discovered a camp of twenty-five lodges of hostiles who were afraid to go in to the agency. Spotted Tail reassured them and sent them in to surrender. His party reached the big camps on the Little Missouri, north of the Black Hills, in March. These were Miniconjous and Sans Arcs under Touch-the-Clouds, Roman Nose, Red Bear, and High Bear. After councils with Spotted Tail, the chiefs pledged themselves to bring their camps to his agency and surrender as soon as the weather permitted them to move. Going to the Little Powder, Spotted Tail found the Crazy Horse group camped in deep snow. Crazy Horse was away all alone on a hunt. Spotted Tail talked to his father, Old Crazy Horse, who told him

by soldiering them. Old Lone Horn, the head of the Miniconjous, had died in the winter of 1875–76, and his sons now controlled separate Miniconjou camps. Whether they were in the Custer battle or not is uncertain. Touch-the-Clouds, one of his sons, had his camp within reach of Cheyenne River Agency in July, 1876, but moved away when ordered to come to the agency to be disarmed and dismounted. Another son, Spotted Elk (alias Big Foot), killed at Wounded Knee in 1890, also had a Miniconjou camp. Roman Nose had a third. They were all in the Crazy Horse camp, in early winter. Spotted Elk and Red Horse then went to Cheyenne River and surrendered their camps. Touch-the-Clouds and Roman Nose, evidently in January, moved east from the Crazy Horse camp to the Little Missouri, where Spotted Tail found them. Spotted Elk (Big Foot) was with the Sioux when they went to talk surrender to Miles in December, when the Crow Scouts killed the five Sioux chiefs and headmen.

that his son had left a message saying that he shook hands with Uncle Spotted Tail through his father and that he would bring his camp to the agency and surrender as soon as the weather made that possible. Crazy Horse's avoidance of a meeting on the pretense of hunting was neither straightforward nor courteous. Spotted Tail did not like it. He sent a Brulé and an Oglala to Crazy Horse, with tobacco and a message, but they could not find him. Spotted Tail then tried to get in touch with Sitting Bull; but he had moved north of the Yellowstone and no one knew where his camp was situated. Chief Four Horns, who had been in Crazy Horse's camp earlier in the winter, had had enough and had moved north. He took his camp of Hunkpapas across the boundary into Canada while Spotted Tail was on his mission in the hostile camps. Sitting Bull with the last of the hostiles crossed into Canada in early May.

Spotted Tail was occupied for fifty days on his trip to the hostile camps and home again. He came back to his agency with a few of his Brulés on April 5, exhausted but anxious to see General Crook at once. He dictated a report to his agent, Lieutenant Lee, and to Colonel Anson Mills, stating that he had left a big hostile camp (Miniconjous and Sans Arcs—170 crowded lodges, 1,500 people) on the Belle Fourche, north of the Black Hills, on April 2. They were moving down from the Little Missouri to surrender at his agency. The chief said he believed the Cheyennes would soon surrender at Red Cloud Agency, and Crazy Horse a little later.[10]

Red Cloud—jealous of all the attention Spotted Tail was receiving from the army officers at Camp Robinson and Camp Sheridan —had come forward, rather late in the day, with a proposal that he follow the Brulé chief's example and use his influence to induce the hostiles to surrender. He did not offer to go to the hostile camps in February or March, but after Spotted Tail had accomplished his task and had the hostiles moving in, Red Cloud offered to go out and hasten Crazy Horse's march. Like Spotted Tail, he was Crazy

[10] *Spotted Tail report*, dictated through an interpreter to Lieutenant Jesse M. Lee, April 5, 1877, in the National Archives. Spotted Tail left Merrival (interpreter) and most of his Brulés with the hostile camp and said the hostiles would reach Buffalo Gap, in the Black Hills, in eight or nine days. He gave the number in the camp as 1,500, but only 917 surrendered on April 14. Perhaps the Lame Deer camp ran away from the main camp after Spotted Tail left it.

Horse's uncle, but he and Crazy Horse were Oglalas, and Crazy Horse would pay more heed to the head chief of his tribe than to Spotted Tail. Anxious to get Crazy Horse to surrender quickly, General Crook accepted Red Cloud's offer, and sent him northward at the head of quite an imposing caravan. Red Cloud apparently started out just about the time Spotted Tail returned home, his mission completed. On April 15, Red Cloud had a half-blood who was with him send in a report that the Crazy Horse camp was on Bear Lodge Creek, west of the Black Hills.

The day before Red Cloud reported, on April 14, the Miniconjous, under Touch-the-Cloud and Roman Nose, and the Sans Arcs, under Red Bear and High Bear, came to Spotted Tail Agency and Camp Sheridan and surrendered. Touch-the-Clouds and the other chiefs had stipulated to Spotted Tail that they were to be permitted to surrender in their own manner. They marched in proudly, the war-shirt-wearers in line at the head of the column, behind them the chiefs with the tribal soldiers, then the column of warriors, and in the rear the women, children, and old people with the moving camp. The column extended back across the prairie to a distance of about two miles. The Sioux rode in chanting war songs; and coming up close to the waiting troops, they threw their weapons on the ground and rode away to where the women were putting up the camp. The troops then rounded up and drove away the Indian ponies and searched the tipis for additional weapons. On May 5, Crazy Horse came in at Red Cloud Agency and Camp Robinson, and this same performance was repeated in the presence of General Crook and his officers. On May 7, Sitting Bull took the last of the hostiles across the line into Canada. Only a small camp of Miniconjous, under Chief Lame Deer, remained in the Powder River country; but the day after Crazy Horse's surrender and the day before Sitting Bull entered Canada, the troops of Colonel Nelson A. Miles surprised Lame Deer's camp, killing that chief and capturing the camp and its contents.

In May, 1877, Spotted Tail's reputation was very high, both among the Sioux and among the officers at the military posts. Colonel Nelson A. Miles and possibly Crazy Horse were the only men who did not share in the general admiration for the great

Brulé chief. Colonel Miles had been quite loud in criticizing Spotted Tail (and through him, General Crook) for practically stealing his hostiles. He complained that Spotted Tail had come to the hostile camps in March with handsome terms of surrender, handing out rations and bags of ammunition to sweeten the terms. Miles was offering plain unconditional surrender, and the way it worked out was that Spotted Tail induced ten hostiles to surrender to General Crook for each hostile who surrendered to Miles. As for Crazy Horse, he did not like anyone who had had a hand in coaxing his people to surrender.

At this time, Spotted Tail had a salary from General Crook, the only Sioux chief who ever enjoyed the felicity of drawing a government salary. It would be interesting to know just why he was paid and how much. One report was that he was being paid as head chief of the Sioux Nation; another, that Crook intended to make him an "honorary major" in the army with the salary of one thousand dollars a year. The critics of the Brulé chief cannot pretend that he was enriching himself at the expense of the people, for it is on record that he insisted on being paid in one-dollar bills and then distributed the whole amount among the poorer Sioux families. The ponies surrendered by the hostiles were the real treasure that covetous men had their eyes on. The Crazy Horse camp was said to have surrendered 2,500 ponies, and to the grief of Red Cloud and his chiefs, the military drove the ponies to Fort Laramie and sold them there at a pitifully small price, impounding the money to be used for the benefit of the Sioux in such matters as farming and education, which did not cheer the agency chiefs at all. They still hated the very talk of farming and schools. General Crook turned over about 1,200 ponies, surrendered by the Miniconjous and Sans Arcs, to Spotted Tail and the Brulé chiefs and headmen as a reward for their good services in bringing about the surrender; and again Spotted Tail gave away all this wealth, giving many of the ponies back to the surrendered hostiles, and his chiefs and headmen followed his example.[11]

[11] The National Archives records show ponies surrendered at Spotted Tail Agency, October, 1876, to January, 1877, 48 head; March, 1877, 60; April and May, 1,243.

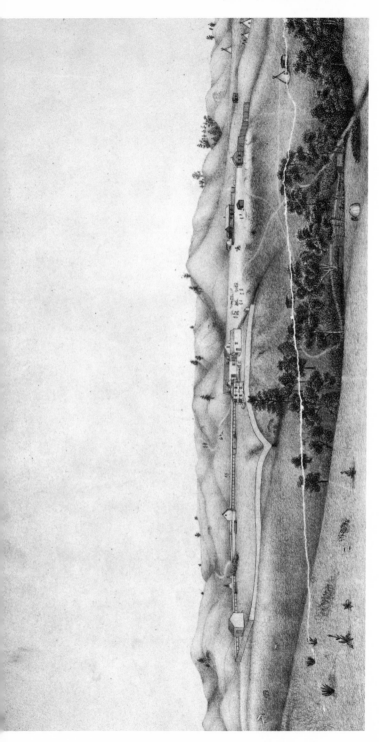

This drawing, by James McCoy, dated May 3, 1879, is the earliest known illustration of the Rosebud Agency, often called the Spotted Tail Agency. (From *The Sioux of the Rosebud*, by Henry W. Hamilton and Jean Tyree Hamilton)

The Rosebud Agency, a panoramic view looking southwest, 1889. (Photograph by John A. Anderson. From *The Sioux of the Rosebud*, by Henry W. Hamilton and Jean Tyree Hamilton)

White Cliffs (now Red Cloud Buttes) near the head of White River, from a point near Red Cloud Agency, looking north. (Photograph by Marvin F. Kivett, 1957)

Chief Hollow Horn Bear, Cut Meat District. (Photograph by John A. Anderson. From *The Sioux of the Rosebud*, by Henry W. Hamilton and Jean Tyree Hamilton)

Spotted Tail's house at the agency, 1889. (Photograph by John A. Anderson. From *The Sioux of the Rosebud*, by Henry W. Hamilton and Jean Tyree Hamilton)

Men of the Brulé Sioux, Rosebud Agency, 1894. *Front row, left to right*: Tall Mandan, Turning Eagle, Thin Elk, Big Head, Picket Pin, Turning Bear, High Bear, Lance, High Pipe, High Hawk, Yellow Hair, Little Thunder, Bear Head, He Dog, Black Bull.

Second row, left to right: Louis Roubideaux (interpreter), Whirlwind Soldier, Yellow Horse, Good Voice, White Crane Walking, Pretty Eagle, Ring Thunder, Stranger Horse, Quick Bear, Swift Bear, Poor Dog, Hollow Horn Bear, Crow Dog, Two Strike, Milk, Sky Bull, Stands and Looks Back, Bear Looks Behind, Colonel Charles P. Jordan.

Third row, left to right: Blue Eyes, Big Horse, Joe Good Voice. (Photograph by John A. Anderson. From *The Sioux of the Rosebud*, by Henry W. Hamilton and Jean Tyree Hamilton)

Group of Rosebud Sioux chiefs. *Left to right*: Bear Head, High Bear, Two Strike, Scoop (Stands and Looks Back), Stranger Horse, He Dog, Swift Bear, and Louis Roubideaux, interpreter. (Photograph by John A. Anderson. From *The Sioux of the Rosebud*, by Henry W. Hamilton and Jean Tyree Hamilton)

Iron Shell, Cut Meat District, a younger brother of Hollow Horn Bear (Photograph by John A. Anderson. From *The Sioux of the Rosebud*, by Henry W. Hamilton and Jean Tyree Hamilton)

II. Crazy Horse and Other Trouble

ONE DAY IN THE SUMMER OF 1877 there was a quiet spell at Spotted Tail Agency, and Spotted Tail and his agent, Lieutenant Jesse M. Lee, were sitting in the office, conversing in friendly wise through an interpreter. Somehow they had gotten on the subject of the sad dearth of honest men in the world, and Lieutenant Lee remarked that you could always tell an honest man by the hair on his palms. With a startled look, Spotted Tail glanced hastily at his own palms. "I used to be ambitious to be honest," Lee went on blandly. "I worked at it pretty hard; but I never did get more than a few sprouts of hair on my palms." Spotted Tail burst into sudden laughter. "How! How! Shake!" he cried, jumping up and shaking hands with Lee. Then he took another look at his own palm and shook his head. "My friend," he said, "I used to have hair on my palms; but shaking hands with so many dishonest white men has worn the hair all off."

These two men enjoyed that kind of a palaver, but they were usually too busy to indulge in it during work hours. Taking care of some ten thousand wild or half-wild Sioux at an agency was a heavy task; and it was not rendered easier by the fact that in 1877 Lieutenant Lee was getting orders both from the civilian Indian Office in Washington and from the military authorities. Many of these orders were impossible to execute; others could be carried out, but only after endless labor and talk.

There were seven hundred Lower Brulés at Spotted Tail Agency, and in the spring of 1877 they were ordered sent home to their own agency on the Missouri. They did not wish to go. Their own agency was such a dull place, rations and other supplies were scanty, and there was far too much talk at Lower Brulé of every man going to work planting corn. Lieutenant Lee got rid of these Lower Brulés, and then an order came transferring 949 Wazhazhas from Red Cloud Agency to Spotted Tail. These Wazhazhas had been rated a part of the Brulé tribe as far back as 1804, but they had separated from the Brulés during the Grattan troubles of 1854–55 and had gone off northward, where they associated with the Red Cloud group of Oglalas and part of the Northern Cheyennes. They came with Red Cloud when his agency was established in 1871, and had been with him ever since. Now the military authorities ordered them shifted to Spotted Tail's agency. Their chief, Red Leaf, was an old comrade-in-arms of the Brulé head chief. Misled by Red Cloud, he had defied the military agent in October, 1876, and had suffered with the Oglala chief when their camps had been taken by surprise, their ponies lifted by the Pawnee Scouts, and the people of the two camps marched off to the agency as prisoners. Red Leaf had never recovered from that shock, and now, when ordered to shift to Spotted Tail Agency, he submitted quietly.

The war was now over, but there seemed to be abundant trouble piled up around the Sioux horizon. In May the government asked for bids for the construction of new agencies for Spotted Tail and Red Cloud on the west bank of the Missouri, and that was a grim reminder that by the so-called agreement of 1876, the Sioux were now at the mercy of the government, which intended to remove them to the Missouri and then control them absolutely. The common Indians did not seem to understand this; the lately surrendered hostiles were unaware of the situation; but when the time came to remove to the Missouri, the Sioux would suddenly wake up and violently resist.

Crazy Horse's attitude was disturbing. Dealing directly with General Crook, he seems to have ignored his two uncles, Red Cloud and Spotted Tail, and there are stories that he despised them for having come willingly to the reservation, settling down and becoming friendly with the whites. The character of this fighting man of the wild Oglalas does not seem very complicated. He was a primitive man of action who hated the whites and all their ways and had kept carefully out of their reach, never visiting the agencies or attending councils. He had come in now and surrendered because he could think of no other way out of his difficulties, but he had no intention of changing his ways. General Crook was making a serious effort to win this wild man's confidence and friendship and was having hard going. There was a plan to take Crazy Horse and some of the other hostile leaders to Washington for councils with the great officials, but Crazy Horse would not go. A visit with the Great Father had no appeal for him. He suspected a trap, and that perhaps indicates his type of mentality. All he desired was permission to take his wild camp on a buffalo hunt in his old hunting grounds on the Powder and the Tongue. General Crook gave a kind of promise—the hunt might be possible in late summer, if the conditions were right. Crook would have instantly rejected any proposal to let the friendly agency Sioux go hunting, but nothing was to be spared in the effort to turn the hostile Crazy Horse into a friendly chief.

It would be interesting to know just what Spotted Tail thought of Crazy Horse. There is no evidence of any friendly visits exchanged between them. For that matter, Crazy Horse seems to have kept away from Red Cloud as well, his attitude being that agency head chiefs were of little account. Spotted Tail left him to it and went on with his work. He was the only chief at either agency who was able to see anything outside his own camp. He had now learned the value of the written word and was using squaw men to write letters that he dictated to be sent to the officials. One thing that occupied him at this time was the fate of the hostages who had surrendered to Colonel Miles on the Yellowstone in October, 1876. The hostages had promised that their families and camps would go to their old agency on the Missouri, but instead of doing so, their camps joined Crazy Horse and then surrendered at Spotted Tail Agency in April, 1877. Spotted Tail wrote letters urging that the hostages be permitted to rejoin their families at his agency. He got Red Skirt, a Miniconjou chief, released; and when Red Skirt came to Spotted Tail's agency and wished to return to Cheyenne River, Spotted Tail gave the family (thirteen persons) twenty-two ponies and outfitted them for their long journey. The chief of the Brulés was constantly performing such acts of kindness.[1]

[1] Harry Anderson found Spotted Tail's letters dealing with the Sioux hostages in the National Archives.

In June, the Sioux held the greatest Sun Dance ever seen on the reservation at a small stream they called Sun Dance Creek, about midway between the two agencies. Twenty thousand Indians are said to have been present. The surrendered hostiles were in all their glory—real warriors, who had defeated Crook and Custer—but when the Sun Dance ended, they were sad that the usual war parties could not be assembled to go and attack Indian and white enemies. What were the Sioux coming to, that white soldiers should forbid them to carry out the age-old custom of going to war at the conclusion of the Sun Dance rites?

A personal item on Spotted Tail may be taken from the agency records. At this time his family was listed as consisting of himself, four wives, nine sons, eight daughters, total twenty-two, to which may be added the family of his eldest son, Young Spotted Tail, who had two wives, a son, and a daughter. Spotted Tail also had several married daughters, who were not included in this tabulation.

Red Cloud Agency had now been turned over to a civilian agent, James Irwin, who reported in August that all was quiet and peaceful at his agency; but Crazy Horse was unfriendly and sullen, and the agency chiefs were beginning to look askance at him. General Crook was getting reports on Crazy Horse that he did not like, and now trouble began to break. Strike riots in Chicago led to Crook's being ordered to send most of his troops to that city, leaving the garrisons at the agencies cut down to a dangerous point. Then a war with the Nez Perce tribe broke out in the lands west of the Rockies, and the Nez Perces—like the Sioux in 1876—astonished the military by their fighting ability, defeating or driving back all forces sent against them. General Crook started for Camp Brown to assemble such forces as he could, in case the Nez Perces came through the mountain passes and down into the buffalo plains, from which the Sioux and their allies had just been driven. The General was badly worried. If the Nez Perces headed toward the Sioux agencies, there might be a violent explosion, with the recently surrendered Sioux joining forces with the Nez Perces. At this critical moment he received news from Camp Robinson and Red Cloud Agency that caused him to drop his preparations to meet the Nez

Perce threat and hasten to Camp Robinson in order to deal with Crazy Horse.

The day Crook came to Camp Robinson the Nez Perces emerged from the Yellowstone Park area and came to the Bighorn River. To head them back was vitally important, and it was almost equally important not to have any fighting with the Sioux. Crook was still being patient with Crazy Horse. He is said to have had reliable reports that Crazy Horse had tried to induce the Miniconjous at Spotted Tail Agency to join him in a flight northward, but Touch-the-Cloud's camp had refused to join in this plan. Crazy Horse had then planned to get away on the excuse of hunting buffalo. He could not even depend on all of his own followers to flee from the agency with him; but if he could get them away from the agency on the pretense of hunting, he could then revive the soldiers' lodge and force everyone in his camp to do his bidding. Crook had these reports and others, yet he set out in an army ambulance to go to Crazy Horse's camp for a conference with that chief.

On the way the ambulance was stopped by Woman's Dress, one of Red Cloud's headmen, who gave the General a warning from the agency chiefs that Crazy Horse had said he was going to kill the General during the coming council.[2] Crook had his ambulance turned around and drove straight back inside the Camp Robinson stockade. He then sent a summons to Crazy Horse and the agency chiefs to come to him inside the post stockade. The agency chiefs all came; Crazy Horse ignored the summons. Crook now told the assembled chiefs that if they did not assist the troops, Crazy Horse was going to get all the Sioux into very serious trouble. He demanded that they aid the troops in arresting Crazy Horse. The chiefs conferred and told Crook that Crazy Horse was a desperate man who would certainly start a fight if an attempt was made to arrest him. It would be much better just to kill him. Crook objected, saying that that would be murder. The chiefs, conferred again and agreed to raise an armed posse of agency Indians to go with the

[2] Captain Bourke stated that this message was sent by Spotted Tail, which seems very improbable. Woman's Dress was a Red Cloud Indian, and Spotted Tail and the Brulés are not mentioned as being present at the council with Crook or taking part in the forming of the posse to arrest Crazy Horse.

troops to arrest Crazy Horse. Crook now issued orders to General L. P. Bradley, commanding at Camp Robinson, for the arrest of Crazy Horse, and he then prepared to go on to Camp Brown to deal with the Nez Perce crisis.

At nine o'clock the following morning, September 3, eight troops of the Third Cavalry and an armed posse of four hundred agency warriors set out for Crazy Horse's camp, which was on the north side of White River, about six miles northeast of Camp Robinson. When they reached the camp they found that the Crazy Horse people had fled. The ground was strewn with camp equipment, indicating that the Sioux had left in great haste and confusion. Following the trail northward, it soon became apparent that Crazy Horse had misjudged his own followers. The trail showed one group after another leaving the main body and turning back to seek safety in the agency camps. One small group had gone straight on northward, but now they were overtaken and forced to give up. Crazy Horse had escaped almost alone by turning back and seeking refuge in a small Oglala camp at Spotted Tail Agency.

This whole affair was a Red Cloud and Oglala tribal matter. Spotted Tail and his Brulés were not concerned, until Crazy Horse came to their agency to escape capture. By that act he brought a load of trouble and dumped it at the door of his Uncle Spotted Tail's tipi. That night a council was held at the commandant's office at Camp Sheridan, which was attended by Spotted Tail and the chiefs of every camp at his agency, including Touch-the-Clouds, chief of the surrendered Miniconjous and Crazy Horse's close friend. Crazy Horse had already agreed to go with Agent Lee to Camp Robinson. The purpose of the council was to get Crazy Horse away from Spotted Tail Agency without angering the Sioux and bringing on a fight. The decision was to have Touch-the-Clouds and some Miniconjou warriors escort Crazy Horse. Touch-the-Clouds induced Crazy Horse to stay at his camp that night.

The next morning the party that was to escort Crazy Horse assembled. There were nearly 10,000 Sioux looking on, at least one-fourth of them surrendered hostiles who might be expected to side with Crazy Horse, but the party got away without trouble. Lieutenant Lee rode in an army ambulance with some of his agency

Brulés and some members of Crazy Horse's band. Crazy Horse rode a horse, and with him were Touch-the-Clouds, White Thunder, Coarse Voice, Crow Dog, Four Horns, Crow Good Voice, Horned Antelope, and others, mostly Brulés. Although they saw parties of hostile warriors on the way, no attempt was made to rescue Crazy Horse. Inside the stockade at Camp Robinson, Agent Lee turned him over to the officer of the day, who escorted him to the guardhouse. Outside the stockade a mass of Sioux had assembled, and two troops of cavalry and a body of agency warriors were on duty, keeping the crowd back. Crazy Horse walked to the guardhouse with the officer of the day, Captain Kennington, on one side of him and one of his own leaders, Little Big Man, on the other. The eyewitnesses disagree about what happened, but either at the guardhouse door or just inside, Crazy Horse made a violent movement that threw Captain Kennington and Little Big Man off balance; he then drew a dirk or two dirks, hidden under his clothing, and started fighting. Little Big Man leaped on his back and tried to hold his arms, getting his own wrists badly slashed by the dirk, but (as he said later on) in attempting to prevent Crazy Horse's killing the men in the guardhouse, he deflected a blow and accidentally caused Crazy Horse to stab himself in the stomach. The other version is that a member of the guard stabbed Crazy Horse with a bayonet. The wounded man was taken to the adjutant's office and treated by the post surgeon, but he died in the night.

The Crazy Horse cult that has grown up during the past fifty years or so is an amazing thing. It was evidently started among the Oglalas at Pine Ridge, and it is still mainly an Oglala movement, aided by some white admirers of the Oglala fighting chief. They depict Crazy Horse as the kind of being never seen on earth: a genius in war, yet a lover of peace; a statesman, who apparently never thought of the interests of any human being outside his own camp; a dreamer, a mystic, and a kind of Sioux Christ, who was betrayed in the end by his own disciples—Little Big Man, Touch-the-Clouds, Big Road, Jumping Shield, and the rest.

One is inclined to ask, what is it all about? When Spotted Tail was asked to surrender to the military to save his people in 1855, he did so and spent a year in prison with a threat of hanging for murder over his head. When Crazy Horse had the opportunity to go quietly into the guardhouse for a little detention, again for the benefit of the Sioux, he started a fight and was killed. Throughout his months as a surrendered hostile at Red Cloud, he does not seem to have considered the interest of his people once. It was the other Sioux leaders who did that, so they are pictured as all engaged in a plot to destroy Crazy Horse. Spotted Tail seems to have been out of all these events, yet we are told that Crazy Horse's family blamed him for the death of their relative and swore everlasting vengeance against him. What they really did was to take Crazy Horse's body on a pony travois to Spotted Tail Agency, bury him there on a Sioux scaffold, and put themselves under Spotted Tail's patronage and protection. The people they blamed for their great man's death were the Oglalas of Red Cloud Agency, the same Oglalas who have worked so diligently to make Crazy Horse out a holy man and a martyr.

With the Crazy Horse crisis ended, the agency chiefs were able to concentrate their attention on a matter that vitally concerned all of the Sioux at the two agencies. Whether they liked it or not, the Sioux had to move to the Missouri River. The new agencies had been prepared there, rations and other supplies were being shipped to the new agencies, and both at Spotted Tail and at Red Cloud the rations and supplies were running out and no new stocks arriving. It meant go to the Missouri or stay at the old agencies and starve and freeze during the winter that was already approaching. Yet the chiefs could not induce the stubborn Sioux to agree to move. In the end, it was the officials who weakened. They just did not dare to starve and freeze the Sioux; and they now suggested that delegations of chiefs from the two agencies come to Washington for conferences with the new President, Rutherford B. Hayes. Thus Spotted Tail and Red Cloud journeyed to Washington once more. Spotted Tail took his oldest son with him, and also the chiefs of the hostiles who had surrendered at his agency. President Hayes sympathized with the Sioux, but he told them that the arrangements for feeding their people on the Missouri had been made and could not be changed suddenly. He gave the chiefs his promise that, if they would take their people to the new agencies for this one winter, in the spring they would be permitted to choose locations for their agencies at any point inside the Sioux reservation. The chiefs were content with this promise, but when they returned home, their people were not satisfied. Most of the Sioux still wished to remain at the old agencies, but that was now impossible, and with the aid of the agents and the military the chiefs got their people ready to move on October 27. Spotted Tail marched from his agency on West Beaver Creek, ten miles south of White River, proceeding eastward; Red Cloud's column went down the valley of White River.

The Sioux were on the wing again. The marching columns extended for miles, and great clouds of dust rolled into the sky. Each column had over one hundred big freight wagons with it, hauling rations and supplies, and transporting poor families, the old, and the sick. Herds of beef cattle were driven along by cowboys to feed the people. Part of the surrendered hostiles with the Spotted Tail column were terribly upset over being forced to move to the Missouri, and at a point near the head of Wounded Knee Creek they broke away from the column and fled northward. With them went Crazy Horse's old father and mother, carrying the bones of their great son. Somewhere in the Wounded Knee district, on the present Pine Ridge reservation, they are said to have hidden the bones; then they left the fleeing hostiles and returned to Spotted Tail's column. These hostiles who ran away were led by Red Bear of the Sans Arcs. Perhaps part of the Miniconjous went with them.[3]

[3] There has always been a mystery concerning this flight of the hostiles from Spotted Tail's column. Red Bear and his Sans Arcs certainly fled; Touch-the-Clouds and Roman Nose disappeared from Spotted Tail's agency rolls sometime in the late summer or autumn of 1877. When and how they left is not known. Joseph Eagle Hawk, of Pine Ridge, was a small boy at the time, and he denies that any hostiles ran away in October. He says that he was in the Crazy Horse camp and it waited until midwinter and then, while camped at the forks of White River, the chiefs decided to go north and join Sitting Bull in Canada, and the camp fled without the whites even knowing about it. That seems to be correct, but the hostiles who fled in October were not with the Crazy Horse camp, which was with Red Cloud. They fled from the Spotted Tail column, with which the family of Crazy Horse was living with a small following of the Crazy Horse Band. As late as 1881, Old Crazy Horse had a camp of his own at the Spotted Tail agency, called the Northerners.

When the agency chiefs had been coaxed and bullied into signing the queerly termed agreement of 1876, the government seemingly imagined that it had the Sioux tied up and helpless, but it now found that these Indians had broken the cords with which an angry Congress had bound them. They refused to live on the Missouri. Spotted Tail's new agency was at the old Ponca Indian Agency on the Missouri, in the northeast corner of Nebraska, while the new Red Cloud Agency had been built on the west bank of the Missouri much farther north, above the Great Bend at the mouth of Yellow Medicine Creek. All supplies for the Indians had been brought up the Missouri in steamboats and unloaded at these agencies, but the stubborn Sioux refused to go near the Missouri. Red Cloud formed his winter camp near the forks of White River, seventy-five miles west of his agency; Spotted Tail wintered with his main camp on Rosebud Creek, a tributary of the South Fork of White River, over one hundred miles from his agency. All rations and supplies had to be hauled to the Indian camps during the winter, the glum officials being forced to pay shockingly high rates for wagon transportation.

Spotted Tail's people were split into factions and were quarreling. Part of the "progressives" (squaw men, mixed-bloods, Loafers and Corn Band) left the winter camp and moved to or near the Missouri. The squaw men and mixed-bloods moved into some houses they found empty, and Chief Milk (*Asampi*) formed a camp on Ponca Creek, just south of the later town of Herrick, in which camp Little Thunder, the old head chief of the Brulés, spent the winter of 1877–78. In the spring more progressive Indians left Spotted Tail's camp to go to the Missouri.[4]

[4] Frank Little Thunder, the grandson or great-grandson of the old chief, says Little Thunder died at Rosebud Agency, he thinks in 1879, in Milk's camp "near Swift Bear's old log cabin on Hay Creek." The Little Thunder family in 1883–86 lived on Cut Meat Creek, west of Rosebud Agency. Standing Bear, in his book, states that his father took the family from Spotted Tail's camp in spring, 1878, and moved to Ponca Agency; the father then sent young Standing Bear to live with a parson's family and pick up some education. Standing Bear claims his father was a full-blood Oglala, head of the Wears Salt Band (*Miniskuyakichun*); but that band was Brulé, and by Standing Bear's own statement the camp was at Rosebud in 1878–80, close to the agency and with Swift Bear's camp. On the agency rolls, old Standing Bear is set down as a mixed-blood, and his conduct indicates that

Spotted Tail and his chiefs had a lively time that winter, striving to keep their people together. The surrendered hostiles were planning to make a run for Sitting Bull's camp in Canada; the so-called progressives wanted to leave the tribe and join the squaw men and mixed-bloods at Ponca to start farming and live in log houses. As it always seemed to happen when the Brulés moved toward the Missouri, the winter camp was full of sickness and death. Lung complaints, diphtheria, and measles were killing the old people and children. One of Spotted Tail's sons seems to have died during the winter. Lieutenant Lee reported on this condition and gave Spotted Tail great credit for preventing an outbreak of wrath and serious trouble. To add to it all, white horse-thieves were preying on the Brulé camps, and hundreds of ponies were disappearing. To the Brulés, champions at horse-lifting themselves, this was an unbearable situation; and they wished to make up war parties and replenish their herds by making raids on the settlers in Nebraska.

Lieutenant Lee, a strong agent and a close friend of Spotted Tail, should have been kept as acting agent. The officials in Washington thought they had the Brulés tied up and wished to keep them tied, but they ruined all that by playing politics with the appointment of a new agent. They offered the position to Henry W. Bingham, former agent at Cheyenne River, who was under some charges involving the defrauding of the government. Bingham declined the appointment on March 12, 1878, and the position was then offered to James Lawrence, former agent of the little Ponca tribe, who was under charges of having helped to dragoon the Poncas into moving to Indian Territory. Lawrence was actually made Spotted Tail's new agent, then thought it over and resigned before taking charge.[5]

he was not a full-blood. He sent his son to live with a parson's family and get educated; he lived with the squaw men in a house at Ponca and then moved to Rosebud and started a store, the only Indian among the Brulés who ran a store in the old days.

[5] Joseph Cook diary and Niobrara, Nebraska, *Pioneer*, April 5, 1877, contain details concerning Lawrence. Joseph Cook approved of Lawrence and was shocked that his bishop (Hare of the Episcopal church) stated that he was greatly relieved that Lawrence had resigned his appointment to be Spotted Tail's agent, as he "is essentially an insignificant man." The *Pioneer* claimed that the appointment of Lawrence was a plan of certain Dakota worthies, who hoped to profit from the arrangement.

Spotted Tail was having one of the greatest fights of his life during that winter and spring. He was battling to keep control of his Brulés and to prevent their taking violent action that would enrage the whites and cause new trouble for the tribe, and at the same time he was striving to prevent the government from taking over control of his people. There were signs both in Dakota and Washington that certain groups were attempting to induce Congress to cancel President Hayes' promise that in the spring Spotted Tail and Red Cloud could move away from the Missouri to new agency sites of their own choice. Lieutenant Lee went to Washington to state the case against keeping the Brulés on the Missouri. Meantime the Niobrara, Nebraska, *Pioneer* printed reports from Spotted Tail Agency (Ponca Agency) of swindling. Buildings not needed were being put up at heavy expense; the hay contract was at the exorbitant price of $5.50 a ton, and local white men were still being paid to cut hay in December. "Our haying season is a long one," the writer added sourly. With no Indians at the agency, the government had paid $6,000 for cutting wood for fuel during the winter.

In March, Lieutenant Lee came back from Washington with the news that the removal of the Indians to an agency of their own choice was definitely approved, and on March 21, Spotted Tail, in his camp on distant Rosebud Creek, held a council and the council decided to have their agency there on the Rosebud. But the Indians still had to wait for a commission to come from Washington to examine the site and approve it, and in the meantime the chief had to be on his guard. Progressive groups of Brulés were slipping away from his camp to join the squaw men and mixed-bloods on the Missouri; Dakota white men were said to be plotting with the squaw men and mixed-bloods, urging them to stay where they were, draw the Brulé progressives to the Missouri, weaken Spotted Tail's full-blood camp, and thus win the battle to remain at Ponca Agency on the river. These men did not know the kind of chief they were dealing with. He did not wait for them to gather strength but pulled up stakes on Rosebud Creek, moved his big camp to Ponca Creek within easy reach of the agency, and put his Brulé Indian soldiers on duty, intimidating the squaw men, mixed-bloods, and progressive full-bloods. In June he held a great Sun Dance on

Ponca Creek, the Brulés whipping up the old pagan Sioux spirit to a high level. The squaw men, mixed-bloods, and progressives sought cover, like little birds when the hawks are awing.

A reporter from the Niobrara, Nebraska, *Pioneer* visited the Spotted Tail camp on Ponca Creek in late May. The camp had seven hundred lodges, six thousand Sioux, and it extended for fifteen miles up the creek. Spotted Tail's family camp was within a mile and a half of the agency, where the chief could keep a close watch on the whites and mixed-bloods. He or one of his men told the reporter that he was fifty-three years old and had been born on White River.

Lieutenant Lee left to rejoin his regiment, and the Ponca Agency was put in temporary charge of an acting agent, W. J. Pollock, a Western man to whom Spotted Tail took an instant liking. The chief and Pollock had their work cut out for them. The Brulés wished to move at once to their new agency at Rosebud, taking the now submissive squaw men and mixed-bloods with them; but in Washington the officials were again shifting their ground, playing for time. In March they had approved removal, to be carried out in June; in June the Interior Department decreed that removal should be delayed until July. Spotted Tail knew a good deal about government methods and delays; but the common men in his camp knew nothing of such matters. All they knew was that the Great Father had told the chiefs in October, 1877, that in the spring the Sioux could remove from the neighborhood of the hated Missouri and go back into their own country. Now the white men were playing tricks. The Brulés were angry and the chiefs had a hard time to prevent their taking down the tipis and starting at once for Rosebud Creek.

The Sioux never knew how terribly near they came in 1877–78 to being shipped off to Indian Territory. The planners for Indian welfare were pulling wires in Washington to have all the Sioux sent to Indian Territory, for their own good. General Sheridan was still in a rage over the failure of the summer campaign against the Sioux in 1876, and he and other generals were demanding that the military keep control of the Sioux and force the tribe to do as it was ordered. All through the winter these matters were discussed in Congress, but no clear decision was reached.

When the chiefs were in Washington in the autumn of 1877, they had met the new secretary of the interior, Carl Schurz. The Sioux looked with surprise at this quaint German bird who, they were told, stood next in rank to the Great Father. The man had whiskers; his face was all hair, and out of it stared two great eyes from behind gleaming spectacles. The Sioux called him Owl and laughed; but Carl Schurz was a man who had fought through a long life for the oppressed and the unfortunate, and (all unknown to them) he fought all through the winter against the theory of the army leaders, that the Sioux were incurable savages and that the only honest policy was to coop them up on their reservation under strict military control and hold them until they died out and became extinct. Carl Schurz's liberal soul revolted at such a view of the Indian, and in the end he won his battle by pledging his honor that if these Indians were put under civilian control, they would go to work and presently be self-supporting.

Spotted Tail must have known something of this struggle in Washington. The squaw men told him what was in the newspapers; but the common men in the Brulé tribe knew nothing of it. The chief seems to have realized that if the Brulés took matters into their own hands and moved away from Ponca Agency without official permission, they might very well be turned over to the army again to be pursued and brought back to the Missouri. He urged patience on his people; but as week followed week, the patience of the Brulés ran out and their anger and suspicion grew. They were saying that the whites had lied to their chiefs again and that they were to be kept here on the Missouri by being fed on further lies.

On July 5 the commission that was to approve removal to the new agency turned up at Ponca. The commission was made up of General D. S. Stanley, commanding the troops in Dakota, A. L. Riggs, Sioux missionary representing the Protestant churches, and J. M. Haworth. With them came the new commissioner of Indian affairs, Ezra Hayt. The tribal council instructed Spotted Tail about how he should speak in council, and he spoke angrily to the commission, ending with the statement that if they did not see to it that his tribe was given permission to move to Rosebud within ten days, he would burn Ponca Agency and start for Rosebud without permission. Staring at Commissioner Hayt's bald pate, the chief remarked that it was his experience that all bald-headed men were dishonest; but after the open council was ended, he met the commissioners in private, shook hands, and told them that he had been speaking as the tribal council willed, that personally he had nothing but friendly feeling toward the gentlemen and knew very well that all this delay was not their fault—it was Congress that had waited and hesitated and changed its mind again and again.

The commission gave Agent Pollock instructions to hold the Sioux where they were and went on up the Missouri by steamboat to visit Red Cloud at his camp near the forks of White River. They found the great Oglala chief in fine humor, friendly and courteous. He had had none of Spotted Tail's trouble during the winter and spring; but had sat in comfort in his camp, making a few visits to his brand new and unwanted agency on the Missouri. There were no violent factions in his camp; the council had decided to have their new agency at *Wazi Ahanhan* (Pine Ridge), as far west from the Missouri as they could go without leaving the reservation. The chief escorted the commission to Pine Ridge. The gentlemen did not like the site much; they preferred a location further east on Wounded Knee Creek; but the military officer who was to supervise the building of the agency (left with no clear-cut orders and having to deal with a horde of chiefs all determined to have their own way) started putting up the buildings there at Pine Ridge. The chiefs had won.

Meanwhile, Spotted Tail and his new friend, Acting Agent Pollock, were having a lively time at Ponca. The Brulés were threatening revolt and war if they were kept at Ponca any longer; Commissioner Hayt was ordering Pollock by wire to keep them there until August, and Pollock was at his wit's end. He consulted Spotted Tail, who advised him to employ the three hundred warriors of the Brulé Fox Soldier group to police the camp and thump some of the noisier revolters. There were two troops of the Third Cavalry at Ponca Agency, but if they had tried to meddle in this affair, there would have been bloodshed. Pollock paid the Fox Soldiers in fresh beef, and they did their best to hold the Indians in camp, but on July 22, Pollock reported that part of the Brulés had

293

broken camp and started for Rosebud. On the twenty-ninth he telegraphed that all the Indians were gone.

The army had awed the Brulés into submission in 1876. Now, in 1878, the Indians had thrown off all controls. The removal to Rosebud, which should have been conducted in an orderly manner, was a riot. Part of the Indians broke away from the camp on Ponca Creek and started. Other groups went after them; and presently they were all on the wing, those with horses far ahead, in the rear the poor families, with the old people trudging along on foot in the burning heat of a Dakota drought summer, cursing the white men who had brought this misery on them. Commissioner Hayt had thrown out the bids of the Dakota men for transport by wagon. He stated that the bids were outrageously high—an attempt to swindle the government—so he threw the bids away. Now Agent Pollock was caught with almost no transport. He got some wagons and teams at $1.25 per hundred pounds, per one hundred miles, and some four-horse wagons at $5.00 a day, to haul indigent Indian families. Commissioner Hayt sent angry telegrams, accusing Pollock of being responsible for the lack of transport. Pollock wired back that it was Hayt himself who had thrown out the bids, adding that in ordinary times it was proper to discard bids that were too high, but this was a crisis in which human needs came above pennypinching. Pollock was in a rage. The whole removal had been messed up by Washington officialdom; his Indians were in revolt and the poor and the old suffering needlessly. He wired for authority to start the two troops of cavalry on the trail of the Indians to keep watch and report.[6]

Alarming reports were brought back from the Indian camps. The Brulés were quarreling fiercely; some men, it was said, had been shot, and a party of eight hundred mounted warriors had streaked off toward the north, perhaps with the purpose of trying to join Sitting Bull in Canada. Later this report was denied, but

[6] The Pollock and Hayt telegrams are in the National Archives. It is rather obvious that Hayt tried to prevent removal, hoping to keep the Brulés at Ponca. He blamed Pollock, and Pollock retorted that dealing with wild Indians when aroused was different from dealing with reasonable white people, that he had tried every expedient to hold the Sioux, but that to do so was an impossibility.

in fact a group did run away, led by Good Bird and Black Yellow Fox. They soon tired of life in Canada and came back across the line to surrender. The Rosebud agent reported their return to the agency February 27, 1880.

No white man reported just what happened during the march of the Brulés to Rosebud. Agent Pollock asked that the two troops of the Third Cavalry follow the Indians. He sent wagons after them with rations, ordered beef cattle driven to the camp, then went there to see what was going on. But when he got to the camp, he was warned off. The chiefs said that this was a Brulé Sioux affair and that they did not want any of the Great Father's meddling in it. The truth probably was that Spotted Tail and the tribal council were soldiering the squaw men, mixed-bloods, and progressives to force them to leave the Missouri and go to Rosebud.

Spotted Tail even had a religious war on his hands at this moment. The Roman Catholics had never given up their hope of starting a mission among the Brulés, and in 1878 they obtained official sanction. Father Martin, who had come to the old agency in 1876, turned up at Ponca and had a number of talks with Spotted Tail and the other chiefs. He and another priest were prepared to go with the Indians to Rosebud, when the Indian Office altered its mind and cancelled the permission for a Roman Catholic mission. Spotted Tail was angry. He did not care a jot about white men's religion; but he had learned to value the ability to speak, read, and write English, and he claimed that the White Robes, who had had a school at his agency for the past four years, had not taught one Brulé child to speak, read, or write in that tongue. He said if the Episcopalians kept school at the agency for one hundred years they would do no better, and he wanted the Black Robes to start a school. The Protestant churches did not want them, nor did the Protestant officials at the Indian Office. Pollock reported that one of the priests brought liquor with him and was drunk during the march to Rosebud. The priests were ordered away. Spotted Tail told them to stay, and on March 17, 1879, he handed Pollock a petition, signed by every important Indian at Rosebud, asking that the White Robes be barred and that the Black Robes be made the tribal missionaries and teachers. Only the squaw men and mixed-bloods preferred the Episcopal church.

Pollock, following the Indians, came to the camp on August 28 and presented silver medals from the Great Father to Spotted Tail and young Hollow Horn Bear, a head soldier and son of Iron Shell, chief of the Orphans. The ways of officialdom are quaint ways. These Indians were flouting the government's purpose to keep them on the Missouri; and at this critical moment the government exhibited high approval of the head chief and the head soldier, probably for past services at the old agency, but certainly a poorly timed mark of honor. Pollock reached the site of Rosebud on August 29. He had his hands full. He had to feed these thousands of runaway Indians and also to start putting up new agency buildings. Commissioner Hayt had made a mess of the transport situation; but now someone (Pollock?) suggested that a big ox-team wagon train standing idle at the old agency in Nebraska be brought to Rosebud, and that the Indians be induced to do their own hauling from the steamboat landing on the Missouri to the new agency. Commissioner Hayt jumped at the plan and took the credit for its inception. Thus he claimed the honor of the first successful attempt to induce the Sioux to work with their hands. But it was Pollock who did the persuading, and it was payment of cash in hand for the work that made the plan a success. All the government's costly farm crusades among the Sioux had been based on the shadowy promises of benefits in the future; but these Indian teamsters were paid silver money in hand at the end of each trip. They averaged twenty dollars a trip, which was better pay than any white farm worker or cowboy was getting. Besides, they had free rations, clothing, and all other supplies from the government. They took to wagon-freighting like ducks to water. It meant travel, and the Sioux were never happier than when on the wing.

After Spotted Tail had moved his tribe to Rosebud and established the agency solidly there, the commission that had been sent out at heavy expense to inspect and approve the new Spotted Tail and Red Cloud agencies *before* they were established, came to Rosebud, looked around, disapproved the site, and then gave a grudging consent to having the agency left where the Indians wanted it. The commission then went off and wrote a report, stating that the agency site was down in the bottom of a bowl, surrounded by a circle of picturesque hills dotted with small pines. It was a beautiful spot for Indians to camp in, but it was a bad location for an agency, and in wet weather it would be most difficult to bring loaded wagons in over the hills. There was no water on the agency site, but plenty where the Indians encamped along Rosebud Creek. Wood was lacking; but there were good stands of timber off to the west, along the South Fork of White River. In effect, Spotted Tail had placed his agency at a handsome location for his people to camp and sit and eat government rations. Red Cloud had also won his desire: an agency nice to camp at. These chiefs were thwarting the government plans at every move, and only two years back the military had had them humbled and apparently willing to submit to all orders. In September, 1878, the Sioux were free again—those led by Red Cloud and Spotted Tail. The Sioux on the Missouri were still being kept meek by the military.

Spotted Tail had established his big Brulé camp several miles north of the agency in a fine location. Close to the agency on Rosebud Creek, the Corn and Loafer bands were camped, for they were never happy far from the white people at the agency. These two progressive camps were now combined and in alliance with the squaw men and mixed-bloods. Spotted Tail and all the principal men of his Brulé camp were conservatives and nonprogressive, which meant that they did not want any sudden efforts to turn the Brulés into farmers and Christians. They also intended to resist any plan of the government's aimed at destroying the chiefs, breaking up the tribal organization, and putting the Indians under white control.

After the strenuous performances of the spring and summer, the Sioux settled down in their camps, watching Agent Pollock's men at work putting up agency buildings. Wagon trains of supplies, manned by mixed-bloods and full-bloods, were constantly coming in from the steamboat landing on the Missouri. Here was one form of work Spotted Tail and the other conservatives did not object to their Indians taking up. This wagon-freighting was cut to fit the tastes of the Sioux. It was not humdrum labor but traveling back and forth between the agency and Black Pole, which was their name for Rosebud Landing, where the steamboats unloaded the supplies for the agency.

297

The trip was 190 miles from Rosebud to Black Pole. The Indian teamsters took their families with them and carried tipi poles, tipi covers, and camp equipment in the wagons. It took several days for a trip to Black Pole and back to the agency; and the Sioux camped at night on some pleasant little stream, just as they had done in the free days before they came to the reservation. Best of all, they were paid in silver dollars at the end of each trip. They had free rations and other supplies, the same as the Indians who sat around doing nothing, and their silver dollars were theirs to spend on articles that they desired from the trader's store. The full-blood teamsters usually made two or three trips and then wished to rest up in the camp at the agency, so they passed their teamster job on to a relative, and he made a few trips and passed the work on. Thus hundreds of Brulés had soon been introduced to this rather pleasant form of manual labor. Following the examples of the squaw men and mixed-bloods, some of the full-blood teamsters began to build little stables and cut hay, and the Sioux ponies were presently horrified at finding themselves being cared for in a stable and fed in winter, instead of being left free on the prairie to scratch a bare subsistence from under the snow. The Sioux had learned that to do teaming work they had to have strong teams and that that meant feeding and caring for their animals.

Except for a few of the Corn Band and Loafers, none of the full-bloods at Rosebud were at all interested in farming, nor were Red Cloud's Oglalas, over to the west at Pine Ridge. Some of the tamer Sioux on the Missouri had taken up the planting of corn and vegetables before agencies had been established. Buffalo and other big game was growing scarce in their country. Half-starved much of the time, they began planting little patches in the Missouri bottom lands in the spring; then they went hunting, coming back to their corn patches in time to harvest. Often the drought and grasshopper plagues destroyed their crops, but some seasons were good ones, and they had corn and vegetables to add to their regular diet of meat. Now the government agents had taken over and were driving the Sioux to labor.

Cheyenne River Agency was almost a model of the conditions the officials wished to establish among the Sioux. The agent was

Captain Theodore Schwan, a German who had come to America as a boy and had enlisted in the army. During the Civil War he had won the Congressional Medal of Honor for valor and a commission as a captain. He had been appointed agent at Cheyenne River when the military took over and had established Prussian discipline among his Sioux, using a force of armed Indian police to accomplish this. Some of his tamest Sioux such as the Two Kettles, had been growing little crops because they wished to do so for fifty years before the agency was established; but Schwan now took hold and drove them, forcing them to increase the size of their planting year after year and punishing any man he caught neglecting his farm work. It was a system of slave-driving, and the Sioux, even those who left to themselves would have tried to grow crops, began to hate the process of planting and cultivating. Moreover, they had very bad luck.

About two years out of three drought and grasshoppers ruined the crops, and when it was not that, it was floods in the bottom lands where the Sioux had their corn patches. Captain Schwan and the theorists in the East who called themselves Friends of the Indians now developed a quaint philosophy. They said that, even without crops, farming was good discipline for the Sioux. It taught them the dignity of labor. The Cheyenne River Sioux violently rejected that philosophy. They saw nothing dignified in being forced to labor by a bad-tempered German and his armed police and then being cheated by an outrageous climate out of the fruits of their labor. The beauty of the situation at Cheyenne River lay in the fact that it was the kind of Sioux the officials called progressive, the hope of the planners for swiftly making the tribe self-supporting, who were being cured of any desire to work by Captain Schwan. Up the Cheyenne River, far west of the agency, the wild nonprogressives were sitting idle in their camps, eating free rations and refusing to plant any crops. They liked conditions at Cheyenne River. They kept away from Agent Schwan and warned the police not to dare to come to their camps. It was the progressives who were getting the cream of the agent's attentions, and were being rapidly turned into rabid nonprogressives.

Spotted Tail had his face set against the establishment of any such methods at his agency, and so had Red Cloud; but Carl Schurz had pledged his word to Congress that he would put all the Sioux to work as speedily as possible. Hardly were the agencies located when he issued an order to survey all the lands around Rosebud and Pine Ridge and divide the country up into forty-acre farms for the Indians. Forty acres! Even the Sioux who had been growing crops for fifty years did not average over one to two acres per family. Moreover, these surveyed farm plots were out on the open prairie. No Sioux would do any planting out on the dry prairie. That meant the officials expected each Sioux family to live in a cabin a mile or more from the nearest neighbors and try dry farming, a process not developed until fifty years later. The Sioux were incurable camp-dwellers. They did not feel safe living off by themselves. Nothing would induce them to leave their camps, and if they did try growing crops, it had to be done in camp communities in the sheltered stream valleys, where there was some chance of obtaining a crop.

Schurz also ordered a police force for Rosebud. That put Spotted Tail and the other chiefs in a predicament. They knew quite well that one of the main purposes of the Indian police system was to take all authority from the chiefs and tribal council and put it into the hands of the white agent. This they bitterly opposed, but they had to go warily with their opposition. Carl Schurz was head of the great Interior Department; the Sioux knew that he stood next to the Great Father, and if they openly tried to thwart him, the tribe might be turned over to the army again. So Spotted Tail and the other chiefs let Agent Pollock organize his police force, but they saw to it that no full-bloods enlisted. The police were all white squaw men and mixed-bloods, who sat around smoking, chewing tobacco, and drawing their pay. There was something wrong about that police force. Every small boy in the Brulé camps knew what was wrong with it, but it took the officials nearly a year to puzzle it out. Then they were shocked at Spotted Tail's duplicity. The simple truth was that the proud Brulé full-bloods looked down on the squaw men and mixed-bloods as vastly their inferiors; and no white or mixed-blood policeman dared to place a finger on a full-blood. Spotted Tail had sold the officials a police force that could act only against white men and mixed-bloods and was absolutely ineffective for the true official object: to control fullbloods.

Having established the new agencies, the next official move was to appoint new agents. They should have kept Pollock, who was an experienced man, knew Indians thoroughly, and had developed a system for getting along with the chiefs. Instead they promoted him to be an inspector, traveling about Dakota and visiting all the Sioux agencies, and in his place they appointed a Michigan man who had never seen a wild Indian in his life. They needed a man at Rosebud who could deal with Spotted Tail and hold him down. So they made a political appointment of a nonentity who would be wax in the hands of the great Brulé chief.

Red Cloud might have had a weak agent, picked for political reason, the same as Spotted Tail, but the Cheyenne troubles prevented it. The Northern Cheyennes who had lived at his agency had been forcibly removed to Indian Territory in May, 1877. They had fallen sick in the south. They were terribly homesick for their old country in the north, and in 1878 they ran away and started northward. Pursued by troops, the Cheyennes beat them off. Troops came down on them from the north to head them back. The Cheyennes evaded part of them, fought the others, and went on north into Kansas, where they raided the new settlers. Troops were rushed out along the Union Pacific to head them off, but the Indians crossed the Platte unobserved and finally came to the vicinity of the old Red Cloud Agency from which they had been sent south, only to find that it was abandoned and deserted. They were then rounded up by troops and taken as prisoners to Camp Robinson.

Told that they were to be returned to Indian Territory, the Cheyenne captives barracked themselves in their prison and resumed the hopeless fight. On a bitter winter night they burst out of their prison—men, women, and children—and fought their way to the snow-covered open hills. Pursued by cavalry, they fought and died in the snow. A handful surrendered and were brought back to Camp Robinson; a few found their way to Red Cloud's camps. When the Sioux beheld the Cheyennes and their women and children—bloody, frozen, and starved—they shed bitter tears and cursed the whites.

The chiefs urged that the Cheyennes be permitted to remain among their Sioux friends; and at last the wicked plan to remove the Cheyennes to Indian Territory, for their own good, was abandoned and the remnant of Dull Knife's people were left in peace at Pine Ridge.

Red Cloud was to pay bitterly for his kindness to the Cheyennes. Major Valentine T. McGillicuddy, the army surgeon who had cared for Crazy Horse when he lay dying at Camp Robinson in April, 1877, had been at this post all through the Cheyenne fighting in the winter of 1878–79. He had then gone to Washington, and just by luck he was introduced to Carl Schurz and made a great impression on him by recounting the story of the Cheyenne troubles. Schurz was a liberal who opposed the appointment of army officers as Indian agents, but he took an instant liking to this vigorous young army surgeon; and as he had been warned that Red Cloud would require a strong hand to control him, he made a quick decision and offered McGillycuddy the appointment as agent at Pine Ridge. Thus Red Cloud, who had decided to change his ways and be always friendly and courteous in his dealings with the officials, was suddenly saddled with the same type of agent as the Prussian Captain Schwan of Cheyenne River, and for the next six years he and McGillycuddy fought it out at Pine Ridge, while the heavens rocked and the frontier editors gloomily predicted that some day these two fighting cocks would go a bit too far and there would be a fresh Sioux war in Dakota and Nebraska.

Cicero Newell was the prize Spotted Tail drew in the selection of new agents. Mr. Newell was a Michigan man, and his appointment was political, with a whisper that money was paid to obtain it. As soon as he received the glad tidings that his appointment had been approved, he opened a jobs shop in Ypsilanti and began dickering with local men, offering them positions on the Rosebud Agency staff on certain terms, so it was said. Thus he recruited a full staff, and in the spring of 1879 he set out for Rosebud with a caravan of Ypsilanti families.

They went by rail; then up the Missouri by steamboat; and by the time they were set down on the lonesome river bank at Black Pole, many of them wished they were back in Ypsilanti. They still had one hundred miles to travel in wagons across uninhabited prairies; and when they got to Rosebud and found themselves surrounded by about ten thousand wild Indians, they were a very homesick lot. Their welcome was cold. Most of the members of Agent Pollock's staff were still at the agency, and they were not pleased at all when the new agent turned up with a complete staff. The Sioux were said to be friendly, but the Ypsilanti families had their doubts on that point; and at night when there was an outburst of fierce yelling in the nearby camps, punctuated by a little rifle firing, the Ypsilanti women and children had hysterics, and Agent Newell ran from house to house, soothing them with assurances that this was not the start of an Indian uprising.

These Ypsilanti families had brought their home-town feuds with them to Rosebud. Newell spent much of his time patching up quarrels. He had some sort of money dealings with most of the Ypsilanti men, and he spent much time dickering with them. Spotted Tail looked on, sizing up his new official father; then he moved into the agency office and began issuing his own orders. Hearing of this, Agent McGillycuddy, the dictator at Pine Ridge, spread it about that Spotted Tail's agent was so weak that he even let the chief open his official letters from Washington and have a squaw man interpret them to him. If there was an order from Washington the chief did not approve of, he destroyed the document and issued his own orders. McGillycuddy denounced this condition at Rosebud, stating that if a strong agent were not put in charge this anarchy would spread across Okiokendoka (Pass Creek, the boundary bestween Rosebud and Pine Ridge) and destroy the discipline he had established among his Oglalas.

Newell wrote hopeful reports to the Indian Office on the farming prospects at Rosebud. Meantime there was no farming, and Spotted Tail was bending all efforts to the planning of a great pagan Sun Dance in June. Newell's incompetence and weakness now showed clearly. Spotted Tail ordered him to write notes to the other agents announcing the Sun Dance and asking them to permit their Sioux to attend.[7] Newell must have known that he would only anger the

[7] Newell to Agent Schwan, May 19, 1879: "You are requested by Spotted Tail to inform your people that there will be a sun dance at a place between Black Pipe

agents, who were striving to force their Indians to farm and would be outraged at the idea of letting the Sioux desert their crops at the critical time in June and troop off to a Sun Dance. The other agents did not even honor his notes by replying to them. Spotted Tail then ordered Newell to issue passes to some of his Indians so that they could visit the other agencies and deliver the invitations to the Sun Dance in person. The military had instituted this system of passes in 1876, and no Sioux were now supposed to leave their agency without a written pass.

McGillycuddy of Pine Ridge made no special effort to prevent his Oglalas from attending the Sun Dance. He had replied to the orders from Washington to set his Indians to farming by telling the officials bluntly that, in his opinion, the Sioux country was unfit for farming and that he objected to the wasting of public money on a farm program. When Spotted Tail's envoys got to Cheyenne River Agency, the wrathful Captain Schwan set his armed Indian police on them, and they were driven off his reservation at a lively clip, the police firing many shots to speed them on their way. Victory to Captain Theodore Schwan, seemingly. But now the Captain learned that many of his Sioux were slipping away and heading for Rosebud. He stirred up his police to fierce activity, but with no success. He asked the aid of the cavalry at Fort Bennett, which was within a mile of his agency office, but even the cavalry could not stop the Sioux from going to Rosebud. The worst of it was that the runaways were the tamest and most friendly of his Indians, mostly Two Kettle Sioux. Schwan wrote to the Indian Office, complaining of Spotted Tail's conduct. Spotted Tail retorted by ignoring the lowly Indian Office officials and dictating an angry letter to the Secretary of the Interior, demanding that Schwan be removed from his position as agent and accusing him of maltreating the Sioux. Schwan was practically accusing Spotted Tail of stealing his Indians; Spotted Tail was retorting that the Cheyenne River

---

and Black Creek next month, in the full of the moon. By doing so you will confer a favor on our Indian friends." The tone of this note infuriated Schwan. An agent doing the bidding of a chief! Talking of the Sioux as "our Indian friends!" Schwan regarded the Sioux as unreliable and shifty people to be driven and to be put in the guardhouse if they disobeyed his orders.

Indians were running away from a tyrant, reaching Rosebud in a half-starved and destitute condition. And they kept on coming, in little family groups and larger parties, most of them deciding to remain permanently. They liked Spotted Tail's fat agency, where rations and supplies were abundant and farm work was unknown.

On the Missouri, to the east of Rosebud, was the Lower Brulé Agency. The Lower Brulés were the stay-behinds who had remained in the old Brulé lands on and near the Missouri when, after 1800, the bold Upper Brulés had pressed on westward, into Wyoming, Nebraska, Colorado, and Kansas. Now, in 1879, the Lower Brulés had a military agent, Captain William G. Dougherty, and he had a police force and was making his Indians farm. Most of them did not like it, but the Captain was a determined man, and they obeyed his orders. In May, White Thunder, one of Spotted Tail's boldest lieutenants, came to Lower Brulé with a party from Rosebud to invite the Sioux to the coming Sun Dance. The captain turned his face against the proposal. He had forced his Sioux to plant larger crops than ever before, and he was not going to have them drop their tools and go off in June to spend weeks at a heathen Sun Dance. White Thunder expressed surprise at conditions here on the Missouri. The Lower Brulés were of the same blood as the Rosebud Brulés; but here they were, taking orders from a white man and permitting a little police force to overawe them. This was a sad situation, so different from the freedom and high spirits at Rosebud. Talking it over among themselves, the Lower Brulés decided that White Thunder was speaking truth, and that something should be done about this.

One day singing was heard at the Lower Brulé agency, and out of the hills rode a large body of warriors. They swept down on the Indian camp at the agency, yelling and blowing eagle-bone whistles. They chased every policeman they saw into hiding; they rode to the log cabins of the police, shot out the windows and shot any of the policemen's live stock that was in sight. Next day the police resigned in a body. The Lower Brulés then made up a big camp and went off to Rosebud, where they spent three glorious weeks of freedom at the Sun Dance, coming home greatly refreshed and happy, as Spotted Tail's people had not only entertained them royally but had given them many ponies and other gifts. Meanwhile part of the Sioux had obeyed the agents at Cheyenne River and Lower Brulé, had stayed at home and faithfully cultivated their little fields, and they had been rewarded as the Dakota climate usually rewarded them with another crop failure due to drought and grasshoppers.

Spotted Tail had won this summer campaign. Most of the Sioux were on his side and were complaining of the military agents and the hard discipline and forced labor that they were diligently promoting. Spotted Tail stood for freedom and the old Sioux way of life, but by doing so he was not only flouting the agents, he was thwarting the policy of the high officials and of Congress. His summer activities brought the Secretary of the Interior to Rosebud in October, and Secretary Schurz made it plain at once that he intended that the Sioux should farm and that a police force should be organized that would do something toward enforcing the government's will. There were councils, and the chiefs gave in and promised that they would not oppose the reorganization of the police.

Spotted Tail came through Secretary Schurz's visit with no loss of standing. He was cordial toward the Secretary, and Carl Schurz exhibited a friendly spirit. He was firm about the police organization, but he ordered Agent Newell to put the runaway Cheyenne River Sioux on the ration rolls and to feed and clothe them. Spotted Tail now sent a Brulé to Cheyenne River with a pass he had ordered Agent Newell to issue, and this Rosebud Sioux told the Cheyenne River Indians that the great man who stood next to the Great Father had taken Spotted Tail's side against Agent Schwan and had ordered that Cheyenne River runaways should be fed and cared for at Rosebud. The result was that more Cheyenne River Sioux ran away to Rosebud. Most of them settled down to remain permanently. Captain Schwan was a very angry German. What was the use of his laboring to force the Sioux to work if the Secretary of the Interior forgot his own pledge to Congress that the Sioux would quickly be made self-supporting and issued an order encouraging them to run away to Rosebud and there sit down to eat free rations in idleness? Captain Dougherty, at Lower Brulé, had about the same view of it as Schwan. Major McGillycuddy, at Pine

Ridge, did not care a pin about Indian farming; but he was infuriated at the spectacle of a chief controlling at Rosebud and the utter lack of discipline among the Rosebud Sioux. Spotted Tail was pleased with all this. He did not like these three agents; the Sioux were on his side, and delegations were coming from the other agencies to ask his counsel. Unofficially he was nearing the rank of head of the Sioux Nation, but there were storm signals flying, and he would be wise to heed them. Even among his own Brulés, some of the younger headmen were turning against him. They said that he was taking the control of everything into his own hands and would not listen to advice or give the younger men an opportunity to increase their standing in the tribe. The chief said good humoredly that these men had no ideas worth listening to, and in a way that was true. Still their growing discontent was a danger that he had to reckon with.

12. The Betrayal

THE BRULÉ CHIEFS, at the urging of the Indian Office, had deserted the Roman Catholics and made peace with the Episcopalians, and Spotted Tail had now announced that the White Robes were in charge at Rosebud and must not be interfered with. Perhaps he meant that no one was to shoot at them or set their houses on fire. He evidently still disapproved of missions and schools and did what he could to discourage them; for when the father of Crazy Horse, now head of Northern Camp at Rosebud, was talked by the Episcopal missionary into saying that he would like a mission and school in his camp, Spotted Tail said to the old man, "You will have no mission or school. I will do your thinking for you, the same as I do for the rest of them." Spotted Tail could be highhanded in this manner on occasion. Someone with a brain had to do the thinking, either he or a white agent, and there can be no doubt that the Sioux much preferred to have a man of their own blood think for them. Many of them admitted frankly that they could not think for themselves. There were too many complicated problems in this new reservation life, and even some of the headmen and chiefs came to Spotted Tail and asked him to make decisions for them.

The Brulé head chief had never been more active in his life. The year 1879 was one continuous performance, and the problems this untutored chief had to deal with were enough to overwhelm most men; yet he dealt with them vigorously and, on the whole, successfully. He was denounced by some of the frontier editors for taking the Sioux away from their farm work to indulge in "a sun dance orgy," and Agent Newell was also pilloried for being weak enough to let the chief use him in sending Sun Dance invitations to the other agencies. The Indian Office officials woke up a bit late and joined in the criticism of the chief and his agent. At this time the railroads were seeking a right of way across the Sioux reservation, and there was much excitement and anger among the Indians. Spotted Tail was accused by some of his own Indians of selling land to the railroads and pocketing the money; but the Dakota newspapers accused him of opposing the railroads, and when the surveyors came on the reservation, he certainly did what he could to stop their work. In August he was dickering with Carl Schurz over the touchy problem of a new Indian police force at Rosebud, and as nearly as can be made out, he managed to sell Schurz a new police force that was loyal to the chiefs and not to the government that was paying the bills. In the same month Captain R. H. Pratt, the superintendent of the new government Indian training school in the old cavalry barracks at Carlisle, Pennsylvania, started out to recruit Indian boys for his school and came straight to Rosebud.

Pratt was an enthusiast. He imagined that he was bringing the greatest of all boons to the Sioux by offering to take their children far, far away into an unknown land and keep them for from four to six years, bringing them home again, if they lived, changed and completely alienated from their illiterate parents. He was stunned when he found that all his talk, made through an interpreter, failed to move the Sioux, and that not one parent was willing to offer up a child on the altar of the god of Education. In despair he took the advice of the Episcopal missionary and made a personal appeal to Spotted Tail to save his school plan from disaster.

Why the chief responded to this appeal is not known. His interest in education was mild, the most he desired being the training of a chosen few sons of chiefs and headmen so that they could speak, read, and write English and act as interpreters and letter writers. Yet Spotted Tail now came forward in open council and spoke in favor of Captain Pratt's new school; and he offered four of his sons and two of his grandchildren to Pratt, to be taken to the school. Other chiefs and headmen, who had refused to give Pratt any of their children, now offered their sons. Pratt got thirty-four pupils at Rosebud and went happily on to Pine Ridge. There Red Cloud used all his influence to prevent any Oglala children being sent to the new school, but Agent McGillycuddy threw himself vigorously into the fray, and Pratt obtained a nice group of Oglala boys.

Spotted Tail had been black-listed by the officials and the leaders of the Eastern church and benevolent groups because of his promotion of the pagan Sun Dance in June, his wrecking of the Indian farming activities, and his other nonprogressive actions; but when these leaders in the East heard of his saving Captain Pratt's new school from being boycotted by the Sioux, Spotted Tail's sins were forgotten, and he became that noble and enlightened chieftain who had snatched up the torch of Education and was preparing to lead his people out of darkness into light. What seems to have really happened was that Spotted Tail wished to have a few boys taught English, and that he also hoped the tribe could profit in non-educational ways. Thus the hardheaded Brulé chief, before he openly supported the plan and offered his sons as pupils, stipulated that his daughter Red Road and her husband Charles Tackett should go with the children to Pennsylvania and should be paid a salary to act as their guardians. Not another chief had the mentality to realize that these children, in faraway Pennsylvania, would be terribly frightened and unhappy if some adults of their own tribe were not there to protect and advise them. Charles Tackett had been interpreter at Camp Sheridan in 1877, and was now running a small store at Rosebud. He was a young white man who spoke Sioux well and was much liked by the Indians. There was a rumor that Spotted Tail had a partnership interest in Tackett's store.

Red Road was being pursued by education, and she hated it. Her strong-willed father had promised to let the nuns take her to Kansas City in 1876, to be educated in the convent. Horrified at this plan, the girl, who was proud as a princess and had plenty of her father's determination, eloped with a young warrior to a distant camp, where Spotted Tail could not reach her. She soon tired of her warrior and came home. Spotted Tail then married her by tribal custom to his young friend Tackett, and now he was sacrificing Red Road by once more ordering her to leave her people and go far away into the white people's unknown land to live at a big school. This time Red Road did not run away. She submitted to her hard fate. She was only eighteen when she set out for Carlisle School.

As the Spotted Tail family have no record of the children who were taken to Carlisle in September, 1879, the list may be inserted here from the National Archives:

> Red Road (Mrs. Charles Tackett), age 18.
> Stays at Home (renamed William), age 18.
> Talks with Bear (renamed Oliver), age 14.
> Bugler (renamed Max), age 12.
> Little Scout (renamed Pollock), age 9.
> Running Horse (Hugh Standing Soldier), Spotted Tail's grandson, age 8.
> Spotted Tail's granddaughter, daughter of Black Crow.[1]

These Brulé children were carried off to Pennsylvania, and only their Indian mothers had any realization of what a wicked and cruel action was being taken in the name of education.

Spotted Tail was now face to face with another urgent problem: the organization of a real Indian police force at Rosebud. The officials pretended that police were necessary to keep order among the Sioux; but the tribal soldiers were performing that duty, and when in 1879 a young Brulé whose sister had died assuaged his grief by shooting a white employee at the agency with an arrow, it was the chiefs and tribal soldiers who dealt with the case, while the agent and his police took no action. As has been pointed out earlier, the truth was that the whole purpose of the Indian police plan was to break the power of the chiefs and to put all authority into the hands of the white agent. Spotted Tail knew that; he also knew that if he openly opposed a police force and employed force to prevent such an organization, he would get his people into most serious trouble. He had therefore aided Agent Pollock in recruiting a police force and was given high praise for his loyal support of the

---

[1] I am indebted to Harry Anderson for this information concerning the Spotted Tail children at Carlisle. He not only found the material in the National Archives but made a study of the photographs taken at Carlisle and identified the boys shown in the pictures. The list with names and ages was made in September, 1879. The fact that the girl taken to Carlisle from Rosebud was Spotted Tail's granddaughter and the daughter of Chief Black Crow is found in a letter from Agent Cook, of Rosebud, to the Indian Office, April 2, 1880.

government, until it was discovered that he had sold the officials a police force of white squaw men and mixed-bloods who did not dare arrest a full-blood Brulé and were therefore of no use whatever. When Secretary Schurz was at Rosebud in August, he kept after Spotted Tail and finally obtained his promise to aid Agent Newell in recruiting a really competent police; but as soon as Schurz was gone, the chief began to hedge. He objected to the low pay, which was five dollars a month, and to the policemen's having to provide their own ponies, arms, and equipment. But Agent Newell seemed to be always ready with clever plans for evading the rules and regulations of the Indian Service. The agent hit on the scheme of getting good men on the force by putting them down on the payroll at salaries of from forty to fifty dollars a month, listing them as extra laborers and ox-team drivers. As Bordeaux, a mixed-blood, was named as a sergeant, it is apparent that Spotted Tail was helping to organize another force that would not dare to meddle with the Brulé full-bloods; but the Indian Office now put its foot down hard. The police pay boost from five to fifty dollars a month was disapproved, and Newell was ordered to stop listing policemen as ox-team drivers and organize a police force of full-bloods at the legal pay rate.

Newell told the sad news to Spotted Tail, who called a council, and the chiefs discussed the matter and agreed to a full-blood police force; but apparently they parceled out the policemen among themselves, each chief nominating one of his loyal warriors to represent his interests on the new police force. The officials were as far as ever from having a force at Rosebud like the one McGillycuddy had at Pine Ridge, which would arrest Red Cloud himself if the agent ordered it, or the force at Cheyenne River, who shot up Spotted Tail's Sun Dance ambassadors on Captain Schwan's instructions.

Crow Dog of the Orphan Band, a headman in Spotted Tail's big Brulé camp, was made chief of police. He was a sharp-witted and fearless man, who had made a reputation as a warrior before coming to the reservation. He had been one of the Brulé soldiers who escorted Crazy Horse in his last ride to surrender himself at Camp Robinson in 1877, and when Crazy Horse was mortally wounded at the guardhouse, Crow Dog rode coolly up and down in front of the mass of enraged Sioux who were threatening to charge into the military stockade, pushing the butt of his gun against the ponies' breasts and ordering the warriors to move back. He is said to have been a nephew of Brave Bear, the Brulé head chief who was mortally wounded in the Grattan fight in 1854, and modern Sioux information is to the effect that Crow Dog regarded Spotted Tail as an usurper who had wrongfully taken the position as head chief, which belonged to the Brave Bear family. As there was no hereditary right involved and as the rank of head chief was one the government had instituted for its own advantage, it is difficult to believe that Crow Dog could have held such views, but he certainly disliked Spotted Tail and was ready to act against him. His appointment as chief of police was a matter arranged between the council of chiefs and Agent Newell. The agent clearly liked Crow Dog and wished to have him for chief of police.

Soon after his appointment, Crow Dog took two of his policemen, one a mixed-blood who could speak English, and rode off into the vast, uninhabited prairie to the south and east of the agency. White cattlemen from Nebraska had slipped across the line and were running their herds on the Indian lands, and Crow Dog had an idea for collecting a lot of money. That evening his party stopped at a cow camp and ate supper with the boss. After the meal, Crow Dog opened the subject of his visit. The white man's cattle were eating the Brulé grass. The Brulés did not mind; but, surely, the white man might show his appreciation of the favor the Brulés were granting him by making a small payment, and as chief of police Crow Dog could take care of the money. The cattlemen said, through the interpreter, that what Crow Dog was saying was perfectly fair; but—look!—here was a paper signed with Chief Spotted Tail's name and bearing his X-mark, showing that he had already visited the camp and collected three hundred dollars for grazing rights on the Indian lands. Crow Dog stared at the paper and had nothing to say. He and his men spent the night, had breakfast with the cowboys, and then rode on to visit other camps; and at every camp the boss had a receipt, signed by Spotted Tail, for money handed to that chief in payment for grazing rights.

Crow Dog was the angriest Sioux on the reservation. When he got back to the agency, he publicly denounced Spotted Tail for collecting money from cattlemen and keeping it for his personal use. The chief retorted that that was exactly what Crow Dog had intended to do, and that as head chief of the tribe he had to entertain many guests who came to see him on tribal matters, and that these grazing fees were his perquisites, to aid him in paying his very heavy expenses.

This affair made more bad blood. It also exhibited how far ahead of the officials in Washington Spotted Tail was when it came to running an agency on business lines. The officials did not even know that cattlemen were running herds on the Sioux lands, and it was not until five or six years later that the Indian Office thought out a plan for collecting grazing fees from cattlemen.

Spotted Tail was by nature a frank and honest man; but it was impossible for any man, Indian or white, to live for years at an agency without having his sense of what was upright conduct blunted. At the moment when Crow Dog became chief of police and started out to collect money (probably for his own pocket) there were constant rumors that the agent at Rosebud had paid money in Washington to obtain his appointment, that he had demanded money from his agency staff in payment for their appointments, and that he was forcing the staff to pay him part of their salaries or to give him expensive gifts. While Crow Dog accused Spotted Tail of wrongfully collecting grazing money for his own profit, Agent Newell was putting pressure on the agency physician. He withheld the doctor's pay checks from Washington. The affair had all the earmarks of a shakedown. The doctor left the agency, with his wife and children, to return to his home in Michigan. Newell sent Indian police after them; and on the lonely prairie east of Rosebud the doctor was arrested and brought back, his wife and small children being abandoned on the prairie. Somehow they got to Yankton, where they had to live on charity. Meanwhile Newell charged the doctor with taking government surgical instruments, although the instruments belonged to the doctor, who had brought them from Michigan; and after holding his victim illegally for a time, Agent Newell ordered him to leave.

Presently Inspector Pollock, who had been the first agent at Rosebud, turned up and made an investigation. Newell claimed the Pollock report exonerated him; he praised Pollock as an honest and fair-minded officer; then he heard that the Pollock report did not clear him, and he denounced Pollock as a low, drunken, cursing man with a biased mind. By the end of 1879 the Dakota papers printed the report that a new agent was being appointed for the Rosebud Agency.[2]

Crow Dog and his friends seem to have developed the idea that this would be an excellent time for getting rid of Spotted Tail and replacing him with one of their own friends. They now came out in the open and began to make charges against the head chief. As winter came on, their hopes rose. American Horse came from Pine Ridge with a message from Red Cloud and held long secret talks with Spotted Tail. Then Spotted Tail rode off westward, telling no man where he was going; but presently a report came that he was at Pine Ridge, in conference with Red Cloud. The schemers at Rosebud took advantage of his absence to whip up new charges against him, but a curious event now transpired to confuse their councils and set them to quarreling.

Present-day Sioux will tell you solemnly that when Crow Dog was dismissed as chief of police, he blamed Spotted Tail for it and threatened to kill him. The contemporary documents show that Crow Dog lost his position with the police while Spotted Tail was far away at Pine Ridge, and that the change in the police leadership was a result of the strange "gold claims" fever that struck Rosebud

[2] The documents referring to Agent Newell's removal are in the National Archives. The letter from Dr. N. Webb, father-in-law of the Rosebud physician, to Senator H. P. Baldwin, of Michigan, February 2, 1880, is particularly enlightening. It claims that the agency physician's wife was enticed from Michigan to Rosebud on the promise of a clerkship at the agency; but Newell kept putting off the appointment, and she then found that the agent never appointed anyone to his staff unless they paid money in hand or gave him a promissory note before being appointed. The doctor and his wife then preferred charges, and Newell retorted by driving them from the agency and then sending Indian police to drag the doctor back and charge him with theft. Newell was also charged with incompetence. He had made no move to start farming, and had wasted all the agency funds on wildcat schemes—a steam bakery that was an utter failure, a dam in the South Fork of White River that a flash flood took out, and so on.

in the winter of 1879–80. Newell reported on February 24 that the gold fever was "playing the devil with everyone here," that the Indians were quarreling over gold claims, that they had gotten Crow Dog out as chief of police, and that he feared the police force would be disrupted. It is only in Newell's letters that this gold fever is referred to. How anyone could believe in gold deposits at Rosebud, where there is no rock and no possibility of placer gold in the streams, is a mystery; but perhaps the ignorant Sioux thought that the surveying activities then going on had something to do with seeking gold. Whatever it was that started them off, they were all staking out claims and quarreling over them almost to the point of fighting. Newell reported that the police took sides with friends who had gold claims; Crow Dog did that, and was thrown out as police head by the tribal council. Newell then wanted Spotted Tail's son to head the police and hold them together.

It was during this gold-claims excitement in January and February, while Spotted Tail was at Pine Ridge for his conferences with Red Cloud, that the opposition to his leadership really got started at Rosebud. This was the first time since he had become head chief that he had to face an open and organized opposition. As far as we may judge, it was among the *Wablenicha*, or Orphan Band, that the opposition first took form. Chief Iron Shell, head of the Orphans, is said to have always regarded Spotted Tail as an usurper who had taken the head chiefship away from the family of Brave Bear. Iron Shell was related to Brave Bear. Matthew C. Field (in *Prairie and Mountain Sketches*), states that Iron Shell was the son of Chief Bull Tail (one of the principal Brulé chiefs of the 1840's) and that in the summer of 1843 this distinguished young warrior killed eleven Pawnees. Thus in the 1840's both Spotted Tail and Iron Shell were notable warriors; but Iron Shell never developed beyond that stage. As a chief in later years, he could not think beyond the interests of his family and his own small group of followers. He was dead now; but there were others in the Orphan Band who were pretending to have inherited claims to be Brave Bear's successor.

Hollow Horn Bear, son of Iron Shell, was now the chief of the Orphans; but in that group the most experienced and influential leaders were Crow Dog and Dog Hawk, both of whom hated Spotted Tail. The Orphan Band was a part of Spotted Tail's big Brulé camp, and thus the leaders of the new opposition party lived in close contact with the head chief and were strongly represented in his camp council. Crow Dog had already denounced Spotted Tail publicly over the collection of grazing fees from the cattlemen, and when he was thrown out as chief of police during the gold-claims quarrels in the winter of 1879–80, he tried to pin the blame on the head chief.

This opposition party posed as the champions of the common people against a head chief who was secretly robbing the tribe to feather his own nest. As far as we can judge, their accusations against Spotted Tail were either inventions or gross exaggerations. They said that he went to visit the town of Yankton (or was it Pierre?) and secretly sold Sioux land to the railroads, coming home with the money, which he kept for himself. This seems to be a false version of the railroad right-of-way negotiations. At the time, the Dakota newspapers stated that Spotted Tail opposed the entry of the railroads into the Sioux reservation and stirred up bitter trouble. He is known to have ordered the Indian police escort withdrawn when the railroad surveyors were laying out the line across the Indian lands, and thus he stopped the work. Another charge of the opposition was that Spotted Tail was having a handsome mansion built for him by the government as a reward for aiding the whites to rob the Sioux. Undoubtedly this tale turned many of the Indians against Spotted Tail, although there was not a jot of truth in it. The mansion being built for him just north of Rosebud Agency was a government project for teaching the Sioux to live in houses by having the chiefs set an example for the common Indians. The government was also building a house for Red Cloud. No one charged that chief with betraying his people and being paid by having a mansion built for him. In fact, houses for chiefs were being built at all the Sioux agencies, and at Rosebud the plan was to build a house for every leading chief.[3] There was no bribery of

---

[3] This second house owned by Spotted Tail, like the first one—the commanding officer's former quarters at the old agency in Nebraska—turned out to be a dismal failure. The chief's wives could not learn to keep house, and after a valiant effort

chiefs in this. It was simply an absurd plan to have the chiefs set an example by living in houses; then (in theory) all the Indians were supposed to desert their tipis and move into cabins. As it finally worked out, the government had to bribe all the common Indians to get them to move into cabins, and it was a slow evolution that took years to accomplish.

What Spotted Tail was conferring with Red Cloud about, we do not know. When he returned to Rosebud in February, he wrote direct to President Hayes, objecting to the removal of Agent Newell; but that already had been decided on in Washington. Spotted Tail was now angered by letters from his son-in-law, Tackett, at Carlisle School, for Tackett told him that the Episcopalians had baptized all the Sioux children at the school and given them Christian names. The chief regarded this as a mean action. He had sent his children to the school to be taught English and writing, not to be turned into imitation whites; but this matter could wait until he went to visit the school.

The officials in Washington had already notified Agent Newell that a grand celebration of the completion of Carlisle School's first term was to be held at the school in June, 1880, and had sent the agent a list of the chiefs who were to be brought to Carlisle to meet the distinguished white visitors who would be present at the ceremonies. Spotted Tail was to lead the Rosebud delegation, which was to be made up of the older chiefs. Agent Newell protested. He wished to have Crow Dog included, although he was only a headman, and he also wished to include Black Crow, as the father of the only girl among the Rosebud children at the school. This little girl was Black Crow's daughter and Spotted Tail's granddaughter. Was Agent Newell trying to promote the opposition to Spotted Tail? He was friendly with Crow Dog, and Crow Dog was making

---

to stay in the dismal, unfurnished mansion, they moved back into their comfortable tipis. Herbert Welsh visited the agency the year after Spotted Tail was murdered and described the house in these words: "It is a wooden structure three stories in height, and when first built doubtless was to Indian eyes of palatial proportions. It reminded us of a third-class seashore boarding-house which was about to be abandoned." The house was two years old at this time. It had cost $5,000—a mint of money in those days—and had outraged the agent, as Spotted Tail's home was much larger and better than his own.

up to Black Crow, who was an ambitious man and hoped to be made head chief when the opposition pulled Spotted Tail down. But the officials in Washington wanted only prominent and influential chiefs in the party that was to visit Carlisle, chiefs who could be impressed with the wonders of the school and who would go home and spread the new gospel of education.

In the first week of May the new agent, John Cook, arrived and relieved Agent Newell. One would have supposed that, after their experience with Newell's weakness and incompetence, the Indian Office would have been very careful in choosing his successor; yet they sent John Cook, who knew nothing about Indians and was evidently a man of even weaker character than Newell. He had been an army officer during the Civil War, but was described in a contemporary report as a long-haired effeminate. He was afraid of his Indians, and they knew it and took advantage of the fact. Spotted Tail treated Cook as a nonentity, and Cook paid him back by siding, when he dared, with the opposition party.

Cook had hardly settled himself in the Rosebud office when Spotted Tail took action against the two licensed traders who had the big stores at the agency. What the quarrel was about we are not informed; but one day Agent Cook heard fierce yelling and, going to his office window, beheld a mob of Sioux surrounding the two stores. He sent his interpreter to find out what was going on, and the man came back with a report that Spotted Tail (inventing something that our labor leaders did not think of for many years to come) had picketed the stores with tribal soldiers and some of the Indian police and had forbidden the Indians to enter the stores to make purchases.

Someone urged Cook to go out and assert himself, and he went with his interpreter and ordered the pickets to leave. A policeman told him that they were taking orders from Spotted Tail and that he was not to meddle in the matter. A quarrel ensued, and Thunder Hawk, a leader in the police, finally took the agent's side and ordered the pickets to go away. Someone had sent for Spotted Tail, and he now arrived and angrily ordered Cook to mind his own business. He said that the police belonged to him, that he would give them orders, and that Thunder Hawk would be dismissed for disobeying.

But that did not end the affair. Cook took advice and called a council of chiefs and headmen; the opposition party was very active, and for the first time Spotted Tail was defeated by an important council vote. The council decided that he was in the wrong and that the police should take orders from the agent.

The opposition leaders were more active than ever. They now posed as friends of Agent Cook and supporters of the government Indian policy. They pretended to oppose the head chief's conservative policy, being young liberals while he was a stubborn old tory. But so were nearly all the Sioux. They did not desire any of the things the government officials labeled Progress in Civilization, and even the young liberals were only giving lip service to the government program in the hope of obtaining official support in their attempt to pull Spotted Tail down.

On May 15 they came to Cook's office with a petition which they asked him to send to the Indian Office. It stated that Spotted Tail disliked the new agent, whereas they liked him and wished to support him. They were progressive; they wished to have the agency sawmill put to work so that they could have lumber to build cabins to live in. They heard that Spotted Tail was to go to Carlisle School and Washington, and they besought the Indian Office to send them a report of every word he uttered while in the East. They did not trust him and wished to check up on his actions while away. The Wazhazhas, while camped with Red Cloud in October, 1876, had had all their ponies swept away by the cavalry and Pawnee Scouts, and in this petition the Indian Office was urged to reimburse the Wazhazhas for the loss of their ponies by giving them work cattle (probably to kill and eat, as the Wazhazhas had no intention of working). The petition showed that the opposition party had recruited part of the Wazhazhas by promising to get them paid for the ponies they had lost in 1876, but Red Leaf and the other important leaders among the Wazhazhas were keeping aloof from this movement. The signers of this petition were Quick Bear (Wazhazha chief), Thunder Hawk (the policeman whose dismissal Spotted Tail had recently demanded), Crow Dog, his brother Brave Bull, some other Wazhazhas, and a number of unimportant men of various bands, including Standing Bear, who was listed as a Loafer, although he was the only Indian at Rosebud who ran a store. The interpreter who drew up the petition was Louis Richards, an Oglala half-blood, who formerly lived at Red Cloud Agency and had perhaps come to Rosebud with the Wazhazhas. The Indians who signed this petition called themselves the White Horse Band, for what reason is not clear. White Horse is not mentioned in the records before 1889, when he was an ally of Hollow Horn Bear, of the Orphan Band, and of Yellow Hair, two men who had opposed Spotted Tail and cherished ambitions for succeeding him as head chief. In 1889 they had an opportunity to exhibit leadership and failed dismally.

When Spotted Tail set out in June on his last visit to the East, he was accompanied by his lieutenant, Two Strike; his son-in-law, Black Crow; White Thunder, the chief of the Loafers; and Iron Wing, representing old Crazy Horse and his camp of surrendered hostiles. There was not one man belonging to the opposition party who pretended to be progressive, although this delegation to visit Carlisle School had been carefully picked by the Indian Office to obtain men who had strong influence in the Rosebud camps. Black Crow was friendly with Crow Dog, but so far he had avoided connecting himself publicly with the new liberal party.

When he left Rosebud for Carlisle, Spotted Tail had a very high reputation among the Eastern church and benevolent groups that were busying themselves in Indian welfare work. By giving his own children to Captain Pratt to be educated at Carlisle, the chief had delighted these Eastern enthusiasts, whose latest cure-all for Indian woes was education, and whose newest bright hero was Captain Pratt of Carlisle. It seems curious that church people, humanitarians, and idealists should fall so much in love with Pratt. He was a quite ordinary army officer who had developed a marked ability for knocking the spirit out of young Indians and turning them into docile students who would obey all orders. Pratt was a domineering man who knew only one method for dealing with anyone who opposed his will. He bullied them into submission. He seems to have originated the system of hiring husky persons as disciplinarians in Indian schools. Years later, when the brutality of many disciplinarians became a national scandal and a bill was introduced in Congress to abolish this class of employees at government Indian schools, Pratt rushed to Washington and filled the air with loud and angry noise. He said that no Indian school could be run without disciplinarians on its staff.

All unsuspecting of the ordeal he was about to face, Captain Pratt happily busied himself in preparing for the celebration of his school's first anniversary. Parties of chiefs were on the way, from Rosebud, from Pine Ridge, and from the Sioux agencies on the Missouri. Bishop Hare of the Episcopal church and other distinguished guests were coming, including a group of Quaker ladies who were fervently interested in the Captain's noble work at Carlisle.

Thus Spotted Tail, Red Cloud, and the other great agency chiefs came to the old cavalry barracks at Carlisle in which Captain Pratt was harboring his new Indian school. Spotted Tail was at once singled out as the favorite chief of the Episcopal Bishop, the Quaker ladies, and the other distinguished patrons of the school. The Quaker ladies insisted upon being photographed with the Brulé chief standing in their midst; he was photographed with his young sons, most of them in the school military uniform; and a big group of all the chiefs was taken in front of one of the wide verandas of the old barracks.[4] Spotted Tail then had leisure to talk in private with his sons and the other boys from Rosebud and found that most of them were miserable and homesick. They were all in uniform and under stiff discipline. A system of courts martial had been set up, with the older Indian boys sitting as judges and condemning small offenders against the rules of the school to the guardhouse and to menial tasks. All the boys had to work at farming or in the carpenter or other shops. Spotted Tail's boy Stay at Home (renamed William), was eighteen, and should have been in training to become a chief. Instead, Pratt had set him to work, learning to make harness for farm horses. None of them had learned English or to read or write.

The thunder began to roll. Spotted Tail went off to Pratt's office with a glitter in his fine eyes. Pratt, knowing no other method for

[4] Harry Anderson found these photographs in the New York Public Library—part of them. Thirty-five seem to have been taken. The one showing Spotted Tail with his sons is from the South Dakota Historical Society collection.

dealing with a critic, attempted to bully the great Brulé chief, and was almost blown through the wall of his office by Spotted Tail's fierce counterblast. The chief later denounced Pratt and his school in front of the horrified Bishop, the Quaker ladies, and other distinguished guests. The other chiefs from Rosebud backed him up. Red Cloud, who usually sided against Spotted Tail, was on his side. He had done all he could to prevent Pratt's taking any boys from Pine Ridge, and he was strong in his support of the Brulé chief. Even American Horse, the Pine Ridge progressive, was on Spotted Tail's side.

Pratt was probably greatly relieved that the schedule for the chiefs' tour prevented their remaining at his school longer. They set off for Washington, and he wrote to the officials urging that the plans should be altered so that the chiefs should not pay a second visit to his school on their way home. But Spotted Tail and the others were determined to come back to Carlisle. In Washington, Spotted Tail had been outfitted by the officials with a long pale-colored linen duster, a derby hat, and a cane (perhaps to put him into a more civilized and gentlemanly humor); but he came back to the school more grimly determined than ever to upset Captain Pratt's neat arrangements. He now demanded a council with everyone at the school, including the Indian boys, present. Most of the boys were Sioux and would understand all that the chiefs said in council. Pratt tried to avoid this, but the chiefs insisted, and the council with all the boys present was assembled in the school chapel. Pratt, fizzing with helpless rage, had to listen while Spotted Tail, Red Cloud, Two Strike, Red Dog, and American Horse made speeches in the Sioux tongue that he reported were offensive and prejudicial to school discipline. The chiefs then demanded that the boys be prepared for travel, stating that they were taking them home.

Pratt was horrified. He pelted the officials with telegrams, and replies came from Washington instructing him to say thus and so to the chiefs. The affair was assuming such alarming proportions that the Indian Office could not handle it, and the Secretary of the Interior began sending telegrams to Carlisle.

Later on, Pratt pretended that the whole of this affair was simply an attempt of Spotted Tail to have his son-in-law's salary as guardian of the Indian boys at the school increased to the shocking amount of forty dollars a month. Spotted Tail did take Charles Tackett to Washington with him, and there was talk of increasing Tackett's pay to make it come to forty dollars a month; but why should Red Cloud, who disliked Spotted Tail, join so heartily in the affair if the only purpose was to have Tackett's pay raised? It is quite clear that the chiefs disliked Pratt and the system he had built up at Carlisle. Most of them probably shared Spotted Tail's view, that the main object of the school should be to teach English, reading, and writing. They said that it was not a school, but a "soldier place," with all the boys in uniform and being trained as common soldiers. Nearly all of these boys were the sons of chiefs and headmen, and it enraged the chiefs to learn that Pratt was forcing them to do farm work and other manual labor like common white workmen.

Throughout this performance at Carlisle, Spotted Tail took the lead. When the Secretary of the Interior brought his big guns to bear, the other chiefs began to weaken, but not Spotted Tail. He demanded that all thirty-four of the Rosebud children should be turned over to him to be taken home. But the official thunders now began to alarm some of the Rosebud chiefs, and they weakened. Secretary Schurz then wired to Pratt that Spotted Tail was forbidden to take any children except his own, and pressure was exerted to force him to give up his plan entirely; but he persisted and put a guard of Brulés over his sons and grandchildren. A final desperate effort was made to prevent the chief's carrying out his shocking purpose, and on June 23 Washington telegraphed that if he persisted in removing his children from the school, he must pay their transportation and other expenses from his own pocket. That was a curious threat for Carl Schurz, a lifelong liberal and a member of the President's cabinet, to approve of. It was mean and cheap, and based on the hope that the chief had no money to pay his children's railway fares.

In all its long history, Carlisle School probably never faced a crisis like this. Spotted Tail took all his children, apparently four sons, a grandson, a granddaughter, and another small boy he claimed as a close relative. He carried them off under guard of Sioux chiefs and headmen, daring Pratt to try and stop him. Pratt was too overwhelmed to attempt that. He had to guard the rest of his school, as there were indications that a general stampede for the train might take place. As it was, some of the heartbroken children who were being left at the school managed to steal away and hide themselves on the train. Pratt's men searched the train and dragged off White Thunder's son and a small Indian girl. At Harrisburg the train was searched again and a little Oglala girl (Red Dog's granddaughter) was found and dragged screaming back to captivity. Red Dog was too afraid of the great officials to intervene. At points along the way back to Dakota, the train was boarded by official messengers to make pleas to Spotted Tail to think again and refrain from carrying out his wicked purpose, but the Brulé chief would not even reply to these pleadings.

Spotted Tail, who had started East as the darling of the church people, educators, and idealists, because he had given his children to Captain Pratt to experiment with, was now a pariah. A number of distinguished persons sent a communication to the Secretary of the Interior denouncing the chief's shocking conduct at Carlisle. Having failed in all their efforts to prevent the chief's taking his children home, the officials began to bombard the agent at Rosebud with instructions. Spotted Tail was to be informed of the great displeasure of the Secretary of the Interior. He was to be urged to repent and send the children back to Carlisle. Agent Cook (siding with the high officials) turned openly against Spotted Tail and reported much disapproval of that chief's conduct at Carlisle among the Rosebud Indians. His reports were a bit biased. It took some time for the moccasin telegraph to spread the news of Spotted Tail's deed among the Sioux; but when the Indians did learn of the removal of the children from Carlisle, the Sioux are said to have approved the act. They approved so heartily that the next time Captain Pratt tried to obtain recruits on the reservation for his school, he drew a blank. Hardly one full-blood family was willing to have their children taken to the distant school.

It was the opposition party, the self-styled White Horse Band, that was registering disapproval of Spotted Tail's raid at Carlisle.

Cook seems to have favored this opposition group. They had gotten Crow Dog back as chief of police, and they were openly talking of getting rid of Spotted Tail. White Thunder (the Wazhazha, not Chief White Thunder, who was with Spotted Tail at Carlisle) told Agent Cook that they would not oppose the official breaking of Spotted Tail, but they wanted assurance that other chiefs who were their friends, would not be broken. They held frequent councils and came to Cook with this proposal and that. One of their favorite schemes was to induce the officials to split Spotted Tail's big Brulé camp in half, the idea being that their own group would gain control of half of the Brulés. They continued to depict Spotted Tail as a thief who was robbing the Indians and the government. Nearly every proposal they made would weaken the tribal council and chiefs and throw control of the Brulés into the hands of the officials, but these schemers were not intelligent enough to realize that.

On Saturday, July 11, the opposition called a council and slyly invited Spotted Tail to attend. A mousetrap set to catch a lion! The head chief sent tribal heralds riding through the Indian camps, proclaiming that all good men should avoid this rigged council, and the Brulés kept away from it. But the opposition held the council and presented Agent Cook with a letter to be sent to the Indian Office, which highly condemned Spotted Tail. On Sunday, July 12, they came back to the agent for another council, which was evidently much more representative of the opinion of the tribe. They now asked Cook to set aside the letter of the day before and handed him another, which had been dictated by White Thunder, the Wazhazha, and written by Leon Palladay. They told Cook that Palladay was the best interpreter at Rosebud, which was a dreadful fib. Like their other interpreter, Louis Richards, Palladay was a Pine Ridge Oglala. He was the man the Indian Office had denounced in 1875, refusing to pay him as interpreter because his services were worthless. In this second letter, the opposition stated that they would not oppose the breaking of Spotted Tail if the officials would refrain from making his removal the excuse for displacing all chiefs. They wished the big Brulé band to be split in two so that they could control at least half of the people in it. They said that Spotted Tail was dishonest, nonprogressive, and an opposer of the government policy.

This Sunday was a big day. Cook, dizzy from many councils and the shifting decisions of these Indians, who did not seem able to stick to anything for more than one day, now had another shock. In the midst of the performance Kimball, the head of the Chicago, Milwaukee and St. Paul Railroad survey being run across the reservation, came storming into Cook's office to announce that runners from Spotted Tail and Red Cloud had come to the survey party's camp and ordered the Indian police escort to leave at once. Thus his survey work was stopped. He could not go on without an escort. Kimball's appearance was a bit of an upset for the opposition. They had been claiming for a year past that Spotted Tail had sold the tribal land to this railroad, but every Brulé present at the agency now knew that both Spotted Tail and Red Cloud were opposing the entry of the railroad into the reservation. Was that not the business that had induced Red Cloud to send American Horse to consult with Spotted Tail last winter, and had not Spotted Tail then gone to Pine Ridge for long talks with Red Cloud? Some of the Brulés now asserted that it was not honest to condemn Spotted Tail while absent, so he was sent for, and he came to the agency. In a long speech he reviewed all the events that had affected the tribe since he had become head chief in 1866. He proved by the course of events that he was no reactionary, as the opposition claimed. He was a friend of the whites, but not so friendly that he had ever failed to stand up for his own people and defy the greatest officials of the government when they attempted to injure the tribe. Agent Cook disliked Spotted Tail heartily; but in his report to the Indian Office, he expressed admiration for this man who had come to a council that had its mind made up to condemn him and, by his frank talk and personal magnetism, had brought them around to the opinion that the tribe had always done well under his leadership and that they had better continue to follow him.[5]

[5] This is the gist of Cook's report, July 12, but I have worded it differently. Cook loved big words, but when he tried to use them, he got tangled up in his own verbiage and fell down. The agent speaks of the weak and vacillating Brulés,

Spotted Tail had won. The opposition, taking full advantage of the rage of the officials at the chief's conduct at Carlisle School, had made a great effort to pull him down; but the events of July 11–12 had demonstrated that a majority of the Brulés were still with him. They had heeded his warning to keep away from the council the opposition had rigged on the eleventh and on the twelfth; they had listened to Spotted Tail and decided that he was the leader they would follow. An event now broke that plainly exhibited the fact that Spotted Tail was the one man at Rosebud that both the Brulés and the officials could depend on for leadership in a crisis.

Ever since they had moved nearer to the Missouri in 1877, the Brulés had suffered from white horse-thieves who slipped into the reservation and stole their ponies. The young warriors were strictly forbidden by Spotted Tail and the other chiefs to retaliate; but about July 23, six young Brulés slipped away and started for Loup Fork in Nebraska to steal horses to replace the ponies that had been stolen by the whites. They stole some horses, but had to kill a white man during the operations. They got home August 2 and openly boasted of their feat. Spotted Tail at once notified the agent, and Cook ordered Crow Dog (again heading the police force) to arrest the offenders, but the young men were of good families and popular in the tribe. Crow Dog, bold as he was, did not dare to touch them. Spotted Tail then used his influence to induce the young men to submit to arrest. He took charge of the whole matter, which was extremely serious. The Nebraska frontier was aroused, and there were demands that troops from Fort Niobrara be sent to Rosebud. If this had been done, there might have been a violent explosion. Spotted Tail sent his eldest son to the fort with messages for the commanding officer. He arranged to have the Indian police handle the matter, and he also arranged to have the prisoners sent to Fort Randall, Dakota, as there were reports that the cattlemen and cowboys in Nebraska were threatening to lynch them. On August 4 the Brulé head chief sent a message to President Hayes, Secretary Schurz, and the Indian Office describing these events and stating

---

of Spotted Tail's wheedling them back to his support by his "strategy and diplomacy," and he describes Spotted Tail as "the magnetic influence upon whose fortune they have hung their hopes for their own perpetuity." Well! Well!

that he had kept his pledge to the President that in the future Indian offenders would be turned over to the courts to stand trial. Spotted Tail now completed a fine performance by raising a defense fund among the Brulés to be used in retaining an attorney to see to it that the young warriors had a fair trial. He had a check written in his name and signed by his mark—the first check ever sent by a Sioux chief—which he mailed to Secretary Schurz in Washington. Informed later that the amount was not sufficient to retain a good attorney, he gave his personal pledge that the additional sum required would be provided. Agent Cook, a weather vane, veering to meet each change in the wind, now forgot his strong disapproval of Spotted Tail and was loud in praise of a chief "whose usefulness to his people is growing more apparent every day." The high officials in Washington had evidently come to the same view, but they were still badly shaken by Spotted Tail's outrageous conduct at Carlisle, and they now renewed their effort to induce the chief to return his children to the school. On August 24, Cook acknowledged receipt of a telegram to this effect from the Indian Office, but regretted to report that Spotted Tail had never exhibited the least inclination to permit the return of his children to the school.

Thus in July and August, Spotted Tail, by decisive action and by vigorous speeches in the tribal council, defeated the attempt to take advantage of his being out of favor in Washington to pull him down. He even won back the admiration of the high officials, who in June had been so angry over the Carlisle affair that they would gladly have seen him go.

The opposition party was persistent and vindictive. In October, 1880, they put forward Yellow Hair, a progressive whose daughter was married to the squaw man Todd Randall, and attempted to have him made head chief; but the tribal council voted two to one for Spotted Tail. The opposition had now lost the powerful backing of part of the Wazhazha Band; but the group, shrunk in numbers, grew more bitter and vindictive. In February, 1881, Crow Dog talked three important chiefs, old friends and supporters of Spotted Tail, into signing a letter filled with childish accusations against the head chief. This letter they asked Agent Cook to send to Secretary Schurz. The letter was obviously nothing more than spite work, and Carl Schurz took no action. At this time he and Spotted Tail were standing together to take care of the young Brulés who had made the raid into Nebraska. The Interior Department chose a good attorney to defend them. Turning Bear had been indicted for the murder of a Nebraska citizen, and the five other Indians for horse theft.[6]

In the spring of 1881 the opposition party appears to have given up. Spotted Tail was too strong for them to defeat him, either in the tribal council or in Washington; but Crow Dog and some others were filled with hate of the head chief and would not give up. They ceased to be an opposition party and began to plot the murder of Spotted Tail. The astute Crow Dog now brought Spotted Tail's son-in-law, Black Crow, into the plot. Black Crow was a chief in Spotted Tail's camp, an ambitious man, but entirely lacking in the qualities necessary to be head chief.

Crow Dog put himself forward, boldly accusing Spotted Tail and making threats. He made no claim to be a candidate for head chief, but posed as the champion of the common Indians against a tyrant. On July 4, 1881, the two met in the narrow space between the big government commissary building and one of the trader's stores. The agency was thronged with Sioux, who dearly loved the American Independence Day, with its shooting, fireworks, and eating. Face to face between the two buildings, Crow Dog and the head chief exchanged angry words, and then the warrior pushed the muzzle of his rifle against Spotted Tail's body. The head chief is said to have dared him to shoot, but there were too many of Spotted Tail's friends nearby, and Crow Dog backed away and vanished into the excited crowd of Indians.

Carl Schurz at this time was in great trouble over the Ponca crisis. The Ponca tribe had been forced to give up their reservation in northeastern Nebraska and go to Indian Territory, and when in 1876 Congress demanded that Spotted Tail's Brulés move to the Missouri, the Ponca Agency and reservation had been made over to the Brulés. But they would not live on the Missouri; they re-

[6] I do not know the result of this trial, but Turning Bear was not hanged, for he was a leading Ghost Dancer in 1890–91.

moved to Rosebud, though the Ponca reservation was still legally their property.

In Indian Territory the Poncas fell sick, as most northern Indians did. Their sufferings were shocking, and a large number of them slipped off and walked all the way back to their old home in Nebraska, begging food and aid from white settlers along the way. In Nebraska a group of leading citizens took up the cause of the unfortunate Poncas. The Indians had no redress in law, but the Nebraska men brought suit against the government and won the case, the government being ordered to restore the Ponca lands.

Carl Schurz was a liberal who had spent his life fighting to right such wrongs as this. The removal of the little tribe to the Territory had been planned and carried out before he bacame secretary of the interior, but now he was being violently attacked by the hot-headed men and women of the Christian and humanitarian groups who demanded instant restitution of the Ponca lands. Led on by the fiery speeches and writing of a young girl, Helen Hunt Jackson, the crusaders refused to see that the Secretary of the Interior could not right the wrong against the Poncas in a day or a week. Schurz, honest and kindly, was being crucified by his old friends among the liberals. In his trouble he turned to Spotted Tail, the man whom he would have gladly pulled down a year back because of the Carlisle School affair. Spotted Tail was known to oppose the restoration of the Ponca lands, as were all the other leading chiefs at Rosebud; but he was a friendly and reasonable chief, and it was hoped in Washington that if the Brulés were offered compensation for the Ponca lands, which they were not using, an agreement could be reached.

Agent Cook was instructed to bring a delegation of chiefs from Rosebud to discuss this matter in Washington, and on August 5 the tribal council met at the agency and voted that Spotted Tail should lead the delegation. Crow Dog had long before this lost his position as chief of police, and he was earning some money by cutting wood for fuel. More probably his wife cut and loaded the wood. At any rate, he had come to the agency while the council was in session with a load of wood, which he and his wife delivered.

They had removed the wagon box to make it possible to haul a larger load of wood; and after unloading at the agency, they started for their camp, sitting on the bare running-gear of the wagon. Their camp was a part of Spotted Tail's big Brulé camp, eight or nine miles from the agency on the South Fork of White River.

Perhaps this bringing of a load of wood to the agency while the tribal council was in session was a part of the well-organized plot. We do not know; but if it had not been planned, Crow Dog's luck was extraordinarily good. He drove his team along the trail deep in dust. He passed Spotted Tail's mansion, now a year old, but standing deserted and forlorn by the trail side. Beyond this point he observed four men coming from the agency, where the tribal council had just broken up. Ahead of the others was a man on horseback, easily recognizable as Spotted Tail; farther back on the trail were three chiefs on foot: Two Strike, He Dog, and Ring Thunder. Crow Dog stopped his team, gave the reins to his wife, and knelt down in the dust of the trail, as if he were tying his moccasin strings. As the chief rode up, he lifted his rifle while still kneeling and shot the chief in the left breast. Spotted Tail fell off his horse, throwing up a cloud of dust as he struck the ground. He struggled to his feet, and took several steps toward Crow Dog, attempting to draw his revolver, but before he could get it out of the holster, he fell backward and lay still. Crow Dog leaped back on the wagon, whipped his team up, and went flying up the trail toward the safety of his camp.[7]

The news that Spotted Tail had been murdered spread like fire, and bands of armed and mounted warriors rode out of the hills, most of them hastening toward the agency. Agent Cook was away, and his chief clerk, Henry Lelar, found the situation beyond his control. He sent off telegrams to Washington. The Indian police, now headed by Eagle Hawk, did not dare to arrest Crow Dog. Lelar had had long experience among the Brulés. He waited until the

---

[7] The eyewitness account, in the National Archives, does not agree in all details with Lelar's story, which was published in the newspapers of the day. The chiefs had a feast after the council, and Spotted Tail then started for home. Red Cloud and his friends were also going to Washington and seem to have reached Rosebud just after the murder of Spotted Tail.

day after the murder for the first fury of the Sioux to wear itself out and then called the tribal council to meet at the agency. The council then warned the plotters in the name of the tribe that they were to stop where they were and not attempt to make any further trouble. The council, by tribal custom, also sent peacemakers to talk to the families concerned and arranged that Crow Dog and his friends pay blood money for the killing of Spotted Tail. They paid six hundred dollars in cash and a number of ponies and blankets for the wanton murder of the ablest chief the Sioux ever had.

When Agent Cook returned from attending to his private business to take up his duties at the agency, he seems to have been contented with this settlement; but the public was now aroused, and the officials in Washington demanded stiff action at Rosebud. Cook got the council to act again, and Crow Dog and Black Crow (who was accused of instigating the killing) were induced to submit to arrest. They were taken in charge by the Indian police and were sent to Fort Niobrara in Nebraska to be held for trial.

Spotted Tail was prepared for burial by his family amidst scenes of intense mourning. He was laid out dressed in his handsome buckskin clothing, which was beaded and had the insignia of his rank embroidered on it in dyed porcupine quillwork. His face was painted red and a piece of suet was placed between his lips to sustain him on his journey to the spirit land. Whether he was buried on a Sioux scaffold is not stated; but he probably was. Later he was reburied in the little Episcopal cemetery just north of the agency, and about 1891 a subscription was taken up among the Sioux and the whites and a white marble monument was placed over his grave.[8]

The Sioux have a story of a beautiful Indian girl named Light-in-the-Lodge who lived on Soldier Creek, north of Rosebud Agency. She was the wife of Medicine Bear (alias Thigh), who is said to have had a broken thigh and was a cripple. Spotted Tail saw this girl and took her from her husband, so the tale runs. Crow Dog, that champion of the distressed, then took up the cause of

---

[8] These details of the burial are from the Susan Bettelyoun manuscript in Nebraska Historical Society library.

Medicine Bear. He got a number of his friends to join them, and they went to Spotted Tail and besought him to restore Medicine Bear's wife. They offered to give the chief several ponies and a number of other gifts if he would give up the girl, but he mocked them and refused to give her up. Crow Dog then killed the chief.[9]

This is a story dressed up to wring the hearts of sentimental modern people, to turn them against Spotted Tail and make them admire Crow Dog. The name Light-in-the-Lodge is not like the old-time names for Sioux women. It implies that the girl was so beautiful and charming that her presence lighted the lodge she dwelt in. It is a name that belongs in the same bracket with Prairie Flower and White Faun, and is not an honest Sioux name. The crippled Medicine Bear is mentioned in the contemporary records as an active member of the little group of plotters led by Crow Dog, and there is not a word concerning the girl in the reports that followed the murder of Spotted Tail. If he really did take her from her husband, it was regarded at the time as a small matter.

Henry Lelar, the chief clerk at Rosebud, knew these Indians intimately, and he reported the day after the murder that Crow Dog had deliberately planned the killing with the hope of ultimately succeeding Spotted Tail as head chief. It was a cold-blooded political assassination, and there was no mention of the stolen wife. Agent Cook then came back to the agency, and on August 10 he reported that the killing was the outcome of an old feud. He said that Crow Dog, Hawk Dog, and Medicine Bear (all of the Orphan Band), and Black Crow, of Spotted Tail's own band, were the leaders, and their plot had been well organized, their purpose to force Spotted Tail out as head chief, and if he could not be pulled down, to kill him. He reported that Black Crow was planning to snatch for himself the rank of head chief. Again, no mention of the stolen wife.

When the law went to work on the case, Black Crow was dropped

---

[9] Eddie Herman of Rapid City sent me this tale of Light-in-the-Lodge. It is also known to Joe Eagle Hawk of Pine Ridge, and Susan Bettelyoun stated that Spotted Tail stole Medicine Bear's wife, as did Mrs. McGillycuddy in her book. It is quite possible that Spotted Tail did have an affair with the girl, but when and under what circumstances we cannot tell.

and Crow Dog was taken to Deadwood in the Black Hills to stand trial for murder. His attorney based the defense on the allegation that Spotted Tail had threatened to kill Crow Dog and was known to be armed, and that Crow Dog had shot in self-defense. But the eyewitnesses testified that Crow Dog crouched in the dusty trail, concealing his identity and his rifle until the unsuspecting Spotted Tail was near enough to make a perfect target. That did not look much like innocent self-defense. The jury convicted Crow Dog of murder, and he was sentenced to hang. Then the United States Supreme Court gave judgment that the Dakota court had no jurisdiction over the case of an Indian killing another Indian on an Indian reservation, and Crow Dog was released, and came home to Rosebud.

The killing of Spotted Tail ended the history of the Brulé Sioux as a tribe. The great voice was stilled, and at Rosebud only the voices of little men were heard, quarreling about little matters. The government took advantage of the murder to start work in earnest, breaking the tribal organization to bits and putting the Sioux under the control of their white agent. The men who had plotted the murder in the hope that one of their own number would be recognized as the new head chief were bitterly disappointed, for the government not only declined to recognize another head chief, it refused to recognize the minor chiefs and went to work to destroy all their authority. The plotters had killed the one man in the tribe big enough to stand up to the high officials in Washington, to thwart their plans, and to protect the Brulés in their rights under the treaties.

It is good to record what one Sioux thought of Spotted Tail at the time of his death. The Little Missouri Sioux Winter Count says: "This year that brave and wonderful chief was killed by Crow Dog."

Indian information about the location of Spotted Tail's house and his camp is confused. The Indians have usually stated that his house was north of the agency and his camp beyond, farther north. Dr. John M. Christlieb, of Omaha, however, has in his collection a letter from Robert Hall, secretary of the Y.M.C.A. at Rosebud, dated May 31, 1911, in which it is stated that the house, then still occupied by one of Spotted Tail's widows, was on a hill south of the agency, and that Spotted Tail's grave with the granite monument, was on another hill, north of the agency. Mr. Hall enclosed a small photograph with his letter, showing the Spotted Tail house, a big plain rectangular frame dwelling, apparently with two tiers of windows, two stories, and perhaps an attic. It stood on the summit of a high hill, surrounded by a welter of hills and narrow vales, with a road winding past the foot of the hill the house stood on. Mr. Hall stated that the lumber for the house was hauled in wagons all the way from Norfolk, Nebraska, and that the house was said to have cost the government $40,000.

Crow Dog, killer of Spotted Tail. (Photograph by John A. Anderson. From *The Sioux of the Rosebud*, by Henry W. Hamilton and Jean Tyree Hamilton)

Chief Two Strike, Two Strike's Camp, Agency District, 1896.
(Photograph by John A. Anderson. From *The Sioux of the Rosebud*, by Henry W. Hamilton and Jean Tyree Hamilton)

Chief American Horse, Oglala, about 1900. (Photograph by John A. Anderson. From *The Sioux of the Rosebud*, by Henry W. Hamilton and Jean Tyree Hamilton)

Yellow Hair and his wife, Plenty Horses, about 1900. (Photograph by John A. Anderson. From *The Sioux of the Rosebud*, by Henry W. Hamilton and Jean Tyree Hamilton)

Epilogue

When Spotted Tail was dead, his eldest son, *Sintegaleska Chika* (Little Spotted Tail) attempted to grasp his father's rank as head chief. He made up to the tribal council and attempted to win the favor of the government officials by pretending to be a progressive, anxious to follow the ways of the whites. He moved into his father's deserted mansion, put on uncomfortable citizen's clothes, and drove about in a new buggy drawn by a nice team. But the tribal council passed him by and appointed White Thunder, the Loafer chief, to head the delegation that went to Washington to discuss the Ponca land matter. White Thunder was described as a brave warrior, a friendly and honest man, but without a trace of old Spotted Tail's qualities of leadership. Not one of these younger chiefs who had resented Spotted Tail's monopoly of authority in the tribe was fit to lead; and when a land commission came to Rosebud in 1882, led by the astute Newton Edmunds, he made fools of all the ambitious young chiefs: Young Spotted Tail, White Thunder, Hollow Horn Bear, and the rest of them. This commission got them to sign away half of the Sioux lands without their even suspecting what they were doing; but fortunately for the Sioux, white men in the Eastern states woke up to the situation and blocked the land deal.

The younger leaders who had opposed Spotted Tail had wanted to divide his big Brulé camp into two, so that they might gain control of half the people. When he was dead, the government adopted this plan, which would be a great aid in carrying out its program of breaking the tribe up and putting it under white control. It cut the Brulé camp in two, naming the two new bands Brulé Number One and Brulé Number Two. White Thunder was head of Number One Band, which was supposed to be progressive, mainly

because most of the men who had opposed Spotted Tail belonged
to the band. Number Two Band was made up largely of old Spotted
Tail's faithful followers, but Young Spotted Tail had already lost
standing, and the band was under the leadership of his father's
friend, Two Strike. By 1884 old Swift Bear had gained his heart's
desire and had a small camp made up from part of his Corn Band,
honestly progressive, trying to farm, and many of his band avowed
Christians, wearing citizens' clothes. The camp was three miles
eastward of the agency, forty-seven families in log cabins with forty-
seven small gardens, proudly listed in the agency records as farms.
Despite Swift Bear's progress, the agent reported that the Sioux at
Rosebud were living on 100 per cent government support. There
was no real farming, no schools, and the Brulés were doing exactly
as Spotted Tail had wished them to do—poking along at their own
slow rate, instead of being swiftly and violently rushed on into new
conditions that were utterly repugnant to them. So far all the official plans for making the Brulés hustle had failed dismally.

Crow Dog, sentenced to hang and then saved by the decision of
the Supreme Court, was back at Rosebud, posing as the hero who
had killed the old tyrant and striving to gain favor among both
the Indians and the whites. He was not very successful; but he had
proved one thing: that a Sioux could murder another Sioux and the
courts could not punish him. Young Spotted Tail, failing in all his
efforts to gain high rank in the tribe, now adopted the Crow Dog
method.

On May 29, 1884, Spotted Tail went to White Thunder's camp,
north of the agency on the South Fork of White River, and stole
one of the older chief's young wives. Returning home later in the
day, White Thunder was infuriated by this insult. He went straight
away, evidently accompanied by his father, who was very old but
who still had plenty of spirit, to Spotted Tail's camp near the
agency, where they took the equivalent of one stolen wife: several
select ponies out of the Spotted Tail herd plus some choice articles
from his tipi. They drove the ponies home and in their rage
killed them, an act which would insult Young Spotted Tail more
than the mere taking of his ponies. Spotted Tail now took advice
from Turning Bear, the warrior who had killed a white man in

Nebraska in 1880, had stood his trial, and been released. On this man's advice, Spotted Tail got up a party—himself, Thunder Hawk, the policeman old Spotted Tail had had the quarrel with in 1880, Long Pumpkin, an empty-headed warrior, and a man named White Blanket. These men rode to a point near White Thunder's camp and set an ambush, and when White Thunder and his ancient father came along, driving some of their pony herd before them, the hidden warriors opened fire. White Thunder was shot dead, but not before he had badly wounded Long Pumpkin; the old father was mortally wounded and left to die. The Spotted Tail party concealed Long Pumpkin in the bushes (he was too badly wounded to ride a horse) and made off before White Thunder's warriors could reach the scene.

The new agent, James G. Wright, summoned the killers to his office. They swaggered in, and Wright listened to their version of this bloody affair; he hemmed and hawed and in the end mildly suggested that, to avoid possible additional trouble, it might be well if they would submit to arrest by the Indian police. This they cheerfully did, and were taken to the guardhouse at Fort Niobrara for a brief stay. Meanwhile their families settled with the White Thunder family by paying blood money, and then the killers were released and came home. They were not welcomed as heroes. Young Spotted Tail (he now had the queer nickname of Tin Cup) lost standing in the tribe, and his friend Thunder Hawk was so unpopular that he went to Pine Ridge and joined the police force. Agent McGillycuddy wanted bold men for his police and did not seem to mind if they were murderers.

Young Spotted Tail sank into obscurity. We do not know when he died. After his death his brother William, who had been taken to Carlisle School in 1879 when he was eighteen and had been brought home by his father in 1880, seems to have been recognized as the head of the family.[10] He had his father's medals, chief-certifi-

[10] The Spotted Tail boys did not rejoin the Brulé camp when they grew up. They regarded themselves as progressives, and in 1889, William was listed in the Loafer Band and Pollock in the mixed-blood band, although he was a full-blood. William died at Rosebud, February 14, 1931, and was buried with military honors. His age was given as sixty-eight. His wife, *Pankeskawin*, Crockery Woman, survived him. She says she was born in 1858.

cates, and other belongings and handed them on to his son, Stephen Spotted Tail, who was still living in 1956 at Rosebud, in the Parmelee district west of the agency.

Spotted Tail would have grieved if he had known the fate awaiting his family. Not one of his sons distinguished himself; but what chance did they have, cooped up on a reservation where the government controlled everyone and nipped every display of native leadership in the bud? After his death his family had no good fortune. He is said to have had from thirty-four to thirty-six children, and Susan Bettelyoun, who knew the family well, stated that the eldest wife had thirteen children, the youngest wife had nine girls, the next youngest, nine boys, and the other two wives, one or two children each. The government census of 1875 showed that the chief then had in his family four wives (one had died at Whetstone Agency in 1870), nine sons, and eight daughters, plus his eldest son, who was married and had two children. Mrs. Bettelyoun, writing about the year 1940, stated that all of Spotted Tail's children were dead and only three grandchildren survived out of the once teeming family. Tuberculosis, induced by bad living conditions on the reservation, was responsible for most of the deaths in the family.

The tribe, unlike the family, did not dwindle away, as the chief had feared it might when placed on a reservation. The Brulé death rate was often very high; but the birth rate was also high, and instead of shrinking, the population actually increased. Before they came to the reservation the Upper Brulés, including the Wazhazhas, seem to have had about 4,000 people. In 1876, Agent Howard certified to about 9,000 (not including the Wazhazhas), but in 1877 the military count showed about 7,000 (including the Wazhazhas). In 1891 the census showed 4,000; about 1923 the figure was 5,466, and in 1956 the Brulés of Rosebud, including the Wazhazhas, were estimated at about 9,000, of which number from 6,500 to 7,000 resided on the reservation at least part of the time.

The humanitarian and idealist planners who longed to help the Indians made the mistake in the 1860's of imagining that the Sioux were exactly like white people. Give white families farms, farm equipment, and free food and clothing for four years, and these families would be on their feet and solidly established as successful farmers. Therefore, the Sioux could be rushed swiftly into self-support from the soil. Spotted Tail knew that this was not true. His people were primitive and centuries behind the whites in their mental processes. He hated all the plans for forcing his people to advance suddenly up level with the whites, and he did all that he could to slow the process down by opposing farming, education, and Christianity, which were the three main weapons that were to be employed in forcing the Sioux to advance rapidly. He brought his people through the trying period of the first twelve years on the reservation, and after he was gone, his tribe continued in the way he had desired. It was the only way they knew or trusted, and no efforts on the part of the government could alter them much. Great sums were spent on farming crusades and on schools; but despite the government's efforts, few of the full-bloods ever showed much inclination for farms or schools. They have clung to their own language, and even today parents who themselves have been through government schools usually have to bring an interpreter with them to talk to the teacher when they place their children in a new school. Generation after generation it is about the same.

This is race resistance to sudden change, and it is what Spotted Tail felt in his bones was the right way for his people to live. There have been great efforts made to hurry the Sioux, but they have all failed. At the present moment the government, for about the tenth time, is putting millions of dollars into a new Indian education crusade which, as far as the Sioux full-bloods are concerned, will fail again. The mixed-bloods are mainly up level with the whites now; the full-bloods on the whole are not much changed from the wild Sioux of the Powder River in 1875, who spent most of the year roving, hunting, and fighting, coming to the agencies at the approach of cold weather to live in comfort under the care of a kindly government. The Brulés of today are not wild at all, but they are still on the wing. Each spring large numbers of them leave the reservation, some to seek work on white men's farms (not too steady work), others to go into towns or to the Black Hills. They still are bitter over the theft of the hills by the whites, but they make more profit out of the hills than their ancestors ever did. Companies filming Western dramas hire hundreds of Sioux, and there is no closed season on hunting tourists. Some Brulés go as far afield as Omaha and Denver. There are Indian colonies in these towns, and the Sioux take kindly to town life. Some of them find congenial work and settle down for a year or two.

On the whole they are a happy people. Many of the Brulés are very poor; but they are living their own way, clinging to their own language, and making life miserable for all planners and controllers. When war comes the young Brulés enlist and insist on getting into a fighting unit. They dislike the draft law. It insults them by assuming that the Sioux have to be forced to fight. They have left their dead in far Korea, in North Africa, France, Italy, and Germany, and they are proud of the record.

The present trend away from the reservation is mainly seasonal; but the Brulés are now within sight of a time when they will join the mass of the nation's population and be merged into it. Perhaps when that day comes, some of them will find the present book and learn to be proud of a great Brulé chief whose name was *Sinte Galeska*: Spotted Tail.

Bibliography

MANUSCRIPTS

Bettelyoun, Susan, Sioux Manuscripts, Nebraska Historical Society
Library.

GOVERNMENT DOCUMENTS

Annual Reports of the Office of Indian Affairs, 1830–81.
Bureau of American Ethnology *Fourth Annual Report (1882–83)*.
Washington, D. C., 1886.
Official Records of the Union and Confederate Armies. Ser. vols.
63, 101, and 102.
Report on Investigation of Affairs at Red Cloud Agency. Washington, D. C., 1875.

NEWSPAPERS

Omaha *Sunday World Herald*, September 21, 1930. Article on Spotted Tail by Alfred Sorenson.
Niobrara, Nebraska, *Pioneer* for 1878.

BOOKS AND PAMPHLETS

Armstrong, M. E. *Early Empire Builders of the Great West*. St.
Paul, 1901.
Bancroft, Hubert Howe. *History of Nevada, Colorado, and Wyoming*. Vol. XXV in *Works*. San Francisco, 1890.

Boller, H. A. *Among the Indians*. Philadelphia, 1868.

Bordeaux, William B. *Conquering the Mighty Sioux*. Sioux Falls, 1929.

Bourke, John G. *On the Border with Crook*. New York, 1891.

Brisbin, J. S., ed. *Belden the White Chief*. Cincinnati, 1875.

Burdette, Mary G. *A Young Woman Among the Blanket Indians*. Chicago, 1906.

Burton, Sir Richard F. *The City of the Saints*. New York, 1862.

Carrington, General H. B. *Ab-sa-ra-ka: Land of Massacre*. Philadelphia, 1896.

Carrington, Margaret. *Ab-sa-ra-ka: Home of the Crows*. Philadelphia, 1868.

Carter, Major General William H. *History of Fort Robinson*. Crawford, Neb., published by *Northwest Nebraska News*, n. d.

Clark, W. P. *The Indian Sign Language*. Philadelphia, 1885.

Collins, J. S. *Across the Plains in 1864*. Omaha, 1904.

Crook, Major General George. *His Autobiography*. Norman, 1946.

Custer, George A. *My Life on the Plains*. Lakeside Classics Edition. Chicago, 1851.

Drips, J. H. *Three Years Among Indians in Dakota*. [Published in South Dakota], 1894.

Eastman, Charles A. *From the Deep Woods to Civilization*. Boston, 1916.

———. *Indian Heroes and Great Chieftains*. Boston, 1918.

Eastman, Elaine Goodale. *Pratt: The Red Man's Moses*. Norman, 1935.

Finerty, John F. *Warpath and Bivouac*. Chicago, 1890.

Foreman, Grant. *Indian Removal*. Norman, 1932.

Frémont, J. C. *The Exploring Expedition to the Rocky Mountains*. Auburn and Buffalo, 1854.

Grinnell, George Bird. *The Fighting Cheyennes*. Norman, 1956.

———. *The Cheyenne Indians*. New Haven, 1923.

Hafen, L. R., and W. J. Ghent. *Broken Hand*. Denver, 1931.

Hafen, L. R., and F. M. Young. *Fort Laramie and the Pageant of the West*. Glendale, 1938.

Hare, Bishop William H. *Reminiscences*. Philadelphia, 1888.

Hayden, F. V. *Contributions to the Ethnography and Philology of the Indian Tribes of the Missouri Valley.* Philadelphia, 1872.

Hodge, F. W., ed. *Handbook of Indians North of Mexico.* 2 vols. Washington, D. C., 1907–10.

Humphrey, S. K. *Following the Prairie Frontier.* Minneapolis, 1931.

Hyde, George E. *Indians of the High Plains.* Norman, 1959.

———. *A Sioux Chronicle.* Norman, 1956.

———. *The Pawnee Indians.* Denver, 1951.

———. *Red Cloud's Folk.* Norman, 1937. (New edition, Norman, 1957.)

———, and George A. Will. *Corn Among the Indians of the Upper Missouri.* Cedar Rapids, 1917.

Kappler, Charles J. *Indian Laws and Treaties.* 2 vols. Washington, D. C., 1904.

Lindquist, G. E. *The Red Man in the United States.* New York, 1919.

McGillycuddy, Julia B. *McGillycuddy, Agent.* Stanford, 1941.

McLaughlin, James. *My Friend, the Indian.* Boston, 1910.

Mekeel, Scudder. *A Short History of the Teton-Dakota.* Pamphlet, reprinted from *North Dakota Historical Quarterly.*

Meriam, Lewis, and Associates. *The Problem of Indian Administration.* Washington, D. C., 1928.

Miles, General Nelson A. *Personal Recollections and Observations.* New York, 1896.

Mills, Colonel Anson. *My Story.* Washington, 1918.

Morton, J. S. *Illustrated History of Nebraska.* 3 vols. Lincoln, 1905–13.

Nebraska Historical Society *Collections,* Vol. XVI, 1911.

Nelson, John Y. See O'Reilly, Harrington.

O'Harra, C. C. *The White River Badlands.* Rapid City, S. D., 1900.

O'Reilly, Harrington. *Fifty Years on the Trail; Remarkable Story of the Life of John Y. Nelson.* New York, 1889.

Paine, Bayard H. *Pioneers, Indians, and Buffaloes.* Curtis, Neb., 1935.

Parker, Samuel. *Journal of an Exploring Tour Beyond the Rocky Mountains.* Ithaca, 1838.

Parkman, Francis. *The California and Oregon Trail.* 8th edition, revised. Boston, 1886.

Pond, S. W. *Two Volunteer Missionaries Among the Sioux.* N. p., n. d.

Poole, DeW. C. *Among the Sioux of Dakota.* New York, 1881.

Priest, Loring B. *Uncle Sam's Stepchildren.* New Brunswick, N. J., 1942.

Riggs, S. R. *Journal of a Tour from Lac-qui-parle to the Missouri.* South Dakota Historical *Collections,* Vol. XIII (1926).

Robinson, Doane. *History of the Sioux Indians.* Minneapolis, 1956.
———. *History of South Dakota.* 2 vols. Evansville, 1904.

Root, F. A., and W. E. Connelley. *The Overland Stage to California.* Topeka, 1901.

Rosen, Rev. Peter. *Pa-ha-sa-pah, or, The Black Hills of South Dakota.* St. Louis, 1895.

Rushmore, Elsie M. *Indian Policy During Grant's Administration.* Jamaica, N. Y., 1914.

Sage, Rufus. *Rocky Mountain Life.* Boston, 1857.

South Dakota Historical Society *Collections,* Vols. IX, XIII, and XIV.

Spring, Agnes Wright. *Caspar Collins.* New York, 1927.

Standing Bear, Henry. *Land of the Spotted Eagle.* Boston, 1933.

Standing Bear, Luther. *My People the Sioux.* Boston, 1928.

Stanley, Henry M. *My Early Travels and Adventures.* New York, 1895.

Stansbury, Howard. *Exploration and Survey of the Valley of Great Salt Lake.* Washington, D. C., 1853.

Tabeau, Pierre-Antoine. *Tabeau's Narrative of Loisel's Expedition to the Upper Missouri.* Trans. by Rose Abel Wright; ed. by Annie Heloise Abel. Norman, 1939.

Tallent, Annie. *The Black Hills.* St. Louis, 1899.

Thwaites, R. G., ed. *Early Western Travels,* 32 vols. Cleveland, 1904–1907.

Truteau, J. B. *Journal,* Part I in American Historical *Review,* Vol. XIX; Part II in South Dakota Historical *Collections,* Vol. IV.

Turner, Katherine C. *Red Men Calling on the Great White Father.* Norman, 1951.

Ware, Eugene F. *The Indian War of '64.* Topeka, 1911.

Warren, G. K. *Exploration in the Dakota Country.* Washington, D. C., 1856.

Welsh, Herbert. *Civilization of the Sioux Indians.* Philadelphia, 1893.

———. *A Visit to the Sioux.* Pamphlet. Philadelphia, 1893.

Welsh, William. *Sioux and Ponca Indians.* Pamphlet. Philadelphia, 1870.

Will, George F., and George E. Hyde. *Corn Among the Indians of the Upper Missouri.* Cedar Rapids, 1917.

ARTICLES

"Big Missouri Winter Count," in *Indians at Work*, February, 1938.

Brininstool, E. A. (and others). "Chief Crazy Horse and His Death," *Nebraska History*, extra issue (1929).

Index

Sam Kills Two (also known as Beads) working on his winter count. (Photograph by John A. Anderson. From *The Sioux of the Rosebud*, by Henry W. Hamilton and Jean Tyree Hamilton)